LOVE, H

LOVE, H

The Letters of Helene Dorn

and Hettie Jones

HETTIE JONES

Duke University Press

Durham and London

2016

© 2016 Duke University Press
All rights reserved
Printed in the United States of America on acid-free paper ∞
Designed by Amy Ruth Buchanan
Typeset in Minion by Tseng Information Systems, Inc.

Library of Congress Cataloging-in-Publication Data
Names: Jones, Hettie. author. | Dorn, Helene, author.
Title: Love, H : the letters of Helene Dorn and Hettie Jones /
Hettie Jones.
Description: Durham : Duke University Press, 2016. |
Includes bibliographical references and index.
Identifiers: LCCN 2016009770
ISBN 9780822361466 (hardcover : alk. paper)
ISBN 9780822361657 (pbk. : alk. paper)
ISBN 9780822374152 (ebook)
Subjects: LCSH: Jones, Hettie—Correspondence. |
Authors, American—20th century—Correspondence. |
Dorn, Helene—Correspondence. | Painters—United States—
Correspondence.
Classification: LCC PS3560.O485 Z48 2016 |
DDC 818/.5409—dc23
LC record available at http://lccn.loc.gov/2016009770

Cover art: Helene Dorn, Santa Fe, 1960 (*left*),
Hettie Jones, New York, 1960 (*right*).

NOV 1 1 2016

CONTENTS

INTRODUCTION

Letters stop time — even old they're always news. "Letters Lift Spirits," declares one vintage postage stamp, another "Letters Preserve Memories," and a third, with reverence, "Letters Mingle Souls."

Love, H is all this as well as a story with a backstory.

Thematically, collections from women emphasize friendship, and a lengthy correspondence unfolds not just a friendship but a sympathetic intimacy, an *I* and a *You*.

So who will you meet here? A couple of plainspoken women, avant-garde by nature, not analysis. Expansive, introspective, reportorial, confessional, two participants in a gradual redefinition.

In 1960, when we began to write, like most women then Helene Dorn and I were married with children. What set us apart were our men and our context: the Beat / Black Mountain / San Francisco / New York bohemia of that time, the Kerouac Ginsberg O'Hara deKooning nexus that has had such a lasting impact on American culture. The place I call Boyland. Each of us had arrived there with something in mind — she to paint, I to write — and then foundered on love, on the hardships and distractions of marriage and motherhood. Still, we were taking it all in, putting things by.

• • • • •

I'd come home from work to a party. In the group with my husband, LeRoi Jones, was a man I didn't recognize, and — surprise! — a *woman*. In 1960, at six on a cold December evening, the women I knew were either home with their kids or warming up at the Cedar Bar.

But here in my house was a tall, beautiful blonde who swooped down, relieved me of my bag of groceries, and with her free hand fingered the fabric of my coat. My outer garment, that is — a poncho I'd pieced together from multicolored woolen samples.

"Did you *make* that?" she asked.

Her husband, introduced as the poet Edward Dorn, pointed out that Helene—this woman, his wife—had made the finely tailored—lined!—silk jacket he was wearing.

In 1960, few women managed to keep their own skills in sight and so immediately presented the evidence. We left the men and went to the kitchen, ready to talk.

· · · · ·

In those days, women raised to believe the nuclear family an ideal safe haven were seldom in places where they could subvert it, or project an alternate reality. Our early sixties bohemia conformed: men in the lead, their wives who accepted this, and the chicks who stood outside, inhabitants of their own lives, looking in at "old lady" and either dubious or desirous. I recognized immediately Helene's refusal, like my own, to acquiesce entirely to this setup. We discovered right away that we had things to say, to exchange, to question. She'd traded an early, settled marriage for a vagabond life with Ed in the rural West, I'd discarded family for LeRoi and the centrifuge of downtown Manhattan.

At dinner that night we kept trying to keep our conversation going across a large, round, noisily occupied restaurant table. That's how it was to be with us—words across distance, sometimes through difficult, even perilous times.

I was planning to write but had yet to figure out what or how. Meanwhile I was two months pregnant, had a toddler and a day job, and a husband on his way to fame. I needed to hear from this straight-talking woman—nothing fancy, just what she was thinking and doing. Like me Helene had fled an intended life. She had three kids. She laughed out loud. Her favorite ending to any art/life dilemma was "Ta *dum* Ta *dum* Ta *dum* Ta *dum!*"

The seven-year difference between us presaged a change in the kind of life a woman might choose, and the result of that choice on her later life. Helene, born 1927, entered our mutual bohemia already a mother, a woman who had felt stifled in a traditional marriage and had been freed by her relationship with her second husband. I, born 1934, entered that same circle determinedly independent, a college graduate already earning her own living.

Although correspondence by the men of that time is available, we have few examples from women. Joyce Johnson and Jack Kerouac wrote for a while (see *Door Wide Open*). *Love, H*, however, isn't a moment in time but a selection from many exchanges—mailed, faxed, and finally emailed over forty years.

And since even the briefest text is a message, I believe the letter form lends itself to contemporary thinking, and that meeting two old pros might inspire its wider range.

· · · · ·

It took twenty years, and some persuasion, before I agreed to write *How I Became Hettie Jones*, my memoir of that sixties bohemia. I'd been working on children's books and poetry and stories, as well as editing and teaching, and I couldn't see the purpose—I thought people just wanted gossip—until, finally, I began to see that particular story as a *way* to teach. Since then, given the book's success, but that it concerns only the 1950s and '60s, people (women especially) have been asking, "When are you going to write '*Remaining* Hettie Jones'?"

Another twenty years passed while I considered addressing this challenge. Why continue the story? Of what use would it be? What attraction? Scholars have tended to heroicize "beat chicks" who lived through that scene and got out alive. But afterward, lacking the anchor of male celebrity, they . . . ah, what did they do? Where did they go? What *kept* them alive? How *did* I remain Hettie Jones?

· · · · ·

In *How I Became* I wrote that these letters "kept me from sinking." Now they've kept time—the right time, because it's easy to be wrong. It was Helene who sent me, as I was writing that book, Kay Boyle's warning against memory's "dreamy evasive eyes." But here, in our letters, eyes peeled, we look straight out from wherever we were.

To correspond isn't to duplicate but to harmonize. Yet what was accomplished in all those years of words that crisscrossed the continent and sometimes the ocean? For us, a record of our separate evolutions, two takes on a possible woman's life. For the reader a glimpse into that process. And what would *this* teach?

Sometimes you have to let an idea reveal itself; I learned this from the men I knew. From Robert Creeley, that one thought should simply lead to another. From Jack Kerouac, that spontaneity can be achieved through writing in the moment *what the mind has been putting by*. From LeRoi Jones and others, that content determines form, and from Charles Olson, specificity, what one word, one tone, can mean. I can't emphasize enough how I value these lessons.

What I didn't learn from the men, though, was to value *my* moments enough to speak of them; for that I needed Helene, who, similarly, valued hers. When we met she'd been married to Ed since the mid-50s, time enough to have figured out how to maintain her integrity—if not her art (the latter, like mine, a story waiting to be told). I learned a lot from her scholarly bent, her excellent eye. And I learned, as I groped toward myself, what it was to have a friend who would herself benefit from our exchange.

· · · · ·

Once we began writing we never stopped, though sometimes there were silences or only postcards when work consumed us, as eventually we both became single mothers / working artists. "Discarded wives"—a definition Helene found—we got over the discards and into the score cards. Naturally, making up for lost time took new time: I was thirty-seven when my first book was published, Helene forty-four at her first show. But we got there, somehow. Or other. "Offline?" she wrote, after we'd progressed to email. "I've been offline since the day I was born!"

But what, after all, is the *subject* of an offline life?

As a poet, I take my thesis for this book from one way to drive the poem, which is to approach its subject from multiple directions. Letters, too, come from every which way, including time. Does their aggregate make a subject? Not guaranteed. But, like poems, they offer voices. As in: the authors have agreed to speak and we, the future, have caught them unawares.

Letters also offer arrivals, as in: at last they brought themselves to the table. Thus this correspondence offers two voices, each of two women bringing herself to the table, approaching from different directions to the other's witness, for forty-odd years. Oddities themselves. Offline.

· · · · ·

The focus of *Love, H* is wide-ranging, and like any story, it has its moods. Ecstatic: "Norway commission verified!" "Book contract signed!" Contemplative: "I wonder what it is that I want, more than this." Reports from the battleground of women's rights: "Nuns for Choice marching alongside well-dressed New Hampshire Republican Women for Choice!" And accounts from the life to which we remained irrevocably connected: "The funeral service was lovely—chanting, and the Kaddish, and little statements . . . the place crowded with people sitting on the floor and squeezed around the perimeter on chairs;

me—a seat away from Bob Creeley—on a little table, since no chairs left by the time I arrived promptly at 9. Everyone up early for Allen."

In making this selection I've been concerned most of all with literature and art and our attempts to locate our own efforts within these disciplines. But art was just one part of the ongoing struggle to sustain ourselves in a culture only beginning to recognize the working woman's place in it, and how she might achieve the necessary balance for such a venture. Given that the quest for this balance is ongoing, my purpose here is to submit some guidance, in the hope that how we remained will help others envision lives of their own choosing, and to offer young women what we lacked, frontline stories of success and failure at trying to be an artist in a woman's life.

Which is opposite the way that's usually phrased. Offline indeed.

I

A woman . . . must be like water.
Like water, you have to know where you are going
before anyone else does. . . .
In times of hardship, in times of heat, you have to steam
only then will you rise.
—*Aaliya Zaveri*

Our first fax, a single page sent both ways, has two phone numbers, two scrawled versions of *Love, H,* and in between—

"it works! we're in business! yeah, babe!"

H and H, two Babes in Boyland:

Dear Helene,
Roi's play opens 2 wks from tomorrow. Do you think I can make a dress in 2 weeks that's fancy enough to make everyone think I'm the poet's inspiration, and sexy enuf to make them think I don't care?

Dearest Het:
Ed very flippy and therefore me too—so I come in here; this bedroom is really groovy, 1st time *I've* had a "heatable" room I could use for my own and he has one too and that's one of the good things about this house— maybe I'll even DO something this year.

You had to learn the trade-offs in Boyland. You had to will yourself part of art's transformative power, while most of its transformations left you the same. You had to be brave and resourceful, a little cunning. And it had to be worse where you'd come from.
What follows are two stories with one shared point of view: we'd fled the norm for women then, because to live it would have been a kind of death.

Helene!

Three men in my kitchen watching the fight of the week (hoorah) and so I left them to squish around on the floor I just washed, muddy, muddy. A Cecil Taylor 33 is playing at 45 speed, someone's trying to fix it, tho it will now not play at all, the record player that is. That is, it needs a new one. Now the fixer is gone too, into the fighting kitchen, all muddy muddy . . .

Boyland offered, at the very least, conflicting possibilities:

Dearest Hettie,

Here's another one of those 1000 drawings I never finished — it fell out of my sketchbook and has been sitting here — "view from the porch, Santa Fe" 1960 at least. Whew. Have just finished (it's 1 am) blouse out of old tablecloth — feels lovely though material so old it's disintegrating. Well, ok, I think abt. you alla time & wonder how things are.

The year before, down the hall from the muddy kitchen, LeRoi had begun the Black Arts Movement which would draw him back to Newark, his hometown, and into his subsequent activist life as Amiri Baraka. "One-half makes you whole," he'd warned when our daughters were born, Kellie in 1959 and Lisa in 1961. Whatever this made me had never been defined; but why, after all, should it have been?

Alone and grief-stricken, only to Helene had I confessed: "I am too out of my brains to write. Sometimes I'm afraid to go to bed because I start to think . . ."

Shit, Hettie, we're so far away and I can't sit down and *write* my arms around you.

But I mustn't mail this without telling you that the letter I started, in ink, on April 30, ended so abruptly because as I was sitting here deep in the clutches of trying to *say* something to you, the doorbell rang a thousand times . . . till I went to stop the sound. And there, in the rainy spring morning, stood two little women, thin bones tight skin powdered faces.

Fig 1.1 Hettie Jones, New York, 1960

Fig 1.2 Helene Dorn, Santa Fe, 1960

Fig 1.3 LeRoi and Hettie Jones with children Lisa (on shoulders) and Kellie, 1963

Fig 1.4 Ed and Helene Dorn, Pocatello, Idaho, 1963

They asked how I was, seeing I was rather upset, and I answered fine, but very busy . . .

O, but we have only come to have a short talk about the second resurrection . . .

I flipped, they were taken aback, obviously embarrassed or confused by the tears — Oh, I'm so sorry! was all I could manage besides shutting the door. I wish I had the power to really tell you what it was like. Anyway, I walked from door to closet, got my coat, went out the back door, and walked around this godforsaken town for 3 hours.

· · · · ·

Helene Helmers Buck Dorn, born in Duluth, Minnesota, in 1927, a time when lucky girls married well and early. At twenty she dropped out of college to marry David Buck, a banker's son. They had a son, Fred, and a daughter,

Fig 1.5 Helene and children: Paul, Fred, Chan, Pocatello, 1963

Chansonette (Chan), then moved to Seattle, where, at a party, Helene met Ed Dorn. After her divorce and remarriage in 1954, she moved with her two children, Ed, and their baby son, Paul, to Black Mountain College, and from there to the West and Southwest.

She told me once that in leaving David she'd been running from a marriage she couldn't sustain. Yet, knowing the risks in any marriage, she'd married again. "But I was so in love," she protested. Clear to us both was that being there—where we were—was worth the trip. The alternative for women then was unthinkable. These are only the facts, though, which are never the whole story.

POCATELLO, MARCH 18, 1965

Dearest Hettie,

Radio just tells me we done made another raid on Ve et Nom, Los Alamos *very* visible by the way to the left of this so-called drawing. *Will* England be any better—new for us, yes, but . . .

Fig 1.6 Charles Olson and Ed Dorn (looking back), Helene Dorn, Gary Snyder, Allen Ginsberg, Robert Creeley at the Berkeley Poets Conference, 1965. Photo: Leni Sinclair

Well ok, am collecting run-over beer cans from parking lot at Buddy's—have some great ones—on this plaster wall now but am going to mount them on black velvet.

The beer cans never made it to the velvet. Shortly afterward, the Dorns left for England, where Ed had a Fulbright appointment to the University of Essex.

COLCHESTER, ENGLAND 10/19/65

Dearest Het,

Imagine buying a nice head of cauliflower & turning the corner to find yrself standing in front of the remains of a 12th cent. priory! Finally get-

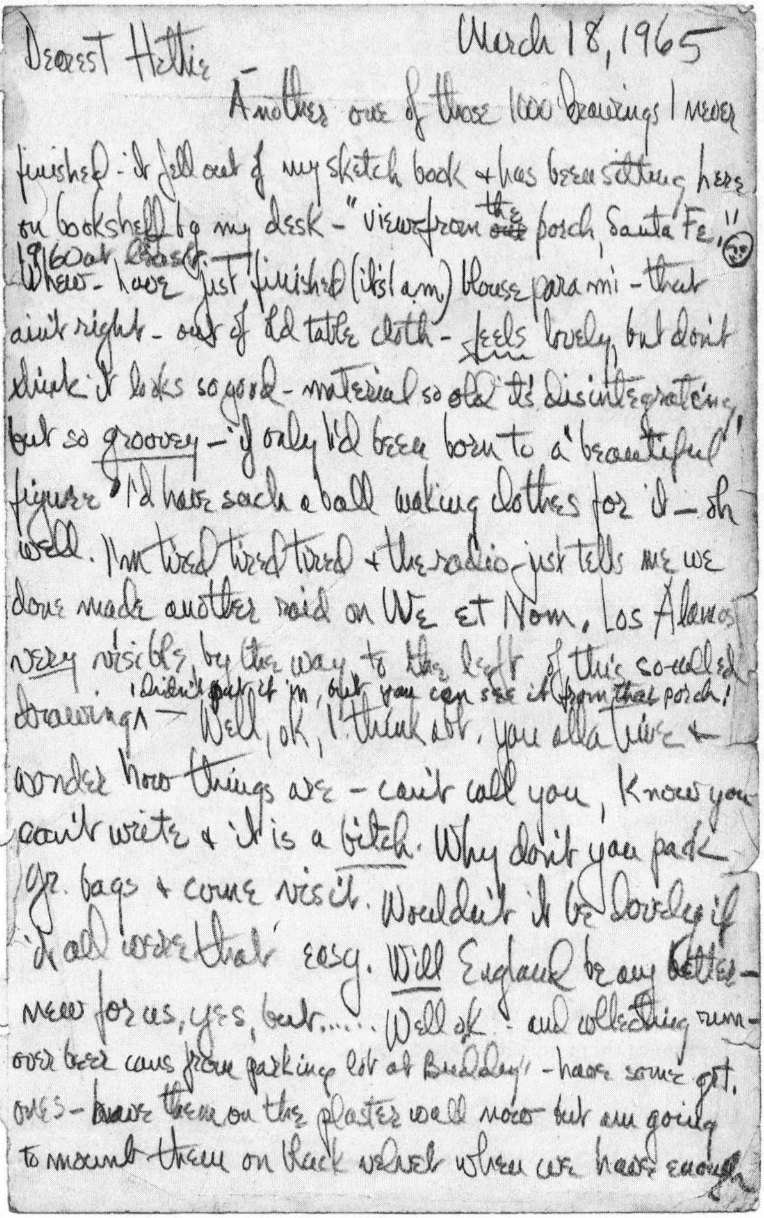

Dearest Hettie — March 18, 1965

Another one of those 1000 drawings I never finished — it fell out of my sketch book & has been sitting here on bookshelf by my desk — "view from the porch, Santa Fe, 1960 or close" ☺

Whew — have just finished (it's 1 a.m.) blouse para mi — that ain't right — out of old table cloth — feels lovely but don't think it looks so good — material so old it's disintegrating, but so groovy — if only I'd been born to a "beautiful" figure I'd have such a ball making clothes for it — oh well. I'm tired tired tired & the radio just tells me we done made another raid on Viet Nam. Los Alamos very visible, by the way, to the left of this so-called drawing — I didn't put it in, but you can see it from that porch! Well, ok, I think abt. you alla time & wonder how things are — can't call you, know you can't write & it is a bitch. Why don't you pack yr. bags & come visit. Wouldn't it be lovely if it all were that easy. Will England be any better — new for us, yes, but..... Well ok — am collecting run-over beer cans from parking lot at Building — have some gr. ones — have them on the plaster wall now but am going to mount them on black velvet when we have enough

Fig 1.7 Letter from Helene to Hettie, March 1965 (fragment)

ting settled & learning the language, which takes learning. A paper cutter, my dear, is a guillotine!

Dinner's ready & I gotta go to a "wives" meeting tonight. Just to let you know—we made it. Please write, I'm suddenly lonely!

Dearest Helene,

Was so glad to get yr card & have been trying to write ever since but tied up with proofreading, colds, school parent meets, etc.

But I now have my very own room—no curtains as yet so I'm available to all of 3rd Ave.! Still it's *very* pleasant to have a place to be that's not the kitchen.

Went to a party at Bob Thompson's two weeks ago and got propositioned four times. A newly available woman, you dig . . . I got bugged, and decided to screw someone—and it was all very swell but the minute my mind started working again, like about 1 minute later—

Roi's poem: "I got nothing against you baby but I got to get back home."

Great news dept: I HAVE A DOG. Named Ho Chi Minh! Marion[1] had promised the kids a dog for Xmas but got this puppy from some girl in a bar on Avenue B—part shepherd and the rest plain mongrel, incredibly smart, everybody's darling, but really *my* baby—

NEW YORK, WEDS. NOV. 17TH

Please forgive me—so many days and troubles since I started this. It's hard to write such lousy longhand and I can't keep up with my thoughts. Still no typewriter . . . I am terribly terribly lonely and can't figure out what to do with myself. Like I should go *out* when there's nothing to do here in the evening, but can't afford it . . .

I will, of course, live. As you know.

28TH NOVEMBER, 1965

COLECHESTER

and it *has* been cole! Hello sweet Het . . .

It was so great to get that long long letter, but I wish so much you were happier, and I don't even damn well know what to say. Except that you've

---

1. Marion Brown (1931–2010), saxophonist.

gotta stop walking from room to room sighing. Somehow or other you've really got to. And you also gotta stop hopping into bed as some sort of out—

This is one of those stupid letters, it's now 1 Dec. and I've about five pgs to type for Ed plus a bunch of quotes to look up and copy. oh yassss . . . It's tenish, the kids have hit the sack, Ed across the table from me working, Coltrane w/ Red Garland on the box. Cars whizzing by outside on their way to London. Or Marks Tey. Or Cambridge, or Tilbury Ferry . . . It's a really groovy foggy foggy night, I've invested in a couple of heavy wool knit dresses, heavy cotton sox, a bottle of scotch and I don't care how cold it gets. England is beautiful. The people I can't stand one day and really dig the next . . .

Kids had their first French tutoring session this aft. at five. Just like inda movies! Mrs. Barrett came and they sat in front of the fire in the living room—tea and soft French sounds . . .

I've got to quit and get to work for Ed.

Look, sweetie, we love you. Which is damn little help, god knows; but I feel so helpless. Especially with now the ocean between us, I can't even phone. Please know I think about you. Please, too, hold on, somehow . . .

Hold on to yr hats—I'm going to be editor of *Kulchur* for a year, maybe more if it works out. Lita Hornick[2] asked me. Gil[3] and A.B.[4] the only people I've told so far—all excited. First thing to do that anthology that Roi began collecting but left here along with other things he no longer wanted . . . Also, whatever ban she had put on political things is off, so if you would like to write about England & politics & Rhodesia & S. Africa . . .

Aside from this I am not fine but it will help and give me something to care about. I think the first cover after the anthology should be *Kulchur 21* WATCH OUT because I don't see the sense in doing anything unless it stirs up turmoils. Do you? I hope I can do it!

---

2. Publisher, benefactor of *Kulchur* magazine.
3. Gilbert Sorrentino.
4. A. B. Spellman.

Grooooovvy!!!! Bless lil'ole Lita's heart . . . Of course you can do it—and how great to get that magazine back where it *says* something. Ed will write you later, am just sending this quickly to let you know how glad we are!

Did I send a card the day Paul and I went to the Tower of London? I can't remember—he wore me out racing up and down those crazy stone circular stairs . . . I felt like I was in a Vincent Price flick!

Kulchur's funder, Lita Hornick, took over this avant-garde literary magazine from its originator, Marc Schleifer, who had begun it as an annual in 1961. Hornick had been publishing it since then as a quarterly, with the guidance of an editorial board consisting mainly of poets, among them LeRoi and Frank O'Hara; issues had been guest-edited by board members Gilbert Sorrentino and Joel Oppenheimer. By the time she contacted me, Hornick, a Barnard graduate who had done graduate work in modern literature at Columbia, was editing the magazine herself and clearly rethinking the whole idea of its direction. *Poems Now*, the anthology that I eventually did edit after some indecision on her part (see below), was the first in a series of books that replaced the magazine format, most featuring the work of poets from the New York School such as Ted Berrigan and Gerard Malanga.

Lita Hornick rescinded her offer 3 days after she tendered it, but I am still to do a poetry anthology though not until spring. Wot a drag, eh—for a few days I felt like everything I get is always taken away 3 days later, or 8 years . . . I am ok, cynical but ok.

Hello dear Het—

I'm so sleepy I can hardly keep my eyes open, but I've got to say hello at least and let you know I'm thinking about you.

Hokay . . . The clock in my room just chimed 10 and the sun came out at the same time. The birds are singing fools and I feel much like they sound. We haven't seen the sun for days and days and days. The gardener is working in "Grandma Palmer's" garden below us—he goes with the house, the contract says. And thinks I want to play Lady Chatterley w/him be-cause I'm all the time looking out the windows (it's a lovely landscape—beautiful trees, red brick walls, tiled cottage roofs, even a greenhouse. And thousands of birds). And I'm sure he thinks it's him I'm digging.

Yup! He just came in. I was looking out the window over the kitchen sink when *blam*—into my view comes his gray hair. Now he's on the other side, raking or something. No, by god, he has one of those magnificent witch brooms (huge) and he's *sweeping* the grass w/it! How about that—they sweep the grass in East Anglia.

But enough of my affair—you'd think that very funny could you see him!

I wish I could write all kinds of soothing things—you *are* a Greek tragedy and it is all so miserably real and it's horrible knowing there's nothing I can say, really. For god's sake write as often as you please, at least it's something I can do, hold it too.

NEW YORK, FRIDAY MARCH 4 66

Dearest Helene,

Hurrah the typewriter is fixed! (Because I took a typing job one day when there was nothing else available, wouldn't you know it wd have to be a crisis.)

Anyway, with help by chance from Joel[5] I've just landed a job as an editor for University Books, unfortunately an hour and a half from here by subway and bus. I go there four days and spend Fri at home read-ing. Spent this week working on copy for *The Encyclopedia of Psychic Sci-ence*—from which you can gather that they publish for what Joyce[6] calls "the nut market" but also the *Psychedelic Review* of Tim Leary and works by Gurdjieff. So it will be good. That is, I am going to make it good. I am tired of wailing and depending on other people for anything.

Kellie has been in the hospital to have a wart removed, Lisa is okay but they are both about to get the mumps because it is all over, Accra the small downstairs Shepp[7] has it now. The washing machine died and needs $75 to come back to life. Have had to stop taking Enovid birth control be-

---

5. Joel Oppenheimer.

6. Joyce Johnson.

7. Younger son of Archie Shepp, saxophonist.

cause of dreadful fatness and exhaustion. It's good to be normal—and if I stand on my head every time I want to fuck, instead of fucking, I'll be all right.

Best news: Lita Hornick doesn't after all want me to do the anthology and sent me $100 for services rendered. I can only tell you that after the work I've put into the damn thing I am going to complete it and sell it elsewhere. I can't let all these people down *again!*

I must get back to the life and times of séances and spiritualism. Did you ever see a verified photo of a medium with ectoplasm extruding from her nose, with pictures of Sir Arthur Conan Doyle in the ecto?

My love to you all, to Jeremy[8] for the nice little squiggle on yr postcard arrived this morning, and to the English ghosts for their being worthy of the literature that's going to keep us in the green!

[On the back of the envelope containing this letter]: Monday, cdn't mail, no stamp. Boss going to lend me $ for car big as a house, drove it tonight. Lita H. *is* doing antho again. Tell Ed send poems *immediately.* Crazy world, no?

COLCHESTER, 11TH MARCH 1966

Dearest Het—

So very good to get your letter—the job sounds crazy: come to me my Psychedelic Bayyaayaabee!!! Looks like we'll be here next year . . .

NEW YORK 3/11/66

Dearest Helene,

I'm cooking a chicken for Marion to take to Buffalo—also, at the same time, finding you on the map. Jesus, those names . . . Wivenhoe, Shoeburyness, Clacton, Burnham on Crouch, Foulness Island—Foulness Island! Cardigan, Hereford, Gloucester . . . Everything from sweaters to cows to Shakespeare, what a language . . .

Editing now a book written by a priest who ran away from his order because of his balls. I like my new job v. much.

Marion has been and gone, with his chicken. Said to tell you he's working the shit circuit (NY, Buffalo, Toronto).

---

8. Jeremy Prynne.

I'm buying a station wagon (Ford '59) from the handsome garage man next door. If boss doesn't come through I'll have to borrow from either Ted Wilentz[9] or Lita. Anyway with the help of god and influence I'll be able to drive to work next week. Do you hear how hard I am? Can you believe me? I am out to take the most of what's available, and screw anyone in the way.

You cannot imagine the kind of attitude that seems to grow up inside one when the only available opportunities for any kind of life have to come from oneself, entirely. I don't mean just money, but all kinds of things. Like I have to anticipate who to come on to in what kind of way, for what kind of advantage. Men, women—if you talk to the typewriter repairman in a nice way, even though he hasn't fixed your typewriter after two days of promises and keeps you waiting 20 minutes with your dog while your children are alone in the house—but if you keep your temper and be pleasant and interested in his work, he will carry the typewriter up the stairs for you so it won't break again when you bump it up in a shopping cart. If you are pleasant to the schoolmarm and tell her your troubles and display your earnestness she will assure you your children will get a scholarship. If you are sweet to the TV repairman who is leching after you, he will fix your TV set three times, and if you look tearfully at the cop and tell him you are honestly *trying* to keep your dog from shitting on the curb instead of in the gutter, he won't give you a summons . . .

I am getting tired, I think, which makes me a little bugged . . .

[POSTCARD: YORK, ENGLAND]

25TH MARCH

Hello Het!

We've been to Newcastle. Spent yesterday w/ Basil Bunting[10] who is a truly wonderful man. Went on the moors & have a sprig of heather for you.

---

9. Owner, with his brother Eli, of the Eighth Street Bookshop.

10. British modernist poet (1900–1985). A generation older than Ed and Helene, Bunting was born into a British Quaker family, and as a conscientious objector had been imprisoned during World War I. After the war he lived in London, where he became acquainted with Ezra Pound, Louis Zukovsky, and other luminaries of that time. Bunting was very much influenced by music; his "Advice to Young Poets" begins, "Compose aloud; poetry is a sound."

Frantic now trying to take care of everything for trip—we leave Sat. at
11 and arrive Sun. in *Florence* at noon. Aiii! Very exciting . . . Jeremy has
gone off to Cambridge w/the heather in his car, I'll have to send it later—
I picked it from the hill going up to the Roman road—which is crazy to
see taking off straight across the moor; it was cold and windy and raining,
very Bronte-esque weather, and we left just as it was getting dark so I said
hello to all those ghosts for ye.

Tonight I'm madly in love with the garage man. He smells of gasoline and
has a brilliant smile, a chipped tooth and a Spanish accent. If I came to
England I would most certainly like your gardener. Anyway it keeps me
cheerful . . .

The job is very interesting, but that seems to be all there is. Sometimes,
like last night, I speak to no one at all between the hours of 8:30pm and
7am, as if in a seminary. Hard to summon from some mysterious source
one's womanhood without reminders. If one can't be the beloved/lover,
at least once in a while??

So here's to Lady Chatterley.

I am facing seven pairs of little girls' tights, all with holes in the knees
or the toes or the asses. And a box labeled, clearly, "K anthology," and a
box full of other mending, and the book I am working on at my job, called
"The Circle of Sex" (more of this later), which I was supposed to be working on all day today instead of dragging laundry. All of it unfinished business of a sort, hanging like a number of stones, always on my conscience,
ding dong bell. Pussy's in the well.

Prisoners' advice: don't serve the time, let the time serve *you*. In this instance
the time had a place, as I would write, "in the middle of other people's wars,"
and a perfect irony in that this territory is called a no-man's-land. The sixties
swirled with revision, not all of it good—imperialism's retreat in Africa vs the
closing of universities in China, for one big example. I watched all but connected to none—reduced, it seemed, to what I alone could make of myself.
Around me, women seemed to be rising from a long sleep, though it wasn't
easy to stay awake, I knew, in face of the real deal, not the romance. Neverthe-

less, I'd just written a poem,[11] the first since my divorce. It's got long lines and needs a lot of breath to recite, and over many years I've given it all I've got, in honor of all that.

Dear Helene,

Where are you? What's happening? I have much news.

#1: I got fired. For presumably not being able to write the kind of selling-book copy the cat required. Anyway day before yesterday he gave me my salary for the week and told me not to come back. So I am again up shit creek for money. Have already, since yesterday morning, phoned the entire establishment—old *Partisan Review*–affiliated friends. Also all the publishing houses . . . So here I sit with my rock n roll radio playing "Monday, Monday," and the window open at last, delighted to be in my dirty old house at 12:25 p.m. with an ear to the neighborhood.

Someone asked me why I had so many extra troubles, like animals and a now useless car, and I couldn't think why. Even if you have to move the car from one side of the street to the other all week, it gives you a chance to go to the trees on the weekend. And then there's the gas station . . .

JUNE 9TH 1966 COLCHESTER

Well hello!

I sent you a card last Saturday from Paris . . . Paris, wow! A beautiful city and I of course fell in love with it, hating the fact of the appeal of that degenerate French elegance, but appeal it certainly has.

I wish things would slow down so I could write a decent letter; I've got 2 months work helping Ed: he's got 3 books to finish by September and just as I found time to do some painting the bastard needs me, but I don't mind, I'd probably flip if he *didn't*, and haven't drawn for so long it's like starting from scratch.

"Your life sounds so *continental!*" I wrote back. "Going to Paris for the weekend! I'm beginning to feel I'll never go anywhere except from here to Grove Press and back again."

---

11. "Paleface," *Drive* (1998).

But I also felt that hard work—freelance copyediting and proofreading—was saving my life, so I'd never again have to give it away because someone else needed it. And here, at 27 Cooper Square, where I'd lived four years, I could put my solitary bones to bed among friends. "Downstairs," I wrote, "Archie is playing the piano very quietly, has been composing for about two weeks now, so every night I have lovely music to go to sleep to, makes me grateful to be here. Things, after all, could be worse."

· · · · ·

It was Helene, I felt, who had it worse:

Dearest Het—

Billie's *Golden Years* on the record player, we've had it on all day.

I *think* I'm getting homesick. Which is a laugh—where *is* home? England is beautiful, but it ain't home. And that swinging Carnaby Street lot is finally the dullest come-on for a long time, and so much a uniform—

Did you go to Joel's wedding?!! We sent them a wire from Paris, I wonder if they got it. Things there look so scary from here. We feel so far away.

Hokay, Mama, just sitting here thinking abt. you.

NEW YORK, 7/15/66

Dearest Helene,

Just read your letter which arrived in the a.m.

I got a great job with Mobilization For Youth,[12] so I've been finishing up a lot of work—during day for MFY and proofreading for Grove at night. My job is a supreme gas—I am going to be writing about the Lower East Side—the whole scene.

Finished Ed's book [*The Shoshoneans*], which Joyce loaned me. It's fantastic and McLucas's[13] photographs are out of sight. We looked at all of them; she hasn't chosen any yet. Jesus, those weird drunken guys riding cows in the moonlight and with flashlights, yet!

Tomorrow is my birthday and it seems I am to be 32 years old. I really

12. One of three New York agencies created as part of Lyndon Johnson's War on Poverty.
13. Leroy McLucas, photographer.

don't understand that! My car died on the Thruway somewhere near Suffern, NY at the end of May, and now I walk. Everywhere. I'm to begin working "in the field" on Monday.

Kellie now one of the big kids, dig, like allowed out on the street alone, and Lisa has lost another tooth, a perfect urchin with a gap that goes from top to bottom!

Marion playing opposite Coltrane August 12. A groove, huh? Such an event might even get me to make a new dress.

Yes, I did go to Joel's wedding, which was marvelous. And he has just gotten a job with St. Mark's Church, with their new anti-poverty money, to run an arts program.[14] I think he'll probably do a great job.

So all in all things are fine. 12:15am. Six hrs. quick sleep. I am homesick for you too.

NEW YORK, 7/20/66

Dear Helene,

I'm in the basement of the Jacob Riis Houses, Ave. D at 10th St., waiting to go shopping with a woman who gets welfare, to see that she spends her money wisely. However I don't think she'll show, as she looked pretty hip when I met her yesterday. But she does what they politely call "mismanages"—and then comes here to ask for food money. This is what they call "resistance." I am learning and learning . . .

Went last night to East Harlem for dinner with one of the workers here, a Puerto Rican black man, community organizer. Ran an ambulance during those summer riots, has been to Alabama, marching, etc. Has a Mercedes and we sped thru yesterday evening's thunderstorms, what fun! Known on his block, people stopping to talk to him as we walked along, very middle-class guy, with *nearly* traditional notions of women. Sees the necessity of P.R. & Negro combined political action, tho that'll be hard to get to. Last I heard the kids were fighting each other in Bedford-Stuyvesant.

Actually this is a fairly simple operation, it's the dealing with *other* city and state welfare agencies that gets complicated. Mostly because they keep on grinding the faces of the poor in the same old dirt. Like, dig,

---

14. This became the St. Mark's Poetry Project.

an employed man is given more $ for razor blades than an unemployed one—and haircuts the same.

Am "observing" 2 bilingual children age 6 and prob 2½. They draw pictures for me, both very well—the so-called "articulate" children . . . The community organizer told me he was introduced as "an articulate P.R. spokesman" at a university conference on China.

My lady never showed. Guess her resistance was up high today.

Dearest Hettie,

I'm initiating my on-sale box of Charta Egypta. Bought it in a funny old stationer on High Street; it had a ½ inch of dust on it—probably no Englishwoman wld buy it 'cuz it doesn't have envelopes to match. Well hello!

We've moved; been here since the 26th of August. It was so filthy it took us this long to just *kind of* get the stench in the background—so crazy to get so involved, suddenly, in our "place." The Weavers' was like a motel, put a few things on the wall and it was okay, not "HOME" but certainly "ours" for a brief period. This place is stuffed full of the ghosts that it really belongs to, and after the getting rid of the filth I found myself caught up in trying to make it ours—a very difficult business and so stupid really. Well, I'm a bit stoned; here in our Ibsen room sitting in front of the fire—and what I really need is the typewriter, to tell you where we find ourselves. It's wild, literally, and I hope I can come through it, which sounds very phony, but if you walked in here you'd understand. Bats and candlelight and musk, Danes and Irishmen, Bloomsbury and the BBC.

As soon as school starts I'll get to letters—just to let you know anyway, I do think of you every day, like they say (do they?)—But I *do* and I'm so much wondering what's happening. Let me hear—just a postcard even.

Dearest Helene,

Thirty days hath September . . . god only knows what I've been doing. The kids back at school, also go to an after-school program, and will begin [ages 7 and 5], this coming Monday, to navigate the 2nd Ave. bus by themselves.

My job is great, I've been writing and my boss is well pleased.

What else? Last Friday this particular staff, ours, called "Program Reporting and Redevelopment," went to Fire Island for a meeting. Talked most of the day but then everyone got loaded in a v. pleasant way—yng man and I had saved a dime a day for a long time and got a nickel bag, so we went off on the beach and got high! Then driving home . . . whew! Oh, I bought a new car, a '53 Plymouth, for $25, sometime in August. Makes things much easier, like picking up tired kids at 5:30 p.m., because five blocks can seem like 50 when you're only five years old and you've been away from home since 8:30 a.m.

Marion has decided that he can't live with me anymore because Roi is going to ruin his career. I am also, in my usual fashion, having an affair with someone else, very quietly.

It's nearly 10:30 and I've been here since 9:15. This place is funded by the U.S. govt and if I don't fuck off a bit not only will people think I'm crazy but I might throw the whole thing—can be construed as sabotage . . .

Your house sounds so nice, ghosts and all. But when will you come back? Kellie and Lisa are very concerned. What's the story? Joyce Johnson's baby is big and fat and red-haired, Archie's wife Garth had a girl they named Bambu, so there are tiny baby noises in our house. We have a new little kitten, all black and brave as two kittens. Must work now, it's really late. Forgive all this past silence, it won't happen anymore, I promise.

COLCHESTER 26TH SEPTEMBER, 1966

Dearest Het—

It's 1:30 a.m., Ed's asleep, jazz on the transistor on floor by the bed— not bad, England swings if you can get the continent after 11pm. Finally getting to feel ok in this house, I just gave in. (Very funny to hear "BBC" English announcing Coltrane, etc. and trying to sound hip for the late-nighters.) Spent much of the day getting all the bug-ridden dying geraniums to the kitchen sink to try to wash them "well." Then to town with Paul, who has entered the pre-teen negative stage. He is ALMOST as tall as I yam [sic] (and twice as obnoxious).

England has been a weird thing for P. and Chan. The minute they get "in" w/their contemporaries it means they gotta lose all interest in learning anything from a book. It seems the whole fucking class/Empire-lost mentality/tradition can't be erased by that ridiculous material-Mary Quant[15] Revolution.

I got lotsa gray hairs. Well anyway, we're trying to get them out of this fucking class structure . . . .

Fred takes the Cambridge exam end of November—please god, his masters at grammar school think he'll make it . . . Is really a fine young man but needs to get away from us—

Aii, Ed stirring again—he's going to wake up and flip that I'm still up . . .

We get the Paris edition of the Tribune plus the London Times, the Observer, Time, Newsweek, etc. but feel even so, very left out, I mean, what the FUCK is happening? Well, shit—I could ask you all kind of questions: what's Joel doing, what's happening to Ed Sanders, Gil, and Grove? Etc.

Whew! I got stoned while writing last night and now I'm on the 12:46 to London and these trains are horribly jiggly . . . It's a beautiful sunny day. Coal yards now and the train is stopping soon, Chelmsford, we're in the station now. I'll finish quickly while I can. This whole letter is hopeless, but am going to mail it at Liverpool Street station anyway. Get stoned and then read it, maybe it'll make sense that way? O dear dear Hettie, *write* . . .

We're having again to make a decision abt staying here another year . . .

NEW YORK SAT AM HOME, V. RAINY/OCT I

Helene! I came home to your letter yesterday . . .

MONDAY AM BACK IN THE OFFICE

Trying to finish writing this paper I've got to have done by the 14th of Oct. Have already been to the Bureau of Motor Vehicles. Monday morning energies fast depleting.

Yes, what if you do come back here? What is there to do? I must tell you that Ed Sanders, last I saw him, was wearing a white vinyl suit. This was in summer, at a recording session sponsored by the *East Village Other*. I am bored by Timothy Leary's guru-ness. Allen Ginsberg came

---

15. Sixties English couturier, widely credited with introducing the miniskirt and hot pants.

to visit during the summer, what I didn't tell him was that the present political failure in this country is indeed a failure of the white liberal to become a white radical. Allen and Peter and Leary and Ed Sanders and all the people I know—I mean the men in this case—should be *out on a limb*, not to make pot legal, but to stop the fucking war and in support of black power. The parents of Michael Schwerner sent around a form letter stating their support for b.p. and underlined that it was *not* a solicited appeal from SNCC—if the parents of Michael Schwerner, middle-class Jews, can do it, where are the rest of us? It's so fucking *safe* for Leary to spend his life turning on. To ease the pain and any guilt you might have at not doing anything . . . Too early for all this jazz!

COLCHESTER, 12TH OCTOBER, 1966

Dearest Hettie—

Such a groove to get your letter yesterday. Ed brought it w/my slippers—I'm in a bed in Alderton Ward of St. Mary's HORSEPISTAL and I can't yet see too well from the hypos and whatever else they gave me yesterday aside from the goofey knife.

I am now recovering from the removal, around 6pm last nite, of a cyst, got 6 stitches and I'm feeling BAD—and I really mean *bayad!* How the hell does one get cysts anyway?

English hospitals are crazy but rather scary for a U.S. cit. like me who's had enuff operations anyway and all the dust, do-it-yourself of this lil hospital scared me plenty! But I took my pre-operation bath, donned my surgical sox and dress and lay down on my bed exactly when they told me.

19TH OCTOBER

Well, I'm back home . . . 6 days in the hospital wow, did this place look groovy! Still can't sit very well and am in some lousy cloud. Try to keep my mind on something for more than 3 minutes but it doesn't work. Weigh 120 lbs. which I haven't for years which is a consolation prize for having a scarred cunt. Dig that.

20TH OCTOBER

Had upset last night and was too jittery to write. Started bleeding for real suddenly and it scared me, finally got Dr. at 10pm and he sez nothing to worry abt, his only advice being to wear a pad! What the fuck he think I was doing!

So you're in your "social workers bag," so what? You got to have *some* bag and that one happens to bring in some $ as well, fuck it, I'm glad you're in it. Useful term, "articulate" — seems to me it applies in that sense to the whole bit of social work/sociology/*welfare*/etc. The Big Show; how can it be anything else when its existence is subsidized by articulate American society, i.e. those members who are smart enough to know they're gonna get their throats cut if they don't get a bigger percentage of articulate "welfare" clients, etc. That articulateness of more razor blades and haircuts for the employed gets even more terrifying in the state employment agencies like yes, we do have this job but we can't give it to you because you got too many children and it doesn't pay enough — all of this you know of course — don't know why I'm rambling, guess it helps get my mind and spleen off my own ill-functioning organism. Yes, of course Leary's beside the point, and Allen and that whole bag of concerns. And yet there *is* that concern and one should be able to get high w/out landing in jail etc.

The problem is far more complex than just the war and Black Power — and seeing that "resistance" through to articulateness by showing a woman how to "shop" is not the point either . . . resistance, wow, *ain't* they got the hippest terms!

It's pouring down very wet English rain from very gray English October clouds so that shoots my walking this to the post. Never mind, tomorrow!

Damn I don't know when we'll be back! Donald [Davie] has asked Ed to accept a post at Essex for *next* year. America doesn't seem to be offering him anything.

I must stop. Your quiet affair sounds nice. The lady upstairs is having a *loud* one w/the milkman (I'm serious!) and it's not so nice because commuting husband caught on and the result almost broke our ceilings — but didn't, incidentally, stop the affair. Love & kisses all around —

· · · · ·

What did stop, abruptly, were her letters — and mine as well, it appears — because sixty-seven doesn't exist in these files. Maybe we both needed to forget it, and writing it then might have proven it now. I remember only the night in July that Newark rioted, LeRoi Jones was beaten, and—"coincidentally"—27 Cooper Square caught fire. At 3 A.M. Engine Company 33 rushed over from Great Jones Street and cherry-picked us off the fire escape. Everyone, including the house, survived.

One evening in February 1968 Helene telephoned from her brother Jack's apartment in upper Manhattan to tell me that Ed was involved with one of his students. I drove uptown as soon as I could, and though a letter makes clear that I stayed late and we talked a lot, I can summon only one image—Helene in a turtleneck sweater pulled to her chin, as if to restrain a scream. From New York she wrote Fred, who was at Cambridge, that I was leading a "pretty awful life," which is probably why I remember so little of it. Still, I've always felt she had it worse.

· · · · ·

22ND WASHINGTON'S BIRTHDAY 1968

BARCELONA, SPAIN

Dearest Het,

Arrived Colchester abt. 3:15pm to find Ed & Jenny[16] in kitchen. No scene on my part—just his. Left Colchester 8:00am week later, same day (Monday)—gear mostly, except for books, packed in trunk for U.S.A.!

Here & *sun!!* Havoc, but we [Helene, Chan, and Paul] finally found apartment . . .

Just to let you know—letters later, am really just too exhausted. Med. *beautiful!!*

Palm trees, etc. Like San Francisco, sweaters & boots & coats needed but in sun you could lie nude in comfort. Too much!

Take care, love to all, from all . . .

LISTA DE CORREOS, SITGES (BARCELONA), ESPAÑA

[smile] write?

· · · · ·

Of course I wrote, but that letter is lost, though she refers to it. The next, and last from her time in Spain, is undated. She had chosen Sitges—very much out

---

16. Jennifer Dunbar, who was to become Ed Dorn's second wife.

of the way then though a tourist attraction now—because she wanted to learn Spanish, and while in New York had seen a poster in a travel agency window.

Dearest Het—

Many thanks for your letter; things sound as bugged as ever—especially the bit about your car. There'll never be another, *never*, quite like that one and I burn effigies of whoever done smashed the windows!

Sitting here having a coffee listening to the sea—marvelous wind today, i.e. marvelous to watch from inside—the palm trees are bending way way over in the heavy gusts and the lovely calm quiet Mediterranean looks more like the North Sea—fantastic foamy spray mist way out . . .

It *is* good to be here, I dig it more every day, the easy life—and I'm suddenly really aware that I'd damn well better take it while I can. Still have no idea what, after this. Dunno, at this point would like, I think, to just stay here away from everything—a real escape this little village in España. Brother Jack wrote in same tone you did of the feeling there in the Apple—wow, what *is* going to happen. Ed sent a wild statement from Charles [Olson]: "The Society / is any American black or white who remains himself in a hostile world." I think much about you there and I'm scared. I so much escape here that I finally don't even read the papers I buy every day. I have Che on my wall in Franco's Spain and that is it for me now.

So, love, things do go on here, and you are very right about the cureall of the sea and sun.

Take care, I'll write a so-called letter soon . . . just to let you know I think of you.

• • • • •

Helene had left school and home in 1947 for two decades of marriage and child support. As an autodidact she was more widely read than I, intellectually rigorous, analytic, a scholar. Yet at forty, as she wrote from Barcelona, she had no idea what she would do next or where she'd fit.

I was glad she thought about me, and I did think about myself, but I thought most about my daughters—Kellie then eight, Lisa six—who didn't have it easy, having me. So I decided to leave them a clear field: they'd be "young, gifted, and black," and I would be what I could. We were all allowed to make ourselves up.

And I was restless to locate myself. I had elected a life in Boyland. Like Helene's thousand unfinished drawings, I'd had fits and starts. With her I could be just another woman with intentions who'd delayed them for a husband who'd left her for his own. Years later we laughed over the term "discarded wife," though at the time we wouldn't have. Still, I was a different kind of discard—a wage earner.

I had also been raised to serve my community, but not in a civil war. Then as now I lived on a corner, a flashpoint of two opposing trajectories, which seemed a convenient conceit. All I could do from here was bear witness.

· · · · ·

In 1969, with her daughter, Chan, and younger son, Paul, Helene returned to the States and settled in Gloucester, Massachusetts, down the street from Olson, on the "Fort" overlooking the harbor. Gloucester answered her question from England: home. One early letter mentions a small drafting table. "So tired," she wrote, "but alive nonetheless and anxious believe it or not to get something going on that drafting table."

Proximity to Charles Olson wasn't Helene's sole reason for choosing Gloucester, though I'm sure having a friend close by was something she considered. Nor was its location—she would later refer to the city as "beautiful, beautiful Gloucester." But not insignificant was its history of attraction for artists since the beginning of the nineteenth century, among them some of the most recognizable and successful: Winslow Homer, Stuart Davis, Mark Rothko, Milton Avery, Marsden Harley, Edward Hopper. Indeed, Helene was to live briefly in a house that looked out on that of Gloucester's best-known native-born painter, Fitz Henry Lane.

When she'd called to report her return, I determined to see for myself. It was midwinter and had just snowed, but I piled kids and dogs into our current rattletrap of a station wagon and drove to the Gloucester motel where she was staying while her apartment was being painted. And there she was, with a broken ankle—having been hit by a car in Spain—but ready, as she'd written, "to get something going."

In *How I Became Hettie Jones*, I wrote of a faith between myself and Helene: "We knew that what was incomplete still compelled us, and hid the same shame at having abandoned it."

Now there was no time to lose. Her first show, in 1971, was a one-person exhibit of mosaics created from glass and metal washed up on the harbor beaches. In her artist's statement she mentions "discards," which "left to lie" often become "extremely beautiful."

Now, decades later, I'd like to linger over her long-ago word choice, for without "discards" we'd have none of the value and challenge of "found objects." I almost want to say that as discards ourselves, we found in art a way to turn one into the other.

Holes to fill were what I fell into, the deepest (and closest) being the absence of people of color in children's books, so I wrote—and sold!—an "easy reader," *The City That Walked*, about Rosa Parks and the Montgomery, Alabama, bus boycott. Inspired, I'd begun researching another when I found myself in the hospital and on welfare like the people I'd just been observing. The social worker there disparaged anti-poverty programs run by people without accrediting degrees. "Stay on welfare and go back to school," she sniffed. "Make something of yourself."

I had no idea what that might be, since I'd always thought *process* not *goal*. "The journey itself is home," Basho wrote. And Olson: "I pose you your question: / shall you uncover honey / where maggots are? / I hunt among stones."

But the politics of art is fluid, and though civil rights weren't yet "history" and my easy reader was never published, my next book for children, a selection of American Indian poems, appeared in 1971, the same year as Helene's first show. I was thirty-seven, she forty-four. "This town is so beautiful," she wrote in March. "I wish you would come now while we've got lamb weather and before they blast us all because the CIA dropt a bomb in a White House john . . ."

I didn't make it up there then, though I would, often, over time. But two phrases from her artist's statement seem to describe, in 1971, the lives we were going for: "the end of pattern and beginning of sculpture," and "found objects, some tampered with, some not."

2

I am is my name and your name, *I am* is
the name we are finding,
I am is the
name who is finding us, is
the one I always wanted to find. . . .
—*Jean Valentine*

The car I'd bought for $25 had come with two free lessons in how to drive stick. Soon I could drive almost anything, even a truck, but seemed always to get stuck with big old wagons that were about to throw a rod. Nevertheless, by 1971 my kids were twelve and ten and in need of rest and distraction, as was I. And gas was cheap. And if the cars died inopportunely, while they lived so did we.

APRIL, 1971, GLOUCESTER

Hello Love—A truly valiant death-of-a-car: in the rain near Sing Sing. Too much! It seems that kind of spring and I'm getting a note off to you right away because I must train myself to take advantage of a quiet moment when it occurs. My house remains Grand Central.

When I can I've been making small tourist "window hangings" from beach glass. It takes a fabulous amt. of time and I'm getting bored w/it because I want so much to do other things, and I wonder if I can find a shop here to take them. I shld have 40 or 50 before I try. If I find I can't sell 'em I'll make a giant mobile or something [frowning face] . . .

Helene often drew on her letters, little self-portraits with varying expressions, one or two perfectly executed lines, no two ever alike, the emoticon's glamorous grandma—and she's looking right *at* you. During the sixties Ed Dorn published *Wild Dog*, a mimeographed magazine, for which Helene had done some covers that show this same fine hand. But it's the life in the little faces I love, as if her hand knew exactly what was on her mind.

It's been v. "social" here—my brother over Easter and two this past week very wild birthday parties. And in between all kinds of people I haven't seen all winter knocking on my kitchen door. To say nothing of parenthetical small dramas sifting in thru the cracks. All of which makes it very difficult to get more done.

And all *I'd* like to do right now is have the ease of spreading out as I feel it, into *all* the rooms in my apt. so I can literally *see* what I've done so far. I feel, wow! do I, a terrible lack of work space and privacy both. Amen.

So my dear I guess this is kind of sending a *yuck* right back but what the fuck sometimes it's a comfort? to know you got company. Beautiful beautiful Gloucester is still here and when that new car turns up outa the blue, you come get a real feeling of it. We'll have a picnic on the rocks at Stage Fort Park and watch the boats and tide come in.

The car didn't turn up too soon; we kept in touch and kept working, though I think it surprised us both to discover the amount of new time involved in making up for time lost.

Within which arrived other surprises. *The Trees Stand Shining*, that selection of American Indian poems, won a Notable Book Award from the American Library Association. It had been beautifully illustrated by the painter Robert Andrew Parker, and since then I'd been able to publish and to get work for hire. I felt grateful and vindicated, inspired to search out other holes to fill. But books for children were and are just as market-driven as any others; like Helene with her window hangings, I could be asked to repeat myself. In April 1973, I complained:

> I'm surrounded by textbooks and pieces of textbookwork and a trophy called *Shining Bridges*, the Macmillan Second Grade Reader. We need to return to either McGuffey's First Eclectic, or the Bible. Whichever, but save us oh save us from the textbookwriters. Dear Lord.
>
> Today I learned how that Lord giveth and taketh away. My agent told me that *Ms* had rejected my little story. Then she told me that my first book is going to be read 9 times by the state of Michigan (!) on some program, and they are going to pay me $300. Then the woman who has become Holt's Senior Kidbook Editor told me that the illustrator who did

2nd book[1] is going to do pictures for Coyote Tails or Coyote's Tail (yes that's it) . . . But that she really didn't like the stories. Now that I remember, it's Coyote's Tricks.[2]

About my daughters, by then teenagers, I had no complaints. As always, having me to contend with wasn't easy, and even more difficult at this time when the word "polarized" was on every tongue. But at home there were no contests, only an intimate peaceable kingdom:

> Sat. night late Kellie and I were up watching *The Seven Samurai* and while we were watching, with no commercials, the rabbit ATE the beanbag chair. Not completely, but enough to scatter beans—have you ever seen them? They're AWRFul!—$\frac{1}{16}$th in diameter, white plastic but rubbery and seem possessed of a marvelous electricity that makes them irremovable.

Unlike me, Helene had grown up bookish. Her family read fiction and discussed it at dinner. When she was married to Ed, they'd read novels aloud. I've assumed, given those times, that like all of us they read men, mostly. For Grove Press I'd proofread Marguerite Duras, and when I worked at *Partisan Review* had read Mary McCarthy, Tillie Olsen, and a few others. Now Helene and I began to read newly available women's work in great gulps—so many stories so unlike ours—but then the occasional eye-openers we could talk about whenever we found time for a visit: "Have you read Jane Bowles?" my April 1973 letter asks, and continues:

> I have *Collected Works* and am reading *Two Serious Ladies*, which is very good. There's a fine used paperback bookstore around the corner—like 50 cents a book or sometimes a quarter. Send me a list.
>
> May I come visit you sometime during the next month? The kids are dying to get rid of me, they keep hinting. Not hinting, telling: "Why don't you go on a little vacation, Ma?"
>
> So I'll round up their favorite sitters,[3] and hop on the train, hopefully

---

1. *Longhouse Winter* (Holt, Rinehart and Winston, 1972).
2. *Coyote Tales* (Holt, Rinehart and Winston, 1974), illustrated by Louis Mofsie.
3. Helene's daughter, Chan, was living and working in New York, and had befriended Nancy Zimmerman, the college student living with me.

before April is over, and we can share the burden of the cruelest month. Tho truthfully I wouldn't want yours and you wouldn't want mine, but it is nice to see another soul with a big jar of Burdens Best and still managing to stay afloat! Afoot! Aloft!

Sometimes I did feel airborne, writing books I saw a need for—in 1974 the YA nonfiction *Big Star Fallin' Mama*, *Five Women in Black Music*, and a book about vitamins, *How to Eat Your ABCs*, which would be published in 1976. Still, the scramble for money was daunting; in 1975, women earned 58.8 cents to every dollar earned by men. In March, I wrote:

> Jan and Feb were the worst . . . I had to borrow money from Elizabeth,[4] the bank, and then from my mother-in-law, in order to eat, and didn't pay the rent for 2 mos or the phone. It's really crazy . . . Anyway soon I'm going to do my taxes and then maybe I can apply for Food Stamps again.

I'd been denied Food Stamps because of the $600 in my bank account. "But that's a book advance, how my money comes," I'd protested. "It has to last for months." To the Food Stamp office, though, money in the bank was money in the bank. "Have I cheered you up?" I wrote Helene. "No? Gee."

That she herself never obsessed over money early on was due first to David Buck's child support and then to Ed's. After that she spent a year or two as an aide at the Gloucester Manor Nursing Home; and beginning in 1973, when federal CETA[5] grants were offered for community improvement, she became a member of the crew that worked to restore Gloucester's historic cemeteries. She piled brush and pulled weeds, did rubbings, possibly drawings. Her son Fred recalls her enjoying the job. Still, in September 1976, after a phone call, I wrote:

> I keep thinking of you in the graveyard saying "What am I doing here?" Which is the same question I ask myself when suddenly the enormity of just being out here dawns on me. When you decide to write a book I think you should call it "No Visible Means of Support," which covers a lot of the aspects (financial, emotional, etc etc).

---

4. Elizabeth Murray, American painter, 1940–2007. After the Shepp family, Elizabeth, her first husband Don Sunseri, and their son Dakota lived for a time in the loft below me.
5. Comprehensive Employment Training Act.

After recommending the title to her I used it myself, for a story I guess I wrote to prove the point. That year I'd done a work for hire—a cowboy novelization!—which had been good practice in writing fiction, the Big Sky Country being far from the life in which I was imagining it. Far riskier, though, was the idea of projecting my own very specific experience onto a character. LeRoi Jones had become well-known as Amiri Baraka. My children had to be protected.

But eventually I allowed myself to try, at least from the remove of the third person, to take a look at *her*, as other women I admired had done. Which analysis couldn't hurt, I figured. I was forty-two years old and should have something to say, at least to report from my "single parent head of household" life, a new category then. I had no time for or interest in nostalgia, and my experience with race and gender kept me alert. I wanted to write, as I would eventually, how, regarding race, "my sightlines had been reconstructed, the angle bent, the light refracted." And I liked the third person; I liked *her*. About public clinic visits I wrote, "Every which way I turned I was *her*."

I did publish some of this writing in small magazines, but didn't expect it to attract much general interest. Neither could it support us, or hold for me the ideal of *service*, as writing for children did. Still, it was more satisfying than the bohemia I'd left. And I did have a changed point of view:

NEW YORK, SUN NIGHT 14TH NOV. 1976

Dearest Helene,

I have for the most part stopped going out (again). It's just making scenes in bars, I hate it, tolerable only if music and hardly even then, small talk, sexual arrangement through alcohol.

Tho everything is all right. I am working on my [YA] novel all the time, with great glee and satisfied farts into my chair. Young man takes me to dinner occasionally—all very asexual and literary, so unlike, as Joyce recalled, people banging on your door at four in the morning yelling because they wanted to screw you.

Kellie and Lisa are among the most amusing people in the world, so full of virtue and voluptuousness their game, they are all curvy and fuzzy, like pears and peaches.

Down here in sin city even at 36 degrees the whores (read young poorgirls) walk around in minis outside my door, I always want to give them hot chocolate.

·····

You are invited
to a reception during the opening
of Gloucester's new art gallery

STAGECOACH HOUSE
at 302 Essex Avenue

from seven to ten o'clock in the evening
on Wednesday, December 15, 1976

On exhibit in a one-artist show will be work by
Helene Dorn, a Gloucester resident

Helene Dorn has said of her work: "There is a religiosity in
these mosaics. I take great care to honor what I find."

GLOUCESTER, DEC. 8, 1976

Which is why I haven't answered yr great pre-Thanksgiving letter—show came all of a sudden, like, w/3 weeks to prepare, I hope I can do it!

O how I would love to have you here—cld. you possibly??? No, of course not, but what a nifty dream—I'm in a slight case of panic—I love you all v. much.

Between her first exhibit in 1971, and this one, Helene had shown her work— glass pieces that grew larger and more elaborate—at eight different venues, in Boston, Cambridge, Bridgeport, Exeter, and several galleries in Glouces- ter. While working, eventually, as a receptionist for Senior Home Care, one of Gloucester's social service agencies, a job she would hold for ten years. We continued to write sporadically, and to apologize for not writing continually:

NEW YORK, 10/14/78

My dear Helene, hello! Are you out there? Where? Are you happy, medium, soft-boiled? The Mayor of Gloucester? Please let me know soon. I have probably thought of you a hundred times without ever get- ting down to let you know it.

I own half a car now, and have use of it every other weekend and most weekdays. I was going to pay you a visit over the summer but I did another novelization, and they never paid me for two months. So though I had this wonderful car there wasn't an extra dime for gas. I can't imagine what security would mean, how I'd feel, maybe I'd resent it or become a liberal and give it all away? First tho, I'd get a Jaguar.

Write and let me know how you ARE.

[POSTCARD: 55 FORT SQUARE, GLOUCESTER]

DEC 12 1978

Well & good Holidays to you all from us all, how can it be that time already! Will be down day after Xmas as usual—will let you know ahead of time so we *surely* get together. You know how I get stuck at Jack's—sometimes it seems impossible to even phone . . . Anyway LOVE & KISSES TO YOU ALL!

[POSTCARD]

NEW YORK, SUN. JAN 7TH, 1979

Deare Ladye,

Thank you again for the lovely pillow and the jazzy sweater which I wore last night to a party in Soho where everyone was dancing to "Roll Over Beethoven." (I left after 10 min.) It was so good to see you and talk with you because nothing needs to be *explained*, even after 2yrs of only postcards like this. Driving Kellie back to school tomorrow and will *surely* come up that way (wrote *that* before!) by Spring. LOVE

[BROCHURE FOR SHOW AT THE BOSTON VISUAL ARTISTS UNION

JANUARY 9–FEBRUARY 17, 1979]

GLOUCESTER, JAN 1979

I have a small piece in Part I should you be in Boston [smiling face] Norway commission *verified*!! Letter soon.

The commission had come from Exportfinans (The Financing Credit Institute of the Norwegian Commercial Banks, Ltd.), in Oslo. Early in the 1920s, Helene's father had shipped out from there, landed in the States, and stayed. His family had remained in Norway, and Helene's cousin, Arild Walder, was a director of the bank. The glass piece she created was installed in the reception area of their new building. Where it remains.

"Yay for Norway!" I wrote in January 1979, "Yay for the piece in the Boston show!" "Yay for (I *just* found out) Delacorte-Dell, who are giving me a contract for 2 novels—the one that's done and the one I want to do! Yay for late-bloomers! Yay for older women!"

· · · · ·

In March of that year I sent Helene a flyer for a party hosted by the *NY Jones,* "In honor of Lisa's graduation, Kellie's Spring vacation, Hettie's book contract, St. Patrick's Day . . ." Billed as "The First Great Social Event '79, The All-Out Party Effect," it promised "We will rock you!! We're giving all you hipsters a chance to get down! We know you've been waiting for the main jam!" In and over these guarantees I typed the following:

> My dear, this is what happens when you live with all who are the hippest. My friend says of a photo of Lisa, smiling on the beach, "she looks like she's been raised with great wealth," but I think it's just they've thought of themselves as beholden to no one, maybe, groups and all, subject to *no* approval (just like us!) How I wish I cd just send my private plane for you so you cd come boogie with us and the other hordes of raggedy NYers as we pretend we are the only ones who ever matter. I am feeling slightly philosophical because *finally* finished that novelization and immediately caught some kind of flu bug, so for past two days just lying around, READING, and other than dog walking, cooking, doing wash, getting addresses for party—I have done nothing. And feel strange. What, where's the work? Do people live like this all the time—easily? Ah, I don't want it. Anyway a beautiful record (Charles Mingus Plays Piano) and pouring rain, a toke (one only because sick) and probably a slight fever, and I determine, as I do when things are calm (and I know you do too) that I wouldn't change a thing, ni past ni present and leave the future up to whatever made those. Soon I will have to start my new book so I'll feel awful and lack confidence and have to do various penances but right now, wow. I am glad to write you for once without complaining. Hope all is well, we'll see Chan the weekend of 24th, everything sounds so terrific. My love to Paul and all Bucks and to you best lady!

Hello hello!

I thought for a moment what a gas to just damn well show up—I *can* be that flamboyant, but the work here is too much, and the $ too little. All you hip New Yorkers have a ball! Your country cousins will be there in spirit!

NEW YORK 3/20/79

Dearest Helene,

I have just this evening read your postcard! The day it arrived was P-day—the actual Party Day, so I put it in a safe place without really reading it, and only today found the vanished "safe place"—the dim interior of my desk—

I use that phrase because my novel has just been edited and one of the things the most-incredible-editor did was change the "dim interior of the bus" to "the back of the bus"—which last illustrates just about every else she did. Unbelievable. Helene, she also had the absolute colossal *gall* to write "parentheses are lazy" in the margin. That made me want to shame her, for someone to call *me* lazy. Anyway everyone, including my agent, tells me to just say no to everything. But the worst was the terrible, transparent racism . . .

Of course I felt bad for a while but after two pages I could see I'd been bombed by a ninny and after that saw all I had to do was insist on my own way. Or: Watch Out For Big Ego Jones, Here She Comes, Offended.

I really enjoyed the party—saw everyone who came at least once but not after that, and loved all the men in their turns—especially *Joel*—first time he's come to my house in years. About two or three hundred folks, they say. I didn't count. But honey, I have a case and a half of beer up on the roof, and it's your share and you should come get it!

But I was the one with the car, the woman seven years younger and more doggedly self-sufficient. Helene was far more fragile:

O Dear Het!!!

I just looked at the calendar and *flipped*. I've been sick—"walking pneumonia" is what the doctor calls it, but I feel on the edge of terminal! Am certainly better but am exhausted & have so much work to do to get the Norway piece really started—they want a 2′ × 4′ to hang flush w/wall back of reception desk—they want me to include their logo, but they want it to be very subtle. Which is like asking an ant out of a firefly. Whew. Anyway, Chan's wedding I suddenly realize is damn near here! When are you coming? It will be so *nifty* to have you here, I'll really need moral support—like I haven't the foggiest idea what I'm going to wear & I gotta stand in a reception line, you dig. Bizarre, Hettie Jones, it's just all too bizarre! Come anytime—but *please*, if you can, at least *one* day before the wedding? Mama, to keep me from getting blind drunk or else to join me in it!

•••••

Dearest Helene,

Well, here it is finally, with the largest type ever seen, good for all my friends who won't have to wear their reading glasses. But who knows maybe the large type will encourage children . . .

Not too long after this YA novel—*I Hate to Talk About Your Mother*—appeared, an organization calling itself the Council on Interracial Books for Children published a strong attack on it. The book tells the story of an interracial teenager's out-of-town weekend with her white hippie mother, during the course of which the girl comes to terms—satisfactorily—with certain ongoing conflicts about her identity. The council's position was that portrayals of interracial children were to be positive, and this book too raw. I can see now what I couldn't see then: that it was just too soon. In 2009, after Lisa mentioned me on Facebook, a woman wrote to ask whether her mother was the same Hettie Jones who'd written that book. As an adolescent, this woman wrote, she'd borrowed it repeatedly from the library, pretending it was her own. I'm glad it was soon enough for her.

But the reception set me back then. I'd tried to be my own consciousness-raising group and it hadn't worked. I felt not only misunderstood, but diminished.

· · · · ·

Dearest Helene,

I feel like I owe you this letter for 2 years, more maybe. I think of you all the time. And here I am with this fancy electric typewriter and I've stopped writing letters. Too much writing. Sitting at the typewriter is like punishment, so HARD! for me anyway. I know I wasn't meant to be one,* in my heart of hearts I know I should've just stayed with music—all feeling and wit, no sense required! (See, I didn't mean sense, I meant logic—after a while language is fuzzy yet that's the way we talk, I hate it.)

*one what? oh, yes, I meant "be a writer"

Thank you for the lovely card. I do think of you all the time. Especially since this last month when I copped the screen you long ago gave Lisa and put it against my brick wall with a light bulb behind. So your screen is the night light of my life.

Everything is everything. The other night I had a very brief, sharp feeling of happiness and thought oh, I used to feel this way most of the time, once.

What I mostly like is this Solitude. Hermit Het.

THURSDAY

A LONG, EXTRAVAGANT DUSK.

Sunday, believe it or not—

God knows what will happen to us all with Ronald Reagan as president. I am trying to ignore the whole thing. Told Lisa the other day that I hoped to make a lot of money soon, as I can see I will be needed to march for abortion rights and will need to be independently wealthy in order to have the time.

My god, will we never improve?

· · · · ·

Sometime during the '70s I had applied for an individual artist grant and was informed that writing for children "didn't fit into their categories." All the more reason, I felt, to continue to do it. As (the former) LeRoi had written: "There cannot be anything I must *fit* the poem into. Everything must be made to fit into the poem."

Accepting this idea had freed me to write what I pleased and to publish only when I was satisfied with it. Thus it wasn't until 1981, following ten books for children, that *Having Been Her*, a chapbook of my poems and stories, was published by #Press, the effort of three twenty-something writer/editors[6] from the Lower East Side's next-wave bohemia, who had "discovered" me one afternoon in the Tin Palace, a local bar. To which I'd been dragged one Sunday afternoon by my dear friend Dorothy White, who'd become alarmed by my continuing withdrawal.

Since writing for children didn't count, *Having Been Her* became what most readers knew as my first book. I was forty-seven. Helene gave it a rave review: "It's a celebration, it's beautiful, & god bless those 3 editors who insisted . . ."

She also mentioned, on the same postcard, having just learned, at 1:45 P.M., that she was to be on the bus at 8:20 the following morning with a "packed lunch" to do a typing job in a nearby town. She'd had other plans, she said, but "I got left 19$ to my name so I toss the plans!"

That's quite a spirited face-off with $19. If I was forty-seven then, she was fifty-four. With Ed, she'd been at times dirt poor, but by 1981 she was an older woman who had never been in a position to market her skills or encouraged to do so. Twenty years later, in the course of our study of women writers, I mentioned the poet Charlotte Mew, an early twentieth-century Brit, and Helene, reading more about her, found the term "discarded wife"—which had us both laughing, though Helene more than once pointed out that, unlike me, she'd been discarded for a younger version of herself. Perhaps there was some redemption in her pursuit of the found object—the "discards" she acquired for her art: *See what I've made from what has been cast away.* But a "career" wouldn't have been possible; in any event, she didn't think so. At Senior Home Care she answered the phone and did a little typing. Part time.

Then again, at fifty-four she might have known better than I that the rest of the time had to be hers. I hadn't figured that out:

---

6. Brian Breger, Harry Lewis, Chuck Wachtel.

Heleeeeeeennnnnnneeeeeeee!

I have in front of me a card postmarked 1pm 23 Jan 1981, which you ended by saying "I say hello to you every day, that pic you sent" and that's just about the way I feel. I also feel like a shit for not writing and have no excuse.

How are you how are you, I hope you're ok, maybe it's just been a strange year.

Kellie graduated [Amherst College] in May, and since the summer she's been here living with me because she's working as an apprentice curator and the pay is low low low.

Are you working? How is your glass? I wish I could see you right this minute. I've been thinking of it, just driving up, but figured I'd better introduce myself first.

I've been copy-editing Barbara Cartland–type romances, for about $1 a page. Titles like *Strange Possession, Burning Passions.* I've been doing this since Aug, when I was faced with that or starvation. Since Aug the sex in them has become more explicit but no less distasteful and it is possible to read them without becoming one whit horny. I am also writing a novel in which I've half lost interest but have to write because I've spent all the advance, and they are pressing me. But if I do it I become a free person, with no contract to fulfill for the first time in 10 yrs.

This is by way of saying that I wish this letter accompanied a new book. But as things are I still don't even have time to work on poems & stories & send them out to magazines (like writers do I'm told). Joyce just sent *Having Been Her* to Tillie Olsen, perhaps I will get known by knowing — but how scary it would be to be out there lacking faith in yr own work — I'd rather just write and let it all get found by accident.

Everything is the same with me I think. I still grow reefer & tomatoes on the roof, also stringbeans, carrots, turnips, shallots, marigolds zinnias mint zucchini morning glories more flowers and herbs — snowpeas are still blooming. It's fun to watch the helicopters fly over my pot plants. I fixed the roof myself this past spring too, the hardest part was trying to get the roll of paper up the stairs — it probably weighed more than I do.

Ms. Lisa is still at Yale and has just decided to become an English major because political science (the language of)—she informs me—deliberately obscures the issues.

I hope you'll write soon and let me know everything!

I keep asking myself what exactly kept us in touch through our long silences, and invariably come back to the faith we had that in time we'd simply pick up where we left off.

Can't even describe how good it was to see you, and felt as though I'd left you the day before. Hard to get it through my head that three yrs had gone by.

What a drag it is that you have to have that job, just when it looks like your work could really take off (that beautiful piece, was it just above the bathroom door?) and the one you're making for Lorna Obermayr—but if it's any consolation most women complain of having reached their 40s and 50s without having "a body of work"—and we all know why. Not that knowing why helps . . .

By the time I did make it up there, I had with me "Minor Surgery," a story about abortion published in IKON:[7]

Hullo!!! I miss you! Been wondering if you Have or Have Not that tooth. I'm still warm from yr visit, and oh, "Mrs. Thompson" what a fine story, what a very fine story! I hope you meant to leave IKON w/me because you did! And I've almost read everything in it. Rhys: all of them checked out of lib. but I'm on waiting list (imagine that!). Easter put me back in studio and to work again FINALLY! Lady, you keep writing!!!!

HELEW HELENE!

Yes, I meant to leave IKON for you, for sure. Still have my tooth—the other day did manage to bite my way through an apple without cutting

---

7. IKON, Second Series, feminist magazine edited by Susan Sherman in the 1980s.

it up in eensy slices. My friend Margaret Wolf says I should just carry a knife, that men think women who carry knives are sexy, but in my opinion women who carry knives are merely armed.

The money thing is making me crazy, have not stopped working since I left you, except for Easter Sunday, if you don't count the 8 loaves of bread I baked that day. However next week I'll probably be shitting bricks because I won't have any work! Am I so hard to please? Today the Salvation Army lady slipped a book in my bag as I was leaving the store; I didn't know what book it was until I got home. The title: *I've Done So Well—Why Do I Feel So Bad?* I thought—sheeeit, do I look like I need *help?* All I want is new clothes!

$$\bullet \bullet \bullet \bullet \bullet$$

One whole month since yr lovely blue letter . . . New supervisor at work and it is ridiculous I am not going to correct any mistakes here on this letter becouase i suddenly hfff a new, first one, my old super never bothered, JOB DEXCRIPTION . . . . . bummer. zI sam opposed to type accurately underlined 50 words per minute which I wonder should I bring my tock climer to work????????????

I must have been full of beer when I stoppt. I don't remember, it is now the 20th. I do think I'm getting slightly senile and like my hearing, 56 is MUCH too soon. And don't tell me to try zink (w/either c or a k). I am at this moment popping so many pills I'm not really all that knowledgeable abt, but I'm getting frightfully depressed because some things are better, but others much worse & my MD is hopelessly against vit. & literal "self help." And he tells me I have 2 middle-aged diseases—thyroid and something else, because he has a very low soft voice I got tired of asking even w/earhorn what.

Shortly before this letter Helene had run a high fever and lost her hearing, partly—as I understand it—because she hadn't gone to the doctor in time. I found her passivity hard to watch from afar, but I did understand that she was dealing with circumstances that had yet to affect me:

I suddenly remember why I didn't mail this! Jean Rhys. 1st. thank you. 2nd. I had got them from library. 3rd. Read *Sleep It Off* first, *Tigers* next, still gassed by writing but going much slower because the weight was too much for what I was currently feeling myself under.

Have just come from an outing—Gov's Conference on Aging. Workshop I chose, "Women and Aging," much too short, but v. interesting.

• • • • •

I hadn't remembered, until gathering these letters, that we'd both arrived at significant crises that spring of '83—Helene's sudden disability and my being thrust into the story I'd never wanted to write. Joyce Johnson's memoir *Minor Characters* had been published that year to well-deserved attention (and the National Book Critics Circle Award for nonfiction), the first notable addition by a woman to the literature of the so-called Beat Generation. In it she had written about me, mentioning that she'd never known anyone "who had orphaned herself so completely."

Thus armed, my agent sent some of my stories around, and there had been interest in my writing a memoir as well. Not of my life as *her*, the person I'd been writing about, but the young married woman I had been.

NEW YORK, FRI 6/3/83

Dearest Helene,

I've been thinking of you so hard these past 2 days it's a wonder your ears haven't burned off.

Out on the floor near this typewriter are all the letters you've ever sent, and I'm going thru them slowly, rapt, trying to find little memory jogs, trying to remember, remember, and all I seem to get is sadder and sadder.

Actually I'm in such a state I shouldn't even be writing but hoping it will help. I've got to begin (and work at) this "memoir"—there's nothing else to do. The novel I finished before coming to visit you, which was such labor for me because so long overdue, has just been rejected, they want me to "rewrite it entirely"—which I won't do—

And—*I Hate to Talk About Your Mother* has been "disappeared"—that is to say, Delacorte Press destroyed every copy they had without telling me. It wasn't selling, because too vulgar, too raw, but they want me to make this second one more like it, so they can hate it too.

I feel so buffeted about, so done in. My agent tried to cheer me, said "if you weren't such a good writer" it'd all be just "chalk it up to experience"—

And no work, though I've got a "summer job" — 15 days in July and Aug I jump in my car early a.m. and go to places like N.J. and Long Island to be a registrar for some seminars run by N.Y.U.[8]

My agent says I'm a victim of economics but it doesn't matter who's the perp the crime's the same. I feel as if I've been hit over the head with a big big hammer and there's a lump in my throat egg-size. All the work I've done has gone to *nada*—what a sensation. Like wasting years of your life . . .

Enough of me, I can't stand me.

SATURDAY

Rereading this I see it was necessary to get the awfulness of it off my chest. And the practice of suddenly shredding books is one that publishers are doing all the time these days; I tell people the story and they say "Oh yeah, that happened to a friend of mine."

Today I'm better, at least resigned. Still the fact remains that I can't, in this conservative age, have my cake and eat it too as before—that is, being able to live off writing . . .

I'm glad your new boss is okay—they should give you a nice peaceful job that doesn't involve answering phones. They should, right, but will they?

I could go on sitting here and writing to you forever because that would successfully put off the business at hand, which is all this stuff still on the floor around me, waiting for me to have some "take" on it (that's movie talk, I hardly understand it). Wish there were a teacher around who'd engage me in a dialogue that would in some mysterious way facilitate not only recall but assessment. That's the fearsome part of this memoir business. I've never done anything save *live* my life, unquestioning—what should I have questioned? *Why* should I have questioned?

---

8. "Working," *Full Tilt, New and Selected Poems* (unpublished).

3

may the tide
that is entering even now
the lip of our understanding
carry you out
beyond the face of fear . . .

and may you in your innocence
sail through this to that
　　　　　　　　　—*Lucille Clifton*

I'm attracted to the French *déraciné*, with its little hint of race inside. In English, "deracinate" is to uproot, first, and then, as if the violence escalates the more you think about it, the second definition, "extirpate," is followed handily by "eradicate."

> HOT FLASH—LeRoi/Amiri's book (autobiog) has just come out. In it he has changed my name to Nellie Kohn. Throughout. Has changed the name of Yugen to Zazen . . . Has changed certain other names too—The Record Changer [magazine where we met], Partisan Review . . . Though not the names of *real* people—like MEN (Allen G., Burroughs, etc.) Tho it beats his trying to kill me for *real*—! But can you imagine? Joyce just read this to me over the phone. Get the book from your library—can you?

How astonishing to be disappeared! But then I gave it some thought, and wrote, "Maybe fear will have a firecracker effect on my lazy ass."

> GLOUCESTER, I#TH . . . FRIDAY THE I#TH INDEED! 1984
>
> Think it's wonderful Mr. Jones did it first—see, the angels are there. That's right, he ain't got a chance to win this one. But stay cool, lady, you got so many heavies all at once.
>
> And did I ever tell you, b.t.w., when my name and that of my children—all of them good—were completely deleted?? I'm sure not. It was such a deep wound I don't think I ever mentioned it. Ed wrote that

there was a new edition of *The Rites of Passage*. He said there were many changes. Book arrived—new title, new format, new printing, new illustration, new cover. The only textual change I could see was complete deletion of dedication:

"For Helene,
and the children
Fred, Chan and Paul"

I was so struck dumb I couldn't more than spot check text . . . but Gerrit Lansing[1] said to me, and he had no idea of what was involved, "I can't see any changes."

If you knew how much a part of that book I was, I mean the writing of it, the remembering, the keeping out of the visitors. And the kids too, be quiet, he's working—all in that one-room shed with the (Red) Garland cookstove. The kids always so helpful. Ed's working . . . And then after they were in bed, the going over of chapters, and the *anger* when I wld say "editing" things . . . Well, that book always belonged to all of us.

Just to let you know you're not alone in literary "besmirch"!

How I loved Helene's words! After that delicious "besmirch" we went right back to art: "I'm starting a fairy tale series," she wrote, "in my head for so long. Snow White & Rose Red . . . I'm working, but it is so slow." And then the unforeseen obstacles:

I come into this part of the apt to open curtains this am & turn on heat (yestdy it was 39 degrees from heat being off for 6 hrs!—36 today, tonight I leave it on low! for my plants . . . ARE YOU SURVIVING? and as I go into studio I see folding light table on its knees, glass all over. Am going for walk to Bucks[2] to weigh this, because I can't bear the thought of trying to repair table. Finishing SNRR today shot to hell. v. frustrating because I've got 7 more pieces in my head, the beginnings on the wall, and where's the time the time/time, time, time!

I am 57 yrs. old + 3 days even. Can you believe?!

---

1. Poet, essayist, editor. Born 1928, longtime resident of Gloucester, friend/disciple of Charles Olson.

2. Helene's son Fred Buck and his wife, Stephanie, had settled in Gloucester and were raising three daughters there.

Now off I go to the kitchen to wash a week's worth of dishes and cook some cabbage and then to Snow White & Rose Red. If you don't get any more work right away why don't you just come for a bit???

I know that's a fairy tale too but they do happen, fairy tales, and just to let you know we're here . . . there are 10 thousand things I've not said, but that's all right.

Goodnight Nellie Kohn, not to worry—With so much LOVE, the deleted

• • • • •

A couple of days before the New Year, I'd written that I was "terrified of this 1984 shit," and almost immediately, as if to supply a good reason, the house into which I had moved in 1962, and "kept extant,"[3] as I wrote, for what my landlord described as "twenty-two *easy* years," was for sale. After at first thinking there was nothing to be done but "shed tears on the way out," my two neighbors and I put ourselves in the hands of a tenants rights organization called GOLES—for Good Old Lower East Side.

NEW YORK, 1/24/84

Some days I do "get the heavies" as you say. I wake up stricken . . . Like what first enters the waking mind is that sense of doom, and then I think oh yes, the house, and then oh yes, I've been Nellie'd, and all that.

A woman just called from the NY Marxist School—I am invited to read "feminist erotic poetry" in honor of Valentine's Day! I asked if I had to be that specific—and she said no, anything sort of in that line would do—oh, these Marxists, still believe in love and sex! All the rest of the women will prob. be gay, but at least I'll get a chance to open my mouth in public—haven't read in a while, which nearly makes me feel I can't anymore. But this NY scene is so cliquey and complicated—despite the fact that I donated hard-earned $$ and filled out a form, etc. to be part of "Artists Call"—a protest against US involvement in Central America— though readings were set up, no one asked. And when I finally did get on the phone with one of the organizers, he said, "Do you really want to? I just thought I'd let you know that Amiri and Amina will be reading." FUCK.

---

3. Built in 1844–45 by William Pinckney, a cartman, 27 Cooper Square had been largely maintained since the 1960s by the artists who had lived here.

In this same letter I mentioned that although I had twelve actual pages of the memoir I'd begun to write, I was "freaked out again over Roi's book," not only disappeared from my past but effectively shunned in the present, silenced, restricted. Had it not been for the support of women I might have given up. "So, so it goes," I remarked, which sounds a lot braver than I felt. "At least the women are generous toward me, and interested, despite the fact that I am a known hetero. To keep up my courage, I tell myself maybe if I tell my story, young women may profit.

"I guess there are all sorts of ways to think about it," I concluded that letter. But the first was the one that stuck.

· · · · ·

Sometime during that very cold winter Helene sent me a copy of a page from the *Downtown Gazette*, a Boston-area newspaper, with an article about the Boston Visual Artists Union show she'd been in, illustrated with a photo of her piece. Titled *Fort Gull*, it's a small arch of glass, metal, and wood, and the "gull" isn't a feather, but something metal with a feathered tail—another of her found objects. It makes you think about form *and* content. "*Downtown Gazette* xerox," she wrote, "got sent me from someone at BVAU. I was so gassed—never had that happen to me before. Out of all the people's work in that show [open to 700 members], she chose mine for her article! I have no idea what the *Downtown Gazette* is, but who cares?"

I did! As I'd have written the writer, the paper, made myself known—a little self-promotion couldn't hurt. Why didn't she? But she didn't like cities, was terrified of subways, and now she was deaf and fifty-seven years old. I couldn't persuade her, and by then I knew that whatever held her back was a good part of what made her tick. Still I never stopped trying. I really did think it would make her happy, as had this.

Anyway, her work was already a part of Gloucester's geography: "Ten Pound Island Bookstore Co. has 7 pieces of my glass in window & store. It's a nice place to be, high walls of books & nice people." It was also right on Main Street in a touristy town. And all I wanted to do was offer encouragement:

Your new pieces sound terrific. What was the third—baseball circle? No, you said baseball/love circle—I can't visualize it at all at all! OK. Thank you for long letter and all postcards. Pleze keep em coming, I so need your comforting hand.

Whoever needed a hand got one; we were always either Babe or Mama, didn't matter. What did was the kinship implied. Though I had reconciled with my family we weren't close, and my mother, who had always (secretly at first) kept in touch, now had dementia and lived in a nursing home.

NEW YORK, 2/7/84 10:50PM

Helene Helene—

Thank you for this new batch of letters. I haven't had the heart to read all through them.

Midnight. (I've been working in between paragraphs.)

I'm going to Florida 3/1 to visit my sister and I guess go look at my mother what a trip that'll be.

Thank you again for the xeroxing, I know it takes time. I can't believe I forgot to mention the gloves you sent. I just now ran to try them on, and they're perfect. Also tres expensive, and even if thrift-shopped . . . puu-leeeze don't I know you watch every penny . . . but I love them ANYWAY also I just ruined my only pair . . . !

Bed.

NEW YORK, TUES. NIGHT 3/6/84

Helene—

A relief to write your name, as something familiar, a familiar act by the me-who-is-me—after that Florida trip!

I can hardly do justice to my feelings just telling about what my mother looks like—a nonperson, mostly because of the *exposed* steel pin in her thigh (no skin left to cover it). But caught between my desire to touch her still familiar face and my sister in the doorway yelling "c'mon, c'mon, let's go, I can't stand it" and me wanting to do what I wanted to do, offer comfort. And why fight? I *want* to like her. Why couldn't *you* be my sister?

The trip back was worth it all, though. The plane was delayed 2½ hrs, but I found a pleasant woman who had a joint and we crawled behind a sign and sat on the grass outside this makeshift terminal where she proceeded to tell me about being a Jewish gay person, and then we were eventually joined by others, discussing the difficulty of being a Jew, all of them having come down to visit parents . . . stoned in the Fla. sunshine. And then everyone on plane very talkative and friendly, all New Yorkers eager to get home to the bad weather that had caused the delay!

Thank you for the words of Jacob Grimm. I so wish I could relate all this family stuff to my lack of self-confidence, if indeed words are thunder, and I can use them, why am I always so afraid? Why do I think they're so piss-poor (my words I mean)? Why does it take me so long to be satisfied with what I do?

Boy, if I continue to earn so much money [$11,000], perhaps I can afford a shrink. Perhaps all I need do is get my ass into that room!

Anyway, here's my new plan: I'm going to lose 10 lbs and then cut my hair. What say to that?

OK. I'm about to take phone off hook and fade into my bathtub, after cleaning the house today I need to transfer the dirt. Everything here looked so funky after all that middle-class Fla. cleanliness. Those people are *devoted* to plumbing. Oy, as they say, vey.

GLOUCESTER, 3/27/84 8:42PM & MILES-TO-GO

To let you know I've not abandoned you . . . if only I had $ to just pick up the phone.

I *am*, we *are* sisters . . . Will someday soon get back to letters etc. Did a "presentation" for an Art Education M.A. "exploratory" class as "visiting artist" and trying to get my fairy tales in some kind of order.

Rumpelstiltskin on the sculpt wheel—I am so caught, I cld go forever, my house piled with fairy/folk lib. books, all back to the Norse thing I got so deep into while waiting for that bank to make up its mind what it wanted. The Baseball/love thing I wrote abt is a mandala.

NEW YORK, 4/6/84

And I always thought: the very simplest words
Must be enough. When I say what things are like,
Everyone's heart must be torn to shreds,
That you'll go down if you don't stand up for yourself.
Surely you can see that.
—*Brecht, last poem in Poems 1913–1956*

Hi—the above was quoted in some endless *Voice* review of Brecht but I wouldn't have minded if they'd just printed this, LARGE. So many times

I do that, trying to stress the validity of common language, and end up feeling that people think it's just corny.

Favorite new word—"domestic"—as in poetry, sensibility, etc etc. Another way to dismiss women; I reckon we'll see an article about it soon.

Well, I buried my mother since I wrote last. She died a week ago yesterday and my sister had a funeral service down in Fla. and then sent her up to me. They also sent a rabbi, who read nicely at the grave, as I mumbled my rusty Hebrew along. My mother, who was always vaguely alarmed by my interest in ritual, would nevertheless have liked that scene too. As surely she would have sighed, thinking, why couldn't she have married a man like that? But it was a brilliantly sunny day, the very first. And then coming home I got lost—not really lost, you can't get lost in Brooklyn, all you have to do is follow the World Trade Center on the horizon—but I took a wrong turn so drove leisurely through parts of Brooklyn I'd never seen, thinking maybe my mother had sent me, as she was born and grew up there.

I've been writing steadily on book and have some 50+ pages now, but I've been delivering all this to my agent, bit by bit, and have not heard one word. It's eerie and I'm terrified she thinks it's so bad that, etc etc.— vaguely discouraged about it tonight, but fuck it. If it ain't good it ain't . . .

Did you get horribly snowed under that last time? and washed out by the recent deluge? What a messy spring—everyone here is muttering and complaining, everyone wants to go OUTSIDE and watch the break dancers.

Speaking of which I will try to copy Lisa's first article in *City Limits*[4]— she tells me she has 4 more coming up, yay baby! Kellie is there this week visiting her.

Restless, restless. Must be spring. Miles Davis on the radio can put me into a spate of labored breathing!

GLOUCESTER, 4/11/84

Hello dear Het:

I'm going to start knowing I'll not finish but that's ok . . .

Call from my sister—and though our lives are very different, she is still my sister, for real, and for that I am so grateful. You are also my sister for

---

4. London alternative newspaper, similar to New York's *Village Voice*.

real, I don't think I have any others—and I have been in state of mourning I guess you'd call it. My mother.

They say her mind went. She got out of residence and across the street (how I don't know, having been told her arthritis made movement very difficult, she'll be 91 in August)—and then down some blocks to St. Mary's Hospital, *looking for her mother.* Guard (do hospitals have such things, like banks? I'm repeating what I was told) realized something was wrong, and she's now in St. Luke's Hosp. waiting for the 1st opening in *any* nursing home.

Her hearing aid had been lost for a whole week. Marie and I wonder how much that had to do with the flip.

And then there's Kate—my mother's sister 2 yrs younger who is not a sister for real, tho blood—who lives also in the residence. When Marie talked to her after being informed about what had happened, Kate said: Should we cancel the order for a new hearing aid?

That word, sister . . . . It has such a rhythm.

· · · · ·

NEW YORK, 4/26/84

Hi Helene,

Agent finally read memoir, says it's too much a poet's book, not narrative enough, I can dig it, of course. And I certainly prefer sense over sensibility when it's necessary. Have this weird feeling that this book is going to be a *process*, that nerdy word.

But oh my suffering ego! And of course the $ is running out, so that vague nervousness underlies everything—

BUT tomorrow I am to read at a place called the Graduate Center across from the 42nd St. Library at the cultural event of the Brooklyn College Women Studies Conference (there, have I got all that right?).

Lisa V. C. Jones is interviewing Germaine Jackson (bro of Michael) this week and Stevie Wonder next; she is also going to be on the radio. She keeps calling excitedly to tell me of this success from various phone booths in the sections where she works as a temporary receptionist while she is becoming a Famous Journalist. We are all incredibly puffed up over her!

Friend of Kellie Jones has just recovered from a kidney infection occasioned by poor follow-up from the clinic that didn't stop her bladder infection, probably caused, they are now finding out, by using a diaphragm which presses on the urethra and keeps in one's pee. Tales from her other friends of supermalfunction of the much-touted Sponge. If I ever get rich I'm going to turn into the Carrie Nation of Birth Control.

I just decided to write a poem about the 3 other Hetties I know of. Maybe that will take my mind off "the narrative" long enough for me to come up with a narrative.

I owe $1200 in taxes on my huge earnings of $11,000 . . . Stanley Crouch came to visit me and offhand mentioned that he'd earned 40 thou and here I fed the dude for 6 mos only a few years ago.

Sorry this letter so disjointed but I'm *dull*, from this writing angst. Oh woe, I prefer ho ho. Write me about yr mother . . .

GLOUCESTER, %?!)?*$>HURRAYS FOR LISA, 5/10/84

Dearest Het,

Bear with me, I can't write. Am in a netherland I don't & yet do understand, & this is to let you know . . .

I love you, and yr memoires (my word) *are* that of a poet. Keep writing. Ms. Jones, what did yr agent expect?!!

NY 6/14/84 6:30PM AND FEELS LIKE MIDNIGHT

Agent liked 2nd submission, I guess I like it better myself. Now I have to write this proposal, which is supposed to be like "extended book jacket copy." She says she'll help, but I have to give it a start. Last night a sudden storm and I went running into my study, found all my new poems soaked, also covered with dust from the construction across the street. I guess it only takes a minute to build a 14-story building these days, and prob by the end of summer it'll be higher than me on my roof watering my tomatoes.

Wish there were more to tell you but nada mas. I have just concluded an agreement to read at one of the hot new East Village cafes on Sept. 11. Also Margaret Randall is putting one of my poems in a calendar (1986)! So all that makes me feel an illusion of success, if the real thing is somewhat elusive still.

Sorry for this rather silly, self-centered letter. But wanted to write you some words. Can't wait to see you, really, and I'm determined to do it one way or another. Fuck paying my taxes . . .

Hello—

Guess maybe you didn't get my response—or maybe I tossed it into the refuse container instead of the mailbox—or maybe I just dreamed I sent quick note to say anytime you can come to this fastly disintegrating nice old fisherman's town, please do.

. . . . .

Since my first, wintry trip there in January 1969, when Helene first returned from Europe, I've been to Gloucester in all weathers, visiting her wherever she landed in that fisherman's town she called "fastly disintegrating." The history of Gloucester parallels the world's history of overfishing. Much of its history exists now as memorabilia collected by the Cape Ann Historical Association. On platforms in the basement of the Association's museum are remarkably small boats that once saw service in the sea, their very size making the point that we have honed our appetites on the brains and brawn of amazingly brave men.

And though there's little enough left of the fisheries that gave the town its character, Gloucester remains an active harbor. Long lines of craft form below the Western Avenue drawbridge. The air and the light, the summoning gulls, remain the same. "And the boat," wrote Olson, "how he swerves it to avoid the yelping rocks / where the tidal river rushes . . ."[5]

. . . . .

Hello hello hello . . .

August seems far far away, I can barely remember yesterday so much has happened. Glad you liked that little clock and I sure would love to hear about your dreams—if they're any weirder than my reality I'd be glad to be in them as a change of pace.

---

5. Charles Olson, "ABCS (2)," *Archaeologist of Morning* (1973).

Arrived home to find the cat nearly dead of nasal infection which turned out not to be cancer but probably incurable anyway . . . and I can't resign myself to putting her to sleep because she's the last of the last.

Was happily continuing to do the little textbook work. Got my stuff together to do my poetry-jazz thing. Rehearsed. Somehow—I don't know how—this brings us to last Sunday night. We returned late from the wedding of Kellie's college roommate where I snuck away between dinner and dessert to see the house where I grew up, my elementary school, and the synagogue—the reception only a few blocks away. So I came home feeling strange and full of chicken and wedding cake—to find a message on machine from Susan Sherman, who edits *IKON*, urgent, call before bed. So I called and she told me she'd recommended me for a job teaching a writing workshop (short story) at Hunter College.

Why me? I asked, I'm not experienced. Call anyway she said. So I did, and on the Tues. following, which was also the day of my poetry-jazz thing, I got up at 6am and dressed like a job interview, went uptown and got the job. I was so freaked out that I didn't do my performance as well as I could have, and my friend got uptight because I was so nervous, he played all the wrong notes and then told me it was my fault, etc. But anyway I now have this job and since I don't know what I'm doing I'm in a state of nervous obsessive confusion. I had to sign a loyalty oath! Am afraid that doing this is going to screw up my entire life by making it impossible for me to write. It wouldn't be so bad if I had a *few* intellectual underpinnings—even a few would do—but I don't know shit from Shinola about *how* to do anything concerned with writing—I've always just done it by ear.

Of course my agent is delighted and all my friends think it's marvelous, what an opportunity. But shit, Helene, I'm not a teacher! And just when I need to be writing I have to start learning how to do something else—completely unrelated to writing!

Right now the whole thing is making me very unhappy. Yet every time I explain to people that being a writer doesn't necessarily mean one's a literary intellectual they look at me as if I'm talking nonsense.

GLOUCESTER 28 SEPT. 84 AFTER A PHONE CALL

Hello & APOLOGIES for waxing so el-oh-quent re writing workshop. odear odear, sd I to myself on hanging up. what kind of help iz that! (none, I know from experience but I did it anyway) owell someday I'll be perfect? Will send $ for that *wonderful* call.

Don't you dare send $ for phone—you have little enuf as it is! Anyway thanks for your sympathy re class—v. much appreciated as no one here really understood my unwillingness and quandary. Still, I know what I am good at—writing—which is *not* supplying intellectual & textual justifications; tra la la—I'm to be observed on Fri—oy vey Yom Kippur eve!

Hello hullo!

Here's the press release for Kellie's first show,[6] which is in a teeny storefront gallery that reminds me of the store we ran the *Record Changer* from in 1957—only this new one is in the very heart of the Lower East Side. K looking spectacular in a suit she'd made herself and blue (yes!) *bright* blue, alligator shoes.

The teaching is less problematic in the sense that I'm not so nervous about it anymore, but it still takes up more time than I bargained for. And the politics of the whole thing. I've yet to "chat" (as he put it) with the head of the Eng Dept. in the interest of getting hired again; inside me there's this tremendous *reluctance*. Went to a faculty meeting and was so put off by the gray-haired, gray-faced, gray-suited *men* (only a few women) and not one black, brown or otherwise colored person in the roomful while outside the door the student body passed, the majority of whom are bl, br, or otherwise c. Oh oh oh oh oh . . .

• • • • •

In one of my stories about the sixties, the narrator says, "It didn't occur to us then that we lived in a way the rich would discover and seize." By the mid-1980s, the coast above Boston was an eastern Silicon Valley, with Gloucester just up the road. Helene, overlooking the harbor, was in the way in a big way. As I was digging in for a housing fight, appraisers and buyers arrived at her door. "Money," I wrote her, "is taking Manhattan . . . and Gloucester."

Under New York's Loft Law I could apply for legal tenancy; informed of

---

6. "Speaking in Tongues."

that, Helene wrote: "Here in lil old Gloucester, there ain't no rent control or squatters' rights." A month afterward: "Am still hanging on what's to happen—no word from no one." And in all this uncertainty: "Sat. at 6pm I'm to be present at a brief formal presentation of my $500 equipment grant from the Arts & Humanities Council—in order to complete my fairy tale series #1— oy vey—and where am I going to put this equipment?? No matter, I'll just have to change from permanent to foldable!"

I have only a fragment of this letter, which she continued on December 3rd, but by that time the house at 55 Fort Square had been sold. She wrote that her mother had fallen and "slightly they think fractured pelvic bone. How can anything be slightly fractured—fracture such a violent term. I feel fractured this A.M. and I do not want to go outside of my nice house."

Then, in a postcard just before Christmas: "No news here yet. Sale was to have been finalized a week ago. Here's to a Brave New Year—Love!!!! H"

· · · · ·

And then two months later:

GLOUCESTER 1/30/85

Am still hanging on what's to happen—no word from no one. Reading for the 1st time Sylvia Plath—"Faun" got me back composing, and "Tale of a Tub"—wow—or do you disagree? I got a *Collected* from library and have only started but how her images hit my eye.

[POSTCARD: JOSEPHINE BAKER]
NEW YORK 1985 [DATE OBSCURE]

I *do* like Plath's images, just her ability to make metaphor is enviable. I can't believe you've gotten an equipment grant and now the same town is going to sit back and watch your studio go down the tubes.

GLOUCESTER, 2/14/85

I need some help—am totally uneducated, except for "names," re women writers, late 19th and 20th centuries. Have you *read* K. A. Porter, etc etc? I have read some—Djuna Barnes and others—but if you are more widely read than I re ladies, please while having bkfst coffee, jot down some names. You won't believe this: I'm also reading V. Woolf, *herself,* for the 1st time. . . .

Fig 3.1 Helene walking home in a snowstorm, January 25, 1985.
Photo: Mitch Egan for *Gloucester Daily Times*

NEW YORK 4/16/85

Hello hello!

Enclosed small present, I've left the price on so you'll see it was re-maindered, and since the store didn't have any paper I figured you'd like a real book as a surprise . . . alla this to stop you from yelling at me—extravagance extravagance!

About Plath, mine's not a well-informed position. I've read her *Collected*—poetry not prose. Maybe it's just me, certainly yes it is, perversity. Katherine Anne Porter's stories—ah, I want to write those! Kay Boyle, too. But my great heroine—for writing style, I guess—is Jane Bowles.

Today's paper announces that the DNA of a mummy has been cloned, which seemed to mean that inevitably we'll re-create the pyramids. Do you think we can each get an apartment in one?

Car partner has backed out of our arrangement and is—this happily—giving the car to me. Kellie has offered to share the expense but it might not work out if she has to move to Brooklyn. Everyone in the city who makes under fifty thou a year will eventually have to move to Brooklyn, which will become very crowded.

This brain stupor [from cocaine 2 days before] is stunning. I think I'll leave drugs to the now-generation, which obviously has more brain cells left to kill. Myself I need all I can get.

Keep chin up, fingers crossed and god knows what else in what position for all of us . . .

It's just a game I keep telling myself—gray 9am and I've a list of 6 landlords to call and put in my name—put in my name—put in my name . . . Oh dear Het, I do need the sun this morning, where is it?

Next nifty little chore is a memo to my supervisor re the A.M. receptionist position, now open, which they are again refusing me. If I could just be mad instead of sad, it would help.

Did I tell you on top of everything else my welder had heart attack?

Lit. talk later, must go.

OH! Here I thought I was so slick and on 5/1, sitting in my morning coffee chair said, "rabbits rabbits rabbits—good luck month," well now . . .

Today I brought myself upstairs tired and wet wet wet from big rain and had just finished rereading yr letter, looking at bad news in newspaper, but looking forward to a rainy day of writing when WHAM big noise from study which upon investigation turned out to be the noise of part of the ceiling falling, not much damage but further investigation revealed water through some books and papers and thru the covers of Roi's and Joyce's and Fred McDarrah's, a bookshelf full of the most important stuff for my book, in other words. . . . So instead of writing I spent the day cleaning and pressing book covers between layers of newspaper, paper towel, aluminum foil—upon instructions from a friend who restores paper . . .

The game is designed to keep us feeling superfluous and dispensable and interchangeable. The whole process of gentrification creating displaced persons who as yet are not given that title but if the shit keeps up . . .

I'm afraid this house will fall about my head unless I finagle use of the rent money (which we are withholding from landlord) to reroof. Which is why I had originally decided not to have a garden, last fall, since roofer had warned me. Forewarned is not always fore . . . I guess being a small woman I never thought about my forearms.

What used to bug me when I worked for Mobilization For Youth was the lack of understanding on the part of people who had never experienced the kind of economic jiggle that keeps you focused only on the present. The big talk used to be that poor people didn't "plan"—but they do that only to keep themselves loose enough to not lose total heart when *next* arrives.

Did write I think 5 pp this week—easy to write about infidelity, so exciting . . . But earlier had one of those awful crises of confidence that attack me like dread sickness. I went to a "literary party" invited by Joyce, party was for a friend of hers, a woman whose short stories had just been published, praised on book jacket by Updike, etc. I could only stand it for half an hour or so. I felt miles miles miles away and had a few desultory small-talks then came home with the book and reading it realized I'd never be able to write that way, grew dispirited that I don't have ways of looking at things that turn themselves to rhetoric, I can't say it but straight out, look this is this and the truth is awful and simple and inevitable. But only—can't write *pretty*. "The unattainable absolute of dark" I just found as good example.

I hesitate to ask you what's the newest in the saga of how why or when they will throw you out, I'm sure it will differ in the days it takes for this to reach you.

Forgot to say we lost the first round in court and now have to appeal. It seems we drew a bad judge, twice, which of course never happens to anyone but us, right? New lawyer says if justice is served we will win, that our case should come out right. Should. Just send money, and we'll keep trying. I do like him, though. His father has a pet wolf, a fact I know because I repro'd the covers of all my books to apply for certification with the Loft Board and when he came across *Living With Wolves*[7] he got all excited and told me about his father's wolf who pisses on people he likes and eats basketballs (chomp).

God knows what time it is.

Descending the stairs for the 4th time last night carrying armloads

---

7. New Macmillian Reading Programs, Series R.

of the broken garden wood, I thought that perhaps at 50 I should not do this, then got mad because that said "do I dare to eat a peach" and so went determinedly up the stairs and down again. So it's this motherfucking determination that I send to you along with this letter. No doubt shit like this will continue to happen to us, therefore the only way to handle it is keep putting in your name, visit the welder in the hospital and keep on struttin. I dunno, I feel stupid lately, recommending only blind faith . . .

Incredible, my dear beautiful beleaguered-equally friend, that photograph you sent of Isadora Duncan! I certainly do see the resemblance to me, facial structure, etc. but what wows me is that I've been there—whatever it is she's saying. I remember a particular night in San Francisco, alone, children asleep, illustrious poets gone off somewhere after intense session at our table. No babysitter so I stayed, thankfully. The moon came in the window and we talked for a very long time. I remember finally just lying down on the wood floor, the white light thru the window covering me.

News, before I eat my lentils and study homophones . . . Homework for the next lip reading session with Anne Miller—Mrs. Miller (she finds it demeaning when people call her by her first name). She's beautiful, I love her, and have, for the first time in my life—I'm not sure that's true, thinking about the welding classes—such a breakthrough. But that was a class—this is individual. Helen Keller, it's that kind of teaching.

I'm (possibly) going to be given, via Housing Authority, dungeon downstairs, but it's still "iffy," to use the young man's word. Had to go to his office and fill out a preliminary application for "assistance." My rent will be approximately 65$ a month, so you see I *must* move into the dungeon, if they'll let me.

My friend Bud[8] said, as I was leaving after several hours visit last Sat and we'd been discussing how everyone having extra heavy problems, etc etc.: "It's been a *disgusting* spring!" I laughed all the way home—

Blasphemy!!! I love it!!!

---

8. Bud Castle, roommate of Harry Martin (1918–76), a Gloucester artist who was Helene's good friend.

Dear Dungeon-Dweller!

Iffy or not, they *oughta* give it to you, mebbe you could cut in a new window or two; anyway the price is right. So I am sending this with HOPE which seems to spring eternally through godawfulness.

The landlord will be around this afternoon, picking up the key from the former occupants of the store, the Chinese people he "vacated"—if I meet him I'll . . . I'll . . . What'll I do? Turn away I guess, ugh. Have been sick-ill and am taking antibiotics.

8PM

In the last light, Sing Foon Ma has all his remaining merchandise on the street, selling to the last, good for him . . . One gets to know people—this couple, their children, two tiny boys not yet in school when they moved in, then the wife's mother, such an elegant, skinny-as-a-rail, chain-smoking woman, still gorgeous at 75. Then watched them through another pregnancy, amnio because she was over 35, then the birth of a girl—girls are better! crowed the mother, in opposition to everything taught—and now to lose them into what Kerouac called cityCityCITY . . . No fair, no fair, their older son one of those smart/kind kids, in the classes for gifted children and always with his arms out to his baby sister, both boys constantly correcting, in slangy American, their mother's incorrect pronunciation ("Not custom, Ma, you mean custom*er!*"). I'm going to miss all of them.

9:25

Stir crazy. Joyce on the phone for an hour, thought I'd try to get back to work but that didn't happen. I have my shoes on and am standing up typing, but nowhere I want to go though feel I must . . .

10:30

Met a neighbor on my walk who told me my restlessness was due to approaching storm, you know, negative ions and that shit. I said good, I thought it was just me and my attitude. These streets are jumping, I wish you could just pop down and check out the bargains on the sidewalks. I remember when "the streets belong to the people" was the word but only this black market has really proved that. Of course the mayor hates it because it's tax-free, but the point is that fewer people are on welfare and the sellers make the world safe for the buyers.

Reading *Machine Dreams* by Jayne Ann Phillips, which is very good, better than her earlier story collection *Black Tickets* which was fussed over. No one is going to fuss over me, I bet, because what's making me crazy about writing style is the I I I I I. I really like she she she she she much better, the elegance of the distance.

But I am happy tonight being I for you here! Outside, the guys who helped Sing load his last truckful are relaxing with the very last of the merchandise that he gave to them to sell. I just bought two baskets from them for $1 and now they are getting drunk and argumentative. This is noo yawk signing off . . .

SAT AM 6/1

At 9:45 AM auto store[9] called to tell me that the landlord showed up yesterday evening and announced that he had sold the building to some Japanese guys who are going to open a restaurant. So where is our lawyer in all this? Out sunning himself? Will keep you informed. What's to become of us?

But there is GOOD news! I am going away for the entire summer! A poet named Janine Pommy Vega just happened to call, and I remembered a little house on her property in which her nephew had been living. So I asked, and he was no longer, and she herself is going to Peru, so I agreed to live in little house for firsts, and then to take over hers when she leaves, mind her cat, stoke her fire, etc. 10 miles out of Woodstock, on a road that winds up a mountain. Behind the place, a beautiful little river crashing over stones . . . Tall pines, a garden. An outhouse and a makeshift kitchen for me at first, then all the conveniences . . .

WILLOW, NY MONDAY JUNE 24 1985

Helene Dear,

. . . Here I am in paradise, truly, in a little cottage with a rigged-up kitchen . . .

---

9. Worth Auto Parts, the business that owned 29–31 Cooper Square and eventually would buy 27 and contribute substantially to keeping it "extant."

Now the shock of isolation! This afternoon by around 2 I'd put away all my books and rigged everything up (lights, action) and then there was nothing to do but work—which is what this whole show is supposed to be about—but I wasn't yet psyched up for it. Weird feeling, you either get in the car and go shopping or you sit outdoors and watch the trees move around!

GLOUCESTER 6/27/85

. . . Thinking of you in the quiet is funny tonight—the beginning of Fiesta—Viva San Pietro—the carnival sounds are coming right thru my closed windows—and the sirens accompanying the state and city and church officials to make their speeches—honky Italian band and a street dance in a semi-noreaster . . .

WILLOW NY 7/9/85

Right now I'm alone in the woods. Was headed for an aerobics class at 6:30 but just at that moment it began to rain, and somehow I felt too old and lazy to take a class outdoors (with only a roof overhead, no walls). So I've jumped my rope for 5 min (not enough) and struggled to jerry-build some fencing around the tomato plant that I brought up here, attacked last night by either the resident raccoon or Mr. Deer—who by the way makes the weirdest sound, like a karate master blowing air out of his lungs! Me so city, I never knew deer could talk!

I do miss my bike. But every morning there's a cool desk to sit down to, none of that humid sufferance I'm used to. It's a miracle. . . .

State of book: I have done first chapter of third section . . . and today began chap 2, after much struggle to concentrate on *what do I mean here*—the biggest problem.

GLOUCESTER IST AUGUST 1985

. . . 5 of the Fairy Tales are in Ten Pound island window, lit at night . . . they look nice—Tinker Bell sold . . . Bud died last week . . . Margaret Flowers, friend from downstairs, taking Harry & Bud's apt . . . if subsidy falls through I'll move in with her—i.e. if the sky doesn't fall in the meantime.

Love & kisses, Henny Penny

Helene!

Minor/major freakout day. Spent four hours on the floor in this room, hardly moving, going through everything having to do with 62–65, incl. rereading the copies of my letters, which somehow, this time around, threw me, don't know why. But now I see it as such an *awful* time, with every stress, to use that new catchall, that a young woman could ever be subject to. And things I'd forgotten—oh god, and things I'd never made connections for, to, about—I can't stand it tonight, I hate to say this but I am blubbering into the typewriter . . .

Tried a beer earlier that didn't do much. Tried weeding the garden and got caught nekked, by neighbor down the road who came to look at his water level in well house. Every time I stop choring, or diverting, the throat lump comes back, now I'm trying a joint possibly that will worsen things I suppose I should just bawl so this is my bawl on y'all got to maintain some sense of humor. My tape playing now is by saxophonist Oliver Lake title of tune "Don't Go Crazy, Keep Your Sanity, You Know You'll Win in the End"—

Ok I'm ok now, wow. Actually it's prob from lack of exercise . . . The car has a flat tire and I have no jack, and the (borrowed) bike has a flat tire and I have no pump. Countr' livin'. But Allah be praised I have a boyfriend who will jack me up early enuf in the am so I can go to this aerobics class and work some of the worry off. What it is, this sending of emotional energy into such a hard part of the past, is a reenactment, to get to the truth where the writing ought to be, right? In one letter you wrote everything you had done in the past 2 hrs of that day that you were mired in, said it helped just to repeat it, and that's what we seemed to have done, just kept repeating it so it wouldn't seem so incredibly destructive, doing things doing things doing things for other people . . . and were passionately in love w/our own lives nevertheless—because *at least* we didn't have to live straight?

So far in book I have quoted a Russian poet (Marina Tsvetayeva) who said that it was precisely for *feeling* one needs time not *thought*—and where's art from anyway

oh oh oh oy vey

My present life is jealous of my past and angry for having taken her pleasure in the Be Here Now and spoilt it thru A Necessary Obsession. That about sez it I guess. I didn't mean to have this boyfriend but Janine—

whose handwriting bears such a startling resemblance to yours that reaching for a spice jar the label confuses me as to where I am! — took me to a party . . . He leaves early and comes back late, just my style, leaving me to freakout in between.

Try to find stories by Alice Munro, a Canadian. I am reading *The Moons of Jupiter*, a collection, and wigging out. Some people have all the insight, I just have events.

Second only to you, of course . . . Bud is surely in a fine place, laughing. I bet he sent you that "flea explosion" you mentioned just as some kind of overload to temporarily short-circuit the emotions and restore insane humor/horror—which reminds me I'd meant to start this letter "Dear Henny Penny" but that was before I got so carried away by my tears—

Thanks, mama, for letting me bend yr ear like this, it's going on to 11pm and now I can read and treat myself to tea, stop thinking. Basil King[10] once said to me, at a party, "Hettie, would you please just stop *thinking!*"

I am getting so gassed out by the prospect of Paul's wedding! A sure-fire affair!

Can't wait.

WILLOW, NY 8/14/85

Will be driving to Boston via the Mass Pike (boring but straight)—tell your kids I can arrive (12th) whenever it's good time for them so no one has to wait for me . . . Sorry about that moaning letter the other day.

GLOUCESTER 9/15/85

We saw you, we saw you!!! On the Mass Pike! Marie: "*There's Hettie!*" Great waving and shouting, but you were so *intent* on the road, the concentration needed after those days, I shall see you forever, now & then that is, in that wonderful green car, going. We didn't really have time, any of us, to say hello before we all left that morning—like a planetary collision we all shot off in our own directions, but we stayed one lap behind you on the Pike for about 10 minutes—till we hit the different turnoffs . . . It was nice for us, sorry you didn't know!

---

10. Basil King, painter, who did a number of covers for *Yugen*, the magazine LeRoi Jones and I published in the late fifties and early sixties.

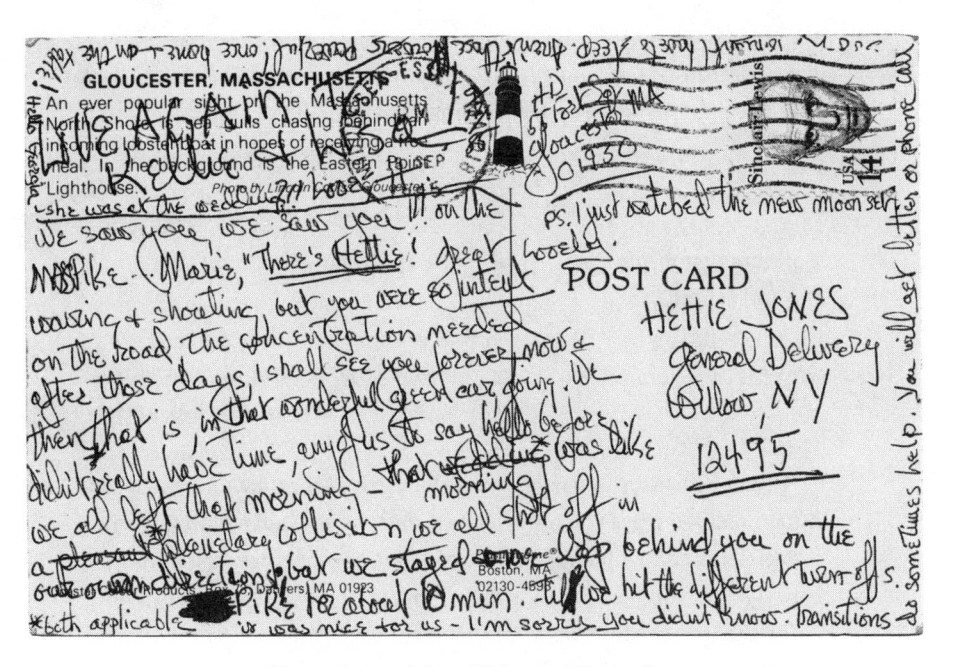

Fig 3.2 Postcard from Helene to Hettie after
Paul Buck's wedding, September 1985

. . . . .

Two days of sneaking into the Xerox room . . . It's helpful, really, to have
these letters to do for you — I almost can't face moving . . . I find it harder
as I get older? I'm not sure that's true.

It's so weird to be dealing w/20 yrs ago and the interim references to
people who are no longer here, etc.

Hello hello!

Thank you again, my dear, for taking the time to ferret out those letters. I apologize again for not dating them, but that I realize now has to
do with my fear — who am I to formalize myself by dating my thoughts;
notice also the little tight letters of my signature. Anyway as I've said and
will continue to say, you saved my life for me, you did. I hope to repay

the favor some way one day, but it's hard to imagine how—maybe I could get rich? HO HO! Let's hope I can write a halfway decent book at the least.

I am thinking about your housing situation all the time and worrying . . .

Building *up for sale* again—real estate and clients in my apt. again oohing and aahing . . .

Hello!

I can't believe yr house is up for sale again. Can they now throw you out for real? Or price you out—same thing? My god, after all that agony of indecision, and that terrible feeling of violation when they come trooping through and you realize (once again) that your home is not your home.

By the way, the homeless . . . This morning I could see, from my front window, someone asleep all wrapped up next to his/her cart right across the street. If I'd stuck my head *out* the window I could probably have seen more than one. And the fucking *shelters* we have are not the answer.

But I wanted to respond to yr "Why didn't you ever mention yr writing?" question when we spoke last. Because I had very nearly stopped writing, except for a poem now and then, because I never found myself with any time, because Roi was the big talent, and because, having been raised in a completely anti-intellectual atmosphere, suspected even for reading, I probably had internalized enough no-nos for a lifetime. I didn't date my letters or write about writing (though I was even then correcting others' work!) for the same reason that my signature is a teeny-weeny *thang.*

But today I am *happy,* despite all long-term problems like the roof scene and the will-I-lose-home scene. Woke up late, did Jane Fonda exercise, hung out a wash in the blowing cloudy day, went to Orchard Street fabric stores on the bike, on an errand for Granddaddy Jones[11] since he couldn't find a certain cotton blend in Newark. Riding a bicycle or danc-

---

11. Coyt Leroy Jones (1910–2002), Amiri Baraka's father, who made dashikis and other African-inspired clothing after retiring from the post office.

ing is always such pure pleasure, therefore accompanied by doubt as to its seriousness yet would I die without it!

The other night I bought a treat, a paperback of Djuna Barnes's *Interviews*—with the likes of Diamond Jim Brady, Lillian Russell, Mother Jones, Flo Ziegfeld—many others! And reading it I felt so vindicated for wanting to hold onto *sound*—she's the best!

I hope you aren't too crazy, though I'm sure you must be. But you are fortunate in a small town in one way—you don't have to lose your neighborhood in as drastic a version as happens here. You'll still meet the same people on Main St., but in the city you just don't go to the same shoemaker as before. I am already in my head structuring a life that includes driving a car with a folding bicycle into the city from far out in Brooklyn. Just to go to my shoemaker, Walter, who knows three languages and survived the Second World War as a child, running . . .

GLOUCESTER 11/7/85

Hello dear Het—

To describe the events of the past 8 days I ain't got the heart for—yr letter a blessing yesterday—am sorting and packing. Will, as the Fates look today, move into Margaret's formerly Harry's apt—i.e., moving in w/Margaret. Bldg. sold—or rather "we are selling" to buyer who wants it tenant-free. Hope to be out and in by Dec. Notations on those copied letters were ruminations, really, not asking for prompt replies . . . i.e. thinking about what/who I was then too.

11/12 I JUST FOUND THIS . . . THOUGHT IT'D BEEN
THERE W/YOU FOR WEEKEND . . .

Oh dear, my head is full of dust in all its many cavities. I'm trying to sort and pack but got that thing called flu I guess which shot this nifty long weekend. You wouldn't believe what a crazy time this is.

Ordered Djuna's *Interviews* from inter-library loan—I've loved her since *Nightwood* which I read in Pocatello when I just couldn't believe how a gem like that was there in my hands. Charles and I wanted to go see her* one of those nights (in which bar?) that time, I think, we all were there [in New York]—o yes what she does w/language is so breathtakingly beautiful . . .

*DIDN'T because we couldn't get anyone else interested . . . that bit.

O dear I kept you up!! But it was so good to talk. To Harry's in AM to make arrangements w/Margaret for clearing some space for me and my gear. Wat a scene . . . back to packing. Hope you dig *Rose & Flo* as much as I did—think finally it's my Munro favorite. Keep the biblio coming!

Hello—wherever you are by now, I just couldn't resist writing that familiar address just one more time. Hope it's all coming together piece by piece. I've been in a funk so couldn't write to cheer you before now, but just spent 2 days cleaning house and feel better, although I have been (not legally) *evicted*. Lawyer says not to worry, still I wake up fearful enough and find it hard to concentrate on my work. Anyway I've determined not to let it drive me crazy and with all this Xmas no time for misery. Hope despite every difficulty that all of you guys will have Happy Holidays—why don't you call me COLLECT for an Xmas present me to you?

Love and Courage—H

4

We lived in a pocket of Time.
It was close, it was warm.
Along the dark seam of the river
the houses, the barns, the two churches . . .
till Time made one of his gestures;
his nails scratched the shingled roof.
Roughly his hand reached in,
and tumbled us out.

                — *Elizabeth Bishop*

To evict is to eject, dispossess, remove, dislodge, this last being the lone word with a picture. You can see that little lodge, right? And the dispossessed lodger? Evict is the past participle of *evincere*, to overcome.

And the chase was on. Having failed to get her dungeon Helene had already moved once, six months earlier, when I got this:

Hullo . . .

This—enclosed copy—"legal termination of tenancy" was stuck on nail on door when I came home from work. I did freeze of course. nono-nonono . . . no! Time all wrong! Good Friday he w/wife behind banged on door 12 noon, I was getting ready to leave. They *banged* on door—Arthur, former landlord, probably told him/them I was a leetle deaf. "HELENE DORN," he sez, "MICHAEL MCNAMARA HERE. I'VE JUST BOUGHT THIS BUILDING AND MY WIFE & I WOULD LIKE TO SEE THE APT." I gave them a few minutes, not speaking, I cldn't; (you must realize I knew this lil whippersnapper way back there on the Fort . . . I never did like him & he knows that).

Akkkkk!

I hate to tell you, it is all valid, and I do have to find something fast. So there you are, I am freak city . . . Don't call because there's nothing more I can tell you.

I think I'm a little drunk. I really didn't think it would be so quick—one month!

A photo of her, trudging through a snowstorm in her Wellingtons, had appeared the year before on the front page of the *Gloucester Times*. You can see what her sister Marie calls "the iron in her." Walker that she was, she tried to take it in stride.

NEW YORK 4/5/86

Helene!

Couldn't believe that letter, its vile officialese "you are to quit and deliver up . . . in good, clean condition"—you should *trash* the thing!

Oh Helene! The wickedness of it all, the denial of what ought to be a *right*—decent housing. The tenants rights groups I belong to call for "housing in the public domain" and I wonder how many generations it will take before we'll see again construction of housing projects like the New Deal stuff. In NY there is a waiting list for such housing of thousands and thousands, aarrrgggghhhh it's my anger renders me helpless . . .

I'm out of space, and out in space. I think you are ONE BRAVE WOMAN and please keep taking your vitamins. Enclosed also some rubber bands to help keep things together although they are not as fat and classy as the ones you wanted they may be of some help and came to me wrapped around the broccoli!

NEW YORK, 5/25/86

Hello . . . last night told your story to some young people whose lives have never been really difficult or unsettled—even at weddings I have to bring along my political head, I guess. And one woman did say, "It does not seem right that a woman should have to give up her kitchen table."

Landlord here today painting over the *No Paseran* sign on the city gate. Looked right at me as I left the house but gave no sign of recognition. It's too weird.

Cheery thought: all the young women in NY this season are wearing large, colorful earrings, bunches of things, the style is very Caribbean, w head wraps and what Lisa has referred to as "overkill"—large chunky necklaces and all in all a Carmen Miranda look, but in the best of temper, as with good intentions. And of course it makes me happy. Contrast them with the sober fem bankers and lawyers I sometimes catch on my nightly bike ride thru lower Manhattan.

But money wins. Nevertheless while it is winning we have color and form. So who has won what . . .

Thinking of you right this minute, 10:51PM . . .

5 REAR CHESTNUT STREET, GLOUCESTER 6/19/86

Dear Het,

Thank you for the beautiful book — what a salve for my poor tired self. It was on the landing when I got home from work. Haven't called because by 11 or 12 I'm all twisted again and don't want to talk to anyone. This is one very crazy time in my life. The new place itself will work but it takes such time to figure how to deal with its small sq. footage. It has a good feeling and I'm looking right now out my window at Fitz Hugh Lane's[1] house and a Canadian freighter heading out of the harbor.

Got to try to get a desktop sawed overnight . . .

Oh Het, dear friend, everything DOES come to pass?

Yet after passing twice, barely a year later:

GLOUCESTER, APRIL 2, 1987

. . . Sit down for this next bit:

Came home from work last Monday to find long-haired broad *w/clip-board* in my kitchen — Steve (landlord) shouting from studio "don't freak, don't freak, it's OK" . . .

You can imagine the adrenaline, turning the key, *tired*, expecting just the cat —

The building is up for sale.

I'm in a small state of something, I'm not sure what. Shock doesn't say it.

P.S. No hot water for last 36 hrs due to real estate people leaving something open . . .

---

1. Painter of maritime scenes. Born Nathaniel Rogers Lane in Gloucester, 1804, he became leading figure in American luminism. In 2007, Helene's daughter-in-law Stephanie Buck and her collaborator Sarah Dunlap discovered his "real" name to be Fitz Henry Lane, and reported this in *Fitz Henry Lane, Family and Friends*.

After three evictions in two years Helene would land, safe for the time being, in a 1764 house owned by the Cape Ann Historical Association. "You won't believe this place when you see it," she wrote, "I still don't and I've been here a month!"

But all that forced removal took a toll, interrupted her work, and—well, let her speak:

Went to libr. after work because I wanted to read some of that [Jean] Rhys prose again—I remember writing you abt her that I had to stop because she tore me apart and I wasn't feeling too strong at that point, but how *beautiful* her prose. And you not quite understanding my reaction because you didn't really have any experience or whatever w/alcoholism . . . And this is just a note to both of us to remember to talk about it when we're together or at least beyond postcards because I find it interesting.

In her 1969 letter to me from Spain, she mentions my saying *no bueno* to alcohol. She once wrote that it helped; I thought it would hurt. But she did her work and went to her job and loved her family and was my friend, my sister. And since she saved my life I'm saving hers because she's dead.

· · · · ·

From *evict* it's an easy leap to *eject*, which shares with *reject* the Latin root "to throw out or off." As in: The editor at Little, Brown, which had purchased my memoir, rejected the manuscript.

GLOUCESTER 8/6/86 AFTER A PHONE CALL

Want to reiterate . . . I ain't known *nobody* who ain't gone through the same o-my-gods . . . it's the same old tired SHIT!!!!

It's o.k. Hettie Jones, dinna you worry . . . hettie jones, what do you think we did in our former lives?????? or this one?

Never mind. Every Thing Comes to Pass.

NEW YORK 8/11/86

My dear,

9:15pm on what nearly feels like "the first day of the rest of my life"— strange, that a psychological blow like this seems to exist only in its physical manifestations—Oh woe and sigh. Spent last 3, 4 days making my files, throwing out, sorting through . . . It was a comfort, the hurt part of the brain just goes to sleep.

Tomorrow night I'm having dinner with agent . . . who when I started whining stopped me sternly and said, "Hettie I *love* this book. You will feel better when you start working again."

Yes, and it's better to write, with things as they are and which will no doubt get worse as the $$ goes to cents.

OK I am sick of myself . . .

Terrible tiredness, but I need to make a few trips down and up the stairs w the boxes of stuff I've got to throw out. At night no one glares when I dump my stuff on the corner, esp. not Dirty Mike, whose corner (car repair) it is. He and I have been friends lately so of course he managed to turn weird and pinched my nipple today. I told him his balls would go if he touched me again and then he got insulted. I'm sure I've mentioned him before, his full name is Dirty Crazy Mean Mike, and once, years ago, he bit my head—the top of my head, to be precise. Then a box of dirt from my garden fell onto one of his old useless parked cars and he yelled at me and I didn't speak to him for 3 years.

Will let you know results of session with agent . . .

Madame!

I wrote you a frantic letter the other day.

What's bothering me at present, even tho I've calmed down some, is that I must be *extremely* watchful. If I've described myself as "a dark, runty Jew" I cannot become "a small, Jewish girl," which absolutely shocked Lisa, for one, because of the sexist tone of it.

But then I thought it's easy to blame but not so easy to write a book so good that they can't say a word. Anyway I just wanted to say I'm recovering, though very slowly it seems.

I didn't send that other letter because now I've changed the beginning, a commitment to go forward I suppose. Wish I could simply get back to work, but it's times like these that make you so aware of *where* the work comes from—and if you have a sore head from having been clobbered, a little healing has to take place, I guess . . .

I seem to be nattering about all this, understandably but then after a while I'm as bored as anyone else with it. Onward, forward march!

Before I began this I went looking for your postcard to answer it—and lo, it had disappeared tho I'm certain I saw it this A.M.?

Someone just walked by, singing at the top of his lungs, "What the world needs now is love, sweet love"—I couldn't agree more but that ain't all. Today's paper reports 600 political prisoners on hunger strike in Pretoria, and the world dragging its feet not wanting to do *anything* against S. Africa.[2]

8PM

Left in Brooklyn overnight, the car is now minus its (nearly new) battery. Now we must get a lock for the hood, installed by a garage. *Caramba*— what next? Am reading a novel by Elizabeth Tallent, *Museum Pieces*. Critical acclaim, good writing, but minus much interest to me, the lives of people who take their good fortune for granted, yet who am I to judge? Anyway keeping you supplied with titles.

How quickly these long summer days disappear. It's nearly dark. Lisa, at 25, thinks she is old. Wait, wait. "How do you feel about my getting old?" she asked me. Old? I said. Jeez.

I still haven't found that postcard!

GLOUCESTER 8/18/86

Dearest Het,

So are you really starting all over again?

Boston Women's Caucus for Art: thank you, I'll write for info. Gregor (bookshop owner) asked me last week if I thought I could get a fairy tale window by Xmas . . . i.e., all of the first 10 we got the grant for, such enthusiasm, and I said I'd try. Fellow from Brookline who does nice stained glass/found glass, think mebbe I told you about him, writes he can arrange show in Brookline Library for next winter/spring.

Have *Later the Same Day*, G. Paley; M. Duras *The Lover* is so beautiful I'm afraid to find *The War* back on the library shelf; T. Olsen, *Tell Me a*

---

2. During 1986, there were daily reports of violence in South Africa and the detention of those protesting the apartheid regime. Two days before this letter, four "terrorists," as the fighters for freedom were then called, were killed in the Transvaal area.

Riddle. She's almost too much for me right now, but I read them at night, somehow if you can just bury yr head in the pillow and think about how fine the writing, it's easier.

Hey Momma!

Yipes! A comedy of errrrrors and it's 9pm and I've no way to get to work tonight so thot I could at least begin this, although I'm up here in mall-land with no idea of where any P.O. is and not an envelope in sight. OH THANK YOU for such a long and welcome letter. It flew in the door just as I was trying to get out of the city yesterday morning.

I was up here all last week, in this fancy house that a friend has let me borrow, being a cat-sitter. So me and the cat was alone, and wrote and wrote, hating what we came up with. Drove home lickety-split Friday night to find landlord's daughter had put up 2 pieces of tin to replace my plastic ceiling. Well, I thought, that's better than a kick in the balls. Then Saturday they showed up in earnest, with plaster and more tin—all 3 children of the landlord. So I'm unable to get any writing done with people hammering and etc. And then Lisa said she'd had hardly any audience at her piece (*Carmella and King Kong*) the night before, so I rode my bike frantically just before showtime . . . Saw performance, rode quickly home to beat an approaching rainstorm, out of breath and sweaty, and lo!—the solution to how to go back to the beginning of the book for real. So I guess what it takes for me is some kind of frantic-ness. Ain't that a bitch?

Zora Neal Hurston, leading woman of the Harlem Renaissance: *Dust Tracks on a Road*, the autobiography, the novel *Their Eyes Were Watching God*, and there is a collection called *I Love Myself When I Am Laughing . . . And Then Again When I Am Looking Mean and Impressive*.

There were blue Concord grapes in the market today, a sure sign of fall.

•••••

Hullo . . .

Thank you for everything: long letter, t. call, postcard re brother Jack [who was ill]. What a lovely lady you are to make that trip and to clarify what was happening w/him.

SUCH A YEAR IT HAS BEEN! Letter coming when I can breathe . . .

Agent likes my new beginning of book but I don't love it yet, maybe soon. There have been 3 bulldozers outside my window all week long—they start at 7AM. We hear that this house may be for sale AGAIN. Familiar?

We had to go to court again, the court fucked up and we needn't have gone, another day wasted. The 2 tenants downstairs got eviction notices; tho I didn't, my garden did—I have to "forthwith" remove my "plants and vegetables."

Meanwhile the lawyers charge, and charge . . .

Just finished reading Martin Duberman's history of Black Mountain, parts of which I had to skim.

Helene, I'm so tired of the past, as tho it were some godawful medicine I have to take every day. And after this book is done I may not ever be interested to write about myself again. I never thot I was an "interesting" person anyway: interesting people are complicated and have problems, etc etc and fears and inhibitions blah blah but as far as psychology I'm so dully well-adjusted! The key is conflict—*agon*—and I've never been conflicted, simply determined. That sounds so self-serving, boo hiss, but then again, I'm probably just a jock who fell in with the wrong crowd.

Told Gregor today I'd let him know by Sat if I think I can get show by 1st Dec.

[POSTCARD: PHOTO BY MARGARET RANDALL OF FEMALE SANDINISTA SOLDIER IN NICARAGUA]

Madame!

Here's a soldier to keep the bad spirits away from your house from now on—just put her up near the doorway, like a *mezuzah*—

[newsclip from "Community" section of *Gloucester Times*]

Beginning Monday, Dec. 8, Ten Pound Island Book Co. will again display the glass mosaics of Gloucester artist Helene Dorn.

Her current series is a group of eight works titled "Myths, Legends and Fairy Tales," and draws on stories as diverse as those of Rapunzel and E.T.

Local residents may be familiar with Dorn's work from earlier exhibits at the Ten Pound Island Book Co., Stagecoach House, Lovisco Gallery, and the Annisquam Village Church.

Dorn's glass mosaics are in private collections in England, Norway, and throughout the United States.

• • • • •

NY SUN 4/27/87

Hello!

This is a cheerup letter going out from 60 degree evening NY . . .

Went yesterday to a conference on Lower East Side history sponsored by some NYU historians looking to find out what to call it—East Village or Loisaida—anyway I decided not to stay thru the history to the present . . .

Had dinner with Joyce and then we went to see Hetty King[3] dance, the dance was not interesting, Hetty was very good, the scenery was terrific, at one point the text (it was narrated): "Women are never really alone in that room of their own," and Joyce said loudly BULLSHIT and later "that obscures the real issues" because (what I've left out) is that the dance was supposed to be about pornography which itself obscures the real issue that the basis is economics. And Lisa, Defender of Woman Faith, said the same thing when I told her about it today.

Enclosed is the card for her party, held on Friday night, for which I cooked 95 chicken wings as who wouldn't for a daughter who so gladdens every heart with a big fundraising party including a terrific DJ and much dancing and incredible entertainment and food/drink etc even a coatcheck and such a beautiful audience! I got to hug all my—there should be a word for those ex-boyfriends—and all the energetic young women I've known since they were small, but the best was riding my bike, drunk on beer and all this love, down Fifth Ave at 2:30 suddenly become 3:30 in the morning! And now, before I get off this piece of paper, just to tell you I cd not go to the opening announced on reverse, because it was also

---

3. Hetty King, dancer with Ralph Lemon and others, daughter of Martha and Basil King.

yesterday, in the Bronx, which is where things HAVE to happen because as the historians will have by this time hopefully acknowledged, there is no stopping money . . .

• • • • •

Unlike many, Helene regularly read African American women writers and had opinions: "Got Hurston's *I Love Myself* from interlibrary loan—find intros *very* innaresting, A. Walker especially—no that's not right, M. H. Washington is equally innaresting!"

So I never had to explain myself or feel insistent about what offended me. In my first draft I'd written that when LeRoi entered the *Record Changer* office I wasn't surprised that he was black. I wrote Helene that I'd been asked, "Because he was applying for a job as Shipping Manager?" "No, *no*!!" I'd protested. "Because it was a *jazz* magazine!"

In 1966, I'd been fired from a job for "black militant beliefs." Now it wasn't about what was in my head but in my face.

• • • • •

Around this time editorial rumor had it that manuscripts written on computers were of lesser value, the writing having been compromised by ease of performance. I had nothing against easy, and found the computer just an easier way to be hard on myself. And it also made possible long (and long unmailed) descriptions—what we called our "blah blah":

NEW YORK NOVEMBER 9, 1987

Helene Helene!

Here is her new computer—I'm too sleepy to feel like myself, so this is *hers*—whoever she is (and sometimes I surely do wonder). . . .

Agent. Went to a party and had 3 vodkas where she informed me I had to get the revised version (what I have of it) to her asap. So came home at 9 (drunk on bike in short skirt in darkness and cold, yum). And sat at my desk reading the thing. Got through the first section and decided I could live with it. That was last Thursday night and now it's Monday.

Right now 9pm and on 5 hrs sleep and up at 6 I am crashing.

Rode bike to 56th St ad agency 7am, worked, rode back 11am, worked at my desk copyediting an essay on the arctic natl wildlife refuge, very stern and romantic so far (for *Aperture* magazine), redressed myself, took subway at 3:30 to chiropractor for shoulder problem, took the crosstown bus from W. 86th to east, through Central Park, in the dark at 5:30pm a winding country lane. Then I walked 10 blocks north, from the Guggenheim to the International Center of Photography where a friend's video was shown; Lisa says video is to film what soap opera is to drama; she appears to be right but I wish I could understand why that has to be necessary. This is the monumental part of NY, where all the old mansions abut the park. It's quiet and so rich and massive that to me it seemed another century that I'd forgotten about between downtown and Madison Avenue midtown where I've been last 2 days. After the video I came downtown; usually whenever I ride the subway I watch the people, since I so rarely have a chance to *study* them, but after a day that seemed so full of people I just sat and read my book, in the harsh light, with all the other pale tired people; in a city where mostly brown/black people ride the subway, it seems they when tired, bloodless with hunger/fatigue, become ashen. Once home I immediately cooked some dinner as I'd had wine and needed *strength*.

You are my reward. It's 10:30pm. Yesterday I worked ad agency for 9 hours, then came home and did private student for 2. I am giving some thought to stopping this. The chiropractor says if I neglect my arm it will further atrophy until I cannot comb my hair or wipe my ass.

Well.

Thank you for that wonderful collection of stuff! Just now read the Beatles/Mandela article—good for the *Gloucester Times*! When I finish correcting the spelling of everyone in NY I will come up there and get to work on the *Gl. Times*—but why not you? Have you ever tried looking into that? What I liked best was that the journalist did his homework and presented statistics in a clear way. How nice for me to have that here, after a morning of American Express copy—the irony that I can't get a card from them but I correct their grammar!

After fifteen years of working with glass, Helene found herself no longer interested and had sent me photos of new work, to which I responded:

I'm saving all my thoughts about those masks you've been making for last in this letter—like dessert. When you're in the presence of that guy with the third eye, it's *scary*. I think they're WONDERFUL! That huge one . . .

I will *not* buy any more grapes.[4]

11/18/87

that was all she wrote.

11/20/87

last night I spent 3 hours getting the printer to work on plain paper, to be able to print out the 186 pp I am now ready to send to agent.

On to judgment once more . . .

Oh Helene, I don't know what's to become!

P.S. on back of envelope: Forgot all mention of house; the 30-day eviction notice up 11/30. Trying hard not to freak and sending letters to Loft Board asking for "speedy" consideration since they've had case since June 1985.

• • • • •

NEW YORK, 1/20/1988

Right now my ½ book is both in Boston at Little, Brown and surreptitiously at 3 other places in New York. I am trying not to shit in my shoes, and fortunately the anxiety over this upcoming poetry class at SUNY Purchase is taking my mind off the idea of being judged again.

Tonight Martha King and I are going to Ladies Night at the local steambath—I could do without this but she asked me several months ago and maybe it will be fun, though I'd rather spend money, if we're talking self-indulgence, on a pair of waterproof boots.

I did a 4-day stint at the ad agency, including last weekend, and that's the end of that for a while. Can't cope with the way it batters my head. Accepted, instead, a copyedit job from Grove that sits unopened—300 pages, each of which must be read twice.

Hope you're getting some sleep. Try to put yourself to bed early, as I

---

4. In sympathy with California farmworkers, who had organized a grape strike locally in 1965. Which, under the auspices of Cesar Chavez and the United Farm Workers, grew into a national boycott.

think I wrote last letter. It does work, although it doesn't seem fair, in a way—I hate losing the quiet hours round midnight. But health matters more. Don't I sound like a Jewish mother?

[POSTCARD]
NEW YORK, 3/5/88

Madame!

Good news—Dutton is taking the book, Little Brown is "forgiving" the original $ **Though you should never send such personal news in a postcard—maybe "overwriting"** and I will get some more with new contract! **(!!!!) is the answer? Get some confusion going? I have plenty of confusion to spare what** Am going to fly (I think) to Boston for Kellie's opening April 19th, but must be **with teaching these two classes and trying to tell myself I can now finish the book by** back in NY for my class next day. Letter to follow—I'm copyediting now. **the end of the year—maybe stop copyediting other people's bad novels like I've been doing all this week and some of last week too.** Hope you're still thinking about Boston 4/19 it would really be a gas wish I could get a new car by then, but . . . Love, Happy Het

90 MIDDLE ST. GLOUCESTER 3/9/88

wonderful!!!

I knew it I knew it I knew it!!!!

GLOUCESTER 4/25/88

[on the back of an invitation to a group show]

You could hop a plane for the event. But since I'm only 1 of 15, I won't insist!

NEW YORK, 5/5/88

I would have flown up for that opening even if you were one of a hundred if I could afford to fly more than once every five years!

Signed my contract last week! You must be working constantly to get ready for other show, but at least it's a sign that folks are beginning to see how *good* you are!

Love and Happy Mom Day

Helene's first word processor prompted serial letters from her, too, full of complaints that she'd work through—which would allow wonderful stories to emerge:

this is the typewriter!

and a quarter past nine I'm too tired to really write a letter, but it's been so long . . .

Was SICK for more than two weeks, went to doctor, which means I was SICK . . . bronchitis he sd. The Kingfisher show opening was a fiasco, she had my masks FLAT, HORIZONTAL, all together on a light box—I was livid. Older pieces look ok in window. Am killing myself now to get two pieces ready for Cape Ann Historical Association.

JUNE 3

Have just come back from taking my 2 pieces over to Association, not fin-ished, but enough on the way to show. I wasn't going to continue if she didn't think them apropos for the "Captain's Collection" exhibition, she being Judith, administrator and my nice "landlady." Well, it took some doing to make myself do it in the first place, what a lonely business we've chosen, you and I, and how I do envy musicians mostly, actors and film-makers and dancers . . .

A friend tells me everything in the heavens is retrograde except Mars and somebody equally ferocious.

To get back to Judith: more than enthusiastic, wanted a "ballpark" price . . . I promised I'd let her know, I just couldn't sort things like prices out, having spent 2 months on 2 pieces for the "prestige" of showing something at the CA. Hist. Assn. Museum when my head is on the masks.

Anyway, I *will* submit them, they'll be shown, and after the exhibition, August, a panel of 3 judges will decide what is to remain in the Capt's Col—a museum gift shop finally is what they have in mind, I'm sure.[5] I dunno, HJ, I dunno.

---

5. These two pieces were either sold or returned to Helene. Currently another is on indefinite loan to the Historical Association, and was last displayed in a 2009 show of women artists of Cape Ann.

After all this time all I'm sending you is blah blah . . . But that's the way I feel. I'm in a kind of funk. All that enthusiasm this afternoon was a relief, but no more than that. I should be singing. I wonder what it is I want, more than that.

Got Spike Lee and Lisa's book[6]—left it in drawer at office, 30 pages into, and it would have been nice to have it to read in spare spaces this weekend but everything is retrograde in the heavens. I was glad Ossie Davis spoke of Malcolm X—

I have a wonderful memory of him—O.D.—standing next to me at the bar the night we all went uptown, was it after the Town Hall debate? I can't remember, to the *Kulchur* people's apt. He insisted the fellow behind the bar get another bottle of scotch because that was what I was drinking, and we *talked!* I'd been so freaked, trying to make some kind of contact with the man sitting next to me in the room where Malcolm was, it was like hitting steel, and I didn't know, until Roi told Ed, that he was one of Malcolm's bodyguards. After Ed told me that, I stopped trying to be what-ever it was I was trying to be . . . but I sure remember Ossie Davis!

I've got to go to bed. This is all me, but I'm thinking of you. Herewith some quotes from Virginia Woolf's letters.

6/6—are you ok? working? what happens w/your summer?—Got big head on "scaffold" this wkend. Planted 6 pansy plants and the rosemary Steph gave me in a plastic window box . . . thought so much of you and yr roof garden while I was doing it—are you ok?

NY JUNE 24, 1988

How Do!

I have your wonderful letter in front of me which I thought was so ter-rific it deserved a real letter answer instead of one of those fly-into-the-middle of your life phone calls. Still you sounded tired and said you were, and so I am worried about you. Of course it helps to *worry*—

Maybe you need to eat more—or, more frequently?

Can you figure out a way to sit while you're in the studio, instead of being on your feet for hours?

---

6. *Uplift the Race: The Construction of School Daze* (Simon and Schuster, 1988).

Maybe eat as much as you can after you get home from work — a real meal then instead of later, with plenty of carbohydrates, which are what put you to sleep . . . rice and beans, ma'am. And then some herb tea and a nap . . .

Oh, sigh, I am always so full of suggestions.

Thank you for sending me Virginia Woolf's letters, how wonderful of her to have described so many things so precisely: "This damnable disease of seeing people" —

Unlike Virginia I have neither lawn nor writing board on my knee but you would laugh to see me now. I once saw a photo of Wm. Buckley on his yacht swiveled back in his fishing chair with his word processor keyboard sort of propped — like but unlike Virginia . . . So tonight I am laid back in my wonderful rolling chair (b'day present from kids), and tho not quite as comfy as either William or Virginia I do have my feet up on the cardboard box under my desk that holds discarded pages of my magnum opus that monkey on my back. Usually I have better footrests, but there's also something satisfying about accidentally stomping into the pile of pages. . . .

The Times today reports that all this heat is seriously part of the greenhouse effect. Weds. it was 98 and the air here like pea soup. I rode my bike in the evening just to create the illusion of a breeze. Tonight, at the Battery, there were little white sailboats running around, and a speedboat, and the last Statue of Liberty ferry noisily pulling away after having disgorged all the tourists.

You spoke in your letter of blah blah — meaning the dailiness of everything, but shit, what are we supposed to talk about? Things that aren't real? Of course I could tell you that Cooper Square park — hardly bigger than a breadbox — is *home*, this summer, to about 30 otherwise homeless people, that every plastic garbage bag in this neighborhood is broken and the contents strewn in the street — every morning — by people looking for bottles and cans to redeem or food that is edible, god knows what — that this situation grows worse while the rest of the city goes on, business as usual —

Which reminds me that I can still hear my complainy voice saying to you "But that will leave me with only $145 a week for blah blah" — makes me feel guilty when you have so little. My boss at Mobilization was a former rabbinical student and once caught me saying "only $25" — and shamed me for it so I remember each time that attitude returns. Last week, when I told a friend about something costing $20, she said "That's *nothing*" and I grew resentful in my heart! $20 is *never nothing*! And speaking of which, your $800 grant is better than a kick in . . . and next time you can ask for more.

A couple of weeks ago I got two letters from little children in Appleton, Wisconsin, who had read a story I wrote mid-70s for a fourth-grade reader, which story is obviously still in print—and this was as you can imagine more reward than anything I can think of. I think when I get done with all this adult shit I'll just go back to writing for kids, who want only honesty and a bit of excitement, and don't give a fuck for your opinions one way or another.

Enclosing this photo of Georgia O'K because I think it's different from the one you have—

When my $$ comes—next week I'm told—I'll call you up and we'll celebrate!

The money for the phone call probably came because my next letter, begun on 8/10/88, contains this line: "You're reading feminist lit!!!!!" I always counted on Helene's literary excursions, so we must have had a long conversation about it.

NEW YORK, 8/11/88

. . . The other day on the street—where *everything* is now sold, especially books—I got a novel by Harry Crews, whose memoir (*A Childhood*) was really good. But I get seriously impatient with men whose female characters seem without rhyme/reason. I am really glad you're reading fem lit. Then you can lecture me on it since I have never been able to get into it; all I know is that I can't read books where women are depicted as insubstantial and their motives totally unclear.

I thought you'd like the enclosed about Tompkins Square "riot"—as of today, 73 reports of police brutality. I read poetry at the mock impeachment of Reagan, glad the cops didn't see fit to come out swinging then . . .

But they've stopped hassling the people who are living in Cooper Square Park. Chairs, mattresses sometimes, but more often cardboard and blankets and makeshift. Bathing in the fire hydrant. Men and women, men mainly. This morning, two guys were cleaning a refrigerator. I rode past on my bike in a hurry and some astonishment but then completely forgot. I should look out the window and see if they've plugged it in any-where, which is the logical next step. God help us.

Kellie went one day to Brighton Beach in Brooklyn, and found that no one bathed, but wet themselves down with spray bottles of water they had brought with them. And the rich folks beaches are also polluted. How cruel it all is . . .

Hello dearest Het,

Yrs. received yesterday in the midst of that heat, how nice to sit here in the studio w/my feet up after work, and air, no matter how hot, blow-ing on the o poor swollen things from sitting in that inner room at SHCS.

Don't count on me for feminist education, I'm just beginning, but I look at things with new eyes.

Adrienne Rich's *Of Woman Born* is a book I think every woman should read; I would give it to my granddaughters but it's not written for young adults.

Dear Helene!

Ugh argh help——an evening of crisis in confidence . . . I had some reference to Patrice Lumumba in this [last] section of the book, and when my agent edited she x'd it out—but now as I'm sitting here (I just looked again at Lumumba's sweet, brave, grieving face on old yellowing news-paper) I realize I've *got* to put him in, he was so important to Roi, and looked, somewhere on his face, a bit like him . . . a young handsome man with glasses . . . Some months ago I spent an afternoon in the library going through newspapers and yearbooks. Lumumba's struggle in the Congo, against what proved to be the CIA, went on for months and months and months . . . And then they killed him![7]

You see? I'm a bit frantic.

I finally had a poem published and they mixed it up with someone else's, did I tell you that? The big feminist collective, *Heresies*. I wrote an

---

7. In 2010, the *New York Times* reported that Lumumba had been killed by rivals, not CIA. The following year the real story appeared in an op-ed by Adam Hochschild, who implicated the CIA, for all time, in Lumumba's death.

immediate nasty letter and got a quick abject apology but as my mother used to say to me, "You're always sorry."

My toilet is leaking, and I thought I could fix it myself but . . . I'm embarrassed at the prospect of a plumber inspecting my attempted repair. O the professionals, like Joel Oppenheimer once wrote.

Joel is sick and hasn't much longer to live. . . .

8/24

A cricket or katydid in the tree outside my front window, doesn't even mind life on the Bowery. Driving back from the beach on Lisa's birthday we passed a section of the highway with beautiful thick trees, alive with singing insects. And the highway a traffic-filled lane right beside them. Noisy and noxious. Do you think environmentalism will be the hot new issue? There's certainly a lot of public outcry. People in NY really did not go to the beaches even when declared safe. But I keep worrying that as the election nears it'll all just become part of the hype, and then, godhelpus, soon next summer . . .

Just read Jean Stafford, *The Mountain Lion*. She was so good, and when she was married to Robert Lowell she used to do all his fucking typing.

This will arrive just after your brother leaves. Hope it doesn't find you too wiped out. I don't know what I would ever have done if I hadn't been able to write to you, all this time. It's as though you had allowed me to verify my existence. You were the only one I knew would understand every word.

• • • • •

NEW YORK, 9/15/88 IN HASTE [AFTER A VISIT TO GLOUCESTER]

Thanks again for such a loverly time. Have, after seven hrs or so, got the beginning of the beginning of Chap 21, and some idea that maybe it'll all end Chap 23. Anyway, I am taking us to Buffalo tonight. Oddly, what I remember is *where* I was sitting in*

beep beep—incredible interruption. Landlord and his translator downstairs in the street to tell me that on Monday morning Con Ed is going to turn off our utilities because he didn't pay bill—we know we are not legally liable but there is the problem that Con Ed wants to take out the meters and it might be weeks before we could get them back. And here I am, hooked up — no electric, no computer. No gas, no hot water, no cooking. Of course tomorrow is Friday and therefore . . .

*to finish that sentence, "the car." That is, on the way to Buflo in 1963,[8] which all seems pretty remote, you betcha, when the threat of being utility-less looms.

NEW YORK, SEPTEMBER 20, 1988

> Tropical Storm Helene, christened yesterday
> by the National Hurricane center, should slowly
> strengthen off the coast of Africa . . .

Hey!

Chapter 21 is, as of this Fri. night, in form if not thoroughly in substance. The lawyer is still dragging his feet about rent arrangements. It keeps getting cold then hot. Various freaky nervous spells on my part over nothing at all or everything and too stupid to describe.

Are you watching all those Olympic children? What skills! What hideous commercialism! What psychologics! Kellie is back with many photos of Dutch canals and the Elgin marbles and King Tut in the British Museum.

Next life I'm going to be a gymnast!

GLOUCESTER, 9/29/88

Hello Hettie Jones:

It's 9pm and I can't call because I've got to buy shoes. But:

1. My little lovely black leather purse has changed my life . . . I think of you daily as I strap it around my waist . . . thank you!
2. Heresies came (all that postage!) & I sat in the white wicker chair & read not only yr. poem-not-credited-to-you, but a lot of other things . . .
3. Have copy of Tracy Chapman tape . . .

---

8. In the summer of 1963, Ed, Helene, LeRoi, myself, and all five of our children spent a month in Buffalo, New York, where Ed and LeRoi had been invited to teach a summer session. We lived happily *en famille* in a large rented house. The owner, when he found out, objected strenuously to the fact that we were not one family, but two, despite there being plenty of rooms, beds, and privacy for all.

4. Made soup the other night and put a whole one of your roof chilies in it—wonderful!
5. I still haven't done any laundry / a few washing-outs of uhnderhpahnts.
6. Jane Brakhage[9] coming tomorrow to make apple pies to get rid of the apples that are going bad in the sack and causing many flies in friend's house where she's staying . . . more about her later, and news of Lucia Berlin.[10]
7. Have got the 1st rune[11] in the finishing stages.
8. Have spent days dealing with dpw re: medical help re govt's MA health ins . . . "working disabled" . . . for which I may qualify . . .
9. I love you and will write . . . can't make head or tail of your housing situation . . . do you have electricity? Here's to Chapter 21!
10. Re Helene: I'm glad I didn't make a very big disturbance . . . got too much else to do, but it was interesting to hear my name on tv . . . and nice to equate what's going on inside of me w/a tropical storm . . . Letter coming when it all calms down . . . WILL IT????

10/1/88 ALREADY, ALREADY!

. . . Slept till 10:30 and there goes the morning. Jane B. here till 11:30 last night. It took us some 8 hours to make the "pies" which because of no pans became sort of odd-ball turnovers, w/ interruptions like time out for borscht & yogurt she brought, and a run to the A&P for freezer bags because what to do w/all these "pies," there being so many apples (she'd picked them in Omaha, Nebraska, a month ago) and time out to send postcards to Lucia & eat the leftover innards Jane put in the oven like a Brown Betty w/out the breadcrumbs or whatever—

And then, before she left, she told my fortune with the deck of cards

---

9. Wife of Stan Brakhage, filmmaker. After their divorce she published *Lump Gulch Tales* and *The Inside Story* as Jane Wodening.
10. Lucia Berlin (1936–2004), author of the story collections *Homesick*, *Where I Live Now*, and *So Long* (all Black Sparrow Press). *A Manual for Cleaning Women* (Knopf), published posthumously, was included on the *New York Times* "Best Books of 2015" list.
11. Aphorism, poem, or saying with mystical meaning, especially for casting a spell.

Paul & I used to play a game called SHIT I learned when I worked at the nursing home. It was an interesting "fortune" — Must get this to P.O.!

Hello Helene,

This is in answer to 2 of yours I think, or maybe I don't think, and mostly because it's too *cold* to think. I am wearing a t-shirt, sweatshirt, sweater and vest on the top, plus sweatpants and knee socks on the bottom and I wonder where any of my gloves are . . .

Our lawyer finally drew up papers and sent them to the new landlord's lawyer; the intent is that the landlord comes back with a counter-offer and we reach a compromise. Meanwhile the old landlord, he who is responsible for the utility bill, called both my neighbor Katy and me today (neither of us home), no doubt to urge us to pay the bill before something happens. Our lawyer, on Tuesday (today being Friday), said that if we paid the bill we'd be throwing money down the drain. Also meanwhile, our middle-floor neighbor, a man who doesn't pay his bills, is hiding from us and pretending nothing will happen if he pays no attention. In order to get the kind of legal coverage we need from NY City we must have 3 people in this building who fit the desired criteria, so we can't kill him, although Katy said she dreamed last night we tore him limb from limb.[12]

OCTOBER 14, ONE WEEK LATER, 2:36PM

. . . Today the new landlord (Worth Auto Parts, our next-door neighbor) is closing on the mortgage, but no one has mentioned when we're to sign our agreement or what terms have been decided.

You probably know by now that Joel died this week. He was only 58. Makes me feel sad. I was just writing about him (how he spent the night on Roi's desk when he couldn't find a bed at our house on 20th Street). Various foggy male voices on my answering machine to tell me the news — people who never call me otherwise.

Hungry. I suppose it's the weather. Despite the cold it's been so clear

---

12. This was the sculptor George Mingo, who died young of a heart condition he'd kept to himself. Had we known we'd been kinder. But he stayed long enough to make that crucial third, and in memoriam we named our new street tree for him. Twenty-five years later, it's higher than the floor where he lived and still growing. RIP, George.

and bright and tempting, and I keep thinking up excuses to get on my bike. This evening for a moment I'm going to an art opening, another excuse. Tomorrow yoga class, another. You see!

OK! I'm just looking through your letters—how I'd love to have my fortune told—although when we lived over the Gypsies on 14th St. I refused, because no one else but me was ever going to tell me about my life! What did yours reveal—you said it was "interesting."

I see that this is now going to be another sheet of paper all empty and needing to be filled, but I daren't even begin. Yesterday, m'dear, would have been my 30th wedding anniversary had I stayed married. I don't usually give in to wondering what that might have been like, because all I need do is look at marriages in general and see how women fare in them. So here's to divorce, if only poverty didn't come along with it.

Glad Rune is shaped up! Keep goin,' Mama!

5

Forbidden to learn Chinese
the women wrote in the language
of their islands
and so Japanese
became the currency of high aesthetics
for centuries
as did the female persona: the pine
the longing. This is the truth.

—*Kimiko Hahn*

Helene the scholar tried hard and long to provoke me to positions, sure in her belief that thinking critically would tamp down my ever surfacing literary jitters. After the first rejection of my memoir, I had begun to feel that maybe what I had to say was nothing people wanted to hear. "Back side are some quotes from V. Woolf's letters," she wrote, "I know you don't cotton to her, but I am really a fan."

"Style is a very simple matter: it is all rhythm. Once you get that, you can't use the wrong words."

". . . reading Katherine Mansfield's letters and feel desolated by them. What a waste!—and how wretched it is—her poverty, her illness—I didn't realize how gifted she was either. And now never to . . ."

"I think I distinguish 'vapid' from 'insipid' only by my ear. 'Vapid' sounds to me heavy, vacant, blank; 'insipid' trivial, frivolous, chattering . . . A vapid man would be silent; an insipid man would dribble along . . .

I suppose the dictionaries might explain. But one writes, I suppose, by ear, not dictionary."[1]

But I no more listened to her than she listened to me, because, as usual, I was headlong into the future:

---

1. To Vita Sackville-West; Lady Ottoline Morrell; Saxon Sydney-Turner.

Hullo dear Helene,

Thanks so much for those quotes — I don't really hate Virginia, it's just that I've no patience with that privilege, no I'm intolerant of it, that's what, so it's my fault, and the quarrel I have with it simply useless — I can't force these people to rise from the dead and give up their body heat.

Kellie gave a lecture at the Metropolitan Museum this afternoon (see enclosed), and after I went up there I went over to an opening on Avenue B where Randy Weston played the piano for two solid hours without stopping and with the most amazing energy, a big man, who once was a lanky man, now in his 60s with a prestigious looking belly, oh!

More later. You're right to push me to letters instead of calling.

But I'd already fallen into the new, distracting next: Janine Pommy Vega had recruited me to take over her poetry workshop at Sing Sing prison, but almost as soon as I got there the money had run out. I knew how to ask for work, but not for money in order to work. A different dynamic, the begging distance between need and help. Nevertheless, after having been dragged behind the teacher's desk, I seemed to like the chair:

TUESDAY 7TH

Calling foundations to see if I can get some emergency $$ to keep this Sing Sing thing going. Made a few good connections, but not for money. I think I'm to visit the women's prison — a group there is looking to have a writing workshop and no one to teach it . . .

One of my students at Sing Sing is codefendant with a woman named Hettie Jones presently incarcerated at Bedford Hills.[2] Hmmn. She is tall, he says. Last night at Harlem School of the Arts I read all my poems about other Hetties — and Jimmy Baldwin's sister Gloria (who was there) said she once knew a Jewish woman named Beulah. How beautiful she is, Gloria I mean, and yet she looks just like Jimmy, whom everyone thought funny-looking!

Reading *A Sport of Nature* by Nadine Gordimer, which has some remarkable passages in and around political theorizing and in whose hero-

---

2. Bedford Hills Correctional Facility, New York State's maximum security prison for women, in Westchester County.

ine (Jewish, named "Hillela") there is—the first time for me—something of *myself.* A "sport of nature" a phrase meaning, roughly, a "mutation"—the name I gave myself in college.

And I was discovering—slowly—that to teach I would have to learn to practice that kind of critical thinking Helene had recommended: "I was just looking again at your letter and those quotes, I think I'll hang them up over my desk, thank you for sending *words*—you've always done that and I'm so grateful."

But I could be distracted for just so long. In that same letter I wrote, "Memoir editor has pushed up our meeting a week," and a few days later: "I'm considering this my last night of freedom."

Though there was, at least, some cosmic comic diversion: "By some weird small-worldishness, my editor is the ex-wife of the man who built my computer. Who, having transferred all my files from one computer language to another, is the only person besides his ex-wife and my agent to have read the book so far."

FRIDAY NIGHT 2/10

If you don't send letters when you write 'em they're yesterday's news! Had a wonderful editor dinner—everything FINE—"I *loved* this," wrote one of editor's young readers, "I think it's marvelous; I cried at the end." Another called it "quite wonderful." I am ecstatic—to please *young people*—who are so critical!

Scrawled at the end of this letter is a signature I could have written two decades later. I keep inspecting it. How could it not be contrived? But there it is. And why is this naive or crazy when clichés that involve body language are deeply rooted in the spoken word? They're active visualizations of human gesture, and I like to write them. So when I look at my name it's as if I'd been freed to show my hand.

· · · · ·

A book takes a year to produce, though, a long enough meanwhile for everything to go back to being everything:

Can you believe the house biz is again unsettled? That we are not out of the woods? That I am about to become irrational? Well, here is Simone, that most rational of women!

GLOUCESTER, 3/29/89

Simone arrived yesterday and I would have called but am in the nasty process of figuring out how much I've overspent my phone allotment thanks to the answering machine I've not started paying for yet. My 92-year-old aunt keeps thinking some stranger is answering my phone, no matter how many times I've explained. So when I get to the phone & hear her hang up I have to call back.

After her brother Jack died at the end of 1988, Helene had been diagnosed with "something rheumatic" (all I ever knew); it was as if her body itself were grieving.

NEW YORK, APRIL 16, 1989

Hi Dearie,

Since I never thought of you as fragile it's hard for me to imagine you skinny, but of course I worry allatime about your getting better and fatter. Rice and beans is it for rounding one out. Cornbread and greens made with a pork knuckle or a smoked turkey wing. Spareribs! You need to come to Harlem and eat some greasy fried chicken!

Now that the weather is better the booksellers are out on the streets. I found an African novelist who also makes movies, Sembene Ousmane — a terrific novel called *Xala*. And some stories by Meridel LeSueur that I'd never read — have you read her? Impassioned recorder of women's lives in the worst of the Depression. Poetic style, like Tillie Olsen.

O, I have forgotten to report the March! [on Washington for Abortion Rights]![3]

Too terrific! A traffic jam on the way home — it took 3 hours to get

3. In order to preserve the 1973 Supreme Court decision in *Roe v. Wade*, then under threat by a Pennsylvania law that would have required a waiting period as well as spousal notification. At that point estimated to be the largest gathering ever to march on Washington.

from D.C. to Delaware, usually about 40 minutes I think! I was so excited—600,000 people, twice that which most of the media reported. Next day I'm telling Lisa all about it—"Mormons for choice—can you beat that? And nuns! And people from Alaska, men and women. Two Southern belles in straw boaters wrapped with chiffon ribbons, and long flowing skirts, gaily flinging their banner—Tennessee for Choice! The Grey Panthers! the Gay and Lesbian Coalition!"—and Lisa says, "Write the *story*, Mom!" And I say, "But Lisa, I've already written one story about abortion," and she comes back, "But Mom, write *another!*" Oh, Helene, you would have so enjoyed the sight of all those thousands of women. Old Ladies in wheelchairs, mother-daughter banners. So well organized and fucking pleasant, all those faces. Well-dressed but casual Republicans from New Hampshire for Choice! All the colleges. People from Missouri, Texas, Wisconsin. We stood on the sidelines, the five of us from our yoga class, cheering. Two women I knew marched past me! We yelled and embraced and I saw that happening everywhere as people who hadn't arranged to meet each other did. I kept yelling when people from far away came past, it seemed fitting to congratulate them, and their faces just split, grinning! Then over the loudspeaker we heard "X, please meet Y at the PortoSans, you have her *plane ticket!*" And the crowning jewel in the day was the fact that not once, not even once, did any of the PortoSans I visited lack toilet paper.

We'd parked the car in the suburbs and then taken the Metro into the city, so it was pleasant on the way out to ride that incredibly smooth, new, unmarked train and watch the Washington Monument recede, and the capitol, looking like my geography book of 45 years ago. Left at 8am, didn't get home until 2am, but the next day I was *wired*.

When there were months between letters I knew Helene was working, and that whenever she did write it'd be something I'd want to read:

GLOUCESTER, 2ND MAY, I DON'T BELIEVE IT.
Trying to get work done on that rune series that I wish I'd never proposed & got the $ for because my head's just not there anymore. That long ellipsis—6 whole months—I'm trying to pull the pieces together so they'll hang as a unit like I proposed and it's all sham . . . They're not a unit at all,

and certainly not what I had in mind some 10 years ago when I started setting glass and metal aside for the runes I wanted to do. SHIT!

Took the *Vogue* someone left in Senior Home Care's "lounge" and brought it back to desk to look at because I hadn't done that for years — & got totally pissed off that all that exists, as I knew I would.

And then of course one starts reading various articles — like *what* was the full p. pic of orange with peelings gracefully falling off in flower-like arrangements/patterns — "thanks to a new process, soon to be commercially available, citrus peels literally fall away from fruit, giving new meaning to fast foods."

One should look at such mags once in a while to get these small details, I suppose, while the world turns & burns w/our advanced technology. It's true comedy I guess because it's so heartbreaking. Like Chaplin makes me so sad I can't really laugh at his antics tho I admire his grace.

From an artist statement in a brochure titled *Driftglass Mosaics: Helene Dorn*:

Rembrandt and the Seattle Public Library taught me to draw; I studied there with Andre Martin in his studio. I got my first real sense of paint from Phoebe Stiles who gave me her box of oils, and some very meaningful night classes at the University of Michigan with a painter whose name I've unfortunately lost. But I do remember Cezanne, whose watercolors I kept going back to. I have Giotto and Redon on my walls, William Blake in my heart.

· · · · ·

If the word for Helene is "stride," mine, I suppose, would be "drive." But you can lean on an image just so hard; as much as the open road, or the taking of the wheel, maybe like any small woman I just wanted a mount. After my last car died, Lisa said, "Oh, you've lost your pet." So I guess the car is the horse I rode in on.

And, in 1989, given the quality of my just-acquired five-year-old Honda — the newest car I'd ever owned — Helene and I decided to go on vacation. We hadn't spent more than a weekend together since 1964, when she and Ed had come to New York with Charles and Betty Olson, and all of them had stayed with us on Cooper Square. But this time just we two would head north to Canada and west to visit Marie on Michigan's Upper Peninsula.

Looks ok for time off 7/31 to 8/11. Postcard from Marie that time ok. Talking to Paul about it last night I got so excited—

Sitting here nervously awaiting the photographer who's to take my book picture and is so far only ½ hr late. Spike's movie [*Do the Right Thing*] causing mucho controversy causing me to get mad at Stanley Crouch article and write a letter to *Voice* which they'll publish. But so happy and excited about making this trip with you!

I can see us driving west into the sunset. Yippee!

Happy B'Day Miz Jones! We'll have a leisurely lunch by the water to celebrate—Almost, now, only a week away, whee! Have a royal day (that should have been regal). Here's xerox of map Marie sent—just to get you gleeful . . . stick it in the AAA info.

I'll call before you come—oh! How much, Mizz Speed Limit Jones, do you figure this vacation is going to cost? I've no way to figure it, even basically . . . Not to worry yr. head abt. it now, but before I call next week, you'll have some sense of it I can figure, & I can go to the bank, etc. with a little reality in my head?

We spent a night at Joyce's house in Vermont, and got to Montreal the next day starving and flummoxed but not at all dismayed by our bad French. We traveled well together; every photo shows us grinning. I'd never seen Lake Michigan, which was all the ocean I needed at the moment. That I couldn't see the other side was a perfect metaphor. Somewhere I wrote, though I can't find it: "This book will change your life. Don't expect this book to change your life."

・・・・・

Dear Helene! Dear dear Helene!

Ooof! It's been a weird slide back to normal, whatever that is, since I feel changed just by the rest—

I miss you! I miss being on vacation! I want to lie around and read books and take pictures. Oh—the *pictures!* There's a whole tale—lost for a week in someone else's package or at some other store. Oh no, says I, my first vacation in so many years and you're going to lose my *pictures!* They had me half convinced that none had come out, then of course I began to worry that the battery was somehow involved—*my fault you dig*—and then they magically appeared—

Today, ad agency 8 hours, first time since I've been back.

Ten pm now and I'm reading *Interview With the Vampire* by Anne Rice, a terrific book (mostly).

There are people lying all over the streets, sleeping during the day on the sidewalk with handkerchief over face, walking shoeless, shuffling in blankets.

I have a story about going to be fingerprinted at Bedford Hills[4] on Monday past. The curler story—

SUNDAY EVE, 8/27—WHERE DID THE TIME GO?????

Your letter arrived yesterday. I'm greatly relieved you didn't get fired but this is too fucking threatening, to come up for review every year, what a toll that takes, and it's so stupid and evil, since there will be more and more "aged" and therefore necessarily more senior home care. It's just like the people lying all over the street here.

Curler story: down to some basement where I was to be photo'd and printed, I'm waiting, 9am, in a group of about 5, 7 people, guards obviously just come to work, inmates. Floor had just been mopped, the whole place smelling strongly of disinfectant. People relaxed, they say "wait here a minute" and seat me at a desk, and there in front of me, just casually on the desk, is a "sculpture"—four hair rollers, pink and black, fitted together, obviously by someone who'd just taken them out of her hair and

---

4. I had learned to beg and had gotten some money to teach there.

was playing. It was so much a clue to the character of the place—I guess I'll have other stories before long!

Speaking of sculpture—I did fix Rumpelstiltskin [birthday glass Helene had made for me], but will wait to rehang it until the poor old broken windows are sealed for the winter—which it looks like I'm going to have to do again since there is no word on our getting new windows because of new refusal from Loft Board.

Enclosed copy of the catalog page with its sensational approach, god-helpme, and the picture that is, as it turns out, not going to be the cover, or the whole cover anyway, though what the cover is going to be is a mystery still. The young man in the copy shop asked, "Are you, etc." when he brought my copies, and when I said yes, he asked if he might make one for himself. "That's funny," he said. "Gerard Malanga[5] always comes in here too!"

GLOUCESTER, 9/21/89

Hullo—this in haste to catch p.o. before closing. Big fat mix-up in reprints so the nicer photos will come later. But these will bring back that wonderful sunset light—and the soup!! which recipe I of course failed to get from you before you left.

Have started getting back to work for real—I owe you volumes, one day I *will* get to the typewriter—

NEW YORK, OCT. 6, 1989

Hi Helene,

Thanks for all those pictures—and the funny cartoons they were wrapped in! How beautiful Marie is. I just looked at us all again and could almost taste that soup . . . Will send recipe later. In five minutes I have to ride uptown to bring back my proofs and make big decision on which picture to use for publicity. Urggh . . . Okay. I'm off on my chariot; it's a beautiful fall day.

---

5. Poet, filmmaker, major influence on Andy Warhol, cofounder of *Interview* magazine.

Photos okay. While I was there editor told me there had been good news, something businesswise, regarding the big wholesaler—or something— in any case there are people "out there" who are excited.

The windows were finally done last week, the mess incredible. I cleaned for 3 days. Mortar dust of centuries (truly). Anyway the windows are wonderful, and baby they are double-hung (like a good man).

New landlord took me out for drinks and confessed he'd been offered 5½ million bucks for his 3 buildings and had refused, but hinted that soon the offer would be one he might not want to refuse. We are still waiting for the one fucking piece of paper that will legalize us, and though the lawyer says we are legal w/o it I don't believe him. I am wearying of the fight even though I realize I might as well not weary since it may never be over.

My sweet grass hangs on the light cord in this room and every once in a while, as right now, I get a whiff of it. Especially on humid days, and then I put the end of it up my generous nostrils and remember Marie's place, and that road . . .

Just had dinner with A. B. Spellman! We walked all over the Lower East Side to Ave C places he used to live, looked at where gentrification hasn't hit—yet—

It's one week since I began this and I have been to school[6] and jail[7] again (have worked 6 weeks now got exactly $200 so far) . . .

Forgot to tell you that there's been a portable generator going 24 hrs a day right in the middle of Cooper Square where the acoustics are best. Necessary repair—the night watchman told me it was the dread asbestos that has been exploding into NYC streets, old steam pipes bursting—lots of noise but better than having white lung. Amazing to see an entire 15 story apartment building wrapped in plastic like a giant Christo while it is cleaned of fibers . . . Here I see backhoes and derricks in a walled encampment painted white with red stripes. They drill at odd hours (I hear one right now, 11:06pm). The generator powers a flashing arrow to detour

---

6. SUNY Purchase, where I'd been invited to teach a second year.
7. Bedford Hills is a half-hour drive from Purchase, so I taught both classes on the same day.

traffic, like the kind you see on a highway. And I'm up here deluding my-self about where I am. A.B. says you don't have to live in NY and of course you've said that all along, but I'm *from* NY and that's different. Besides, it still interests me . . .

"I never thought I'd want to be alone," wrote one woman at the prison this week, and went on to describe her feelings about being alone, and the process of self-discovery: "I'm here / just me / Mona . . ." She *sang* it too!

Driving up to school on Weds., such a beautiful fall day, mucho sun-shine on the highway, the little car purring along, I was seized by desire to *just keep driving*—I'd have stopped to pick you up!

Full moon Saturday night, am writing a moon poem which doesn't seem to end right . . .

FRIDAY 10:30PM

New landlord said they would put in front windows and fix the doorknob that comes off in your hand some mornings.

Well here we are at Cooper Square. I listened to Joe Termini, one of the two former owners of the Five Spot, on the radio the other evening—and was relieved to get all my facts corroborated . . . "In one direction Cooper Union," he said, explaining, "and in the other—the Bowery!" As if those distinctions could carry much weight in Milwaukee! I hope it'll make him happy to get a copy of my book in which I've told how he treated me to a brandy one day when I was cold. I didn't even know he was still alive, so that's a pleasure.

I am also pleased to report that because I couldn't work I of course found myself in the Salavation [*sic*] Army . . . At the prison the above mentioned young woman asked me if my new shoes were Joan and David's, which are very expensive, and so I raised my feet to show the $8 written in magic marker on the arch where it'll never be worn off, and the women all laughed and laughed. This week I read them some Meridel LeSueur, from *Harvest* . . .

· · · · ·

A couple of weeks after I finally managed to mail this long letter, an article about the artist Martin Puryear appeared in the *New York Times*. "Why Martin Puryear?" it began, and continued: "What is it about his work that made the distinguished group of museum curators and directors on the Federal Advisory Committee for International Exhibitions select him to represent the United States [at the São Paulo Biennale]? Why did he win the grand prize . . . as the best artist in this exhibition? Why is he the first black American artist to be singled out for international attention?"

I'm telling this story because I was only one of the three of us who made herself up on this corner. The article goes on for two pages full of detail and art history, with a couple of large photographs. Nowhere, however, does the name of the curator, Kellie Jones, appear, though this was all her doing.

· · · · ·

GLOUCESTER, 10/30/89

Have just come from about six hours trying to finish off very large mask I started so long ago and now realize is a self-portrait. In the process of supporting it I had to change all kinds of lines and I've been working on it for weeks—the process so slow, I have to wait for one piece to dry before I can add another, & it's piece by piece w/out being able to see the whole.

The tedium in this process is understandable, but she'd chosen it. Why? Chan once said she wished Helene could have gone to art school. Fred says she never got the matrix right. Sometimes I wish she'd taken up the pen. But she did what she did, and while waiting for things to dry, she was my valued librarian:

[POSTCARD]

NEW YORK, 12/7/89

Hi Kid—Thank you—I'm so grateful—for those articles you sent— I've promised to read to my students. Today I agreed to a redesign of book jacket—everything last minute. Ted Wilentz called to tell me of great Kirkus review—that sells books, I'm told. Ted's wife grew up in Laurelton,[8] so did my new editor's mother. Life keeps turning circles . . .

No time for letters for a while—I've just taken a BIG copyedit job (*Samurai Widow*, memoir by Judy Belushi, John's widow), worth money I couldn't refuse. The HEAT bill will be enormous with this weather.

---

8. The neighborhood at the outer limit of the borough of Queens, where I lived from age seven to seventeen.

... Yr schedule makes me dizzy. Your book will not only sell, it is going to be a Best Seller and you are going to make enough money to do what you want to do. Only put all that in the present tense & repeat it over & over! I'm being trained, sporadically, in the power, by Jeri Kelsey, who has moved in downstairs—it really does seem to be working for her, but my thoughts are always so scattered ...

I'm listening to Coltrane, the studio door shut to keep in the heat. Got Leslie Marmon Silko from library. She's wonderful. I'm totally illiterate in Native American women writers. There's so much to *learn*.

Hope you are OK & that you all had fun over holidays. Send my best to Jeri—glad that's working out, nice to have a friend close by.

OK! Happy 1990—jeez, I still can barely say it, much less *write* it!

Hello my dear ...

Your funny birthday card arrived on the 19th—and thank you! It was so wonderful to laugh! Fred took me to Rhumbline and we got totally sloshed, as he'd put it, so it didn't matter that the food wasn't that good ... some incredible coffee drink to end it all. How many brandies I don't know, whipped cream piled on the top—

Marie turned 70 on the 24th. I sent her seven roses and she was so gassed (that outdated term keeps coming into my vocabulary). She said "you idiot," when I called ... what joy to do something special with money you don't really have for someone you love ... She was feeling kind of depressed, "I feel like I've made this long climb and now I've hit a plateau"—but she did *eight* of those wonderful "rising to the sun" or whatever, I can't remember the yoga name for what she did at your house first out of bed,[9] and said to Harold, "Not bad for a 70 year old"!

---

9. When their brother Jack died, Helene and Marie came to New York and stayed with me while they attended to his affairs. For them this made a hard time easier, and for me was a chance to get to know Marie, who had sent me an article from her local paper about Kellie's appointment to curate the São Paulo Biennale. "It'll probably gas you," Marie wrote, "that such news has made the *Kalamazoo Gazette*!!"

I am trying to write this in a hurry, which I never can do . . . want to send on this quote from Louisa May Alcott's journal, December, 1856:

"December—Busy with Christmas and New Year's Tales. Heard a good lecture by E. P. Whipple on "Courage." Thought I needed it, being rather tired of living like a spider—spinning my brains out for money."

My phone is out of order and so am I. I've been workinking—that is such a beautiful typo I have to leave it, regardless of the "th" left out between the k and the i—it's very much what I spend a lot of my time doing, though I do have one new thing in the process of finishing. . . .

· · · · ·

My memoir was for the most part praised for its measured tone, its value as a social document. (A little meanness was added to the mix to keep me on my toes.) Helene sent the *Gloucester Daily Times* review, with the advice that "15 min. [of fame] grows like a pebble thrown into the water makes all those wonderful waves go out & out." She also taped my radio interviews:

[POSTCARD]

NEW YORK, 4/2/90

. . . the tape arrived—THANKS—I listened once and felt OK, that I had indeed done all right, but think I should *study* it to avoid making similar mistakes—learn to sidestep the shit and try to focus on the writing . . . Slowly returning phone calls & letters. I think all this is like hanging a show except it won't stay still—but then neither does art hah hah—

Some of the young people brought me red tulips and pink roses to the Fri. reading!

NEW YORK, 4/10/90

Hullo!

Full moon has me going—blank mind!

How are you?

They're going to send me to San Francisco! June 21, or thereabouts. I haven't been to S.F. since 1968.

Sarah Vaughn has died. . . . She is singing, right now, "Thanks for the Memories." Oh, Oh!

I guess my biggest problem has always been being smart enough to know I wasn't good enough. Enough for what you may well ask—probably to suit my taste in writing. So anyway, now that has changed, now I am good enough, now the point is to get my point across, necessitating a *point* . . .

On Weds., at the prison, we began the long, argumentative process of editing what will become the book called *More In Than Out*. This is to be printed there (they have a print shop, do jobs for the state). Book paid for with donations from rich Westchester County people who do charitable stuff . . . I will put two of my poems in, which will give truth to the "out" part of the title.

So this is the up-to-date *moi*. On the edge between feeling so great from all the compliments and feeling strange because not intently involved in a new project. But how can I complain? Nice letter from Ron Loewinsohn, said there was a review in *SF Chronicle*. Today I got, from Don Sunseri, Elizabeth Murray's ex-husband, a copy of the big *Voice* ad with different color shiny stars pasted all over it, and under my current pic the words "Hubba hubba"!

Please let me know how your show is up, is getting up, got up, etc. And whether they have okayed your new hearing aid, and when you start to pay your new rent, that godsend. Please tell Fred that his picture on my wall was noticed and he has been pronounced "Fine."

Stay tuned, I feel like a one-woman soap! Big hugs and kisses to you.

Had the nicest letter from Henry Louis "Skip" Gates. I sent him my book after he appeared on cover of *NY Times* magazine and big pic of his interracial family inside. He was Lisa's teacher at Yale and I met him and his wife at her graduation. What I remember (this 1983, I think) is a moment, even in that protected academic environment, in one of those oh-so-Yale-rooms, when I sensed that they were again having to insist on their relationship, publicly, I could feel it, feel that estranged-ness. They were young, to me, again in a hostile atmosphere. Boy oh boy. It's amazing how things like this get remembered. What is it? You just have to bear witness.

I am to meet a movie producer this weekend. My agent doesn't know anything about him, except that he loves my book. Well, he can buy me a

Fig 5.1 Hettie, 1989. Photo: Colleen McKay

drink. Perhaps he looks like Marlon Brando. M.B. looks better these days, as if he'd finally got through menopause.

You know why I love you Helene? Because nothing impresses you— I suddenly had a vision of you being unimpressed by the sight of Marlon Brando! Though I do know you liked the sight of that young man with the earring who came to inspect your house. You said, on the phone—*you* (meaning me) would have taken him to bed! But maybe *you* should have! Remember that movie *Harold and Maude* with Ruth Gordon?

SAT. 5TH

Yesterday, trying to clean the closet, I knelt with vac in hand, and a large piece of the remaining linoleum came up, revealing a floorful of news-papers—the *New York Post*, the *Journal and American* (as it was called) and the *Daily News*—all from 1937. Fascinating reading! The fashion figure of the time was a pencil-thin body with square shoulders, and abso-lutely no hint, none by golly, of pelvis or belly or ass or hip.

Just finished *Beloved*, a hard book to get through but the language was fine in places. Now I'm reading both Chester Himes' *If He Hollers Let Him Go* and *Eva Luna* by Isabel Allende.

Voice still hasn't reviewed my book but Nat Hentoff hinted that they would next month, so I'm waiting. I feel too spring-fevery to care. [They never did review it.]

GLOUCESTER, 6/17/90 5PM

Found your message when I got back from wandering on Pavilion—It was wondrous—fog not yet lifted beyond the breakwater around Stage Fort Park, all the weekend sailboats Seurat-esque in the mist . . . Crazy, wonderful ocean coast weather.

Gathered a bunch of glass & stayed a lot longer than I'd intended. Did some work on requiem mask I've somehow got to do tho at this point it seems a disaster & I wonder why I continue—all this shit I have to get out of my heart/soul I guess. Quit when I realized I couldn't see what I was doing. No more masks unless I can discover some transparent ma-terial to support the convex background necessary to make the head hang plumb—it's a bitch, H. Jones.

So now I'm sitting in the sun on my little porch having a beer and sev-eral cigarettes, my 49 cent bright red sun hat on my head, Squirrel at my feet, surrounded by pansies & basil & all my house plants. The wind in the trees a truly lovely sound—like the ocean connecting w/the beach earlier—I would like a month of such days.

I've just come in from planting the ginger root that sprouted while sitting in wood bowl on kitchen table. Louie Siminoff, crazy mathematician friend way back 10 thousand years ago in Pocatello, told me I could grow it in a long container—that it was a beautiful plant. But I'd never tried it. Back then, mama, we had to travel out of town to the Chinese settlement left over from the railroad days to purchase such things. And he *loved* food & cooking; and me—I loved him too, but not that way, & thinking of it just now I realize how I used his adoration—o aren't we all leeches at some point in our lives! His funny yellowed recipes fall out of my ancient cookbooks when I open them to check out something I've forgotten.

[POSTCARD]

SAN FRANCISCO SUN. 6/24/90

Hi Helene! I just bought this card on Telegraph Ave in Berkeley . . . Pretty pretty city . . . The irony is that the big interview this Sun. in the *Chronicle* went to Judy Belushi!

GLOUCESTER 6/27

Call from Marie—our beautiful little mother (97 on Aug 21st) has flu not expected to come out of it & I may be off to MN at any point. I'm all choked up because I want her to go for her sake but I don't want her to go for mine—

GLOUCESTER, AUGUST 13, 1990

and here I am sitting at my NEW desk! . . . IN MY BEDROOM-SITTING ROOM!!!!

Taking one brief moment just to feel it . . . It's a total mess at the moment, and has been due to being stoppt once again by my mother having no pulse—last week was a nightmare, she rallied again, I'm sitting here w/500$ in travelers checks, etc.

Today, having a very deep need to resolve SOMETHING, I threw caution to the winds and bought my beautiful white melamine desk which isn't a desk, it's a typing return, or some such thing . . . on casters, so I can move it around easily . . .

I still can't believe it's actually IN here! When young man who delivers asked where I lived, I plaintively sd. 90 Middle, how soon can I have it? And he sd. the white house on the corner? I sd. yes, and he sd. I'll carry it back with you, how's that for service. I sputtered, can you really do that?? And he did, on his shoulder, across Pleasant St. & down Middle & up my front stairs, and into the studio. And when I told him he could just leave it there, I could get it where I wanted it, he sd. are you sure & I sd. yes. We must have looked so funny coming down the street.

So there's my story for today, mama, what's yours? Now that I have such sweet space, mebbe I really will start writing letters again. I really love this room, & in the winter I can close it off, be not so expensively warm in my little cozy nest. Thanks to Gov. Dukakis, Jack, and the Mass. Housing Assistance. AMEN.

NEW YORK, 9/10/90

Helene!

Hello from *my* new desk!

I'd already written that once, then something was wrong, and in leaning over to reposition the monitor I pressed a wrong button and whoosh! it was all gone and I had to turn off the machine to lose

9/13

And now, obviously, I've lost 3 whole days! So, again, I'm at my very new desk, this again the first writing I'm doing from it. For so many reasons . . .

First, how are you? [Helene's mother had died.] I know, so strange to have made all those old connections, and under duress, and then to be thinking about it, the place, the life, David's sister, etc. and all that water under all those bridges . . . whew, I still sometimes think about my mother's funeral, my Aunt Fannie's . . . But I hope you're stumbling back to "realtime" whatever that may be, people are beginning to use that word in their writing, it jars me the way "vibrations" used to.

Still have a few more boxes and miscellaneous shit to go through in this great study rearrangement, but the situation improves daily and I am *so happy* with my gorgeous new desk, etc. and it's all so comfortable and sane. I could almost feel professional.

The situation with people sleeping in the streets is unbearable. Every day there is some worse degradation to see. People sleeping in broad daylight in all kinds of attitudes of complete exhaustion. This morning there was an absolutely filthy person, such a young man I thought it was a woman, writhing on the sidewalk. A cop was saying "Are you sure?" as the guy managed to stagger a few steps and lean against a parking meter. A woman beside me said, "Are we living in a Third World country or what?" (as she hailed a cab)—Forgot to tell you I finally heard from Rena,[10] who had just read the book and said she'd gotten "hungry" to talk to me. Said she finally was enjoying the great pleasure of being alone and not taking care of a man. Can you imagine, all these years doing that.

• • • • •

[POSTCARD]

GLOUCESTER, 9/21/90

Tomorrow rent D-Day. I spent yesterday going over all the figures again. Woke up this a.m., sensibly quiet in heart—somebody must have talked to me while I slept. *Why* get so traumatized over something over which one has no control! It either happens or it doesn't. Yeah, Mama, where is bohemia now?

Though she still had what bohemia had long ago held out:

Measured the case at library & did some more finishing work—have a week to get it all together. It's a very small space, but it's been so long since I've shown anything I'd like it to be right. Do-it-yourself bit, like your book party.[11]

---

10. Rena Oppenheimer Rosequist, big sister of my youth, first wife of Joel Oppenheimer. Owner of the Mission Gallery in Taos, former chair, New Mexico Arts Commission.

11. To celebrate the publication of my memoir, Helene, Marie, and Marie's husband Harold Bahlke had come to New York to help out at the party held at the Hatch-Billops Collection.

Squirrel asleep on the chair by fridge — & I want to haul out my crayons he is so beautiful! Maybe one day I will — what *is* this desire to record — but that's letter talk. Time to put dinner leftovers away & get some sleep; tomorrow, no matter the outcome, will be a relief just to *know*.

Helene — Hello!

Migod, I feel as if I haven't spoken to you in about twenty years . . .

Nothing new except *The New York Times* has included me among the 200 best books of 1990, a certain honor I guess, out of all that were published, and I have begun a new story, which so far is kind of strange and not formed, and I have taken on an enormous copyedit job, a novel about werewolves. I read it once last week, feeling disgusted and quarrelsome all the while because it's stupid and amoral as well as badly written.

How was Thanksgiving? We ate mucho. Some people stayed until 1:30 in the a.m. Sooner than anyone wants, it will be Christmas, and New Year's. The English publisher who is not going to publish my book has sent the remaining $ to honor the contract. I am thinking of not doing any other kind of work except my writing for a certain amount of time over the winter, like maybe 2 months, just to see if I can. I should really go to a writer's colony. This man I know says I am a depot, as in train station. These winter nights I think it's midnight at 8pm. I've been invited to read in Buffalo in March, and in Franconia, NH in July — remember driving through Franconia Notch?? Please tell everyone nice in Gloucester that I love them. Mostly I love you for putting up with this *mishegas!* And I hope you are well and working!

• • • • •

HELENE DORN

RUNES, 1988–1990

ONE FOR LINDA

TWO FOR JOE

THE FOUR DIRECTIONS, THANK YOU BUD CASTLE

ONCE UPON A TIME

ISS

From an artist statement with this show:

I don't start with a shape I want to explore or a message or an emotion I want to express, but certain pieces of my found media that say things to me, provoke images. I love lines, shapes, space, color, light, textures—and I must work with them, not talk about them.

This work was made possible in part by the support of the Massachusetts Arts Lottery, as administered by the Gloucester Arts and Humanities Council. And I thank them.

6

Someone has been painting
NOTHING IS IMPOSSIBLE
across the backs of bus benches . . .

Did some miracle startle
the painter into action
or is she waiting and hoping?

Daily the long wind brushes YES
through the trees.
                    —*Naomi Shihab Nye*

Hullo Helene, it's . . .
    Monday
    A gloomy day and I woke up with a sore throat—kissed too many people yesterday. But how to stop?
    Debating whether to teach at New School. "A good credential," says Joyce. I almost feel that I do not need any further "credentials"—to whom must I prove myself? Aaarrrgh!
    It was so good to talk with you though you did sound a bit stuffed in the nose.

Love and kizzes!*

*That biographer of S. Plath took exception to the fact that she signed her letters with xxxs and oooos—like a *child* is what he thought, and this was evidence of her disturbed mind.

• • • • •

Hullo — Wondering if you're still there. I'm still here, but vaguely . . . Have lost track of time — I got totally stopped by that war.[1] Did a small mask while listening to pub radio "news," so aware of what's not being said about what's going on in those other places. Bought new sound system w/ tax refund & therefore rearranging studio shelving. All of which is mind boggling on top of other things. All of which is just to say I'm freaked, how are you?

I was getting the hang of the proper response. At readings from my memoir, I'd had to confront, again and again, the fact that I'd opened my life deliberately and here was the consequence. But everyone has a limit, and after a while I felt compelled to do away with having been "Nellie'd." Unpublished until many years later, I sent the following to Helene in the spring of '91 when it was finished:

A NEBULA OF NOTEWORTHY NELLIES

for the Nellie in a recent literary work

for strength I give you
     Nellie Taylor Ross, the first woman
     governor. Elected by Wyoming, 1925

and for inspiration
     Nellie Monk, wife to Thelonious

and though I've read of nervous Nellies
     and fussy Nellies

Nellie, f.y.i., is a form of Helen, that beauty
     who caused such havoc

and sometimes Helen is confused with *heleane*
     a word describing a planetary aura

---

1. The "first Gulf War," a UN-authorized conflict, August 1990–February 1991, when Iraq invaded and annexed Kuwait.

named by sailors for their patron saint:
St. Elmo's fire

and when two electrical conductors meet
the air is ionized, changed
in a coronary discharge
called St. Elmo's fire

So burn on burn on burn on Nellie

GLOUCESTER, 4/2/91

Hello m'dear—this is just quick to thank you for pome—I laughed &
cheered & it set me up out of a doldrums I'd been in—bless you! Made
copy to send to Marie which figured wld be ok w/you—I know she'd
really dig it too.

Nice letter from Bob (Creeley), & copy of his palm-sized autobiography—caught me up on family—a surprise & very nice thing to find in the
mail. He spoke of your reading as "very moving."

Forgot to tell you on phone—Birch's Drug Store on Main St. is now a
Salvation Army Store—bad news, just around the corner & I can't resist,
spent 2 hrs today, I'm sure, going through the books . . .

In response to the war and a subsequent spurt in oil prices, social services
saw a definite trickle-down effect, though not in the usual sense. In this letter
Helene also reported that at Senior Home Care "we've all had to take a week
w/out pay." And then a few days later:

4/5

70 degrees out there!

In haste, weirdly frantic day at SHC & I'm going to post this & walk
around for a bit to loosen up my nerves. Am told Mercury is retrograde
again, which causes much disruption, for instance: since I started this the
sun has completely clouded over & it damn well just might rain. Like they
say 'bout N.E. weather—if you don't like it, wait a minute. . . .

Hello Helene!

It's midday and one of those weird times when I can't bring myself to open up the *big new* copyedit job because I glanced at it yesterday—it's the FBI files on Malcolm, intact repros of the originals (with blacked-out passages). I just finished another book, all last week and weekend, it'll add up to a month's rent & gas, I am back to living like that, chalking up a month here or there, and not quite making it each month, frugal, frugal, parsimony (like those words on the wall in the Bible)!

Today is prison day. They have held up (literally) the book of my students' work and are giving me a vast runaround while I keep calling (long distance) and requesting, etc. First a proposal ltr to the Deputy Supt (as instructed by the Supervisor of Volunteer Services) who after 3 days of unreturned calls finally told me I had to write a formal proposal to the Superintendent, this is weeks now, and I can't get the final set of proofs from the printer there (even though he has my $300) because he runs scared too. Everyone is scared of this meager book of poems, it's so preposterous, so—eeek, stress!

A gray day, perfect for bed, nothing else, not that I've ever. Have been snatching moments to read, late at night (after a day of reading, not too good) Lee Smith's *Fair and Tender Ladies* which is marvelous.

THURS.

A wicked ride back from the prison on the curvy, foggy, puddle-filled highway last night. The water reflecting *in color* the green highway signs and their white lettering.

Kellie was here overnight . . . so cute! She came in this afternoon with lilacs, trying to cheer me up I guess, I'm just complaining all over the place.

But I haven't asked about you, or not enough, feel so focused on myself, yuck, this only happens when something's out of sync. I think maybe spring? April is the . . . memory and desire—but not that, in particular, it's the fucking frustration, and the economy, and the ecology—oh, that bird-watching piece you sent! And here we have displaced and murdered so many people since the beginning of this 1991, where will it all end? My landlord again mentioned selling this house . . . though I was ready to paint the walls have given up the idea—I think of all that painting you did. . . .

Please keep your spirits up about the job thing, or at least don't succumb to panic, although of course I'd never blame you if you did. Some fucking place this country is . . . Remember how we used to say it would have to get worse before it got better? Well, we had the right idea.

Anyway, "as long as you have your health."

[POSTCARD: LIBERTY, POLYCHROMED WOOD,

BOSTON, MASSACHUSETTS, CA. 1868]

NEW YORK, JUNE 1991

Another H. Dorn lookalike! One of your foremoms surely passed by— or maybe even through the hands of—the sculptor Henry Leach! Hope you're doing okay, now, a century-plus later. Just found out they ok'd prison book, but I have to charge *sales tax*—

· · · · ·

I'd been coaxing Helene to buy a word processor, because I knew she'd like all the design aspects. Eventually she got a computer, but it was this first machine that began to make our correspondence, as she suggested then, even more of a conversation.

GLOUCESTER, JULY 13, 1991

I DONE oyes O YES!!!! I done it. And now I got to get used to the keyboard which I'm not sure is as well-planned as it might be, but it was on sale and once I get used to it mebbe I will get to my resume, etc.

Have to watch the time, I really don't believe I've been playing with this machine for 4 hours! Lib. about to close, must return overdue books, will put this on disk, yeah, & return soon . . . I'll really miss the Borzoi *Turgenev* . . . I devoured all 801 pages while coming off cigarettes. Started on him directly on top of rereading Jane Bowles . . . don't ask how that happened, but as usually happens, my instinct was right, it was a perfect juxtaposition. OK, to the library not the lighthouse, hi Virginia!

LATER

Other news: SHC is moving on Sept. 1 to the Blackburn Industrial Park (horrid) to occupy floor above our Adult Day Health Center. Necessitated by budget cuts. Was freaked but didn't have a chance to query about lay-offs . . . Anyway it will be a bus trip and of course an hour and a half out of my day as well . . . a real drag, will have to be on Main St. by 8:15 a.m.

P.S. It's of course now Sunday and I think it was midnight when I fell drunkenly into bed having printed out I don't know how many of these testing margin changes . . . finally stoppt around 10:30, made a sandwich and watched the latter part of Bette Davis & George Brent taking care of Henry Fonda, was it? By the time I switched on the set he had cholera and they just showed him as lump on bed. . . .

NEW YORK, FRI. 7/19/91

Hi! Thanks for b'day call! This is not a little answer to your long computer letter—ain't it *fun*? Will call this week if I can't find time to write—finished painting hall floor last night, wrong color brown I think, but maybe it'll grow on me, and I'm not into 2nd coats. Could I visit you after all my gigs? Weekend of Aug. 10–11?

Summer visits were our spring tonic. We hadn't planned for the release that August of *Thelma and Louise*, but drove happily to a mall to see it. "Thelma? Louise?" she teased. "Your choice!"

GLOUCESTER, 8/24/91

Hullo . . . Just quickly to thank you for parcel waiting for me when I came home from work yesterday . . .

AUGUST 26, SAME YEAR

The phone rang & I never got back to this because then I was hungry. Had partially defrosted two turkey thighs and decided, having drunk 2 beers, that this was the ideal time to test recipe I'd clipped from *Globe* because I love garlic & it sounded v. good, and I've always regretted that I didn't get my lovely friend in Sitges to tell me more exactly how she made that Catalon stew for her husband. It was so wonderful to see: big ol-time soup bowl filled with a many-vegetabled beef (I suppose) stew, directly in the center of which sat one totally intact bulb of garlic! "Ah, Helena, it's easy!" Victoria was her name. Something about dipping the bulb in boiling water to make the skins easy to pull off the cloves . . . I watched him devour the whole thing, pulling cloves off one by one. Well, anyway I decided to make Paula Peck's Chicken and Garlic Stew. I actually stood at the stove and peeled about 25 cloves! Salivating all the while.

Heavy pot, olive oil, layer of garlic cloves, parsley, celery leaves, tarragon, pepper, allspice, cinnamon, dry white wine, chicken. 2nd layer of garlic, etc. Cover, bake 375 for abt. 1¼ hrs. Paula P's recipe was for a lot more chicken, layers & people, and of course I added some things, like mushrooms that needed using up; I figured I was making 2, if not 3, meals.

It was so tasty, I ate it *all*, Hettie Jones. Woke up yesterday a.m. wondering what on airth I'd done to myself!

Walked the length of the boulevard twice . . . Saw this wonderfully handsome gray-haired woman, walking with three others, holding one edge of her wide brimmed straw sun hat against the wind . . . and she smiled at me in a way that was a recognition, and in my heart of hearts a blessing. Happened one other time, in NYC . . . Park Ave., I'm sure I've told you, freaked & walking against cold, nasty wind, having checked out tourist bureaus, where to go, what to do[2] — and there, coming in the opposite direction was this woman whose eyes met mine and her smile was an embrace. She was so full of joy, all these sour people around her, the boy walking next to her glowering at me. And the hostility of those men on either side of them . . . Such a wide sidewalk Park Ave. is — or was it Fifth? I don't remember. I just remember her greeting, I can see her even now, all these years later, flanked by all that FBI, her son . . . Didn't realize til I got to end of that v. long city block that it was Jackie Kennedy who had touched me with her eyes.

AUGUST 28, SAME YEAR

It is so miserable here, still 90 degrees. Packed up everything in office today. In this incredible heat, water cooler gone . . . OK Louise. Tired. Ordered Lorraine Hansberry's *To Be Young, Gifted & Black* from inter lib. loan, been reading Gordon Parks' autobiography . . .

---

2. In regard to leaving her marriage to Ed.

Hello!

I've just come back from the boulevard. Crystal clear, sunlight dancing on the waves. Some gulls very loudmouthed out my window. Work this week, it's now Thursday, has been devastating. No one knows what they're doing. If my head were more political I'd start a union.

Am really getting pulls toward the studio. Zzzzzzzzz, like mebbe I'm not dead after all, we'll see. Below from *Boston Globe*.

QUICK FIX

Jamie Pearson, of Bolton, won the $1,000 grand prize in the recent America's Best Gordon's Bloody Mary contest. Her recipe:

> 2 oz vodka
> 4 oz Clamato juice
> 2 oz spicy hot vegetable juice
> 1 tsp horseradish
> 1 tsp hot salsa
> 2 dashes Worcester, ground black pepper, lemon wedge. Shake all ingredients together & pour over ice.

that's for next time, ok thelma?

9/8 ADDENDUM

Senior Home Care, Inc. is falling apart. Turns out director himself is applying for jobs. Also the fiscal manager, and the assistant director for grants & planning. The assistant director for home care has already left. It is totally insane. In the midst of all this they made that move! I learned yesterday that we're only funded to Jan. 1, 1992. . . .

Jack's Buddha smiles down at me from the shelf. I look at the lines formed in that soft slack skin on the inside of my left elbow and I think of fish scales. Aging is interesting. And awesome.

• • • • •

New York, Sunday eve 8th Sept — fyi my calendar says that the grape strike began on this day in 1965, so it's more than a quarter century these people have tried to take life in their hands, and we're still not free of the pesticides and the hideous working conditions. Also the day that Ford pardoned Nixon, it's all one thing—

hi helene!

There is a cute sounding cricket above this room in my garden, or out on the street tree. Other than that a cacophony, as usual. This is to thank you for your wonderful letter! That typing machine has freed you up to tell whole stories—just the way I feel about my computer, kisskisskiss it!

That woman on the boulevard probably went home thinking she'd had a wonderful encounter on the street with a "wonderfully handsome gray-haired woman" and felt validated forever.

Did a successful reading at feminist bookstore Judith's Room, nice crowd filled up the place, including a woman I lived with briefly 35 years ago when I was going to Columbia. The store owners were really happy. But I am standup comic, you know, not a writer, so it's easy for me to do that and hard for me to write.

I think about you and that stressful job of yours and your straining to hear every word coming at you from a million different directions, oh oh—Can you find the *Voice* for this week? Or just the Literary Supplement, because a big picture of Lisa is on the cover, and it is so *cute* (that word again), or rather she is, her dear little feet propped up at her desk, and in the background a painting by Whitfield Lovell,[3] who went to Music & Art H.S. with Kellie, a portrait of his grandmother—all this in the newspaper, so fragile—

Whitfield is little and pudgy and gay, and his family is incredibly supportive, they come to every opening, they are always in evidence when anything important goes on with him, it's wonderful to see.

MINNEAPOLIS, MN TUES. NOV. 26, 91

Helene!

Snow on the Ground! Snow in the Air! Snowing the day I arrived—Saturday past—snow expected today—

In the airport I saw two guys who resembled Fred, and a woman like Chan—"Sons of Norway" on a building up the street from here—

---

3. Sculptor, painter, MacArthur "genius."

Sat. night we went to a big opening party at the Walker Art Center—
people later said the show (*Interrogating Identity*) was best that had hit
this museum yet, "most exciting"—so KJ is a star, front-page news in the
Arts section of all the papers—

Proud mom, me, wearing my Salv. Army combat boots amid much
finery—

· · · · ·

Happy (Belated) Birthday!

NEW YEAR'S POEM, 1992

Not Yet, Pals—

not yet payday
not yet paradise
not yet panAmericana—

Need Your Participation!

Thank you for that marvelous cartoon about teeth, I laughed long and
hard and *loud*—

Viking has published *The Portable Beat Reader*, with a piece of my
book in it. In the bio I am called "a secretary"—too bad someone had to
get info about me from Baraka's book instead of asking me. It's little shit
things like that . . .

Enclosures here[4] are both to appear in magazine called *Frontiers*.
Please let me know what you think. I feel that I pare things down too
much, so that the reader has to bring a lot to the story, but I hate senti-
mentality.

Sorry for being in such a bad mood—I'll get better.

---

4. "Enough of This" and "How She Recognized Her Last Fling When She Found It" (fiction),
Frontiers, A Journal of Women Studies 13, no. 2 (1993).

Hello m'dear . . .

Your letter & ms. sitting here on the desk.

2/24

Thought I'd written a lot more than that! O well. One 2 hour moan session, that phone call yesterday, but what a blessing to be able to.

Call from Marie about 7 pm. Our Aunt Kate died at 5:10pm. People
at nursing home were with her. Rie said they really loved her. I just lost
one entire page of talking to you—pressed the wrong button. I want to
scream, but what good would that do. SHIT!

[POSTCARD]

2/28

Hello again—figure you need an everyday cheering. Can you explain to
me what is the "virtual reality" they're working on in the computer sci-
ences? To ask why, is of course ridiculous. Had a wonderful ride home on
the bus today. New driver & she shouted—HOLLARED . . . a story longer
than a p.c.

To send you a flower.

NEW YORK, NEW YORK, FRI MARCH 6 92 THE ANNIVERSARY OF

THE DRED SCOTT DECISION IN 1857 AND ALSO THE DAY

THAT ROOSEVELT CLOSED ALL THE BANKS IN 1933

Hello Helene!

Thank you for the beautiful Bleeding Heart postcard. I will now attempt to explain "virtual reality." Started with the stereopticon, if you'll
remember back to that. Then 3D movies. Now they give you some sort
of headset device which I suppose gives you the illusion of being inside
a hologram or the like, so that you actually feel as if you're part of whatever is happening. Just another thrill from the makers of thrills—and as
I recall it had its origin in military planning/training. I know very little
except from a few articles—there was one in *Voice* last year—but I've got
all the reality I need right outside the door, and it smells worse. . . . And
you can be sure that civilian use will be for games and more games . . .

Thanks *mucho* for the Sandra Cisneros stories! I had heard so much
about "Woman Hollering Creek." As good as I suspected.

My blood pressure on Weds. afternoon (at the clinic for a gyn checkup) was "good," said Mrs. Sanabria who, with Dr. Ang, has been taking care of me for 10 years now. They wouldn't lie, those women I wrote my "Pause That Refreshes" poem about. The one I called "the slender nurse" in the poem is stouter now; when I walked in she hugged me and said "I thought we'd lost you!" Actually I *had* tried to get an appointment at the HIP clinic where I could have gone for free but they did not have a woman gyn. I said *never mind*.

SUNDAY EVENING

Susan Sherman has suggested to the people at Parsons School of Design (now affiliated with the New School) that I propose a writing course. If I could just think of a catchy title, and propose it as a way to improve the writing skills of all those art majors . . . I wouldn't mind, I like those art major types.

I didn't realize until just this minute that today is International Women's Day; in 1908 women demonstrated in NYC demanding end to sweatshops and child labor—but the Triangle Shirtwaist fire was in 1911. Guess it always takes a tragedy.

GLOUCESTER, 3/11/92

Hello . . . 5 min. after 5pm . . .

My morning stint waiting for the 8:15 bus is a story. It's a bitch losing that time, but I see the bank employees going to work, the addicts going to Nuva for counseling and a shot, the "homeless" men, one of whom has a check from somewhere waiting for the bank to open its 8:15 window . . . that seems to be only every 2 weeks, where do you suppose the check comes from? I love them, they smile sometimes, we wait in the same space, and when the window opens the older man goes with his check— thinking of it, it's probably only once a month and it's a s.s. check . . . any- way it's beautiful the way they both walk slowly up the bank side of Main St. after the money is in hand, talking.

NEW YORK 3/14/92

Hello Helene!

I loved your story about waiting for the bus . . . I can see those two men of yours walking companionably up "the bank side of Main St."

I liked that LeGuin story you sent up to the end, which would have been more satisfying if she (the protagonist) had, even tentatively, risen over her limitations. But then, I'm for heroic women! Nevertheless the writing's so clear and un-fussy. It's the fucking fussers I hate, truly. They're always describing emotional states that I want to shake the characters right out of. Oh, let's face it I'm opinionated and too direct.

I can't possibly describe to you, although I would so much like to, the conversation re the color of black people that went on in the *Friendly's* across from the Woodmere, Long Island library, where (after I read at library) I sat last Tuesday night with an 89-year-old lady, a friend of my mother from Laurelton, and her son and daughter-in-law. It must have started when I said that black people come in all colors, apropos of I don't know what. But then the old lady went on about her son's neighbors, and how light-skinned they were, as though, were we to wait another few generations, all black people would lighten up, and then the son, possibly seeing my consternation, or something, said, "Well, it could just as easily go the other way." Honestly, Helene. That's the sum but not the substance of it.

I am hired to speak at Middlebury College on April 23, and they asked for a topic, something about women and writing, they hoped, so I just sent them "Women Writing Change," which popped into my head because you can read it different ways. Hope they don't think I'm too weird.

· · · · ·

With a legacy from her aunt and divorced spouse social security benefits, Helene was finally able to quit her job, though she still had to work some hours to qualify for Massachusetts health insurance. I finally convinced her to try freelance proofreading, and arranged for her to take tests at a couple of New York publishers, which she of course passed, and by June I was able to report: "Joe says there's been no work but will send you some when he has. Laura is on vacation till Thurs. Just to update you!"

GLOUCESTER, 7/11/92

Hullo m'dear!

Thank you for having a birthday so I could send you this card. Beautiful day—I'm going to eat, then to the porch to sew new elastic into my old bathing suit (bought when I went to Norfolk, VA to visit Paul when he was in the Navy—I'm sure that was at least 15 years ago). I tried on at least 7 new ones last week, determined to ignore the outrageous prices and buy one, but they all had loose elastic too. Must be something to do w/my "hanging bottom."

Funny, what happens w/age: Ten years ago I would have announced my resignation the very day the bank called [about her inheritance]. What is it, lack of faith? Lost my Zen again for sure. Mebbe if I go out into the sun & take this to the P.O., I'll get it back—Anyway—I do love you, thanks for being born!

GLOUCESTER, 1/10/93

Hullo . . .

Am in a snit—met w/tax man last night. I owe all these dumb dollars to social security. Oh well. He tried. I sat for an hour watching his computer and him. What a wonderful merry-go-round. And there's no work. Called Joe Monday, today called Laura, nothing for at least 2 or 3 weeks.

I'm trying to clear out my house, which I'm sure has more to do w/the snit than finances.

Yma [granddaughter #3] got her driver's license. Is going to cut my hair tomorrow and take me to Ames to get an on-sale TV table because mine, a hand-me-down from some 15 years ago, is no longer moveable. I found it about to crush the VCR one morning around Xmas. Kettie [granddaughter #1] is now Office Manager of the fabric design co. where she's been working. She has her very own apt. in Cambridge, 2 kittens, & a lover. Niva [granddaughter #2] turned 19 2 days ago. I gave her a pair of long, dangly Peruvian earrings which she almost didn't get because I tried them on, and they looked & felt so good I wore them all that afternoon— took great fortitude plus love to put them back in the box!

1/13

Was up til 2 a.m. putting the damn cart together—remember the days when you cld buy something already "assembled"? However, my television is now fucked up. Think about me next Tues when Paul calls. Long distance consultation from the TV Doctor takes great patience on both our parts. Me & my bifocals searching for the knobs he's referring to while at the same time frantically trying to keep the phone at the right angle so my hearing aid works. Straight out slapstick.

Read Toni Morrison last week. Have neglected to read any current reviews of anything, not even checking out the plain, ordinary, completely depressing, "News." I can hear you clucking, lil red hen, but there comes a time when all that doesn't matter. I'm just clearing my own dust right now, and don't need the world's on top of it.

Ok. To the bath to wash my gone-from-waist-to-shoulder-length hair, make me presentable tomorrow night for a party to celebrate the publication of my friend Claire's son's first book. A novel abt. baseball for which he got mind-boggling amounts of $. And a movie contract I think already . . .

The weather has been typical New England—pouring snow and then pouring rain. And bone-chilling cold.

Are you alive & well?

I was, but very busy. On a recommendation from Joyce Johnson, I'd been invited to spend the spring semester of 1993 as visiting writer at the University of Wyoming in Laramie. Despite having complained about "credentials" the year before, I'd agreed immediately! Except for my recent trip to California, I hadn't been to any of the western states since 1968 and was very excited, as I'd written Helene: "Forgot whether I told you I rented house in Laramie that's got washer/dryer, study, carpets, heat—a luxury 5 months!"

2/17/93 IN LARAMIE WYOMING AT 10:05 PM

Probably about 5 degrees out there—last night it got down to 19 below! On the radio, the wonderful NPR program that saves my head, Sam Cook singing "Bring It On Home to Me." Yesterday I wrote a fan letter to the guy who produces this program; I brought with me a tape I'd made of it while I was packing—only to find it broadcast here not once but 3 times a week—plays all the wonderful old r&b songs—Marvin Gaye, Wilson Pickett, the Shirelles!

It just occurred to me that in New York I hear music *all the time*—out the window, passing by, in elevators, the subway. Radio's great when the only other sound is the furnace. (Bless furnace.)

hello helene!

Thank you for the picture—you look gorgeous and mean as shit. And now you have cut your hair all off? Your TV table and my TV—my tenants wrote to say it had no picture. Well why should it, it belonged to my parents and was shipped to me from Florida in early 80s. Since I never watch it, it didn't break for me. I dig your snit about owing $$ and then having no work, ugh. But it will come back, it's just seasonal according to their publishing lists, that's the way it's always been.

Tomorrow night I discuss my book with a group that has been reading it—couldn't refuse—you don't refuse in small towns, right? And they bought the book, right? Sat. I read at the local bookstore.

I'm down to 28 students in the 2 classes. The memoir class is terrific; it's the kids I am wrestling with, they are slow to trust, shy, so hidden behind themselves. Weird socialization. The repressed violence. The boys write gory stuff, real anger.

Today I had to bring some things to the bookstore for publicity, then drove onto a road I'd noticed called Vista Drive,[5] which went out onto the plain and then paralleled the interstate, like being on a great white snowy lake. Houses built on flat plain with nary a tree in sight. Then in the distance, through a white haze, the mountains, like dreams.

Ate one large and one small sweet potato and an entire bunch of asparagus! I've been forgetting to mention the microwave, haven't I? Well, I haven't been forgetting to use it!

2/18

Five minutes before the lady comes to pick me up to go answer questions about my book. I'm thinking about your not wanting to hear the "news" but I know you prob. get it by osmosis; keep thinking about what I'm not learning being out here. Wonder, if you'd come back to the West after Europe, what you'd have gotten into.

2/20

For some stupid reason I balked at bringing with me the only camera I own, manual focus, takes film hard to find. So I didn't have a way to take pics of all this gorgeous snow, and by the time I got my ass to the Wal-Mart to buy a disposable, the snow had lost its beautiful pristine quality. So here I am wishing for more even though I'll have to shovel it! They don't plow the streets, and so everything was muffled—I walked home

---

5. This is probably where Matthew Shepard was murdered five years later.

about 6:30pm and the snow under my feet was squeaking, that wonderful sound I guess I've mostly read about. It was an unusually wet snow for this area, and clung to each branch of all these majestic cottonwoods and amazingly tall, perfectly shaped firs, like a Currier & Ives print, oh the snows of yesteryear! Anyway, minus that "bone-chilling cold" you mentioned, that wet rawness I know so well, it takes on different qualities. Though the wind here can be adversarial!

I've just come off 8.26 miles on the exercycle in the basement, which I'm slowly figuring out how to adapt—high enough to stretch the legs, but how to fix the seat so it doesn't gouge my ass bones?

Recommendations! Josephine Herbst, *The Starched Blue Sky of Spain*. Gorgeous, for the most part. New novel by Dorothy Allison, called *Bastard Out of Carolina*. I'm in the middle and it's good, for the most part— always that qualifying, because there are good parts and not-so . . . What else? A memoir called *The Bookmaker's Daughter* by Shirley Abbott, I've just started that. *Black Ice* by Lorene Cary, good but too young, in a way. Also the novel *A Thousand Acres* by Jane Smiley, which won Pulitzer. I plowed through it (forgive the pun) but again couldn't relate all that much.

The women in the reading group I spoke to asked about you—I told them I was in the middle of a letter to you and they appeared very pleased, as though that represented some kind of "normality" on my part—a long-term friendship.

Yay, friend!

xxoo

[UNDATED POSTCARD FROM CODY, WYOMING]

Went for a little trip and stayed in Buffalo Bill's Irma Hotel—there's a branch of the Whitney Museum in Cody! Saw lots of scenery and several towns just like this one—

I've had the slippers I'm sending you since Xmas! Hope you're OK— Kellie's show opens in July—14th I think. See you then (in Boston). I'm *home* on 6/4—yay!

xxoo

Hullo . . .

About half past ten last night, bleary-eyed from hours proofing *How to Have an Orgasm . . . As Often As You Like*, I finally pay attention to Squirrel who has been racing, ears back, from one room to the other. He ends up at the front door (studio) so I open it and let him out into the hall and he races down the stairs. I go into the kitchen & make some stir-fry to put on yesterday's rice because I really need to eat after dealing w/all that sex while checking for single & double quotes & English versus American usage. I do eat, get myself ready to sleep, & remember Squirrel is in the hall. I turn on the hall light & see him very comfortably curled up by the basement door. "You're there for the night, I'm going to bed," sez I, leaning over the banister. Which is when I saw yr. pkg. sitting by the mailbox. I bring it upstairs, Squirrel follows me. I shut & lock the door. Take yr pkg. to the worktable & open it and totally break up!!! What timing! "DEAR-FOAMS," flowers on the soles, soft, *perfect* for masturbation.

Aside from all that, they're wonderful, thank you!

7

If we have not struggled
as hard as we can
at our strongest
how will we sense
the shape of our losses
or know what sustains
us longest or name
what change costs us. . . .
— *Kay Ryan*

Hello!

It's so great to be back here, to once again have chance encounters. I was putting out recycling earlier when a guy asked to help, and proceeded to tell me it was his birthday, and that he had managed to make it all the way to 31, thank god, and that he collected cans for a living, and— shit—31, just a *baby!* I told him I hoped he'd make it to 100, and he said he was hoping to be Methuselah. . . . I've been doing nothing but cleaning—actually washed all the windows, including the ones in the front which are newfangled and open in, so that one is standing on a ladder four stories above the street with nothing but a collapsed window between oneself and The End. I managed to fuck one of them up so that it no longer stays open, and of course it had to be the crucial one for throwing down the key.

Forty years before this letter my father's response to my first Village apartment was, "Ach, why live like this!" So I had by this time long lived like that—in a walkup sans doorbell or doorman—and thus thrown the key a lot, often into astonishing weather or event. The question was never why, but why not.

· · · · ·

Helene!

Just had to send you Jennie's first story right away. After first Parsons class she said her English was so bad she wasn't sure she could take the class but her friend had recommended it. Today So-Young wrote one called "At a Bar" which I haven't had time to copy, which includes the sentence "The lights were shooting those drunk souls like X-rays." (It was an exercise in metaphor.) She describes an empty table as "alienated" and "as if it was desperate to be taken by one of those black dresses." Students told me that no other writing class has allowed them to be creative. And they really dig it!

Must try to print this and go to bed. Hope you're well.

GLOUCESTER, 10/1/93 AND SOMEHOW I REMEMBERED TO SAY RABBITS 3 TIMES, WAKING FROM A WEIRD DREAM, SUN IN MY EYES, SQUIRREL CURLED ON MY SHOULDER, HIS WET NOSE SNIFFING MY NOSE, THOSE LOVELY LONG WHISKERS BRUSHING MY CHEEKS. WHEW!

IF I WEREN'T A CAPRICORN, I'M SURE I'D BE A SODOMITE!

Jennie Lau's "Dim Sum" is BEAUTIFUL . . . I wait for So-Young (Such a name!)

10/5

I will get this off—but I've lots of kitchen-table things to talk about, put off again, call from Laura tonight—250 pp coming Thurs which she wants back Tues. which means I send it back Mon which means I run around doing all those things like laundry which I put off thinking I had a space and lots of time in the studio (terrible trouble with a little mask—have torn it apart 3 times), sorting and clearing glass and, you know, just being me, in my house, doing my thing and loving it no matter the frustrations.

Folding this up to put in envelope I see I never put no "Dear Het" at the beginning—but it *was* writ to you!

• • • • •

The following spring I went for a second stint at the University of Wyoming:

Helene!

Happy Birthday to You!

Corthell Rd travels *up*—and the study is even better than last year, with 3 desks. And let us not forget the carport, which allows driving right up to the door, where the first sight that greets me is my new bike, chained to the stair rail!

Although I haven't quite *come to* yet. Which brings me to what I wanted to say—

Thank you!

Last night I finally had a moment to pay a little attention to myself, you know, to what I was up to, so for openers I read Le Guin's *Fisherwoman's Daughter* which you so kindly sent, and it has cleared up a mystery for me.

Mystery: do you recall a letter I wrote to you early sixties (while I was still married I think) with lots of crazy convoluted and half intelligent and poorly written ideas about men and art and women? Well, I haven't looked at it for years but did when I started to write the memoir. Have ever since been puzzled as to what I was trying to feel out there, because my ideas were so basically unformed. Anyway it appears to me now that I was trying to refute—no *distance myself from*—that Great Artist myth Le Guin talks about, trying to connect *our lives* to something that could be art, and refusing to relinquish my dignity, my respect for my own womanly life . . .

Solved! Thank you. Thank you!

Are you finally gonna get some studio time now that the holidays are over and you're so snowed in? I hope so.

Happy Birthday To You!

Hello, I think I need a computer, this machine has been doing such weird things lately.

Backside of this paper is copy of *Glouc Daily Times* article with recipe, "Nine Raisins Soaked in Gin" remedy for arthritis that I cldn't resist trying because I had this big bottle of gin left over from 2 years ago when Steph's mother was visiting. But then it got too much, trying to gauge when to eat the raisins so the alcohol wasn't depleting everything else my body needed to survive. I think the ladies who could move better were probably just tipsy. I got no argument w/that. And the raisins *are* v. tasty!

If I'd had my head abt. me, which I very much don't seem to have these days, I'd have described the section of the AIDS quilt I put stitches on. Sometime I'll tell you about all that, the stitches, the waiting in line, the ceremony.

Three images were all she needed. I took such pleasure in this writing, in the act itself and her choice to perform it. I suppose that's a sisterly feeling; I never thought to assess it, though I always wanted to express it:

[POSTCARD: PHOTO OF GRACE RAYMOND HEBARD,
UNIVERSITY OF WYOMING PROFESSOR OF POLITICAL ECONOMY,
STANDING ON A COVERED WAGON, CA. 1920]
LARAMIE, 2/20/94

Only you deserve this great woman! Dig those sexy boots—and that skirt! And is that her dishpan—why yes!

GLOUCESTER, 3/23/94

Hullo m'dear . . .

Your letter in mail this morning . . .

It's been ages & ages since we've sat together in yr kitchen or mine, 2 years, I think. Weird . . . I mean the phone is wonderful, but it ain't the same, I agree.

Re the Wyoming silence you mentioned—am sure it was John Chamberlain who was visiting us in Santa Fe, sd—"It's so fucking quiet!!!!" Made him nervous—

LARAMIE, 3/28/94

Hi (as you say) Keed!

I've been assembling this packet for you—the article on the information superhighway[1] came from *Z* magazine, I thought you might be innarested (also as you say).

---

1. Early name for what eventually became the Internet.

It's "snow showering"* at the moment, and has been disgusting this past week, down to below freezing at night, 29 right now, 10 above tonight, this is spring in Wyoming. Lisa tells me there are buds on the trees in NY, sigh. Anyway I'm making chicken soup.

*2 hours later & the "showers" are still at it, everything all white, it's *winter.*

• • • • •

In my last letter from Laramie I enclosed a brochure about a conference on the Beat writers to be held in May at NYU, which for the first time included a panel of women. About the title: "Women and the Beats"—what was this conjunction? "Beat shit, which is the way I'm thinking about it," I wrote Helene. Like every other box, I felt, it was just another way to set you straight. Yet I had no quarrel with the motives of younger women who wanted some clues toward their own survival. That seemed to be my mission, anyway. Lisa had taken to calling me "mother to the masses." *Carpe diem.*

• • • • •

NEW YORK, 9/1/94 WHERE DID SUMMER GO?

Hi!

I've been cleaning and moving shit for days.

Have 4 boxes of books to sell or give away. Trundled home on my luggage cart 2 little file cabinets, on top of which sits a better desk. Physically, things look good. Now all I have to do is work. Just got the proofs of *Big Star Fallin' Mama* reissue; editor said "Would you add a little mention of hip-hop?" (I have 2 weeks to do this, and read the proof, during which time I also have to prepare for my classes).

Margaret Wolf [then an editor at Carroll Publishing] stopped by one day this week, said again that you were wonderful. Well, of course. Hope that book is not kicking your ass.

GLOUCESTER, 9/7/94 9:30PM

Margaret sent me *another* book just as I was in the process of saving the 2nd mask & had figured a studio agenda—oh well. So that's where I've been—as well as to the laundromat. I dunno, Hettie Jones. Where did summer go, where does anything go! And while wondering that someone comes along and sez "Would you add a little mention of hip-hop?" Well, mebbe you can just say *no*. Something I've been thinking about while doing this book, which is *not* interesting.

Helene!

Was glad to hear you're alive and well, as you said in your message, but you sounded like you were working—anyway I thought I'd write—

I've written some poems but feel totally blank. I don't know why it's called "blocked," or maybe that's different. This is blank, as in nothing.

My stories have been rejected 2x so far. First by Viking, which didn't know how they could sell them. Second by Scribner. Editor there said the stories were "provocative," but "visited the same material as How I Became" and the prose "failed to engage" him. So I guess I'm depressed but not surprised, as I didn't really think I had much chance.

See if you can get hold of *Charlie Chan Is Dead*, edited by Jessica Hagedorn, an anthology of Contemp Asian Amer Fiction.

I just spent the last half hour or so not writing this letter but working on a poem (not a very good start but I'm desperate enough to push it— or maybe I just need to learn to keep pushing until it appears, even out of a not very good start). You were talking not long ago (on phone, not in letter) about the whole shame thing, and pressure, and wishing you weren't so vulnerable to it. Well, here it seems to be. I don't think I have an answer, though lots of people have asked the question, or talked about the feelings engendered, all the pleasure/pain shit. How art is such a gas, and then the other part, the no-good turd part. But sometimes I feel less than ambitious, want to just lie down and rest I think, just lie down and think maybe. Then I never do, and it's perverse of me not to.

I am thin! Very good for doing yoga. And wearing clothes. Next week there's an opening at the Whitney Museum and then a party and since I'm supposed to look good so I won't shame my children, I took a "personal day" last Thurs and went to Domsey's Clothing Warehouse and got the most amazing collection of new clothes for $38, including a power suit just in case I need to show some power, if I have any left. Why should I have to apologize for wanting to do nothing but write poetry?

The phone rang and I talked for an hour, then had to work on this poem because of dying of shame feeling, as above.

Thinking of applying for unemployment. If not, it'll be a big scramble — but part of this "blankness" thing is that I feel a certain inertia about scrambling. Is this age?

Thanks for sending that article about the hoof strengthener — *Times* also had an article about it, though I've yet to prance up to Saks Fifth Ave to find out how much they soak you for it.

Hope you're okay, I keep feeling anxious despite your "alive and well" message.

• • • • •

At this juncture our conversation shifted. Though I had always written about age — birthday poems and the like — now it was as if the sky had 60 written all over it.

NEW YORK, NY I/I/95

SONG AT SIXTY (FRAGMENT)

If you want to know me
you better hurry

Thought you'd like my New Year greeting. How are you? Have things quieted down some? xxoo

GLOUCESTER, 2/9/95

Quote from "Confronting Ageism," Shevy Healey, *Sojourner*, 1990: "I am tired of hearing that the less I look like and act like my own age, the better I am! Studies show that in old age there is the greatest diversity in behavior, physical and mental capacity, and personality than during any other developmental stage. Our society is able to patronize and insult old women in large and small ways because nowhere is there validation for the bravery, courage, beauty, and endurance of old women."

Hello dear Het,

I'm making carrot soup with a whole lot of celery thrown in for my bladder thanks to your book's advice.

This is to send the little calendar I meant to get to you as a Christmas card—oh well. I am trying to follow my pontifical big brother's quiet advice over the phone (how many years back?) when I was freaked by all I needed/wanted to do: "Do it as you think of it and it will get done."

He didn't, I think, realize how fast my thoughts go—no way can my body keep up. But I'm trying. Which means everything I do is helter-skelter—there's no "order" in doing it as I think of it, but it's interesting.

Helter-skelter, okay. I could forgive her that—everyone has a process. Nevertheless, I was always pushing her to do *more*:

Helene!

My last letter to you written in June, jeez, I wish I'd get better about this, you've mentioned the same "we used to write much more," but I guess that reassurance of hearing the breathing body is important.

Though it was wonderful to get your review! I loved it, you gave a good idea of what the book is about, and your feelings about it, which is what any author wants, and in a page and a half, not bad baby. Maybe this is the start of a new career!

Some time ago I bought an anthology titled *Postmodern American Poetry*, which I haven't found useful for teaching because too difficult for beginners, but having promised to bring some more "experimental" poetry to prison, I've been reading it this evening. Got stuck in the lovely early years, Kenneth Koch and Frank O'Hara, James Schuyler, Barbara Guest . . .

That's to reward myself for not freaking out when my car muffler came loose on way up there last week, and had to be taken off for return trip, resulting in an entire new exhaust system.

Feel like a good night's sleep is in the offing, so I'm off to off it!

Hullo . . .

Torrential rains all day, you had them too, I'm sure. Little red ants all over the sink & stove when I came out to the kitchen this morning . . . Mercury, please stop retrograding! I tore open 4 tea bags, spread the tea all over where I thought they were coming in, and spent my first, first hour of the day killing ants, I mean even before coffee, it was like having the DT's but they were real. A Daymare . . .

Shit! Sixty-eight years old and I still don't know how to deal with life.

Hullo.

It's 9:50 p.m. and I'm stoned and tired and need to eat the still too chewy lentil soup that should have been done 20 minutes ago. Shit!

If I had a fax machine you'd have had the enclosed long ago. Mebbe that's what I shld. buy instead of a computer with a fax modem which for my use means investing in a scanner, etc. Technology is wonderful, but it's driving me up the wall.

If they see
breasts and long hair coming
they call it woman,

if beard and whiskers
they call it man:

but, look, the self that hovers
in between
is neither man
nor woman

O Ramanatha
—*Devara Dasimayya (tr. by A. K. Ramanujan)*

Don't ask me, I've no idea where it comes from other than the page be-fore the preface in the paperback I pulled out from the new nonfiction shelf at the library this afternoon: *Women in Praise of the Sacred* edited by Jane Hirshfield. I just leafed through it, like I do, and there were some lovely things and if the plumber wasn't coming tomorrow at 8 AM (!) I'd take a hot bath, curl up in my bed and read it through . . . but the plumber is coming.

I really think I need a shrink, Hettie Jones. Went yesterday with Fred to check out laptops, all too violently expensive. But I did almost buy a Canon fax/copier. Have to do something before Jan 1st.

12/7

Call at noon today from Chan. She passed her orals (PhD, English Literature) with all kinds of accolades!

GLOUCESTER, UNDATED FAX

Hello—think Paul via phone just got my tax* machine working—I had the right things plugged into the wrong places—how like me! If you're home, could you send me a fax?

*this is *not* a typo—

FAX SENT BY: HETTIE JONES 12/22/95

Merry Christmas!

• • • • •

Faxing proved to be an irresistible temptation to tell the whole story:

NEW YORK, 12/29/95

Hello!

Oh woe is me, I am injured! Fucking incapacitated!

A week ago, I slipped in the slush and caught myself. And though I felt a weirdness, nothing hurt and I went on about my business. Yoga, stretching. Walked 2 miles to get haircut.

Christmas I had to take Tylenol in order to have a good time. And we did. Next night I sent Katy out for Advil. Day later could not go to prison. Could not walk. Went to chiropractor.

Sacroiliac. Chiro said I could walk, so I did, home, thought I'd faint before I got here. After making soup and corn muffins, I sat on an ice pack in my rocker all that night talking to Joyce who came down to keep me company. But next day some people came in from California and I hung out with them in a restaurant, a coffee shop, and finally a bar, for about 5 hours when I should have been home icing my butt. I have the coldest butt in NY.

Having got rid of some work I had to do, I have taken off the icepack, smoked a joint, and written this. I forgot the coda to the story. A guy I know who lives down my block, amused watching me gimp to the corner for the paper, after an exchange of 2 sentences, seized me, lifted me into the air, and squeezed me and nearly broke my ribs while I screamed "Stop! You're Hurting Me!" Lucky I was wearing my Wyoming down jacket. Ribs hurt every once in a while, at a sudden movement. The chiro said they would for a while. I can't believe it.

And how are you?

GLOUCESTER, 12/30/95, THE 1ST DAY OF STEPH'S 49TH YEAR!

O winter! I'm so sorry for you m'dear . . . what a consummate DRAG . . .

It's 11:45 a.m. and I've the shakes from too much coffee and no breakfast so this is just quick. Found your fax on the floor last night when I came in here at about 1am after watching, back against the hot pad, *The Bodyguard*. (Dumb film—but Whitney Houston is fun to watch. I've decided K. Costner is this generation's Charlton Heston, a tiresomely perfect hero, and ALWAYS Kevin Costner.) I was testing the rehab'd tv Paul brought me—BIG screen which makes tapes almost like movies—and treating my back at the same time tho I should have been flat-on-my-back-in-bed. (I fucked up my back hauling too much heavy stuff in preparation for Xmas Eve. Plus shoveling heavy wet snow and lifting 20 lbs of rock salt, etc.)

So here we are, at the end of the year, two old ladies—one on ice, the other on heat—ain't that the shits!

My new neighbor gave me *Breath, Eyes, Memory*. My most favorite gift. Okay keed, we're fax tax city. I'm gone.

· · · · ·

NEW YORK, 1/19/96

How could I have forgotten your birthday when I have it written down on the 2nd page of my address book, right after my own name! Helene, 1/19 it says. And 1/19 it is!

Happy Birthday dear Helene!

Mea culpa. I have been totally self-involved, aware of my body at all times and freaked that this injury would never go away especially since I now have things to do. Going to SF to read at St. Mary's College, lve NY 24th, retn 28th. On 30th I have to speak to another audience at the Whitney about being a beat woman. Beat bat bit but.

I think your stationery is gorgeous, did Steph do it? You'd have fun on computer if you cd get graphics. And your poem!!! [So there you are / and here I am / 69 today / and still OK.] Send it to Marie, she'll love it. I have to find her letter with her poem about seventy-five—I think it goes "Seventy-five and still alive alive alive!" And when I give readings I'll put them with my "Song At Sixty"! Do you give me permission? With due credit of course.

I'm wiped. Reading *The Stone Diaries* by Carol Shields, which I like. Hope your nonorganic veggies were good. Okay, Ms 69 today and still OK!

NEW YORK, 3/7/96

Good afternoon!

Hope you're doing okay. One more reason never to go to jail—last night I had to meet my class in a different room, one that contained a couch and a soft upholstered chair, and one of the women sank down and said, "Wow, I haven't sat on a couch for *eight years.*"

Of course I thought of you—I've never known you to have a couch. Me, I don't count, I have a futon (though I've never had a *real* couch like last night's example).

Along with the above I sent an article from that day's *Times*, a consideration of the word "old." "We need to rescue the word," said one woman. Americans are "fearful of aging," the article reported, thus giving rise to such euphemisms as "senior citizen" and "silver fox," as well as more weighted terms like "elderly." Various older people were asked what term they preferred. "Got any thoughts?" I scrawled on the margin.

GLOUCESTER, 3/8/96

Hullo—

Read the *Times* bit—it's all nonsense, of course. I call myself Helene Dorn. And respond to, and use, "senior citizen" when it means a discount.

I've also at times referred to myself as an "old lady." The term old woman (or old man) has always conjured (for me) a positive image. "Mature American" — what bullshit!

That this debate has continued into the twenty-first century is clear from a *Times* article dated February 17, 2009, which reported a new stylebook for the media to guide professionals through the problem. "Elderly" should be eliminated; "senior citizen" and "golden years" are discouraged, as well as the adjectives "feisty," "spry," "feeble," "eccentric," "senile" and "grandmotherly." At least one of these has already been used by the *Times* to describe me.

· · · · ·

GLOUCESTER, 3/15/96

Hello . . . 6:25 pm.

Standing here at the worktable where the machine still sits . . . Am working on this mask, re: Chekhov's "The Black Monk" (which story mesmerized me, I'm still not sure what he was saying) and I just now put it up on the wall so I could see what I'm doing and I see I've given this monk who's been traveling in space for a thousand years a drinker's nose. And I can only laugh. What one has in one's head and what one's hands do!

NEW YORK, 3/15/96

Hi — I've never read that Chekhov story but I keep looking at the title and thinking of Thelonious's "Blue Monk"!

Made a good garbage soup this afternoon. I told Alexander Smalls,[2] who loves soups and stews and casseroles, that you called it that and he laughed, liked the name. Kellie says the food in his new restaurant is fantastic. That's where we'll go when you come to the city, when the weather is warm and dreamy!

---

2. Whose memoir/cookbook *Grace the Table* I was then writing with him. Proprietor of Café Beulah in the 1990s and at this writing proprietor/chef of The Cecil, and executive chef at Minton's, both in Harlem.

I doubt if I saw even one Irish person today though I did see a girl quite greenied up yesterday—

The gym in the store downstairs is moving. We may get a Thai restaurant. *La vie continue*, isn't that someone's title? How is the Monk, with his drinker's nose?

GLOUCESTER 3/18/96

The Monk was a total disaster last night, after *hours* of work, but today I think I can do it. Maybe.

NEW YORK, 3/18

I finally got the reading [with Cornelius Eady] together about half an hour ago. It's going to rain tomorrow. But we got written up in *New York* magazine. That's something, out of all there is in this city, so I better be good!

Sorry about the Monk's behavior yesterday, but I'm sure he'll be more cooperative soon. He'll probably fall in love with you.

GLOUCESTER, 3/26

I've put the Monk on hold. He sits here above me on the wall back of my worktable and looks down at me with his smile and his wishbone earrings and his blackbead eyebrows and maybe I'll just keep him there. Something for myself. To remind me that perfection ain't everything.

NEW YORK, 3/28

I am here, on Weds. night when I'm usually at the prison, because I had planned to bring 2 guests from an organization called Justice Works Community who were going to teach us to fold origami flowers, for a Mother's Day demonstration at City Hall, to call attention to incarcerated mothers, the problems of foster care, etc., and to encourage alternative sentencing. BUT the woman whose room I have been using in the prison called me at noon to say she was sorry, I couldn't have my group in her room, she had to use it. The arrangements had all been made, for several weeks, clearances arranged, many phone calls, etc etc. And then I had to cancel 3 hrs before we were to leave. It really makes you feel like shit.

· · · · ·

Just to say hullo. If you're like me you're freaking out about everything you have to do before you board that plane for California two days from now (I think I'm right on the date?).

Additions to the Monk, which I shld abandon but somehow can't, drying; Squirrel outside in the snow!

Mailed today a very short letter to R.M. re: Panna.[3] In the process of all that remembering I lived through past Hells during the day in my thoughts and at night in my dreams. And I thought about you, how did you do that memoir without going totally bonkers? A whole different situation, of course, but even so, those fucking hurts thought dispelled, erupting . . . You can shut them off during the day, but they come back at night in dreams.

Oh hello, thank you for writing so often, it keeps me from freaking.

My sympathies for your bad thoughts and dreams re Panna. How did I write that book? Cried a lot, smoked a lot of dope. But I seldom dream — and when I do it seldom has anything to do with anything. Fortunate, in some ways, but then I've always wondered what it might be like, to interpret, etc. Maybe have some clues about oneself . . .

I think I could sleep if I could move from this chair. I'll probably write you tomorrow with my latest freaked out discovery or whatever. Maybe I won't have time, maybe the sun will shine. *But I will say I knew you wouldn't abandon that Monk!*

Hi!

10:10 p.m. and nothing as yet in the suitcase—have to gather jewelry and cosmetics and something to read, hah—*

*At 5pm I get this fax from Simon & Schuster—do you recall I did a little kid's tie-in book with the TV show produced by Lisa's friend Maria?[4] Did this last Sept., it was all okayed and I got paid. Now this fax comes

---

3. Ralph Maud, scholar; Panna Grady, a wealthy '50–'60s Beat supporter, who gave away much of her fortune. Helene mentions Panna's kindness to her.
4. *Gullah Gullah Island*, produced by Maria Perez.

with the manuscript all over again, with apologies from the editor, but they've changed it, and I have to sort it out. So I had to cut up the fax, copy it, find the original ms to check it against. All this must be done while I'm away as they need it back Monday.

Then, having dealt with that, I made corrections to my speech and began to print it out. But nothing was printing on the paper, and as I stood up to find out what was going on, one of the wheels fell off my chair. Luckily I had an extra ink cartridge. Got the pliers, put the wheel back, etc etc.

Anyway, thought I'd say hello. I went rushing to buy a pair of shoes this afternoon but found I had a flat tire, so walked bike to bike store, dashed around corner while they were fixing it, and then rode home, looked carefully at shoes from fancy Soho store, and discovered they are not leather. I repeat, *not leather.* They even smell like leather, I swear. If I don't wear them in Calif., I will return them.

Nevertheless. Okay. Off. LOVE!

Thank you for saying hello, I was going to send you a quick funny bon voyage. How can they charge $$ for non-leather shoes? Easy. They put on a price tag. OK. Will be thinking abt. you in that Calif. sun . . . LOVE!

• • • • •

hello i'm home!

AND HAD A GREAT TIME. Everyone liked my speech and I got lots of good questions, and the other people on the panel were good—especially Nancy Peters, who is now the co-owner of City Lights and a lovely woman. I had such fun with her and Ferlinghetti—we snuck out between panels and went to lie on the grass in the wonderful warm sun—ah! And I didn't wear the plastic shoes, though I took them along. Today, however, I took them back. Plastic, I said, and got a refund right away.

Anyway I wanted to say hello. I quoted *you* a few times, too!

Hello and glad you're home safe and sound and had a great time. This is to say that and quickly tell you a very funny story, the moral of which is

NEVER GO TO THE SUPERMARKET BEFORE BREAKFAST EVEN IF YOU'RE OUT OF CAT FOOD, AND ESPECIALLY NOT IF THE WEATHER FORECASTERS HAVE PREDICTED TORRENTIAL RAINS & WINDS FOR THE NEXT 2 DAYS.

I got the cat food. But the salmon steaks on sale looked so lovely and I was by then, hungry, so I bought one thinking how nice to have it broiled, some rice w/peppers & scallions, a lovely dinner for myself in the rain . . .

That was yesterday. I got working on the Black Monk; talked a long time w/Paul; cldn't stand my dirty hair any longer, washed it & my body; heated in the microwave a can of pork & beans . . . and went to bed at 3 a.m.

Well. I did do the salmon tonight—but turns out the red stuff I had in the paprika jar was cayenne. Good thing it was old. The oil, wine, lemon juice, garlic, & paprika basting calls for 1 TBS. of paprika. Since you are working on a cookbook, I thought this wld. amuse you like it did me. What a bummer, I can't even give my cats the leftovers!

And while I was broiling this oh-wldn't-that-be-nice-in-the-rain salmon steak, the smoke alarm started screaming and wldn't stop no matter I opened the porch door, letting all that rain and 40s weather in. And my cats, naturally, are driving me crazy with all their smelling of this salmon . . .

I will never again eat salmon. I don't care who cooks it, or how well it's cooked, I will never again . . .

· · · · ·

Viking had produced one small paperback edition of my memoir, which was soon out of print. Regarding a reprint, I was told the book couldn't stand alone, and that I would have to wait until there were other books by "Beat women" to accompany it. As if they needed a chorus line.

Today I finally got the word that Viking is "considering" the reprint of my book—I don't know whether that means they might not do it at all, or whether they're thinking of putting it off again. The editor, whom I called last week, never returned my phone call.

So that threw my heart into double speed. That's what it felt like, *shock*.

They will know in a week or so, I was told. But right after that I had to go downstairs and meet the owners of the 2-month-hence Thai restaurant. Katy, my neighbor, just loved them, but later told me their food isn't any good. Great.

Don't feel defeated—you know those pricks—you're *not* alone. Have just finished reading *Listen to Their Voices*—really nice interviews—Lucille Clifton's I'm going to copy.

I just tried to call you but there was no answer so I guess you've gone to bed.

Have just finished an enormous paste-up typing job to make the program for the PEN Prison Committee event which is on Thursday. It took me hours and hours and hours of experimenting with type face, size, spacing, etc. I will never, ever, do that again.

Have been partying since Friday, also, when I went to hear my friend Dagoberto Gilb read as part of a Latino writers festival that PEN put on. Managed to get drunk and stay out until one. Got up early to go to yoga but found out at last minute that there was none. Then went out last night to hear some other Latino writers and ended up hanging out until 3:30 in the morning. Now you *know* I'm too old to do that. But I got up at 9:30 and worked on this fucking program again and then went to the Public Theater with Lisa to see 2 Adrienne Kennedy plays. If you've never read anything of hers you might like to. She's very nonrealistic so I don't know how they read but she also has published a beautiful autobiog called *People Who Led To My Plays*. Anyway she herself was there today, it was closing day. Lisa interviewed her a few weeks ago for the *Voice* so they had spoken of me. I'd forgotten that she won an Obie Award same year as *Dutchman*—she took my hand and happily said, "Last time I saw you was in 1964 and you were so happy and were wearing a beautiful hat!" I was so touched that she would remember me!

It's raining and if I don't go to bed I will pass out. I have no further news about my book except that I did call Grove Press and I did call my agent so I have at least made some attempt to set things in motion.

Good night!

It was Dagoberto who had introduced me to the editors at Grove, who'd expressed interest in publishing a paperback to keep on their backlist, in the company of many of the writers whose books I'd worked on so many years before. Fanon, Duras, Genet—a long list I never kept. I suddenly wanted this like crazy.

Happy Mother's Day, Gram!

Oh what a week—I'm so glad it's over. Stood out in the burning sun this morning for 2½ hours at Columbus Circle as part of a rally to protest incarceration of mothers, at which I read poetry—and got a sunburned nose and chest! Very exciting though—the borough president spoke, our senator, representative, and Ossie Davis among others!

I cannot work another minute, have been somewhere or done something every single night since I last wrote you. Party given by my new agent to celebrate 20 yrs of being in business, Weds. Then Thurs the PEN Prison Writing Event complete with nervousness about program, then dinner with the PEN people. But it was successful, and scored points. A *wonderful* poet named Marie Ponsot read for us.

Yesterday a book party for one of my students (I didn't stay long, but still . . .)

Trouble with all this partying is people ask what you're up to and you have to tell them. Then it gets real and they get expectant. If you're lying, you feel like shit.

Let me know how you are.

And happy M's day to you in return.

I am exhausted & going to bed—been working on a rainy-day dream mask—mixing pigments that when mixed w/my mash end up not what I want & I'm totally frustrated & tired & depressed, but not—because I'm venturing on a new way of working—so I'm excited & depressed all at once—Going to Ket's for M Day brunch at 11:00am tomorrow—will sit down and talk one day soon—Yes!

G'night—your week's schedule makes me dizzy!

Hello! That was so much fun—to have an unexpected phone call!

This is to explain that I've started the process of getting rights back to *How I Became*. I just got fed up and Grove said they were still interested.

It's making me nervous.

Hope your process problems get sorted out. But how fortunate to have an obsession, I think, even though it drives you crazy.

GLOUCESTER, 21 MAY 1996 12:45AM—HOPE YOU'RE PEACEFULLY ASLEEP

Have had an incredible week & book coming tomorrow from Carroll & Graf so I've been tonight cleaning off the debris from all over my house to make that kind of work space possible, but got interrupted w/phone calls and Jane was here yesterday and I've been working on this mask and finally figured out how to make my own beads to hold feathers and that took a lot! of time and I had an opossum! on my porch (thought I was hallucinating, but knew I wasn't after he went back down the steps & I went out onto the porch to look & tell myself I was really OK and watched him meander around the maple tree just like my cats do. *Well.* I just ain't never *seen* an opossum, read abt. them a lot, but never had a description—and here in the middle of the city.

Also got waked up (after going to bed at 3am) by sound of phone at 6:15. Went back to sleep knowing if it was emergency I'd be called back—found fax on my floor from Coca Cola Bottles Philippines, Inc. asking for Jim Buckley's "best quote for one unit Alexus Sniffer complete w/the usual spare parts, kits commissioning and training."

And then I had a bird in my house—that took some 3 hrs. & the help of my neighbor to set free—

P.S. You've never told me abt. Minneapolis—reading??

PPS—if you stick this upside down on yr wall it might be more interesting than reading it right side up!

GLOUCESTER, 5/29/96 7:40PM

Hope yr home—how do I deal w/this?

> "He just called me," Jordan told the old maid Bernie had as a secretary. Taylor decided years ago that no one would have willingly

worked around dead bodies as long as she had if they'd possessed the personality to acquire a less gruesome job.

What do I say—"something less male chauvinistic"? I really want to make a notation but not sure how to put it. Help!!!

You could remind the author that terms like "old maid" are now found offensive by at least some of the people who read his books, and he shouldn't risk offending his readers (and losing sales). Also he should try to summon a little empathy for any working person who spends her years in a morgue; a job is hard to get these days. She might be supporting someone, how does he know? If he wrote a character sketch for that person, would he give her a *completely* vile life? If so, he is a schmuck and a fartface and should stop publishing. I could go on!

Hello, finally—!!!!

I am home having had a glorious time.[5] I got tremendous applause— I mean the most applause I've ever gotten in my life—sure does make you humble. Allen G. was really good too.

It's too late and I'm too tired, just wanted to tell you it was a terrific program.

We had record rain yesterday, at least some of which came in through my skylight. But tonight it's cool and I've been working for myself all day—business but still mine and that felt good. Then I rode to the Battery and looked at the bay and the gulls and the fog and the condom in the water and rode home and back to work, phone, etc.

What's with you? How are you and what are you doing?

• • • • •

Like many divorced women, Helene and I had sometimes to deal with the reappearance of our former husbands. I had just been through such an event

---

5. A speech at the Guthrie Theatre in Minneapolis, program in conjunction with the Whitney Museum's *Beat Culture and the New America* exhibit, which had traveled to the Walker Art Center.

when I wrote, on June 30th of that year, "Well, you've lived through it, despite it," and then went on:

But doesn't it always leave a . . . residue of feeling? Took me *days* to get over that snub from Roi this spring. But I did, as you will. Why??? That's my answer to your "After some 25 or so years, why?" I can't imagine anyone ever getting over it, though they do. But why can't the hurt just vanish? You got me, kid. I think we've done our level best to banish it. It's just a *situation*. It's something to carry, and that's that.

Write me if you have time but mainly try to chill, absorb yourself in something mindless while your mind heals. "Become a pearl / of a girl / yeah momma!" (Hee hee, isn't it great to have a poem for an occasion?)

Hope you're asleep, resting, reading, something, anything but brooding. But if brood you must, then do it to the max—and then it'll be done, it'll get *boring*. Good night!

A LITTLE LIGHT VERSE FOR HELENE

This was the first verse about us—
Heartbreak Hardship Humiliation
(cross the nation)

And this was the worst verse about us—
in/ in the teeth of it g(gritting ours
the bite it took the meat from our
      bones   poems

But the last and best is a little light verse about us—
the sea light around us
the light your glass pictures
soak, spill as we make
   light of it

glaze that core with a bright shine
become a pearl of a girl, yeah momma!

the way your glass holds light
we take hold take the light
   heart

Hullo . . .

I'll talk about it all later, just to thank you. For always being there . . . yeah, Momma.

Love, H

8

We make too much history.
With or without us

there will be the silence
and the rocks and the far shining.

But what we need to be
is, oh, the small talk of swallows . . .

in the present tense, in the present tense.

— *Ursula Le Guin*

I can't sit down at machine because I've been dealing w/print all day & I want to sit here at kitchen table & not look at another printed word.

Fred & Steph off to the west coast for 12 days—Lorna sending me $500 to come visit in October—plus a whole lot else that has my head whirling—wish we were just sitting around the kitchen table so I could spill it all out & you cld respond. Yeah, Momma!

Hello it's late but I've had coffee!

I wish we were at the kitchen table too and I'm hoping to get there. This morning I finished all but the 2 last chapters of Alexander's book, and he turned in the recipes separately, bless him, and his agent, who was pushing, is off on vacation.

It's been raining since morning—hard at times. Everything damp damp damp, fishy, rain coming off the sea.

Will you go to Seattle in October? That would be great! When you can read again, *Krik Krak* by Edwidge Danticat.

Almost midnight—Rabbits, etc.

Love!

Evning, Mizz Jones . . .

S. O. Jewett—have you read her? I mean lately? I have to thank her for getting me through this period in my life.

G'night . . . 10:10, yr fax just here. We're both tired from different things. Ain't it sompthin' that there's that care across states . . . I am ok but not ok, and nobody but you all those miles away has any sense of it.

Mas tarde!

Hello—Great that you were writing me last night just as I was thinking of you. I was majorly tired.

I don't think I've ever read Sarah Orne Jewett, unless excerpts in feminist text. But I really can't remember. I was just thinking about all the things I haven't done in my life (like travel), and high on that list is reading books I've never had time for and seeing movies. Almost wish I were an insomniac.

I've been so distracted that this week I 1) tried to get on the subway with $1.25 when the fare has been $1.50 all this year, and 2) forgot that to get on the bus one needs exact change. These events occurred Tues and Weds and made me feel terrifyingly senile (my worst fear, of course, considering my mother and aunt went that route).

I haven't told you about the "family" reunion.[1] The drive there was grueling, as the hotel people had said "under 2 hours" and I found myself late and having to speed to make it to lunch. Most interesting encounter was with the man whose daughter has had 3 interracial children (I had been begged, literally, to come talk to these people). The daughter, a high school dropout, first kid at 16, etc. was present but not the kids. Her father admitted to me that his wife did not show photos of her grandchildren to anyone besides "family," e.g. did not show them to co-workers, etc. And he and his wife are both *schoolteachers!* When he said that, it was as though a gate went down—BAM!! Anyway I managed to escape by 9:30pm and drove as fast as possible but did not get home until after midnight. . . .

---

1. Some of my father's cousins had found me and asked if I'd drive up to a hotel in the Catskill Mountains to meet them.

I have signed the new book contract with Grove Press.[2]

It promises to be a good sleeping night; my wind chimes are blowing, a good sign. Wish I were in your kitchen drinking the 4th beer of the night and talking shit in general. Maybe I've never learned enough about *carpe diem*—I should drive up to see you one day on the spur of the moment. But I promise to call first!!

Hope this finds you in good spirits despite windows that won't open and etc etc.

GLOUCESTER, 8/11/96

Well jeez, keed, how very nice it wld be if you just appeared at my kitchen door, like Jane W.! (She did leave an hour's notice on my answering machine but I wasn't here to get it till ten minutes before there she was, in all her smiling wonderfulness, on my porch hollering "Are you home?") So please do come, and spur-of-the-moment will save me a lot of cleaning time—we'll just set in my dirt and enjoy. Yeah.

Thank you! for last night's long letter. Don't worry abt. senility, H.J.—I wld be a basket case after all that.

5:45 p.m. Took time out to call Marie. It ended up being a long call. We've not written or talked to one another for months. I'm playing Vivaldi's *"L'Estro Armonico"* which my brother sent me how many years ago. I don't know nothing abt. music but there are sections of Vivaldi that make me think of Coltrane.

Please do come.

NEW YORK, 8/11/96

Hello again, this is a quick one because I'm having a Personal Day! Thank you, I wd love to come, of course it all depends on Alexander.

Last night about midnight I decided that what I needed to do was slow down, so I let myself sleep and then rode bike to Macy's and bought Lisa her birthday present. It was lovely this morning and I stopped on the way to say hello to the bike man I flirted with all last summer while looking for the bike I never bought. He reached to shake my hand and then kissed me—almost on the lips, I caught the corner—oh!

---

2. For a *How I Became* reprint.

Then I came home and replaced the mildewed shower curtains in my bathroom with supposedly mildew-proof ones that I bought six months ago and never had time to . . . etc. Also fixed electric switch. Also fixed (temporarily) the top hinge on the bathroom door. Doing this shit makes me deliriously happy.

Then I wrote letters,* worked on last version of Chap 17, made copy for Alexander, rode it to his apartment at Madison Square. Met another handsome man** on the way home, an artist. Talked art shit with him. Came home and ate a humungous bowl of salad, watered my little garden, wrote more letters, and *then* worked on my stories for the past hour or so, which I'm beginning to like again . . . A perfectly lovely day.

Now I'm going to finish *Krik Krak* which has been good all the way through, I'm happy to say.

Love and kisses, H

*Sent note to Marie with titles of Marie Ponsot books.

**He kissed cheek 2x, having lived in Europe long. All NYers doing that now, pretentiously, most.

Having managed to get there—to Gloucester—I have no idea what transpired, see below:

GLOUCESTER, 8/30/96 4PM

Hello—

I've been meandering about in a stupor, doing bits of errands—we drank, each of us, 4½ 16 oz. bottles of beer between 9:30pm and 3+a.m.— I glad I didn't check this morning! Rest up if you can, Mama—I love you, thank you for coming!

NEW YORK, 9/1/96 RABBITS RABBITS RABBITS!!!

4½ beers—how could we have done that? I'm amazed!

NEW YORK, 9/8/96

I bought the *Collected Poems of Kay Boyle* (all out of print until this edition):

"ADVICE TO THE OLD (INCLUDING MYSELF)"

... Do not dwell on other times as different from the time
whose air we breathe ...
Have no communion with despair; and, at the end,
Take the old fury in your empty arms, sever its veins,
And bear it fiercely, fiercely to the wild beast's lair.

GLOUCESTER, 9/8/96

Kay Boyle!!

Reading Breyten Breytenbach for the first time.

Breytenbach quoting Jean Genet: "The Blacks in white America are the signs writing history: on the white page they are the ink giving it meaning."

Well there's a lot more, but I need to eat my garbage soup and get some sleep.

NEW YORK, 9/10/96

Hello — this is in answer to two of yours, no three I think. First to thank you for the funny story by Margaret Atwood, a welcome entertainment yesterday, at some point when I managed to sit down.

Today I taught my first class at Parsons. Last year I had 10, this year I have 25 students. 25 students in a writing workshop. It's insane. I have the responsibility to teach each of these kids for 15 weeks, and I get little more than $100 for each one. It's total exploitation. How will I manage to hear their work and criticize it every week when I have only 2½ hrs — and within that a 10–15 minute break? They all seemed so interested, it breaks my heart to think they're getting such short shrift.

NEW YORK, 9/12/96

Well I've done the Killer Day. Am totally wired on coffee, but the NYS-CA[3] meeting was okay, and now I am sorrowful because that was the last meeting I can attend, and much more fun people have just appeared, including nice, smart, not-uptight white guys, whom I seldom meet and

---

3. New York State Council on the Arts, where I had been serving on the Literature Panel.

would like to meet again. Interestingly, from upstate. Friendly men, with sparkly eyes and easy bodies. And Elizabeth Murray's second husband — remember she used to live downstairs from me with her first? — anyway her second is Bob Holman,[4] one of the nicest men on the planet. He recently had a TV program called "The United States of Poetry" which of course I missed, but maybe it's out in video. And that reminds me that Jessica Hagedorn's new book is called *The Gangster of Love*.

Last night I was going to ask you whether you'd called C&G lately, but it turns out I didn't need to ask. Hope the book you're getting is something good, and if not, something that'll at least piss you off with its ghastly mistakes!

GLOUCESTER, 9/14/96

Hello —

A novel abt. filmmaking, clean ms., good copyeditor, interesting reading, author is trying to say a lot & I'm curious to see if he pulls it all together. I'm only 80 pgs into 289 . . .

Standing here looking at the little mask I was working on when the proof work arrived. It's driving me crazy because it says it close-up, but across the room it's a blob.

According to my calendar it's Rosh Hashanah — I always thought it was Rosh Hosannah — !

NEW YORK, 9/17/96

Hello, I'm alive! Sitting here with a sweatshirt draped over my head because the house is still open, and fall is pouring in on this wave of dampness. . . .

It's 11:05 and I just wanted to let you know I'd survived another Killer Day. The only mess was riding my bike home from Parsons, on a very wet seat. But later there was such a cute 3-month-old baby at the subway station, who smiled at me. Don't know that those are two opposing events, but here they are!

---

4. Bob Holman went on to found the Bowery Poetry Club and to host *Language Matters*, a TV film on endangered languages.

MEMO

DATE: 9/28/96

TO: LA COMANDANTE JONES

FROM: LA COMADRE DORN

RE: REPORT 17:58

Monday Yom Kippur—book packed up and sent to C&G. Urine sample packed up & sent by Yellow Cab for $8.00, one dollar less than if I'd taken it myself by cab, thank you for advice. Got workspace back to normal and spent a lot of time reading abt. my new Vitamix totaljuice machine.

Tuesday—Orange juice plus for breakfast. Housecleaning again due to fleas. Still studying book re: machine.

Wednesday—I'm sorry, La Comandante, I can't remember. Think that was day John P. from library lent me his own 2 books on Eisenstein. One of the blessings of small-town living. I'd asked him abt. the *Que Viva Mexico* video. It was the film I wanted to see again (some shots take my breath away), but the one book on the shooting of the film has big format & lotsa pics . . . The book is so pristine and I usually read while I eat and tho I'm careful, I just might splash some Totaljuice or Totalsoup. . . .

Thursday—Checked 2 mo's worth of bank statements and paid bills. Tested more juice and soup. Decided to keep Vitamix machine if only that it does clean itself and I therefore keep my kitchen clear because I can't bear to throw 1½ cups of hot detergented water down the sink so I pour it into my plastic dishwashing container and wake up to a clean counter— that's worth 369$.

Friday—Mopped and vacuumed again and did the Laundromat, thinking I should probably spend $ to have house defleaed. Checked receipts: 7/29/88, 8/31/92, so I guess it's time again. Got hungry for something sweet at midnight & made a strawberry yogurt freeze which I didn't process long enough in machine so it was sort of crunchy, but next time I'll know better. Sent check for machine off today. I'm committed to Vitamix.

Saturday—here I am, OK. I can't believe it's almost October. Met young man I worked with all those years ago (in the cemetery), in the parking lot of the Star Market. Hey, Helene, did you see the lunar eclipse? No, I didn't. He promised to call me in 2001 the next time. . . . If we're both still here. He assured me we both would be. Such a sweet young man. While we were working in the cemetery he'd told me about using dogs in

Vietnam . . . he can touch plants and make them grow. And while he was pruning trees he fell from some incredible feet, came out of it, and as he explained to me, again in the parking lot, he can't remember some things, names, etc. But he got mine right.

OK Comandante, here you are. I'm going to make a vegetable soup — no, I don't microwave it, it cooks in the machine. I am OK. Just totally spaced.

P.S. The moon is still lovely—not full, but bright inside all the floating cloud covers—g'night!

NEW YORK, 10:40PM SEPT SOMETHING

Thank you for the long missive! Sorry for barking orders at you . . . I didn't know the machine could *cook* too!

Yesterday a wonderful event: My neighbor George's nephew Tracy has been living here for a while, a pleasant, quiet young man. Turns out he can fix things, so I asked him to fix shower head. Well, I have these new windows . . . opened the bottom part and realized I'd completely forgotten how to clean the top. Called Tracy in a panic: he came up and cleaned all four, then fixed my bathroom door so it closes for the first time in maybe 10 years. Shower head is next, and I can think of *many* things. I hope he doesn't move away!

I loved your story about the young man you met in the parking lot.

Love to the Machine Wizard of Soup! And to You!

GLOUCESTER, 10/1/96

Can't quickly answer to your frustration over not writing—You *are* getting on w/yr life . . . Anyway that's a consideration I need to think about for myself, & a whole philosophical question: what *is* getting on w/your life? Scrubbing floors, mebbe; if it makes you feel good.

NEW YORK, 10/1/96

Hello again. I am unwinding by writing to you the way I used to when I was young, when everyone was finally asleep and out of my way and I could *think*. I suppose there wasn't as much to think *about* then, except my total responsibility for everyone else and my shame at neglecting myself.

While cleaning my study I discovered I didn't have too many copies of *Big Star* left. Then began thinking that I'd *never* rec'd a royalty statement since publication in Jan 1995. So I called royalty dept, and discovered that not only had the book earned back its advance, Viking Press owes me $648 and three weeks ago sent it to ICM, the agent for original book [published 1974]. ICM pocketed money! My editor at Viking has left the company. But I called editorial, finally got someone in charge, told him this, wondered how many books were left because I wanted some, and then casually mentioned that former editor had said there'd be a paperback if sales went well. "Oh," sez he, "that's already in the works, it'll be published in Feb. '97!" "What!" I scream. "You didn't even notify me?" Well the paperback editor says she sent me a copy of the brand new cover on 9/5. Possibly she did and it got lost in the mail, but for shit sure I never got it. Anyway the guy, exec editor or something, I forget his title, messengered me a copy of cover, which is LOUD!!! But fine, let it be, the blues are hot too.

Tomorrow after various errands I can come home and vacuum some more and wash the floor in my sitting room where I never sit because I don't have time. I know you must think I'm crazy but it just makes me too *sad*, like I'm not being nice to myself, when the dirt is too disgusting.

None of this is addressing the "What is getting on with your life?" question. But I did have fun on the subway today. A man and a woman next to me had an argument because she, sitting down, didn't say "excuse me," and he accused her of sitting on him and having no manners. Which got into a question of family. She told him she was old enough to be his mother, no his grandmother, she corrected herself, but he didn't give a shit, he said, only that she respect him. Last words: "I know who your father is." "You don't know nothing." No one, of course, intervened, least of all me, hidden behind my dark dark shades, feigning sleep. I could see them *both* hauling off and slugging me if I said something!

GLOUCESTER, 10/2/96 . . . 8 SOMPTHIN P.M.

No, I don't think you're crazy; cleaning is cleansing. I've got the cleaning in my head, but I'm totally crazy. . . .

And I'm NOT doing any work in studio though I think about it a lot; I'm working w/my head but not w/my hands. So what. Again this is philosophical . . . all those things I've done with my hands, who sees them, & if nobody does, what's the point? I ask myself that a lot, but when I'm working that's not on my mind; I'm just totally involved in what I'm doing.

How you deal with all that shit you deal with I don't know!

Here is my lecture:

Even if you are not working in your studio and are working in your head you are working. Writers do that shit all the time and no one criticizes them for chrissakes. And the point — if there's any point to art — is in the doing. You know that, that total involvement you mentioned. It makes one's *self*. And your things *do* get seen, wherever they land.

I think you should *make* yourself start something in the studio, and then what will immediately happen is a book to copyedit will come and you'll have to put shit away and will get angry!

Got a psychic card reading at Ket's yesterday . . . have never done that before. Nice 40ish woman w/no come-on. Told me to start working w/my hands. Well, there's more . . .

What you need is a microwave so you can cook when you have time, freeze it and then zap it. My machine is wonderful! It makes hot soup in something like 5 mins. . . .

10:15pm — Say hello to SanFran for me.

Hello!

Much to say about California . . . it wasn't as exciting a trip as it could have been — largely because all the *real* action had gone on the previous weekend: Ginsberg, David Amram, DiPrima, so I was on the "B" list.

Wanted to write tonight but I think I should not sit up at computer. Tomorrow for sure . . . Cover of new Grove memoir is *beautiful*. Will fax. Designer was so amenable to slight changes. I felt blessed.

Re California trip: Day began at 9:30 a.m. with radio show, which was okay but I didn't get to go on 2x as planned because some asshole fake beatnik was jiving with dark glasses and a "jazz" band . . . oh California.

Then I signed copies of the beat women anthology that's coming out, in the museum, but no one who worked there had any responsibility for me. So editor of the book took me out to lunch, finally, at 3:30. Panel at six, I was the only one prepared with a text. Asked, the moderator shrugged. I thought we'd just talk, she said. Hadn't been told I'd give a presentation, so she was so glad, and put me on first. Bullshit. To her credit she took pity on me and drove me back to hotel, because no arrangement had been made to get me back from Golden Gate Park at 8:30 at night. On the plane I wrapped myself in blankets and read *Push* by Sapphire which Joyce had lent me, and some of *Loverboys* by Ana Castillo, which got better as it went on.

Monday I bought some Chartreuse, my friend Marilyn Colvin's cure for any respiratory ailment. I swear it worked! I think I am normal but there's still something wrong with my head, and I think it's the sin of pride, which always worried me as a child. That I fell into feeling bad about being on the "B" list of beats is a sign of moral decay. No one should be attached to shit like that, but then it has continued to happen: At the next SF show, in November, where the beat women book is to be celebrated, I am on the panel I have decided to call The First Wives Club, but of course Anne Waldman and Diane DiP are not paneling, but reading their work. So I whined at the editor today and was told I was indeed reading other places, but that no one had made this clear to me. Oh California. Still, that needle again. Known for one's liaisons, not one's work. And of course I realized once again that in that scene I will never be anything else.

I suppose this is how you finally develop humility, by fits and starts, but it's weird, usually I don't have that trouble, never feel competitive, or left out, or whatever. Have so much to be thankful for, proud of, etc.

Hope you are well in your clean digs. Hope the electrician didn't make you wait all day. It was a beautiful warm day here. I hung clothes on the roof and stood looking at all my dying plants, not guiltily. They seem to be enjoying the twilight of their lives. How hateful I am!

I made garbage soup today, first of the season, and thought of you. At the greenmarket there were all kinds of little kids interviewing the farmers, walking around with clipboards!

I think you should do what that psychic says. I find that the longer I stay away from what I'm supposed to be doing the more difficult it is to get the balls to come back to it, and the terrible shame just builds in you and fucks up your head. It's a great relief to just *do* it, makes you feel so much better, like the human being you think you are in your best moments.

Now I'm a dead pigeon.

GLOUCESTER, 10/17/96

Moral decay, bullshit—that needle pricks & I don't think it's a matter of pride, really, tho' mebbe yes, but how many of us are Zen "saints." It's easy enough to know better, but not so easy to stop emotions. Humility, I mean *real* humility, that you feel inside, I'm sure you're right, has to come in fits and starts. I dunno, I've often thought of going on some kind of retreat to get a real sense of what a small speck I am, get out of myself & into the universe (that sounds New Age but I've thought abt it long before New Age—see, these days you can't even take a breath w/o its being labeled).

NEW YORK 10/17/96

The reading tonight was really good, I'm happy as a pig in shit. 30–35 in the audience, maybe. Then I rode my bike home, slowly, wearing helmet (always helmet in the dark, always slowly), in the incredibly warm October night, and up the stairs waiting was your fax with its wonderful encouragement. My first thought was what would I do without it? Once a student asked, "Who nurtured you?" (in the days when nurture was that new word) and I said "myself," but I think that's not entirely true, though of course we both "nurtured ourselves" because no one else was around— all of which is to say I appreciate you, your fine intelligence, the way you read things. A pearl of a girl, you!

Re: "It's easy enough to know better, but not so easy to stop emotions." This is true, but since I can't bear the pain/worry that comes when I feel bad, I work with great haste to get out of what's causing it. So I trace it back to my own pride—true humility means you do have to get rid of that ego, no you have to ride it first and then laugh at it. I'm so convinced of the mind-body connection that just coming to the decision to get over it—or this particular manifestation—is a great relief. I *have* thought about "the sin of pride" since I was in elementary school and learned the term from Joan Sullivan, my Catholic friend. Because of my family, and how they felt about things, and how threatened I felt they were by my accomplishments, I learned to curb myself very very early. I have guilty memories of when I failed to. So it seems I flew out to SF as a Beat Queen and found I could be, well, less. And I *am* less, we're all less, and it doesn't matter. Of course I'm also saying this under the influence of a shot of that wonderful tasting Chartreuse and a couple of tokes, after a successful performance. Still, we're hardly talking "literary establishment" here — this is not the 92nd St. Y, where I'm only a teacher, but a downtown below Canal St. coffee shop!

Am reading 2 books — *The Art of Fiction* by David Lodge, which Joyce reminded me to read, and which is just wonderful. And the memoir *Paula* by Isabel Allende, which seems to be good, haven't read much of it yet.

Why *don't* you go on a retreat — not New Agey, people have been retreating since before the term, it's more like Old Agey, among the religious, no?

Let me know also about computer, when you might get it. Now I'm going to read either one or both of those books, drink tea and eat an apple and then fall out. I love you —

GLOUCESTER, 10/19/96

Just quickly to say I appreciate you, too, Mama — Yeah! Watch that Chartreuse —

Gilles, in Spain, introduced me to it, respiratory conditions far from his mind — did I ever write or talk to you abt. him? My gigolo lover who introduced me to that whole (very French) underworld & kept me from learning Spanish because he wanted to bone up on his English . . . But he was otherwise a friend in my time of need. Whew! haven't thought about him for a long time — or that spell in Sitges —

Storm [Hurricane Josephine] coming, whirling winds but no rain yet. I think abt those Cubans who got the brunt of it & this stupid country's boycott — oh yes, the U.S. is so interested in human rights —

NEW YORK, 10/20—OOPS VERY LATE

Yeah, the whole thing about Cuba makes you sick, right? Have you read Reinaldo Arenas? *Before Night Falls*. His view of it, but anything is better than the policy we have now. I saw a photo of women with foam mattresses on their way to some shelter, human rights, yes.

Speaking of photos, Fred McDarrah has a new book on the Beats, and there is the most wonderful photo of me that I had never seen. I am sneaking a hug from behind off Remy Charlip, one of my favorite people, and he is turning in pleased surprise, it's just so great and I still had teeth! (You know that one, I know.) God, that shit makes getting old a bit easier—at least I *once* was cute! And you—*beautiful!*

It's raining again. I hope you didn't get swamped up there. I think I'll have some Chartreuse in honor of your gigolo.

GLOUCESTER 10/24/96

Rain was coming in my house thru windows and the fireplace in studio . . .

I am an old crone and I take offense at your saying "I *once* was cute"—that's a pile of bullshit and you otta know better—what's your head going? Zapping into the media-youth syndrome? Why are you worried abt. getting old? It happens. And it has its compensations, like *not* worrying abt. lost teeth, etc. Oh!!! If you were here in my kitchen I'd "shake you till your head rattles"!

NEW YORK, 10/24/96

OH! I have been corrected!

Actually, the reason for the cute business—I got the contact sheets of photos taken of me last week, and honey, what can I say? Not as cute. I think the photographer was attempting something that wasn't working—and I've been looking a bit tired lately because—I am tired! But I'm over it, I promise, mama.

Last night after Bedford I went up to friends Marilyn and Peter in Pawling, and today we walked 3 miles to town and then back and then ate wonderful soup and then I drove home just as calm and peaceful as can be. And oh the leaves—there were 2 red maples on the way, and that smell . . . So I've been on a minivacation and tomorrow I have to work 9:30–5:30 in an ad agency, so hopefully it won't be too bad. And I have Parsons homework for the down time . . .

Croney! You're a crone in the marshes, singing—like my poem![5]

---

5. "Aftertune," *Drive* (1998).

Hullo . . .

Just changed all my clocks. Kitchen & wrist say 7:45. Fax sez 19:43, phone sez 7:42, VCR, 7:48. At least it's all p.m. I hate these time changes, but it was nice to get some "extra" sleep. Wish you'd been here to see the huge moon rising tonight—I was making a quick cig. run, and it stoppt me, in the middle of Middle St.—a slice less than full.

Hello—just arrived from prison in a foul mood because the guard at the gate, a woman who's usually nice, refused to look for my misfiled ID, which meant that I had to get another guard to escort me, since without ID I'm not permitted to walk alone.

That stupid *Women of the Beat Generation* book came today and I really can't bear to look at it. Under my name I'm called "Mother Jones." Of course only people of a certain age will know that Mother Jones was a radical,[6] no one will see anything but the literal meaning, just as forever my poem ["Hard Drive"] will be called "teddy bears on the highway." I don't know how I'm going to get through this trip [to San Francisco] without getting angry, since I already have such a good start.

This is to say hello and I'll certainly write when I return Mon night. If psychic said for you to go out, that's fine, but if your psyche says fix house, fix house. You know what I mean?

Hello! I'm exhausted & have laryngitis, but it was a good trip. Am trying not to get sicker.

Will write soon.

And I'd promised myself I'd start working with the sun but here I am still up . . . mostly because I got mesmerized with the media reporting of the election [Bill Clinton vs. Bob Dole] . . . Went to kitchen door to let Chili [new cat] in, and THERE WAS A POSSUM ON MY PORCH AGAIN!

---

6. Mary Harris "Mother" Jones, prominent American labor and community organizer.

Advice from an old lady: mebbe you should let yourself get sick for a day. Just rest. There is a ladybug crawling all over my machine as I write . . . whew. ladybugs and possums.

I sure don't want you to get sicker, so think abt. what I sd. above. . . .

Hello . . . I still haven't really come to because I don't I know where to come to *to*. I just made a list of everything that had to be done over the weekend so that I won't be worried about reading at Modern on Tues night, which is of course to me a big deal so I'd better be good. . . . Your advice to rest well taken, mama. I did *not* sweep the hall or water my plants, I sat still all day and then had a nice walk to PEN in rather warm air.

I just read somewhere a letter telling of an infestation of ladybugs, and though I don't recall the exact explanation, it had to do with looking for warmth. Probably the possum on your porch looking for same thing — hey, maybe *you* are the peaceable kingdom!

Did you ever know Joanna McClure? She was on the panel in SF with Joyce and me and made many good points.

I still haven't written much about SF. Sat afternoon was panel, a huge crowd, and then Sat night a reading at Borders, not well attended, after which long dinner . . . On Sunday Joyce and I took a cable car to Nob Hill and then walked all through the streets down to Chinatown, where we met Tillie Olsen for lunch! She is totally weird and scattered but such a lovely woman, and so kind. Told her the story about William Phillips at *Partisan* saying "What?! You've never read Tillie Olsen!" and me spending my lunch hour reading "I Stand Here Ironing."

I think I'm going to sneak a look at one of my unfinished, maybe never-to-be finished, poems because it's 11:15pm. In my flaming youth that was about the time I'd have my second cup of coffee of the night, and then that silence wld settle all around me, and then I'd have the third about 1 a.m. Oh memory . . .

Marie Ponsot is 75 and her next book is coming out in 1998. She is reading poetry for the Prison Writing Contest. Still my hero!

OK. To kitchen to make tea, put up feet, read some of Isabel Allende. Hope you are well. Weird weather here, too warmish and the air dirty. I'm looking for the rain and then the wind. Indians called north wind the cleansing wind, I remember. Yeah, we need it. Big love to you, mama!

7:25pm & I've no idea where yesterday & today have gone!

Not sure abt. Joanna McClure . . . just really remember Michael's elegant talking bird. That time is so fuzzy in my head re: women . . . It was so much all men. In fact, the police (2) came one night. Ed was out working, driving for the Mafia. There I stood at the top of the 3 flights of stairs, aproned & trying to deal with the kids in the bath having slopped water over the sides which went into apt. below whose occupants called the police because they thought I was running a house of ill-repute & the water was a good excuse. The police were stern at first, came up a few steps, threatening—but I was exasperated trying to clean up the water and take care of the kids and I started shouting at them and they retreated and actually apologized . . . Well, it's understandable those downstairs neighbors wondering about what was going on in our apt. Men, and men only, coming up and down our stairs at all hours of the day or night.

I envy you all those walks in SF. I envy you SF period. How I did love that city!

Hey! You had lunch with Tillie Olsen . . . in what way is she "totally weird and scattered"?

T. Olsen dominates conversation and talks compulsively, goes off on weird tangents in a soft voice, almost like someone who can't finish a thought. I thought *Silences* had a bit of that. But she was so nice, so affectionate.

End of my page! Will let you know about MoMa—

I'm thinking about you—want to have a "hello, trust it was a grand success!" waiting for you on your return . . .

I know I should be in bed, but I was *starving* when I got home, and Lisa was here and starving, so we went out to eat and then I just came back and did stuff and now all I need to do is brush my teeth and fall out. . . .

The reading was great! All my old students came, and my new ones from the Y, and the place (the museum café) was pleasant and they had free soda and pretzels . . . And Ed Sanders was terrific with his little stringed instrument. And there was really quite a crowd—more than a hundred, I'd say, though I'm not good at guessing . . .

Anyway this is just to say thank you for that fax, waiting for me—

Love!

5:25pm and I'm waiting on chicken soup I'm making because you and Paul, who has terrible cold, passed on over the phone whatever bug is causing all this . . .

Hullo!

Glad it went well, but of course I knew it would. Just a few notations while my ailing body waits for soup. I'd been to the Sal. Army store, just on instinct, to check books, abt. a week before you went to SF. Found Robert and Jane Coles' *Women of Crisis*. First thing I did when I got home was to read Tillie Olsen's "One Out of Twelve," which I remembered . . . written in 1971, it's still timely. Anyway, Tillie Olsen has been with me for a couple of weeks, I've reread *Yonnondio* (I wish I knew how to pronounce it), and so it was a rush for me when you wrote you'd met her for lunch.

Well, the soup is done, and I'm going to put my almost-70 body to bed. Trying to get to the S.F. memories . . . I do have a faint memory of Joanna, but my head comes up with their Mynah bird and dramatic Michael . . . I remember he pissed me off with his dramatics—I was too much involved with trying to keep things together to relax and enjoy him.

San Francisco, whew!

Oh no, now *you're* sick!

Yo *non* dee oh. Which I just loved so much, for its subject, the quality of the writing. When we had lunch, she (T.) complained about not being able to write, to sustain anything. Joyce admitted to me that T.O. was reworking things endlessly, that she couldn't give things up. Well I know about that problem, since I also have it, but it's not enough to make you as seemingly scattered as she. Joyce says she has the teeniest tiniest handwriting she's ever seen. And, indeed, she carries teeny weeny writing pads, maybe 3×3 inches, eccentricity magnified I thought. Or reduced, in this case. Though I did so *like* her.

Hope my faxes haven't been too cantankerous . . . I'm in a weird period, mood. No patience for anything, screaming at my cats . . . who of course don't understand anymore than I do, why?

Meant to write last night but was tired from having worked both ends of the day. From 9 to 11:30am with Alexander going over the editor's queries and then at the prison at night.

Got up this morning and went to Alexander's by 9am once again, but he is so jovial and intelligent that we worked well and continuously for 3½ hrs until we were done. Yesterday he sent me home "like a Jewish aunt, always trying to feed you," he said — with a big plastic container of rice pilau with okra, corn, some kind of great sausage, and shrimp. There may have been more in it but I was too busy eating when I got home to notice!

Yes, you have been in a pissy mood, I have noticed, which — if you want my opinion but certainly have not solicited (wish I could put one of your little smiley faces right here) — could be due to not working and having no forward motion. You mention stuff in studio to be fixed and finished but not doing it or starting something new . . .

Anyway, that's the kind of feeling that drives me crazy and makes me cranky, so I'm just projecting here. Joyce called me this eve, returned from Shanghai — and she says I sound "uncranky" — though I was hardly that when she left —

Which I swear is because I wrote those poems last night, which are far from done, still they are there, and their "notdoneness" I find exciting. Before they are there, their lack of existence is first annoying, then grating (anger) and then terrifying. But I am 62 and not 69 so you are ahead of me in certain ways that I don't know.

Such beautiful weather. Frost on my car windows when I came out last night, and stars in the sky.

10:45 and I'm finding it hard to focus. Have you read Harriet Doerr's *Tiger in the Grass*. I just finished it. Good stuff, if you've read the other books, and we have. Little outtakes, were how I thought of them. But it's really great to read someone you don't want to edit!

... Me. A strange, overwhelming ennui I can't seem to come out of. There *is* a big difference between 62 and 69, I think. It's stupid psychological shit, but I do wonder if I'm dreading turning 70. Why? I really felt good about being 60 plus . . . alive and doing my thing. Alive in my head, with a kind of calmness that does come from years lived. Well, I've other things I've thought abt., like how frustrated I get when I read abt. things I want to see or do and nobody to do them with and no way to get there. I get totally depressed. Hettie, I'm stoned and will try to get my head right to write you later.

When did you start to feel this "strange overwhelming ennui"—it seems recent to me, very recent in fact. When you started making the masks you seemed "alive and doing your thing." When you mention "things I want to see or do and nobody to do them with and no way to get there"— it seems as if *no* avenues at all are left to you, and that can't be true. You spend more money on your cats than you do on Helene. Why don't you get on the train and go to Boston and look at art? And the work thing— have you called Adam Dunn? If not, why not? Can you get along w/o the proofing $$? But what I meant to say, most of all, is that it might be helpful to focus on what you *can* do. Reading about old people for years, I've come across countless admonitions to stay busy. I suspect I'll have to slow down some when I get to 69 but see the wisdom in the fight. I hope this is encouraging, since it's meant to be, and not nagging.

Just before Christmas, Helene wrote that she'd gotten a book to copyedit, banishing all talk of old age, ennui, etc. And I had good news to offer:

... My memoir with its new, beautiful cover is in the window of the St. Mark's Bookshop. Bless Grove Press, they really did exactly what they said they would do, get it out—

11:30pm The kids both arrived, and now they have left, with all their stuff and their wonderful energy and hugs . . .

And I'm glad to be alone.

Let me know how the book is progressing and whether it's gotten any better . . . and how everyone is up there . . .

Love and rockets (something K & L used to say!)

Hello & thanks for your letter which came thru with a lot of sentences unreadable—your machine or mine? Was up till after 2 a.m. finishing 1st run of book which got to be sort of relaxing, like watching an Errol Flynn adventure flick.

Nice! abt. yr. memoir in window . . . I'll order it and you can sign it next time you come . . . Xmas is absurd! I gotta stop. Lots more to say. Love! And rockets too!

9

When we learned the language our grandmothers
spoke
it was to weave fabric from past to future . . .
         the antiquated
language of dialects gone awry
Kitchen table talk. . . .
      On the table you put your feelings
      in a box and said they were whole. . . .
                   —*Ava Chin*

GLOUCESTER 1/16/97 10:45PM

Hello, my fingernails are stuffed with plastilina—but it feels good.

Re computer, I'd thought abt. getting a tutor . . . and will do when Fred checks out people he knows. No way am I going to answer an ad in the paper—I'm usually not uptight, but my instinct tells me I shld be now. I hate it. I've never locked a door in all my years . . . but now the door on Middle St. has to be locked—neighbor discovered someone smoking in the hall. He ran out the door—it was Xmas and so *cold*—But what can I say? It's true, someone like that cld set this house ablaze and old as it is it cld go so fast. So here I am locking, & it's a terrible drag.

Of course to me, an unlocked front door on a main street—even in a small city—was incomprehensible. But I see this as a marker: as we aged what hadn't seemed to make much difference—the seven years between us, our histories, and the directions our lives were taking—all gradually began to matter as much as our locations.

NEW YORK, 1/17/97

Was great to get yours of yesterday. Sorry you've had to start locking your door, but Gloucester I'm sure has a shelter, you don't have to be one. Write to the paper!

Rena was here today—did I remember to tell you she was coming? We had a fun lunch. Lives over her gallery, in two rooms, happily.

HarperCollins is doing a poetry anthology called *The Plain Truth of Things*, and wants the poem about my mother and father that was in *Hanging Loose*. Just got today the anthology *Ladies Start Your Engines* with 2 poems in it about driving, made me so very happy to see one of them especially, written in 1966 and never published anywhere.

Are you making a mask? I took a photo of the Black Monk at your house but it didn't come out. I like to imagine you working—it's cheerful!

We wrote nearly every day of 1997, close to a ream.

Hello—this is in answer to many of yours. I've been over my head . . .

And today I had the most wonderful conversation with a famous former New York City judge named Bruce Wright, who's going to be the keynote speaker for the PEN Prison Program Ceremony in April. He hated sentencing people to prison because he thought it did no good, so he was known as "Turn 'Em Loose Bruce," and the powers-that-be finally moved him from criminal to civil court. Anyway he was full of good humor and said, "I'm pretty old, I hope April comes soon so I can make this ceremony!" (He's 79.)

So you'll have to wait another 9 years before you can say you're old!

. . . flying in 18 different directions with nothing to hold them all together. Trying to keep early hours and it's a struggle to get out of bed when it's still half dark and cold. The people who do it have my respect, by golly.

Okay, let me know how you are now that you're Slick and Seventy!

I'm okay, just sloshing through 1st week of Seventies . . .

As for getting up in the dark cold—thanks for reminding me. I did that for a bunch of years, to the nursing home by 7am and to Senior Home Care by 8. Once I had to sit down and slide to the street, the front steps and walk solid ice. And then, when SHC moved, I had to be on Main St. to catch the 7:45am bus . . . So I feel better abt allowing myself my own time clock (I always feel a bit guilty), but I've paid my dues!

GLOUCESTER, 2/3/97

Finished mask last night . . . Printer unpacked, huge, and dismaying . . . Such a story! One big fiasco, my trying to enter the computer world. I order over phone, Hewlitt Packard fellow sd. you have a laptop, you want a portable . . . I sd yes . . . and I got next day this totally huge, unportable printer.

To me the computer meant words; as long as I could read, it suited me fine. Not so Helene—soon she fell head first into the visual. We had discussions about, of all things, emoticons; she discovered elaborate fonts with female names. "Love from me and *Desdemona*," she wrote one night. For the next few months she abandoned her studio and sat for hours, often staying up all night, trying to figure out everything the computer had to offer without benefit of Internet or any instruction. On February 6th she wrote, "I'm just so crazy trying to make this fabulous machine work," and as a sort of apology: "I love you, *if it would fax I'd do it in purple!* YEAH!"

· · · · ·

That year neither of my children was living in New York, though New York was often where they needed to be:

NEW YORK, 2/15/97 8:15PM

On Weds. Kellie called and asked to spend the night on Friday. She arrived yesterday morning at 10:30, then hung out with a friend, and then we had dinner together and then she went off to a party and I (finally) sat down to work on my reading. So it's 10:40pm and I'm at last concentrating when the phone rings and it's Lisa asking to spend the night as well. To make a long story somewhat short, I ended up undoing the futon carefully made up for one, and with Lisa's help remaking it on the floor for 2, getting out 2 sets of pajamas, head scarves, socks, extra pillow, etc., and didn't fall into bed until 1 a.m. having left note on door for Kellie: "Watch it! Sister in Bed!" Rushed off to yoga this morning though I would have loved to stick around with them, they're so *funny* . . .

Oh, I haven't told you the great news! My Bedford students' poems appeared in the *New Yorker* that just arrived today! The only poems in the issue, a double one, devoted to crime and punishment. I am proud, of course. Fee Dawson, jealous, said, huffily, "Well, how did you swing *that!*" My name, I might add, appears nowhere.

It really sounds like Saturday night out there, horns blowing, etc. But at about 6 or so, when I went out to get my spinach, the sky was still blue though full of half-moon light. Spring is coming.

I bet you're still playing on that machine!

Love!

Helene's reply: "Children are so wonderful, no matter the interruption. Can you even imagine, I have 3, plus 6 grands, plus 3 great-grands." But she complained about my having been given no credit for the poems in the *New Yorker*. "No way would the NYer give me credit," I explained, "but I did make clear that there was only *one* writing workshop at Bedford":

That's a funny story: Alice Quinn, ed., asks me, how do I write the contents page, "a writing workshop at the BHCF?" No, sez I, ego rising, there's only one. I usually say "*the* writing workshop at the BHCF. And I capitalize ww."

Well, maybe because I asked for 2 things, I got one: they printed (under heading POEMS) "from the BHCF's writing workshop." It's the *the* that counts!

The following week at the prison I didn't have my usual room, for the usual bureaucratic reasons, and thus had one student only, Judy Clark, one of the *New Yorker* poets.

NEW YORK, 2/26

Judy's mother has been dying of cancer for at least a year. She'd been getting really bad lately. Just before she died, last week, Judy was able to send her proofs of the poem, and then people began getting their subscription issues of the NYer in the mail and calling her up to congratulate her. *Nachus*, Yiddish for this kind of happiness. That, to me, is worth the price of the ticket.

There is a coda to this story. Fifteen years later I learned that Sister Elaine Roulet, the nun who worked at Bedford, had brought a printed copy to Judy's mother. "Know what she did?" said my informant. "She kissed it!"

• • • • •

Hello . . . March 7, 1997 . . . and it's 11:48pm so I'm just starting this and will continue tomorrow since I'm again very tired but wow, I've been to a movie! Imagine that! *Michael Collins*. Not one I would have chosen but am glad to have seen.

Now 7:19 pm. 3/9 . . . A long "tomorrow" because after I finished all the things I had to do yesterday and sat down at this stupid wonderful machine to write you I started fooling around with fonts and letterheads and trying to figure out page layout and multiple copies, etc., and ZAP it was 1:45 a.m. and I fell into bed crosseyed without having added so much as one word to the above paragraph. It's not my new computer, it's my new labyrinth.

Back to the movie: Ireland's fight for independence. I missed a lot of the dialogue as did my "date," Jonathon, who also wears a hearing aid. Directed by Neil Jordan who did *The Crying Game* . . .

So I've been out in the world and now I want to go to the movies nonstop. Ho!

But she had been copyediting a book and I'd been asking and asking what it was about—selfishly because I loved her writing:

The book was another Rex Stout novel that had been printed in serial form in a story magazine circa 1900. *Her Forbidden Knight*. A mystery of sorts. I understand he wrote a lot of them. Beautiful, innocent, orphaned nineteen-year-old behind the telegraph desk in once grand now seedy hotel on Broadway, I think, befriended and protected by ex-prizefighter, 2 actors, a French palmreader, a typewriter salesman, the villain, and the hero, who took to passing counterfeit ten-dollar bills in NY after being falsely accused of stealing $ from the bank he was vice president of back in Ohio and thus disinherited and sent away by wealthy father. It ends happily ever after, even Poppa comes through with a "Come home, Son, the ill-doers have confessed; I was wrong"—and in between the sweet young thing does all kinds of gutsy things to save her love, the hero. The characters Damon Runyon–like, tho' that may be wrong, I haven't read him in years . . . A lot of suspense and a lot of laughs. Which made up for the obnoxious that-era male/female ideal. That isn't said right but I'm tired and hungry and must stop.

So now I have told you what that book was about! :-)

When she finally got everything—computer and huge printer—properly set up, which took some doing, she wrote, "Oh my dear friend, can you realize what a relief it is to finally get this machine to work? I can see what I'm doing and—oh, I'm so happy!" And she was ready to move on, or at least thought she might. After saying "Goodnight, it's now 3:24 a.m.," she typed "Well" and then continued by hand: "I seem to be using that word a lot, but it's how I feel: Well . . . . . ?"

Hidden between explanations of how involving she found the computer— "Trouble is, if I sit down at this machine I can't just write a note"—is this little toss-off paragraph:

And I really do have something in my head to do . . . editing and making a little book from letters in the late 60s, when I first came here. It wld. be interesting for my kids. Especially since every time I start making notes for a memoir, I get totally spaced out. It wld be a start.

I'm not sure whether she meant her own letters, those she'd received, or both, but I wrote that I thought her "little book from letters" was "a wonderful idea," a "great start," and now I regret failing to push her to it. A few days later, having stayed up until seven in the morning fooling around, she wrote, after a paragraph in *Lucinda Calligraphy*, as if to reassure me, "Well, this is *Maiandra GD*. It's such a game, Hettie Jones. I hope I can put it to good use once I stop playing. I *do* have in mind putting together all those letters I discovered going thru files from the time I first came here . . ."

But the project stayed in her mind. Some of her papers, though, are with Ed Dorn's at Stanford University, in case anyone wants to take a look.

• • • • •

Feeling a bit down—sad, I guess. I suppose since you haven't mentioned it that you don't know that Allen Ginsberg died. This morning. I'd known since last week that he had liver cancer. There's a funeral service at a Buddhist center on Monday morning.

No, of course I didn't know Allen was sick . . . and now dead . . . such lovely memories of him I have . . . I can hear his voice, see him sitting at my Fort Square table, oh dear, I cld. go on and on . . . England, Santa Fe, New York (I still have the elegant fur hat he bought me that 1st visit Ed & I made to New York) . . .

Whew! Death . . . If you do go to the funeral service on Monday, please say goodby, hello, for me.

Allen—I've been thinking abt. him all day. He was so gentle & caring & quiet, offstage. It used to bother me at times, watching him perform, because that wasn't the man I knew.

The funeral service was lovely—chanting, and the Kaddish, and little statements from people. Roi was sweet and funny, Peter said little but was very dignified, Anne Waldman was visibly upset, Gregory Corso read a wonderful poem called "Toodle-oo"—which was, he said, the last thing Allen said to him last week . . . Oh, what Peter said: They'd wheeled Allen home from the hospital (close by), helped him out of his clothes and into pajamas, then Allen asked to have Ma Rainey put on the phonograph, got out a book, and was singing along—"See see rider, see what you have done . . ." And Peter said that was just about the last thing Allen said. I got big lump in throat over that one. Tried to write a poem yesterday but ended up bursting into terrible tears that surprised me . . . but I didn't mind weeping for Allen, after all. Was happy today to speak with his brother, Eugene, whom I'd met years ago. The place was crowded with people sitting on floor and others squeezed around the perimeter on chairs, me—a seat away from Bob Creeley who looks great—on a little table I'd found, since no more chairs left by the time I arrived, promptly at 9. Everyone up early for Allen.

· · · · ·

Like Helene's approach to found objects, I've wanted these letters to bring our story, to "work with them, not talk about them." So I've only reluctantly acknowledged that there are three voices here, and I'm trying to get the matrix right. Matrix being both source and what holds it all together. Though I still feel this is cheating, since Helene, were she here, might just as easily construct another:

GLOUCESTER, 4/26/97 10:55PM

You wouldn't believe all the letters spread out on my floor. Trying to get some kind of order, but it's like going thru photos—I start reading instead of just looking at dates . . . and, Mama, it's such a story, our letters.

5/3/97

Hello, it's 11:03pm and this is just a quick note to tell you I did do it, got all our letters and others filed. There's still a mess of things on the floor, but I feel better. I've tried, over the years, to keep a journal or diary; I can't do it. It just finally feels too weird, writing to myself. Although I do it on little bits of paper, things I see or read or think abt. But I've just now thrown them all away and it feels good no matter I lost some gems—who can deal w/such clutter??? And, of course, here I am at the computer . . . Oh well. Anyway, just to say you are my diary. There are others, of course, but you are the main one . . .

Good night, I'm more than a little freaked from all this sorting.

And, having once again fallen into the computer, she ended by saying, "I'm sure there's a way I can put love inside this egg but that means hours, and I'm not sure the egg will print . . ." And then handwritten, "Love," with a disappointed face and "the egg didn't."

The following night she sent sixteen lines of type and a couple of decorative borders in a large oval. Got it all in the egg. I loved that kind of prickly determination. But I worried about her drifting into received images, the very ideas of pattern she'd avoided—letters bordered with birds, stars, balloons, butterflies, cupids. Nevertheless, a few days later, after I'd asked her whether she'd read Charles Baxter's novels, she said she hadn't "read ANYTHING. Just wasting my time on this machine." So she knew what she was doing. Until she wrote one evening around eight that she had to stop writing and fix some food, "which I've had none of all day," and I wrote back, "It scares me when you say you're not eating," since I knew she was drinking—because soon after Allen died, Ed Dorn, too, had been diagnosed with terminal cancer.

GLOUCESTER, 6/7/97

Hello my dear friend!

6:20pm and cloudy . . . It's been a strange day, weather-wise and me-wise . . . but I want to thank you for last night's phone call.

I'm going through such changes and I don't understand them. Like *why* are all the past devastations and resentments coming into my head??? Things I've buried, I thought, but obviously haven't . . . and this is certainly no time for that. I don't know what to do. I'm trying to put my head in a positive direction, which I can during the day, but while I'm sleeping, no way!

So here I sit. Trying to remember all the good times. But I'm so terribly out of them . . . and at this point, till my head gets into another direction, I could care less. I'll probably die before he does.

NEW YORK, 6/7, 10:30PM

Glad I helped out, and don't chastise yourself for your resentments. They're legitimate. Probably that happens to everyone in situations like this. I don't doubt that it's a common reaction. You'll remember the good times "whenever." Wish I could write more to comfort you but it's too late. Hope you're fed and asleep.

6/9

Hello, it's Monday, only 9:15. What a beautiful day here! Hope it was for you too and that you're feeling better. I've been thinking about you, worrying some about what I know are complicated feelings. I find that people are frozen by their guilt. Not that I understand men in the least.

Nor did I understand, fully, the effect of all this death and dying on me:

Good morning! Kellie has gone off to breakfast with friends . . . we've been packing boxes since I got here, but as usual whatever is done with Kellie is more fun than anything else, with much stopping to collapse giggling.

It's more than nice to be away from my regular life. Especially at this time of year. Driving the Merritt Parkway was like walking through the woods.

I've had many thoughts lately about why the age of 62 was set as retirement. Even if you still have energy, there's a desire to sit back and reflect. I feel that coming over me more often than ever. I want to catch my breath.

GLOUCESTER, 6/18

Fax just now from Fred . . . Ed has been put on this new drug. Sounds as if he will live much longer than me . . .

NEW YORK, 6/19

It's good news about Ed, I'm glad. But you keep saying he'll live longer than you as if you thought you might drop dead tomorrow and that is *scaring me!!!*

GLOUCESTER, 6/21

Thanks for your 6/19 fax which I haven't answered because it's been birthday city here as well as full moon. Big lobster fest last night at Bucks. And this is just quick: an answer to your concern abt. my not eating. I do, but sporadically. And have made appts. w/doctor to check all my body weirdos . . . I hate going to doctors, even tho I like Tom Pearce. He's misdiagnosed me a couple of times, but sent me to a specialist who reversed his opinions. Besides that, he's a Buddhist. You can tell I'm talking myself into this.

OK . . . a quick hello. Did get some work done in studio today.

NEW YORK, 6/21

What do you mean, you eat "sporadically." Explain, please! And what "body weirdos"? You must tell your Buddhist doctor that you eat "sporadically." (Is he cute?) Why don't you invite your friend Jonathon for dinner? Or better—get *him* to invite *you* to dinner . . .

Hey, you got some work done in studio!

Crazy days . . . Yma's best friend, Meghan, age 20, found dead Sunday am, asthma inhaler under her hands, straw and white residue found on dresser . . . Yma told me yes, she did snort heroin now and then, but was not hooked, like they say.

Possum on my porch again, after one year. It was so lovely! Possum under chair, Chili sitting in front of chair just looking at him/her. I disturbed it all by saying a quiet "hello"; possum came out from under chair and went slowly down the steps, his long tail making wonderful arabesques.

Goodnight . . . I *do* eat . . . but I drink too much and smoke too much . . .

6/27

Just cleaned up all the past 2 days' kitchen mess and *must* clean, now that I've space, all the dandelions and lettuce I bought because of a sale and for once, everything appeared fresh. But it ain't gonna keep, stuffed as it is in my little fridge—

So, you see,

I *do* eat : > but then you don't get letters . . .

"I'd rather you ate more and wrote less," I answered. Still, I counted on her help. Thanks to a Soros grant, a West Coast designer, a New York printer, Helene's careful proofreading, and not least the women of *the* Bedford Hills Writing Workshop, I had succeeded, though it took the better part of a year, in getting together a *real* book—with a spine!—from the workshop. On 6/24 I wrote: "I'm going to get *Aliens At The Border* tomorrow!"

And now, every time I read that line, I wish I could have taken Helene to Bedford to meet the women she'd helped. Especially then, when she was going through so much.

I wrote the above before rereading my letter of 10/3/97. Same never granted wish.

• • • • •

Kellie has been doing some work with the dancer Bill T. Jones (for the Walker) and so has gotten 2 free tickets to see him dance tomorrow night in New Haven. He's ½ of a famous dance team with a guy named Arnie Zane, who died of AIDS. They were an "unlikely" couple—Bill a tall black guy Arnie a short Jew—but they supposedly were great dancing together. Though I never saw them, I've seen lots of photos and read about them. So I'm looking forward . . .

6/30

Dance concert was great even though Bill T. Jones himself didn't appear in it, but the company and their ensemble dancing wonderful. He also uses people with "nontraditional" bodies, that is, there were 2 fat people!

Penn State [which a month before had asked about a course] called me today to ask if I were still interested, and I chatted the guy up and found out I'm high on the list. They'll decide around the 6th or so . . . It has me on tenterhooks, the meaning of which I really can't say, but it does sound like something in a meat packing plant, no?

What are you doing? How was Fiesta?

GLOUCESTER, 7/1/97

Hello Het,

I did remember to say rabbits, which I seldom do.

Got yr. last night's fax this morning. I was minus sound, on cushions in studio reading Henry Louis Gates, Jr's introduction to *Thirteen Ways of Looking at a Black Man*. Which I pulled off the new book shelf at library because I've read, here and there, stuff of his and liked it and I noticed there was whole "chapter" on Bill T. Jones.

Tenterhooks . . . I looked it up because I've always spelled it tender-hooks: "tenterhook: a sharp hooked nail used especially for fastening cloth on a tenter." How that equates with being in a state of uneasiness, I can't figure . . . language! Communication!

Speaking of communication: went to audiologist today—dear Celia!—because my phone hearing aid got its battery stuck, and she freaked see-ing how old my machines are; they've improved so much since 1989. Even if my insurance won't OK a programmed one, she sd the new ones like I already have are so improved, it will change my life. And she's gonna get me a free phone that she sez will make talking on the phone OK . . . Whew! What a lift!

Hello Hello Hello, What Great News About Your New To-Be Sound!

Oh, I'm so pleased for you! And I'm glad you're doing sporadic work in studio, better to do that than not to. That's what I'm doing here and sometimes putting time/space between the idea and the next time is good, better.

Near midnight. Maybe I'll turn on the radio and catch some version of "Round Midnight." Maybe I'll put myself to bed.

The washing machine and I have a hands-on relationship at the moment. I help it through the wash cycle by moving the agitator, since it slows down by itself. Like an old dog. Tracy has named it Janie Summers, for the actress who played the Bionic Woman on TV. Of course I never saw this, but I think it's charming that he thought of it and excellent that he feminized it!

You sound so good. Here's to New Sounds—

An hour later I faxed her a copy of an email I'd gotten from a friend, with a note I'd scrawled on it: "Looks kind of cute, I think. This is my first attempt, thought you'd like to see it. As you see, I've still not gone to bed—12:51!"

I don't know what Helene expected when she'd written, "If you go on-line w/your new computer I'll die!" But I had replied that I would, "because that's one of the main reasons for getting it." I had to keep a place in the world, whereas she seemed to be drifting away. I hoped the new hearing aids would counteract this.

• • • • •

Hullo—just finished vacuuming and mopping—call last night from Paul saying they'd be here abt. noon on Mon. (tomorrow)—oy! veh! that's phonetic—on their way to a 3-day vacation at Sasha [his wife]'s uncle's house on a lake in New Hampshire. Fred off that same day for a couple of weeks w/Steph in England . . .

Back from Laundromat at 3:30pm today & there was HO! call from Carroll &Graf. Whew! What a relief!

P.S. It's weird having both your sons gone off, and a daughter so far away and I seldom hear from her but it's my fault because I don't have e-mail, and I'm sure, anyway, I'm the one who owes her a letter . . .

Hello, a very quick note because it's already nearly 11. Great about that c&g job—what is it?

Well, if both sons are gone and your daughter far away you still have those three gorgeous healthy grands around you.

If this were e-mail, all I'd have to do would be "point and click." For saving, the same. And it would print as example I sent you—Of course I'm eventually going to agitate for this; however for now I'm content to explain!

. . . and you're going to insist on e-mail too . . . even my audiologist did. Right now I have to cook some broccoli and eat more of that chicken I fixed last night. I'm going crazy with all my non-functioning legs and arms and hands, and losing weight (98 and sometimes 100 lbs) and I have to wait till end of month to see dr., but I've found that eating fat seems to help.

Yes I have those beautiful granddaughters. Ket caught me on the street yesterday. "Hey Gram!" . . . those bright eyes and that smile . . . Babies all around her.

Good night . . . I'm off to fat and all that!

. . . Please eat fat, please eat all the fat you can, 98 lbs is not enough, that is 7 whole lbs less than I weigh, and I am so so much shorter than you. But now I'm worrying—a meal of just one chicken leg? No rice? Potato?

I've forgotten to tell you that I GOT THE PENN STATE JOB!

So I will drive 4 hours to State College, PA, every Thurs starting August 28th, soon enough. Graduate students, no more than 12, said the man. I am excited! I may have to spend the night—the head of Eng. Dept said, "Oh there's a nice place on campus, it's *only* $70 a night." Shit, I got an AAA book and there are motels for $35. Anyway I'm psyched!

Okay, I know you don't have time to read all this blather, just wanted to tell you the good news. Hope you're having fun with the c&g book despite . . .

I'm to be on a conference call tomorrow re the PEN Prison Program. You remember Radical Chic? Well, get ready for Prisoner Chic, it's coming . . .

Hello & Happy Birthday!

Am hard at work—didn't call because I knew you were having confer . . . Anyway, am thinking about you, my dear pearl of a girl—and here's to your 63rd!

Thought this excerpt from interview with crime writer would interest you. I am, by the way, gaining a real respect for that genre of fiction, which I've always thought of as pure entertainment—that's the nice thing abt. c&g—the books I get from them always are interesting & that makes up for the low pay—yeah Momma!

Thanks for sending that interesting stuff from the book . . . Yes, for the most part c&g does good stuff, as they ought to, since both of them came from Grove Press originally. Which is why I never minded working for Grove, it was like getting paid to be interested.

hullow!!!

Had the first physical in some 15 or more years this afternoon. It took hours . . .

This is in haste. Got some new clay, self-hardening, thanks to visit to gallery and talking to Joy Dai Buell.[1] She was answering my questions abt how she did what she did in her collages . . .

---

1. Cape Ann artist.

Hello—

Thinking about you but I just can't write—New aids in my ears & I think they *really* are an improvement, but it's gonna take some time to deal w/what adjustments need to be made . . .

Renewed Skip Gates's book today because there was so much I wanted to reread—and as I told my lovely audiologist who wanted to know what I was reading, I've learned, on all these doctor bus trips, to keep title by my body—because all the wonderful Gloucester ladies who ride the bus & talk to one another look at that title [*Thirteen Ways of Looking at a Black Man*] and then at me and then at one another . . .

I've just sat for an hour trying to get to know my new cellular phone, an amazing object. Everyone said yes, get it, you won't regret it. But I'll use mine for emergencies, I think, so I hope I won't use it at all. People all over NY walking around with their cell phones to their ears.

They've added 1 person to my class at the Y, this year it's 13. It's to be 12 at Penn State. With Parsons that makes 45. 45 Stories. Yipes!

• • • • •

Hullo, this is just that . . . not a letter.

Big wind coming in windows, that's nice. I am not well but seem to be improving. Not to worry, all tests, and I've had so many, have come thru okay. I'm not going to drop dead tomorrow from physical things at least, am dutifully taking medications.

Hullo . . .

Just to say that. I can't seem to do much other than try to get my body back, can't write letters, respond to all you are doing. I think I'm disintegrating, which is an interesting proposition. Did nothing more today than vacuum and use a lethal spray to clean up all the cat spews. It's helpful to have a sense of cleansiness . . . that misspelling is on purpose.

At something like 3:30pm I received a *14-pg* fax from Lockheed Martin telling me how, "for your review" to utilize the FAA Explosive Detector . . . so to whom were they writing and why? O this world. Will the FBI check me out since I got unsolicited info?

Call from Fred earlier . . . Ed remaining stable and drug seems to be working . . . makes me sure of what I've felt . . . I'll go before he does.

About what, exactly, she was dying of, she was vague: "It's so difficult to describe—wrists, knees, and ankles too," she wrote. "It's not 'hurt,' just a nonworking weirdness, like butterflies in my joints . . . Now HOW are you going to tell a doctor abt. that, even if he is a Buddhist!"

GLOUCESTER, 8/27

Hello, Wed. & you go tomorrow for first stint at Penn . . .

Just to let you know I'm thinking about you, hope it all goes well . . .

My blood pressure is down, but my VCR no longer works. The clay I've been testing also doesn't. Oh well, nutz.

Love, and some birds in flight [a border]

NEW YORK, 8/27

Thank you for your note and the flying birds. You'll be pleased to know that I made myself a neckrest pillow for the car out of red fabric with black birds that look very much like yours flying all over it. Kellie was tickled— a scrap from one of her high-school dresses!

I've been in an advanced state of nerves all day trying to get shit together for this trek. Would you believe, I washed a shirt I thought I'd like to wear, hung it on roof, and a bird shat on it!

The Supt. of the prison called this evening and ordered 20 copies of *Aliens*! Other volunteers are using it to raise money for the college program—I'm so happy—not only is it a good book, but now it's being put to some good use.

Okay momma. You sound okay except for the clay. What were you trying to do with it?

• • • • •

Hello! 8/30/97 and the traveling teacher has returned . . .

I forgot to look at the odometer after I came home but it was 248 on the way there. What saved the trip home was a book on tape. As for the students, there were maybe 2 or 3 good writers out of the 12 . . .[2] And of course it was great just to loll around a motel room for a couple of hours. But the best was stopping for breakfast both mornings. On the way home I found myself in a place meant for truckers—with showers and TV rooms and lots of telephones and a store as well as a restaurant; it was fascinating and I could've just hung out watching . . .

So I was going to take it easy today, but ended up walking to Canal Street with Eric so that he could show me where to buy a talking watch. I need this object for the car, so that I won't be distracted by a clock that might not glow in the dark.

GLOUCESTER, LAST DAY OF AUGUST, 1997

I remember those truck stops—the amenities I'm sure have changed— the basics were there, but the truckers slept in their trucks, no TV rooms, etc. The food was OK, the atmosphere nice, we were all on the road, and the kids felt at home (at least I thought they did). Whew! That conjures up such memories!

I am trying to finish off an age old mask that I've been looking at for days and days and think I've finished but won't know till tomorrow.

WHAT is a talking watch? The thought of it gives me the creeps. We live in such different worlds outside, but inside the same?

Reading this now I want so badly to bring her back to reassure her, to say that yes, of course we were "inside the same," just as years before she'd written, reassuring me, "We *are* sisters."

The talking watch was needed for the car that replaced the blue Honda, which had burned after eight years and many thousand miles, and had even been stolen for two months and found in the Bronx by an alert policewoman. But now I had a little red two-door Toyota named Ruby My Dear after the Monk tune. The family opinion? Mom got a sports car!

---

2. The best of these students was Lyrae Van-Clief Stefanon, who has since won awards for her poetry.

Sporty or not, Ruby had to get us there on time but had no dashboard clock. And I had to keep my hands on the wheel, which was where I strapped the watch. "You just push a button and it talks to you," I wrote Helene.

I've been asked, about this book, "But what's the *story*?" Literally, you might say it's the tale of two Babes from Boyland who saved each other's lives. And since I've always wanted the letters themselves to tell it, maybe we're getting to that now. Maybe they were, simply, our talking watch against the dark.

10

In the foreground, two women,
their squinting faces
creased into texture. . . .

Around them, their dailiness:
clotheslines sagged with linens. . . .

One woman pauses for the picture.
The other won't be still.

Even now, her hands circling . . .
— Natasha Trethewey

One night in early September 1997, beset by medical problems, Helene began a letter with the simple admission that she was depressed, but then went on for three handwritten pages into a story I'd never heard:

Gloucester, 9/5 8:45pm & mebbe you're back from Penn — or off doing something else. I get so dizzy, I can't remember what you've sd. you were scheduled to do. Oh! Not to worry abt. bld. pressure — "If it stays that high for 20 yrs you'll be in trouble." Dr. gave me more of the pills. I know in my heart of hearts what I need to do is stop drinking and smoking — which I've done in various periods of my life, but right now I can't summon the strength to do it, and I don't know why. Maybe I want to die.

I thought I did, years ago, in the miasma of going back to David & my children — because I couldn't face being in a life that my heart did not want, but I wanted my children back. I had left them to find myself in the new world I found w/Ed after exploring a bit on my own — which was hard. I went to bars, etc., trying to draw, sketch, people, & everywhere I got come-ons I didn't know how to deal with. But then there was this man who wanted me to go home w/him and I said no and we got to talking & he said go see my friend at — (a very big store in Seattle & I can't remember the name!) and that friend gave me a job in the "Tip To Toe" department—I outfitted women to go on their various vacations, taking them from department to department—but it was so hard for me, because I was so set on my own criteria. I wanted them to dress like me. Oh! Such a long time ago & I'd forgotten I did that!

Back to my wanting to die, and David—years ago—I stood on the balcony railing, high up, wanting to jump, but couldn't. I was hysterical because I couldn't do it. David came out, gently lifted me down and drove me back to Ed's apt. David Buck was a true friend. Not the husband I should have had; I thought when we married we were going to do all these wonderful things—him writing, composing music, me painting. Turned out he just wanted to be a family man . . . which is ok but wasn't my gig—

Oh dear—I'm not going to reread this—

P.S. If you don't have time to read it, no matter, I've got it on file . . . I think maybe I'm flipping with age—as well as too much beer.

NEW YORK, 9/6

Hello—

I am dreadfully worried about you. I don't really think you want to die but I do think you are "in denial" as they say. Not making the connection between pain and awful tests and everything else with the alcohol that your body is rebelling against. I *do* understand why anyone wants to change consciousness—either chill out or speed up, depending on what you need—get high or get low. But you said once that "it helps" and I remember that very clearly. Now it has ceased to help and is hurting. As for the story about your leaving David—I can appreciate that fully, not wanting to be swallowed into that life, I too would have wanted to die. But why would you want to die *now*?

The very first day I ever taught a memoir class a woman about my age confessed to wishing she'd led my life: "How did you *know* to rebel?" she asked.

Surprised, and having no ready answer—in fact I considered the question unanswerable—I finally blurted out: "If I hadn't, I'd have died."

So I understood Helene's impulse, but that we were "inside the same" didn't manifest outside. "Everyone has theories about how to help other people," I went on in my letter of 9/6:

. . . and I am especially meddlesome. But I do love you and don't want you to be in pain and feeling lousy about yourself. I guess that's why I've nagged you so about working—because it has seemed to me that whenever you've had a book to work on you've been happy, then gone back into studio with renewed interest, or into the computer, or whatever was most compelling. Not that proofing is the answer—just one of some you could think of. Surely there are things to do in Gloucester. I *know* that my busyness is not only put upon me but a position I seek out, a state of being that keeps the focus away from what's incomplete in my life . . .

It's hardly helpful, I know, to be recommending work to a sick person. As for the smoking, you stopped for *three years*. What were you doing during that time? When you say you can't summon the strength to stop drinking and smoking, how can you then summon the strength to endure the pain?

Anyway I'm just writing to say I love you and wish I could encourage you to love yourself enough to do right by yourself.

Write when you can.

GLOUCESTER, 9/6

I woke up at 5am having to pee and my first thought was omygod I *sent* that letter—and there was no way to get it back! I went back to bed feeling very sorry I'd laid on you a bunch of things I was really just saying to myself . . .

The onus of not feeling comfortable writing into a journal; guess I need to be saying something to someone other than myself—only way I do that is on bits of whatever paper is on hand and if all gets lost because they pile up and I end up, tired of scatterings, throwing them in the paper recycle bin—that letter shld have been on one of those "bits of paper."

I'm going back to bed. Have been there most of today and want to be up and around tomorrow. Please don't worry Mama . . . I'm okay. Think mebbe I'm going into a 70s trauma which I'm sure can be heavier than the menopause one.

This was followed by a wonderful self-portrait with crossed eyes and a smiling mouth and three flowers in and around the handwritten "Love, H" and then a P.S. written the next day: "The hours disappeared again . . . Anyway, thanks for your concern."

I wasn't able to write again until the following week, and even then, with "as of this week 29 homeworks to read and correct every single week," I apologized: "This isn't much of a letter. I'm just writing to say hello. How are you? Any better?" I didn't get an answer, but wrote again a few days later, ending "Hope you're doing okay—please let me know!"

GLOUCESTER, 9/14/97

Hello back . . .

Am ok. Last 3 days in hosp. for some awful tests . . . which I did live through but thought I wasn't gonna, no matter how positively I made myself think. When was the last time you downed castor oil—2 ounces!—after taking some hours earlier 10 oz of magnesium citrate or something and then . . . never mind, you don't want to hear it. Watched, when I cld, my innards on the screen. It was in color & like traveling through a labyrinth. Everything looks normal said the jovial surgeon . . .

If I don't die from ailments, I will from tests. Just joking! Not to worry.

As usual, or always, those academic jobs sound great, and the $ are there, but . . . O Het, I'm tired. Just commiserating over all those mss you have to read. I used to correct Freshman English papers for Ed in Idaho and I know how they pile up, etc.

GLOUCESTER 9/20

Hello—

Crazy weather . . . so hot today and now after a beautiful Beethoven thunderstorm the air blowing in my windows is cold. And the wind! The trees are dancing!

Last night I watched the Allen profile on PBS, which came from NY so you've seen it or heard tell of . . . I think it was nice, but I was so caught up in that depiction of all those years, on camera . . . whew! that's so immediate. I got lost in myself watching what they were telling me I was. *It was a strange experience.*

9/26

Hullo, this is just quick. It's been some days, but I'm still here. Ket drove me to Dr. yesterday which saved me some 3 hours. Have to go for another damn test on Monday. He simply wants to make sure. And I've no argument with that. Blood pressure pills up 2.5 mg. I am so sick of all this, and sick of being sick.

Chan may be coming for Xmas . . . Yma is pregnant. Amen.

P.S. in the midst of all this I *am* getting bits done in studio — just bits, but it seems to be coming back to life — that room, that space, that kind of thought . . .

Don't forget to say rabbits tomorrow . . . I always do. You haven't written for a long time it seems . . . everything OK?

Hello —

You're right, I haven't written in a long time. I am trying to keep cool in the face of all this stuff to do, but there doesn't seem to be *any* time to just sit down. Today was my first day of Parsons afternoon / Y evening. I was getting ready to go this AM when I found there was no water in the house —

Anyway I hope this finds you much better. It's 11:15 and I have to be up at 7 to bring car in for oil change since I've put so many miles on it in one month.

Is Yma happy?

Please get well! Love xxxoooo

Hello, it's me, I think it's me tho I'm hardly sure.

I am surrounded by what seem like hundreds of pieces of paper all of which require my attention. Next weekend mucho preparation for reading at Penn and a guest appearance in someone's class — so I'm there Weds. eve as well as Thurs. I hardly slept at all on Weds. night after coming back from prison rehearsal, don't know why. So had to go to Penn on 3rs sleep and drink mucho coffee to stay awake. Listened to *Death in Venice* and a speech and interview with Jimmy Baldwin and a story by Nadine Gordimer on the way home. I love these tapes!

My Y class promises to be good. They're all "good," I suppose. Just a big fat involvement precluding everything else. Next Weds. is the Bedford reading; I'm bringing 2 carloads of people up there from the city; the women are very excited; I wish you were coming as the official proof-reader!

I'm going to bed. Just dragged out my recycling (meaning I carried 2 weeks worth of the *NY Times* with its new unnecessary sections on my shoulder). Yoga tomorrow and then the vacuum. I could use a househusband but then I'd have to feed him.

Please let me know how you are even if just one line or so.

GLOUCESTER 10/3

11pm—Just to send that line you asked for—I'm OK. Details later. My head, when it gets itself together, will get me to computer and I'll send you a letter you won't have time to read—I've done my bit of worrying abt you, too.

NEW YORK, 10/10/97

Hello! I'm really way too tired to do anything, it's been such a week. But sitting here is at least relaxing in that I'm not either standing up in front of people talking or driving or rushing from one place to another.

Between my Parsons class and my Y class on Tuesday I had dinner with Marie Ponsot and a poet named Jean Valentine, the two of them really really nice.

The big Event at Bedford happened on Wednesday. So of course there was a major traffic jam on the parkway and the 9 of us who had traveled up together had to rush through dinner and just made it on time to the prison. But all went well; in fact it was fabulous. I even had a call from the superintendent while I was away telling me she'd heard it was great. So I feel we did good—after all these many years, finally a reading where the women could truly present themselves.

Then there was Penn, but the drive was amazing—to see all that incredible color as I drove through the mountains. Listened to *White Noise* by Don Delillo on the way home—which did hold my attention and was, I suppose,

10/13

and there I stopped and never got back to you . . .

So what's going on? The last fax I have from you is dated 10/3, and in it you promised to get out computer when your head was together and send me a letter I won't have time to read. But I will have time, even if I have to cart it around with me. Anyway I'm here until Weds. morning at 11 and then home on Fri. afternoon. The weather's really changing, I think, so I can just haul out all my black sweaters and get through winter!!

Hope you're well! Love!

Hullo—

It's 7pm and this is just quick to get back to you . . . and then the phone rang and it's now later. Great news that the Bedford reading was such a success. Again I am putting off letter because I have to clear off the mess on this little desk and put computer on top of printer because, thanks the gods, I have a book, 2 books, coming tomorrow from Adam Dunn. I was really getting uptight abt. no $ coming in, so that's a big relief. Had lunch with Gerrit today. His some 40 year companion and a lovely man, Deryk Burton, died last Friday afternoon. He'd been very sick for a long time, Gerrit's life has been taken up for 2 years caring for him. Well so I'm dealing with all that plus 174 over 96, new bp medication which I think makes me feel weird, Squirrel is sick and I gotta get him to a vet tomorrow. I am in full moon.

Love, H

Hello!

I was so happy to get yours of 10/14; you sounded like your old self and that's great about the books from C&G.

Please, although it's rather late, send my condolences to Gerrit, or better yet, send me his address and I'll write him. I did meet Deryk when I was there for the Olson thing—I still remember the lovely afternoon on the porch, with you and Gerrit and Jean and Deryk, who had the most beautiful eyes . . .

I'm trying to sleep a lot and keep calm and keep doing my classes etc. This past week was the reading at Penn, and that went very well, but I was even happier to see home after being away for 3, not 2 days.

Grove editor just sent me his wife's book to blurb. Couldn't say no. It's about her year as an observer in an alternative school. Not uninteresting at all, but oh . . . I barely have time to do what I do, and now must struggle to fit this in.

Well, but I didn't mean to complain. Kellie's finally coming home tomorrow after 3 weeks in South Africa; last I spoke to her she said she *definitely* was happy to be coming home. I'll be glad to hear her voice.

Hope those books from C&G are somewhat interesting, but then they usually are, so I'm imagining you happily at work. Write when you finish or have time.

10/26

Hello and Happy Standard Time!

Write me when you have a second, I haven't heard from you for ages.

GLOUCESTER, 10/27

Hullo—

I'm just still so *sick*—that's why you haven't heard from me—Dr. appt. 10am tomorrow. Managed somehow to get the last 2 books off today. All I want to do is sleep. anyway, bear w/me—I am truly truly SICK and at my wits end and if Tom Pearce can't help me tomorrow, I'll slit my wrists!

And of course being sick I can't get a flu shot . . .

Lots to talk abt but I can't—have to eat my garbage soup & get under the covers . . .

Good night & love—

10/28

Hello—quick update to last night's wail—bronchitis—swollen feet due to pressure medication—I am so tired of pills, but at least now I have some codeine cough med. So here I sit, foreign things in my body. But this is *it* for any more antibiotics this year, I've promised myself. What on earth has happened to my body's immune system??? Can it be age?

Love, later—just not to leave you w/that wail—(for which I apologize!)

NEW YORK, 10/29/97

Well! Holy Mackerel! Sick! Shit!

Hello—

I don't know about age and immune system, it seems that a lot of people have been getting bronchitis: Lisa, as well as a friend of hers in

Italy . . . I think it's what we breathe rather than how old we are. And you probably did have the flu to begin (as I had last year for 2 months). Ugh, *winter.*

I am now pushing at the last of the hard hard weeks, the one I've been dreading. Tomorrow to Penn, back Friday, then the weekend to do Parsons homework, prepare for the reading in Indianapolis on Monday (plane leaves at 7:30, I have to be up at 5 the latest, *oy vey,* arrive 9:30, be a guest in a writing class at 11, then probably some kind of dinner, and *then* the reading). Then back Tues a.m. same time, get ready for my 2 classes that day. Rest Weds. while doing Penn homework, Penn Thurs, Fri home, then a reading in Westchester, the one to benefit the prison college project, with Glenn Close and Pete Seeger. After that, on my way home, I'm supposed to go to someone's 60th birthday party on the Upper West Side but I'm not sure I'll make it. Can you believe this?

I left out the book I'm supposed to blurb, which I've got 100 pages to finish and won't be done in time.

BUT—after all that above is over, there won't be any extra stuff until a reading—at the Brooklyn Museum!—in December. And one day there will be the Christmas madness plus the endterm papers to read and grades to get in, but *then—then—then!* Just me and my computer, and . . .

I'm glad you got those books off. When you're feeling better, tell me about them. Oh I hope you *are* better!

GLOUCESTER, 11/5

I'm okay, getting better but still totally exhausted—2 more days of Cipro and by then, please, all my gods, will not want to sleep all my days away . . .

In 2001, during the anthrax scare, Helene would write that Cipro, a very strong antibiotic, was "not to be trusted." She gave no reason, though by then she'd had extensive experience with it, and we have since learned a great deal about the continued use of strong antibiotics and how this affects the balance in the human body of crucial, beneficial, bacteria. When she wrote "What on earth has happened to my immune system?" she knew exactly what she was talking about.

· · · · ·

I'd write but am too tired—driving home in ice & sleet. Up since 6:30. *Big Star* and *Trees* both to be remaindered by Viking Penguin now called Penguin Putnam or The Penguin Group—so I'm out of print again. Boo.

Anyway I owe you 2 letters. Maybe tomorrow or sun—this time *will pass!*

I don't really believe all the time that has passed. Working on a collage to try to make sense of the October I totally lost. It's slow, of course, because I want to put 2 masks in it and they take so much time, but it's a healing process and I get all involved in how to do it . . . and no way can I keep track of your mind-blowing agenda.

Hello—I wonder how long it's going to take me to get over all this insane activity. Will I crash? It's so cold here, I can only shiver imagining how it must be up there. But as long as it doesn't sleet/snow/whatever I don't mind. I had enough of that on the way home last Friday—Thurs nite after class my car was covered with ice, a little red jewel, and Fri morning was worse. I sure was glad to see Cooper Square, where it was merely raining . . .

I never did tell you about the reading with Glenn Close and Pete Seeger, which was a great success, especially the reading of the poems from *Aliens*. I sold $600 worth of books! I've almost made enough $$ to cover the cost of the printing, and all this is due to the coincidence of the "College Project" beginning at the prison. Anyway it was a wonderful evening.

Sorry for not writing all this time . . . Have a lovely turkey day with all your wonderful generations!

And now it's Thanksgiving and I'm to spend Wed thru Sat with Paul and Sasha and those 2 grandsons who are suddenly teens . . .

Well! Your fax just coming in!! *Stop* apologizing for not writing!

Hello—I can hardly hold my head up. It's 11:45pm and I've just returned from the reading at the Brooklyn Museum, where I was handed an almost copy of my poetry book—just the cover and the forms, unbound. It all looks great and made me so happy! Wait till you see, it's so *colorful*—

But I'm dead meat. Drove home yesterday through first rain, then snow, then rain again, as if crossing borders.

Hello, are you in the Christmas madness?

Tomorrow evening I must go to a party to eat *latkes* (potato pancakes), the traditional Hanukkah dish; for years I've avoided doing this, but recently encountered the hostess, who said "You *never* come . . ." Truly I'd rather stick to rice and veggies for several weeks . . . but that ain't in the cards right at Christmas!

Have to say I *do* know about *latkes*—I love them—terrible rich awful food, but so *good!*

I'm totally frenzied, of course, trying to stash all my working stuff to make house look like Xmas for one evening—And figuring how to buy food tomorrow for next day etc. I'll think about you Tues, and write later . . . I'm totally tired.

Hello!

It was great talking to you the other night—you sounded so good, and I'm glad I called then because today I'm a mess! I was happily working on my poems when suddenly I felt a *loud* pain in my sinus . . .

shit!

Would you believe, a student from Penn State (in her fifties, mind you) emailed me a long letter protesting her grade of B+! Where I come from, that's a great grade—but nowadays nothing but an A will do.

I think I'll lie on my futon and read a book, something I haven't done in months—maybe it'll improve my mind. About 2 feet from where I'm sitting are 15 unread books (I've just counted). That should keep me busy, no?

I wish you could see me: a *lined* ski hat over a kerchief wound around head and neck, a turtleneck plus 2 wool sweaters and over that a puffy vest meant for the outdoors, long johns and sweat pants, cotton socks plus wool socks plus down booties. Yes, the heat is on, and the house isn't cold. Why am I not sweating? I'm quite comfortable. What is this weirdness?

Well, despite this "woe is me," I do feel cheerful and hope you are the very same!

GLOUCESTER, 12/31/97

8:41pm. I did go to hear Megawatts [Fred's band] for abt. a half hour, though my sick body just wanted to be home, overclothed like you, sitting by the heater. But they are always great and it's a delight to watch how they make people dance and have a wonderful time. The BRISK air was probably good for me (it's incredibly cold here) and it was fun to see Main Street so festive and all the people, especially the little kids. Masks and costumes and all that in this fierce cold! Gloucester's first First Night. A couple of really fine ice sculptures, a marvelous Gloucester Sea Serpent and a railroad engine on the library lawn. The time and care involved in making them—it has been two days—they were sawing away at midnight last night, and today until close to 5 pm—whew! Makes me think of sand painting . . . they'll be gone with the next warm air current. That's love.

And when I stopped across the street from Harborlight Futon on my way, I saw a mime in their window. I love mimes—and she was beautiful, all black and white, making slow movements in that huge display window, nobody paying any attention to her. I stood watching her thinking what a drag it must be to perform w/no audience, and then my nose started running and I pulled a Kleenex out of my pocket and blew into it while I was watching (from across the street)—and she did that beautiful slow movement thing mimes do, drew with her white-gloved hand a Kleenex from her pocket and mimed a noseblow exactly like mine. I laughed and gave her a finger-up sign which she returned! I realized then that she'd been mimicking my movements from the very beginning. I love her and wish her well. As I do you, Mama . . . GET WELL!!!

HAPPY NEW YEAR . . .

• • • • •

Soon after the New Year Helene sent our horoscopes, noting that we each had been given four stars by the *Gloucester Daily Times*. Since our local papers were the subject, I apologized for not yet having addressed her teasing: "Do you actually *learn* anything from reading the Sunday *New York Times*?"

"I've clipped 2 things so far to send you," I wrote in defense, but after I mentioned a party for a literary press, she wrote, "I am so out of that world, Hettie Jones, wasn't even aware James Laughlin[1] died—so you see, I should go out too, every Sat. night for the *Times*."

Of course this was followed by one of her funny drawings. And when later that month I wrote that despite the rain I was on my way out to get the paper "where I'll read all about Clinton's dick," her rejoinder was to ask whether that dick had been worth the trip. For me this banter balanced the effect of some of my other trips:

NEW YORK 1/29/98

The scene at Bedford last night was amazing. An entire floor of women was made to move all their worldly possessions to different cells on different floor in different wing. As I left, a little after 9pm, there were women dragging plastic bags of clothes, carrying boxes, etc. They'd all been up since 5am, when they're awakened and made to stand in front of their cell doors with a hand in the little window, to be counted.

For Helene, our back-and-forth offset her despair about the world she was aware of with or without the "newspaper of record":

GLOUCESTER, 2/14/98

Tell me, are we going to bomb Iraq, will Clinton survive, and what does the Afghanistan earthquake say about what's happening on this planet? Whew, that's something to think about, but of course it's been happening all through the ages and will continue. Still, when you read about all those villages just zapped, buried, all those people going about their lives like we do, zapped out . . . and we think we're so important. What a joke!

But we really are, day to day, to one another. Hope this doesn't wake you.

---

1. James Laughlin (1914–97): established New Directions; published W. C. Williams and other well-known twentieth-century writers.

Oh, I shit sure hope we aren't going to bomb Iraq . . . Is this what we need to galvanize Generation X? Must they die for oil?

A quick Sunday night hello since we both missed our usual Saturday. I had *two* Margaritas I don't know how to spell them but I certainly enjoyed drinking them . . . and a long-delayed get-together dinner with my crazy friend Claire Baker whom I dearly love. When I arrived, a bit late, there she was at the bar, looking lovely and half through a White or Black, I can't remember, Russian . . . anyway we had a wonderful time just talking about ourselves and what we are doing now (we did eat).

Came back to wait for Larry, her husband, to come pick her up . . . had said he wld. do this so she cld. have a drink (he disapproves) . . . and there we were sitting in the studio w/the blinds opened so we cld. see when he arrived. Suddenly through my kitchen door, he arrives and shouts that he's here . . . whew. Neither of us cld. believe it. So I get a call from her tonight worried that I don't keep my door locked . . . "YOU MUST!" He's an ex-KGB higher-up who defected and I guess he was really freaked that he cld. walk into my house like that. Well, I suppose he's right. All my doors are now carefully locked as of 7:57 pm. Oy Vey.

It's snow/rain/sun/wind . . . Totally March . . . I love it.

Okay, the magic moment, 10:25PM. I'll get paper and turn the pages on the Clinton shit, which simply obscures the business of government, as if we were back at the beginning of this century, scandal scandal. We need another age of enlightenment, or something. If you know, let me know.

• • • • •

Hello Het . . . it's a noreaster Sunday and here I am w/all these videos a friend lent and I feel obligated to get them back at a decent interval. It's just that movies demand my whole attention. I suppose what I need is that television set one reads about at the foot of the queen or king-sized bed, remote handy on the bedside table . . . Well!

I was amused to find this reference to a bed, since for all the years I knew her, Helene slept on a futon on the floor, which though healthy enough proved difficult whenever she was sick: "I've got to get Squirrel off my bed and fluff it and mebbe even put on fresh sheets if my back holds out . . ." She seldom revealed what was wrong, but did admit that she needed to quit drinking and smoking. "I've tried, but never succeeded. Mebbe I need a shrink???"

Why the fuck not? You take your cats to the vet, don't you? Perhaps it will be fun, even if it's stupid it'll be *innaresting*—your word!

Okay, this is my Easter-Passover sermon. Rebirth. I have on my desk a bumper sticker that Sister Elaine gave me after my Honda was found. It's one of those Jesus things and says "Expect A Miracle" in some reflective material. Well, the car died but you never know when there's another miracle in sight.

Love and many kizzes and I hope this finds you feeling better . . .

When I had no reply for a while, and wrote, "ARE YOU OKAY?" she sent back my fax with a note scrawled on it:

11pm—yes, of course I'm crazy,* that's a given—

*in my haste I read "okay" as "crazy" . . . I don't want to think abt. the psychological meaning of that—But *am* okay, just feeling reclusive, trying to clean up after my sick cat & sick me. Clean up my act, like they say . . .

Hello. Sunny Spring day here, and I haven't exactly wasted it, but have spent a lot of time watching and worrying abt. Squirrel who I'm sure is on his way out. Hope my answer last night was not too abrupt . . .

What I am is not really reclusive, just sort of totally spaced. The books on my kitchen table say it . . . Lorca's *Collected Poems* (bilingual), Jean Rhys's *Good Morning Midnight*, E. O. Wilson's *Consilience*, *The Complete Poems of Emily Dickenson*, Aldous Huxley's *The Art of Seeing*, and all of it not really random, I cld. tell you why each one is on my table but that would take a lot of time and might bore you and I need to go fix something to eat besides the rice which is done and waiting.

I accepted this desire on her part to zone out, even if it meant not hearing from her, and not seeing her, even when I read in Boston that spring. She apologized, said she was scared to travel, had no sense of direction, etc., though on the night of the reading, she wrote: "I've been thinking how nice it wld. have been to be there, hear you, see Kellie, etc. You're being wined & dined right now I suppose . . . Just wanted you to know I've been thinking abt. you and yr. reading so close by that I've missed."

I'd gladly have shared all that wining and dining, but hadn't expected. She *was* reclusive — or spaced, whatever she wanted to call it — and uncomfortable in crowds, and I didn't want her to feel guilty, so simply told her the story, as usual. Now I can't decide whether this was the right response, although it was, after all, the only way she'd have been there:

NEW YORK, 5/8/98

The kids tricked me! Kellie said, before UMass reading, "I just have to stop at the bus station to pick up a package some temp secretary sent via Greyhound instead of UPS." So we stopped, I waited in car, and lo! There came Lisa, holding a sign that said "Surprise! Happy Mother's Day!" They came to both readings, bought me flowers, and took me out to a lobster dinner in between, and afterwards we went to a party at Skip Gates's house and hung out with all the hot shit black intellectuals of Harvard [and a few white ones]. Woo Woo! as they used to say.

Today I've been a Jew on a panel about identity at St. Marks Church.

GLOUCESTER, STORMY STORMY 5/9/98

Hello! I'm feeling much better, it's a matter of figuring out what did it.

Chan has sent me her first two chapters of dissertation and it is very very interesting, and of course so well written . . . more on that later. This was meant to be a postcard!

My lovely next-door neighbor has got himself a press, to make prints from his woodcuts. He brought over the first, and was so excited, we both were. So I guess this is an up time, all around. Like he said, so exhilarated, "I got my Christmas early."

To celebrate Mother's Day tomorrow I'm supposed to be at the Gloucester House for breakfast at 9:30AM . . .

Plate 1. Fort Gull, 1975. Photo: Kenn Schrader

Plate 2. Lobby window, EF Logo, Eksportfinans Bank,
Oslo, Norway, 1981. Photo: Kenn Schrader

Plate 3. Superhero series, c. 1995. Photo: Kenn Schrader

Plate 4. Helene at her light table, 1984. Photo: Kenn Schrader

Plate 5. Black Monk, 1996. Photo: Kenn Schrader

Plate 6. Big Joke, c. 2000. Photo: Kenn Schrader
Plate 7. Rainy Day Dream Mask, c. 2000. Photo: Kenn Schrader

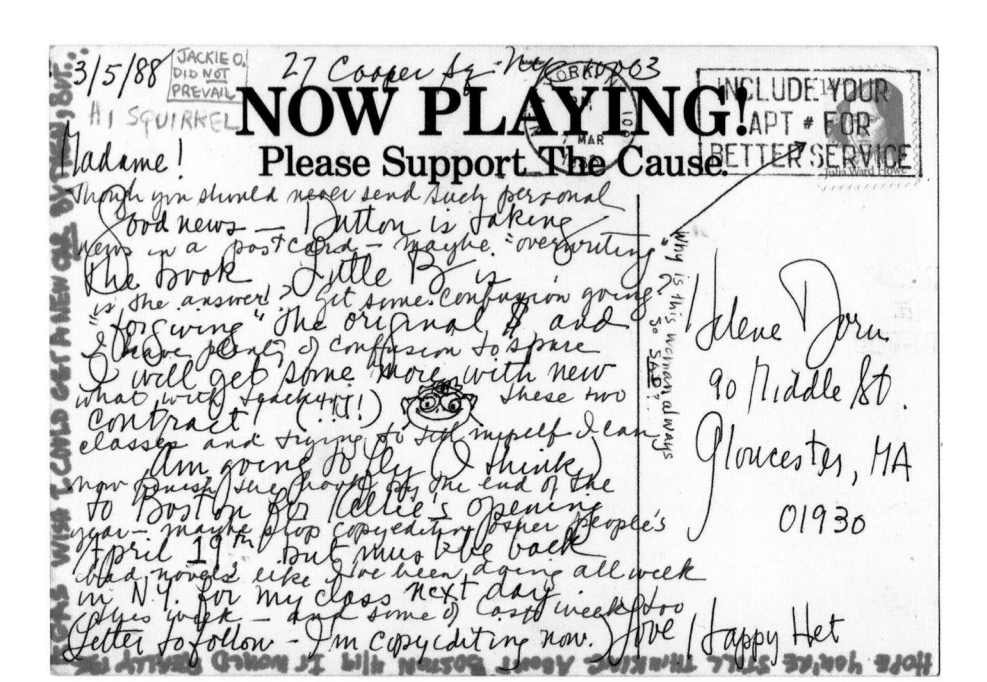

Plate 8. Postcard from Hettie to Helene, March 1988

Plate 9. Helene and Hettie at Marie's, 1989

Plate 10. Hettie and Helene at Marie's, 1989

But she wrote later that although she loved all "those little mothers and mothers-to-be" so much, it was hard to keep up with what was being said, and she wondered if her physical presence was important to any of them—which she doubted. And she ended, after more worry over her cat, "Oh dear, I think I am what is called a drunken old lady," with a funny drawing to deflect the charge.

"I think you underestimate your importance," I shot back. And then, after a while:

For no reason I can figure I got very angry with myself and have cleared off all the light tables and am back in studio after *months* of walking thru on the way out the door for stupid errands thinking "tomorrow." I blame, in part, the computer, but that's not fair. Think it might have been ticked off by my going thru files to find a photo of the piece Cape Ann Historical gave back to me to fix (at least a month ago!) because, of course, only one of the 3 missing pieces of glass was in the box. Anyway, even if it's just repair, it's a start. And maybe will get me out of my mind and back to my hands . . .

Reading this I remember Marie's comment that one was not to underestimate "the iron" in Helene. Soon as the meds got (somewhat) figured out, and the cat had died and she had mourned, she wrote that in the local supermarket her great-grandson had challenged her to a running game, and "we covered every aisle of the store and startled a few customers, but had a great time. And I'll never see Star Market the same again." And now I want to say, as she might have, Amen.

II

At the horizon's lit fog rim
earth keeps in touch with sky.
I call this the end of the beginning.

In its mist, frayed ghosts of selves drowse;
I call them my lost selves.
Lately they drift close, unaging,
watching me age. Now & then, one or some

flare up, known shapes in known clothes. . . .

— *Marie Ponsot*

Hello —

I've been in a fog since Saturday's mail telling me my Massachusetts Common Health coverage will STOP 7/28/98 because my assets are over the program limit of $4,000. Called yesterday a.m. — and the very nice sympathetic woman explained that the fact that I was over 65 had been ignored somehow. "Consider yourself lucky," she said. Hear this, Hettie Jones: *Under 65 you can have any amt. of assets, over 65 you can have no more than $4000 savings.* That's age discrimination, I sd., and she was silent. Then I asked her to explain and she said "I can't, it's just a state regulation."

So there you are — guess I'll just have to manage to be well.

The seven-year difference in our ages provided some lessons I never could have anticipated but was grateful to learn early. Age discrimination, I discovered, took many forms. I suppose any late-blooming woman should have expected to be tested later in life, but I was always surprised by having to continue proving myself, to justify, by referring to others, what I knew from experience to be worthwhile:

Yesterday, out of the blue, I got a call from the man who runs the writing program at Lang College, part of the New School. One of their poetry teachers is ill, and they needed an immediate, experienced substitute, someone with a poetry book out, and here I was. So I had to stay up until 1 a.m. writing a course description, which I faxed to them in the middle of the night and is now in the catalog, and I start on Sept 14th. And now I don't have to work in the ad agency (but I do have to think up a poetry course). Whew.

Last night I read Fenellosa (edited by Pound) on Chinese poetry, all his difficult but fascinating stuff about language, in *The Poetics of the New American Poetry*. I'm trying to figure out this poetry class and wrapping my mind around stuff ain't easy, since I basically know what works and what doesn't. Not much theoretical underpinning from this drama major . . . Still for me the big questions revolve around structure (of the class not of poems)! What's the first assignment to be? And the second, third? And what does an *intermediate* poet know?

Whew . . . Fenellosa . . . Pound's translation, you take me back years. One of the books that got sold when I was totally broke on the Fort and one of Fred's knowledgeable friends came, went thru my library, took the gleanings to NYC, and came back with enough $ to see me through a very bad, scary time. But I do remember being totally enchanted with that sense of language.

Still have not written the introductory lecture or planned the first lessons, though I did manage to get through *The Poetics* with lots of stickies on the pages to look at again. Also looked up a lecture I gave at The Frost Place some years ago and some notes I made before teaching poetry the last time, and it's all pretty much the same way I feel still: "the heart to the breath to the line," just like Charles said. And the stuff from Fenellosa, re active verbs and images. I loved your story about that little book. Saved by poetry.

Letter from Lucia last week describing what she'd had to do—*page after page!*—to provide the powers a reason for her being reappointed to the creative writing department. The only thing she cld. remember of what she turned in was that she does know in one of the *five* demanded pages on her "poetics," she wrote: "As Miles Davis said, 'you know, those dark Arkansas roads at night. That's the sound I'm after.'"

Lovely, no??? Is it a familiar quote? In all these years of being a Miles fan, I don't remember it, and am sure I wld. had I ever read it.

That wonderful reference, though not the exact quote, comes from the autobiography Quincy Troupe wrote with Miles. [The roads led to his grandfather's farm.] But oh how I sympathize with Lucia. I've started trying to write the syllabus they want, and I suppose it's a good thing to get your brain in order, but I find it an interruption—how can I know what's next when I haven't seen what worked the previous week? Each group is different! And all that stuff—five pages on one's poetics!

Which reminds me I have an appointment at SUNY Purchase next Thurs. to talk about the class in Poetic Techniques I've applied for this spring. I don't know poetic techniques from those dark Arkansas roads, man.

Now it's 11:15 and I have to put on shoes and find my glasses and wade through the wall of children out there partying in the east vill. I hope to see the moon you spoke of in between their burly shoulders.

Hello—

I thought you'd be pleased to know that your scholarship again saved my ass at that interview on Thursday! Do you remember sending me something by Ursula Le Guin titled "The Reciprocity of Poetry and Prose"? You must have sent it years ago . . . In any case I've referred to Le Guin many times but there she was, on the tip of my tongue, when they asked something about poetry/prose. Oh, I sounded so smart, as if I'd found that myself! All the while I was thanking you . . .

Love to you and all the Ghosts of Gloucester!

• • • • •

A quick Sat. nite note . . . Got lost in a Bronte family biog. which is some 900 pages of small print, don't ask me why except I stopped in lib. to see why Lucia had sd, a long time ago, that my house reminded her of theirs. It just came into my head to do that & she was right . . . but of course I started reading it there in the lib., and brought it home no matter the back of my head told me not to do so. I guess I just do that, and it can't be helped. I am scattered, always have been, & that's why I never get much done . . . (lecture to myself).

Born later, college educated, trained at an art school, she might have learned shortcuts, blasted through the scatter, developed the back of her head more. But I write this half a century after women have been working hard to get the front and back—and sides—together . Like other women I've known, Helene just came along too soon. And why, at seventy-one, should she have had to berate herself, or apologize for her scholarly interests? Why even consider this, I ask myself, especially since so often I was the beneficiary?

That fall she kept me supplied with cartoons to cheer me through a season in which I had sixty students in four classes in four different places. She made good fun of my devotion to newsprint, my Saturday night trips to get the *Times*. In October, with the note "Bet the nyt can't match this!" she sent a photo from the Gloucester paper showing "Nathan Hale," a 1914 life-size bronze, too valuable to be left unattended while an exhibit was installed at his City Hall home. The solution to this problem had been to lock "Nathan Hale" into a holding cell at the local precinct, where he was captured gazing heroically through the bars.

• • • • •

We also had fun with age and appearance when I was on my way to San Francisco:

Hello, it's *very* late but I just had to do something with my brain other than choose my clothes. Whew. It's a job trying to look cute and be comfortable at once on a Salv Army budget.

Hullo . . .

You keep using the term "cute" which, for some reason, bothers me . . . so I've just now looked it up in my trusty Web 10 —

> *Cute (ca 1731): 1-clever or shrewd often in an*
> *underhanded manner 2-attractive or pretty esp. in a*
> *dainty or delicate way 3-obviously straining for effect.*

I do love you, my dear friend. And I wish you wldn't worry quite so much how you look because it's what you say that counts in the long run. I'm preaching . . .

Hello —

Please don't apologize . . .

Well, in defense I use "cute" sardonically; after all, at 64+ how cute can you be? OK. I'll write when I come home. Keep preaching, Momma.

Sat nite hello, 11/21/98 . . . can you believe it?

Just a quick note but want to send because I'm thinking of you and laughing . . . I've just spent a lot of time working out a comfortable, warm, easily packable to carry on my back, outfit to wear on Thanksgiving . . . to look "hip" mebbe? Certainly not "cute," I'm too old and weatherbeaten for that . . . and *why* I feel the need to do so, I've no idea.

When you have time [*HO!*] tell me abt. your time in SF.

I'm truly tired and going to bed. It's v. late. I'll send this tomorrow, but while I write I'm thinking you've gone out for the paper, have read it, and are now totally informed abt. what's happening in the world and have gone to bed.

That's nice.

Hello — I was feeling so *good*, having almost finished all the Xmas buying. Turned on TV to catch tomorrow's weather and got nothing but pics of exploding bombs, etc. I called Fred, he sd. he didn't know anything except we've bombed Baghdad, had just turned on the news himself. Well, shit!!!

Here again all these men playing war games, & the public will probably love it. Fun to watch, like the Gulf War, was it?—

So here we are—Merry Xmas all you poor innocent Iraqis—

Hello—

The fact that they named this action in Iraq "Desert Fox" has offended and shocked me. ANYONE who was alive during WWII and knew of Rommel—oh I can't even bear it. To name this after a NAZI!!! The govt got some stupid guy to say, "Oh, it's really ok." But IT'S NOT OKAY, NOT WHEN MY UNCLE DIED IN THAT WAR!!!!

This is a rant, as you see. Love! Merry Xmas.

Solstice tomorrow—we shld. be out dancing!

Janine Vega told me today that the solstice begins a time of putting things in order. I certainly hope that's the case, as we've a lot to figure out.

· · · · ·

In the months before the turn of the century, amid the many preposterous world's-end predictions, we never considered a possible end to the world as we knew it. After I'd had hints about "market-rate" rent, Helene wrote, "I can't understand *any* of that, but it's *truly scary*, and I remember, coming home on the train from visit to Jack, seeing the lights in all the houses and crying— I can't even recall which eviction, but I had no place to go I cld. afford."

The previous summer she'd written of a fire on Gloucester's waterfront: "Another wharf gone, another stab at the still-working fishermen, and tourist city, condo haven, here we come . . . The developers are already here en masse."

En masse, yes, but she didn't know how close:

People here today to check out house for "insurance purposes" we were told. Which was weird. Anyway neighbor Paul was as nervous as I abt. "why?"—No matter he works for the museum, he had no idea, and didn't like it. Woman w/insurance man is very involved in the historic houses in

Glouc. & restoration, etc. — who knows, we may be booted out . . . something I refuse to worry abt. till it happens & by then I'll probably be ashes thrown into the harbor.

Re your house inspection, *very alarming*. Is there no way to ask what is going on?

I keep returning to the idea that we were being chased — no, she chased and I *squeezed*. But this recurring threat of removal felt like just another result of our inadequacy, a built-in lack of preparedness. Helene's response was to predict her death, mine to complain: "I always feel underprivileged and under-educated."

"But like Frank O'Hara said," I added, "you just go on your nerve."

"Dislodge" is one synonym for "evict," interesting for the violence implied, its root that little lodge with its woman (no doubt a woman), her belongings beside her on the street. "It's a game," Helene had written, so many years before. But if so, it was a serious one:

Hullo it's almost 11pm and this is very quick because I must get to bed since people from the Cape Ann Historical Association board are due at ten tomorrow morning and I intend to be awake to ask them why this sudden interest and intrusion on my life.

Have been listening to all these CDs — Wynton Marsalis Baroque Music for Trumpets is so nice . . . but they are due back to lib. tomorrow and I must not listen, just go to bed. If you don't own your own house, you have to deal with the people who do. As you so well know.

2/6

Those gentlemen from the CAHA gave me strange answers, like they were new on the board and just wanted to see the building and what repair was needed. Oh don't be ner-vous, all smiles. I dunno. Paul-next-door asked them outright when they were in his apartment if they intended to sell the building. If so, said they, it will be a very long-term thing and you certainly will have plenty of notice. So I KNOW something is going on . . .

This is just quick because machine is on and it seems a long time since I've heard from you and I'm wondering if you are ok. Probably just overwhelmed w/work, I'm sure. My head is swimming with all these things I want to find out about, none of them related, though are sort of, but I can't organize the "sort of" . . . for instance, the warrior moon goddess Coyolxauhqui.

I think we both needed some armor, or a little divine assistance. I had become chair of the PEN Prison Writing Program's volunteer committee and thus was responsible for the yearly reading to publicize the program's writing contest for prisoners:

NEW YORK, 2/9/99

I'm just overwhelmed. The PEN stuff is all consuming and I have complicated it by having to do it a new way. Now I'm involved in video and I can't believe I didn't write you about carrying a 13-inch TV in its big box on my shoulder all the way from Broadway, the only woman under five feet in lower Manhattan doing that at that moment, I suspect. Then ran somewhere else to buy a table and couldn't find the screws supposedly in the package which it turned out were screwed into the poles how was I to know that it said nothing about it in the directions, oh oh oh oh . . .

Finally last night I sat down to watch the videos I'd been trying to see for a week. But there's also a lot of other stuff, interpersonal relations, etc. In any case it's a big, unpaid job.

That stuff about your house sounds ominous, are there any protections at all—senior citizenry or anything? Oh god that's the worst, as you know already.

Goodnight. I promise to write something coherent soon.

GLOUCESTER, 2/10/99

You may not be home yet, but thought I'd send a hello. Wish I cld. fax you some of the chicken soup which is smelling good . . .

There is no point in worrying about house. If it happens, it happens. I've been thru it before, tho did think I was safe at last. How could any right-minded woman in her 72nd year on this earth think such a thing?

No matter. The sun and moon still exist and do their thing. How stupid to ask for any other safety.

Don't worry about writing.

2/11

Chili left at noon with no food and hasn't been back since. It's 7:38PM. He's done that only once before. He cld. be locked up in City Hall or in the library. Or, and I can hardly think of it, caught by a car no matter how streetwise he is. Hopefully he is just out with a friend.

9pm. Chili still not back. Obviously, I am very upset. Sorry! There you are w/all those frantic meet-the-schedule-things and I sit here worrying about my cat.

NEW YORK, 2/11/99

Oh, but I do understand, having had all those cats and the dogs besides and the rabbit—I'm sending all kinds of hopes and prayers up there with this.

Dear Chili, come home now!

• • • • •

Maybe the cat knew something first. I never got the full story, but after a while he was "mending well." As was Helene herself, who eventually wrote, in a very shaky hand:

Chili still gone. Fell after I wrote last Thurs. and have been fogged out since. Happened to be right by phone Mon. night and picked up call. Talked for some min. & then had to ask who I was talking to! Well, she brought me to, and next a.m. I somehow got to Emerg. Room. Brain scan proved (I hope!) I did not injure my brain but did break my left, thank God, wrist, and am suffering post-concussion fog which they promise will pass in a couple of weeks. Much help from all, plus visiting nurse, etc.

Not to worry! But I can't write for a while (cast on for 6 wks) plus other details . . . just to explain my silence—

Around all the anxiety re health and home, we still had time for jokes. During the Clinton/Lewinsky scandal that winter, she'd written: "I've ignored it till now as a bunch of boring shit, but seeing those scary staunch right-wing faces, I got freaked. Damn Clinton and his wandering dick . . . What's to happen?"

"Were Wm. Burroughs alive," I answered, "he'd end this scenario with all those guys fucking themselves to death."

· · · · ·

ANNOUNCEMENT:

THE POETRY SOCIETY OF AMERICA HAS AWARDED DRIVE BY HETTIE JONES ITS NORMA FARBER AWARD FOR A FIRST BOOK—

$500, THE PURCHASE OF 500 BOOKS, AND AN AWARDS CEREMONY ON APRIL 23RD, WHICH HAPPENS TO BE THE BIRTHDAY OF THE POET'S MOTHER!

Hope this doesn't wake you! I'm as excited as a 3 year old!

That's *wonderful* news!

This, written in a much surer hand, was followed by a drawing of a champagne glass with bubbles ascending, nine additional exclamation points, and, of course, "Love, H"

Hey, it's the great American Sat. night! Hello!

Is the cast off?

What I'm up to right now is piling on some clothes and tumbling out of here to get the paper. Even if the news is all bad.[1] I grew up with the idea that we should never step into the Balkans and now of course we see why. No doubt there will be more photos in the paper of weeping, displaced people, all of whom must blame their situations on internecine wars of the 14th century. Bah humbug.

But NY is full of daffodils and even some tulips, and in the green-

---

1. The Kosovo War between Yugoslavia and the Kosovo Albanian rebel guerrillas. There ensued a massive displacement of population, close to a million people.

market this morning not only pussy willows but actual greens—collard and broccoli rabe and spinach—wintered over and a wee droopy, but I remembered how sweet those were and bought them all! The best, though, is that from my front window I can see 6 baby trees all in full bloom—white flowers as if covered in snow. Even if they were planted to raise property values I can't help loving them—AND BIG LOVE TO YOU

· · · · ·

Oh dear, how long it truly has been that I've been a'ailin'—

I've no idea why I decided to go online, I just did. Concussion aftermath???? Anyway, the line is in but I haven't done the rest. I'm nervous that I'll fuck it all up somehow, no matter my sons tell me it is a simple matter (other than the extra 20$ per mo which I've stopt mentioning since it gets a shrug of the shoulders from Fred, and from Paul: "What are you saving your money for, your 'old age'? You're already there!")

I have little to show for these months. Got into the Bible last week, and yesterday realized all that old testament blood and guts was totally depressing me so hauled out Tolstoy's fairy tales & fables to go with my dinner and felt much better—he had me laughing.

Dinner is done and I must eat. No I've not gained a pound. Weird! Oh! Also read Farai Chideya, *The Color of Our Future*, which I found really interesting. Then read Danzy Senna's *Caucasia* because she had mentioned it.

I can't believe I've almost finished some note I've started!

Another "Board" person here at 9am to inspect the house. I called Judith ["landlady"] after he left and she sd. yes, they are putting the house on the market. Amen. At least I know.

Love & thanks for yr patience w/my looooooooong silence—

I am ashamed now that in my whirligig of self-involvement there's no mention in my next letter of the impending sale of that house. Maybe we spoke on the phone. Maybe our letters crossed, since both were written the same day. But I understood her relief—"at least I know"—because all I knew about my own situation was that any rent increase meant I would not be able to stay where I was.

Today was weird, hard—I dunno. I see the result of overwork, one's mind goes crashing, skittering—

9:45 Tues night the head of the 92nd St. Y Poetry Center calls and says they've organized a reading of "Howl" for next Monday night and could he possibly ask me at the last minute to fill in for Larry Rivers who no longer wanted to do it after having initially agreed. Was I to refuse? I have to write a 4 minute speech about Howl or America or something about Allen. The pay is $350 and I am not in a position to say no. But now I am reading Sat in Staten Island, Mon at Y, Weds I have 2 classes, Thurs reading from *Aliens* & showing video at John Jay College of Criminal Justice ... Friday from my own work at a benefit for Planned Parenthood. This does not include *life*, such as taking the car to the garage because the wheels are not yet balanced and so the steering wheel shakes as soon as I hit 60, and going to Social Security to see about "my future," having Lisa here tomorrow night and brunch with Kellie on Sun and taking her to the airport thereafter.

I thought, this morning, that I was having a nervous breakdown. I felt angry at everyone, or envious—because I won a prize (500) but not the 7,000 state grant for poetry I'd applied for.

Yes, tomorrow is the award. And I'll get to see my kids and have a good time. But all the rest ... It must be a physical thing, something to do with *flow*—

Aren't you glad you got better so you could hear my complaints again? I'll write a better letter soon. Now you must bear with my insanity ... thank you!

xxoo

P.S. email, internet stuff not hard but get someone else to install it for you.

On 4/26 Helene sent a handwritten note about having had "a couple of bad days." No wonder. But on Mother's Day, with a "lovely spring evening in store," she wrote:

OK. It's 4:28pm and I thought I'd be able to send you an email but having problems and need to contact the 800 people. Yesterday I gave myself a heart attack break and didn't even turn the computer on.

And that break really started when Pat, the package mailman, knocked on my kitchen door and handed me your [Bedford video] tape, "Something from your pal" . . . I undid it right away, of course, then went out for my daily walk, did my exercises, then sat down to watch it. THANK YOU!!! Whew. Those women. I love them . . .

Long Mday call from Chan, nice! and a funny stop-in at Bucks. Steph greeted me, vacuum in hand, "Happy Mothers Day." I sd. TY and the same to her but what was she doing vacuuming on this day? She only smiled, I walked on in, and there was Fred sitting at the table, one foot immersed in a plastic container of soda water. He'd gone to pee barefoot in the middle of the night, got a splinter in the ball of his foot and cld. hardly make it back upstairs to bed. Cldn't get it out by himself, woke Steph, who also cldn't but could see that it was glass. I fumed and sputtered, of course, don't leave it in there, go to the emergency room. They looked at me and laughed—you're a fine one to talk! I sputtered some more, and then laughed too. Then somehow we got onto a Welsh pudding beginning with F. but I can't remember the rest, and I'd heard of it, and Steph suddenly remembered Mrs. Bean, an English basic cookery book from 1850 . . . It was in there but then she started reading aloud from other things, like how to deal with various fowls and the like and we got semi hysterical, it was just very, very funny but I had to come home and fix food so I decided not to listen anymore because I wld have all those images of violence and vinegar in my head and not want to eat even vegetables.

It's now 6pm due to phone calls, etc. I'm going to send this, do the dishes & fix something to eat. It's still beautiful out my OPEN windows. Must be same there, hope you're out in it—AMEN

Hullo—I sent you an email a while ago. Date w/Steph tomorrow AM to go get herbs for my porch . . . who knows how long it will be "mine"??? Oh how that hangs over my head—

Dear Het,

Got yrs of yesterday this a.m., was nice to have with my wake-up coffee. I'm totally stressed out which is why, I'm sure, I slept some ten hours! The bldg. has not yet been sold, I have no idea how much time I have left here, but it is inevitable that whoever buys it will want me out. Amen. I think a few more nights of 10-hour oblivion will bring me out of the daze I've been in. I cldn't even get my head straight enuff to fill out the application for Central Grammar (just up the street, elderly housing w/nice apartments), when I came to the question "Why do you want to move to this property?"

This is just a quick get-back. Learned from my big sister that age doesn't catch you, it just slows you down. Which I know you refuse to do, but you ain't old yet, mama.

Am sure I'll still be here in July, please try to come. Even if someone bought the house today, it's gonna take time for the legalities and they have to give us 2 months notice. If you think I'm crazy to be so freaked, there is a 2-year waiting list for Central Grammar, the apts. listed in paper want more $ for a one bedroom per month than I have coming in, and the other, city-owned, elderly housing is just awful, but there's only a 6 mo. waiting list. I really feel too old to once again have to deal with an act of commerce—act of god one simply says ok; I dunno, mebbe it's the same thing. I ain't got time to be philosophical, but it has flitted thru my mind that if the house burned down and I lost everything it might be easier.

With that I leave you. Not to worry, I'm ok, just spewing. It has been a truly lovely May day, everything in bloom, even the daisies in the courtyard.

NEW YORK, 6/1

Hi—

I certainly do *not* think you're crazy to be so freaked; I'd be totally freaked in the same situation, in fact even more so since I haven't moved in so many years.

GLOUCESTER, 6/5/99

Hullo . . . A Sat. night note. oy vey, more people here today going thru my house but I left my keys w/neighbor Paul so I wdn't have to be here. Went instead w/Ket and Elaina, Keyra, and Alexis to do their errands up and down Main Street. Then we went back to their house, and Ket showed me how to use the Internet, sort of, and she checked out real estate agency, which ain't yet got this house listed which is in some way quieting. She checked historic houses on Cape Ann, still not listed. Which made me feel better. Tho I don't know why it should. We cld. have sat there for hours, oh! the Internet!

Paul told me people here were v. innarested in my glass. So was the man from Rockport last week when I *was* here. Mebbe I shld have cards ready to hand out? I think I'm slightly drunk and need to stop & eat. More people coming next Tuesday. I shouldn't hate them, they just want to buy a house, I shouldn't hate the real-estate lady, she just earning her living, I shouldn't hate the Historical Assn, they just don't want to spend the necessary money to keep this house in shape. I know that but I still HATE THEM ALL!

6/8

More people here today, one hour past the time they sd. they were coming. Paul next door has found a place to live, now I gotta do the same. Chili seems to sense there is something terribly wrong, sitting here on desk and rubbing against my arm . . .

So much for the two months' notice about which she'd written *twelve*— TWELVE—days before. Two days later wrote that she'd rented something and felt much better. "Small, and of course paneling on the walls, but I'll make it work till Central Grammar comes thru."

Nevertheless, though I sent her "much encouragement and sympathy," and begged her to "PLEASE KEEP EATING," she wrote, on 6/19, "Not sure I'm going to live through this move."

She did, but not without another fall. Though "at least I wasn't concussed," she wrote. Some comfort in that, I suppose. Not concussed but chased. Dislodged, in twelve days, after twelve years, without care or compensation. Displaced. Discarded. Later she would write, "I took care of that house as if it were my own child."

· · · · ·

GLOUCESTER, 6 RIGGS STREET, 8/1/99

!!!! And *Hot*. If you're there, send me a short message so I'll know if it survived the move (not sure I have)! It's a sauna out there & in here. Which wld. be fine if one cld. get out of it & jump into a snowbank, which we did in Idaho. It *is* improving but so *slow!*

Errand today so got out at last—clocked it—6 min. to Fred's, 12 to lib. So I have come out of my cocoon (sp?) . . . I wonder which box my dict. is in?

So to the "dis" list could be added "disorder." There *was* something disorderly, I can see now, about the end of the century:

Hi—So much going on, the NY Public Library pursuing me for workshops, which is great. I haven't told you I'm probably not going to work at Bedford anymore, have I. Well, it's complicated. With 7 library workshops I'll make up the money. As for the sentiment, that's something else.

And I had begun to mistrust email after encouraging it: "I keep thinking we'll lose all these words—even the lists of stuff we write—the casseroles and papers to be filed and me and my hithers and yons." But paper was itself a problem:

GLOUCESTER, 8/17 RETURNED EMAIL, HOST UNKNOWN
DATE: MON 16 AUG 1999
TO: HETTIEJ@EARTHLINK.NET
FROM: HKDORN@EARTHLINK.NET
SUBJECT: FRNENZIED

Frenzied was what I meant to write/ Hello! WHY am I breaking my back & my head finding a place for all my correspondence for some 20 years WHERE am I going to put it now WILL I ever do anything with it and if I don't WHO wld. be interested.

At least I had some foresight about this, even though I still viewed us as adjuncts to the real thing, and answered: "Do NOT throw away correspondence, please; it will be of interest to any university that eventually holds Ed's."

As before mentioned, see the Edward Dorn papers at the Stanford University Libraries, Stanford, California.

• • • • •

Hello! What are you doing? I haven't heard from you in—forever. Are you still unpacking? What's going on? Let me know how you are!

Of course she hadn't written because immediately there were disasters—fallen ceiling, no water, no shower. To how many unsettled women of limited means has this happened?

I'm just by now completely BORED! with moving in. Stuck again till work resumes upstairs and I can get all the stuff I had stored off the floor & back in the closet. Met former neighbor, Paul, who tells me they've sold 90 Middle, so bear with it & be thankful you have a roof over your head. He also hasn't yet got back to painting.

I dunno, every time the phone rings I quake, likewise a knock on my door . . . Such another time in my life . . . if I'm alive a year from now I'll laugh at it. I still can at moments, but the moments don't come often enuff to stave off the depression that creeps over me. Which makes me feel guilty, looking at the "world at large." I shld be down on my knees w/ thanks for my lot.

There shld have been a dear Hettie at the beginning. Here it is at the

And that's where this email stopped, as if a signal. I worried.

Hello!

What's happened to our correspondence? Are we both so caught up that we can't write? I feel terrible to not be in touch with you. Are you still dealing with landlord's fixings and falling ceilings?

Here's much the same, only in the ether. The boy in the middle floor, Tracy, whom I liked so much, has been shot dead in Atlantic City, "allegedly" in a robbery. Landlord, after 3 years of refusing to accept rent from this dead boy, just on Friday decided to relent. Tracy was basically a good kid. Oh god.

Tues I must go to Lincoln Center to watch the work of my Bedford students, who have become the writers discovered by Eve Ensler, who claims that now she will be the voice of the voiceless women in prison.

Here I must differ with this approach. It was never my intention to be the voice of those who are "voiceless," when they have as much a voice as each of us. I simply taught them to use it. That, after all, was the point, wasn't it?

What else? I had a wonderful group at a local library on Thurs, and the librarians so helpful and warm. And the place, when I walked in at 4:30pm, filled with happy children, oh. The real Lower East Side; I felt so privileged to be teaching for the library.

It rained all day today; I didn't mind since I had to sit here doing homework anyway. I don't actually mind the homework, to be truthful, it's just that there's never ever enough time to get everything done, and I begin to feel out of breath, ever anxious . . .

I wonder whether in all this I am really having a life? I remember coming across an Inuit verse — "Is this real, is this real, this life I am living?"

12

My dissent is cheer
a thankless disposition
first as the morning star
    my ambition: good luck

and why not   a flight
over the wide dilemma
and then good night to
    sad forever
        —Grace Paley

NEW YORK, 2/26/00

Hi—

A gray, weird day. Lots of action around NY re the Amadou Diallo case; 4 cops shot this unarmed guy 41 times and there's much to say but I won't. They moved the trial to Albany, where the cops were acquitted of all charges today. Ah. And my Purchase students responded to an assignment to write a poem of rage or protest by claiming they had nothing to be angry about.

Looks like the Rita Marley book [a memoir I'd write] is coming through.

NEW YORK, 4/16/00

Hello—

I signed a contract to do the Marley proposal, to interview her in Miami next weekend. Her manager called this morning to say I'm not going to Miami but Jamaica (fine with me!) and on Sunday not Saturday. These people are going to drive me crazy.

Hello—

Jamaica was terrifically interesting. There *is* a Rita Marley story (as I suspected) and I'd love to tell you about it, but I can't write it all in this email because I haven't written it down yet!

From the hotel balcony I could see a huge vacant lot where guys played soccer from dawn till dusk and there were goats grazing. All this next to a fancy hotel . . .

I got home Tues afternoon and Rita's manager called Weds at 8:30 in the morning asking when would I be done with the proposal. Then he called again Thurs morning to say that Rita wanted me to hurry up as the publisher was waiting.

Ah . . . . .

Last night I went to a book party and there spoke with a guy I know who is head of sales for one of the big publishers. Hyperion, which wants the Rita Marley book, has tons of money because it's *Disney*. Should I pray for money? Is that moral?

At Naropa, where I'd gone to teach, I met Helene's old friends, the writers Lucia Berlin and Jane Wodening Brakhage, she of the 1988 "odd-ball turn-overs," whose work I'd read via Helene's introduction. When I returned mid-June I wrote, "What you and I need to do is drive out there at least once before we all croak." But nothing enticed her.

Hullo, hope you're getting rested up. Got the poppies & rocks you sent in mail today. Knew you'd seen Jane, got an ecstatic email note from her—what a celeb you've become!—but had no idea Lucia had been to that reading too. Lotsa questions, of course, but will wait till I figure you have some space to write. Food waiting, the air in here so wet I can't see out of my glasses. Put article from AARP mag. (am sure I'm the only one I know looks thru them) which I thought you might dig, in envelope, no note enclosed, and *actually* had to look up yr zip code! That's what email does. Later, love H

Hi—this isn't really an answer, because it just occurred to me that I could play a CD while I was working. I've been reading about reggae music for hours, after my agent again rejected my proposal yesterday, saying I had to put more history in it. That is, I had to write the book before writing the book. Last night I tried the internet and got nowhere so went out and bought 2 books with photos—one of them published first in the 70s when reggae first came out of Jamaica. And of course I fell in love with the correspondences, the history that completes some of what I already know about African-derived musics . . . Seduction! So tonight I had to go get some CDS.

Right now Bob Marley is singing beneath my fingers "Burnin' and Lootin'"—I just read an interview where he claims it's metaphorical—and I thought immediately of Roi's poem, the one he got so attacked for—"Damballah / murder my friends in their beds" . . . Anyway I'm all jacked up on sentiment, looking at pictures from the 70s and realizing how little has changed.

Sent you something else via snail mail today.

Okay. After this tune he's going to sing "No Woman No Cry" and I might have to stop it because that one . . .

You can email me in the country through the marvels of technology, since I'll be hettiej wherever I go. Re my being a celebrity, hah. Oh no, here it comes . . . and the whole audience (in London) is singing "no woman no cry" but he's such a tease he plays a *long* intro before he actually sings—"In this great future you can't forget your past"—oh!

Helene did write again that year, as I know from mine of July 5th, which begins "I turned this thing on specifically to write to you, and there you were, twice." That so little of her voice from this time survives is my fault. When she asked me not to use "that dumb reply bit," I didn't fully understand email's potential for loss. Now, without her words in my hand, I read this: "That story of you and the dish and the pot is priceless!"

Hullo, as usual, my dinner is fixed & staying warm in oven . . . but am wondering how you are and miss updates on all the dilemmas—figure you're up to yr. neck in busyness, plus probably dealing w/new computer.

Thought I would be too, but Fred obviously didn't have time this weekend to get the Mac.

OK, a bunch of nonsense just to say hello and let you know I'm thinking abt. you and wondering!

Hi—I'm so pleased that you're walking and doing, etc. Yeah, I do appreciate that everything you do is heavy. I went to see the film *Pollock* last weekend—lots of stuff required by anyone who makes art. But then again, you get to move around a bit. Play with substances. There's a great Yiddish word for it—*potschke*. As in "Why do you want to *potschke* around with paint?"

Tho this ain't a letter, you know I'm miraculously still breathing . . . This machine is so much easier on my eyes I'm gonna get one & tell myself it will take place of $ spent on glasses . . . ho ho. But, once learned, it will I'm sure lower my blood pressure. Yeah.

Am leaning over Fred's Mac to type this. Mas tarde. Happy Mother's Day—Fred arrived for a tutoring lesson w/a case of beer and a dandelion and a kiss. How about that.

Got this job through my agent: was picked up by car at 8:15am and taken to a school auditorium, where I saw a wonderful performance piece by nine kids (high school age) who'd been coached by George Faison, who has done lots of Broadway, etc. The kids were selected through many auditions and wrote all the material—most of it cautionary tales about sex, drugs, etc. but really sincere, and not a flubbed line in the 45 minutes. Some singing and line dancing. The kids in the audience were 7 & 8 grade and so responsive. What a treat!

Then I came home and wrote 853 words about the kids onstage and the kids in the audience. Not a bad gig. I get so turned on by these new baby children who, in NY anyway, are amazingly multiculti.

I've been in touch with Chan and we're going to hang out when I'm in SF.

Seems a long time since I've heard from you . . . You OK?

LOVE, HD (I thought icon Macintosh HD simply meant this machine was registered to me. Talking to Fred on phone, he sd, go to the hard drive icon at top of screen [Macintosh HD]. I didn't tell him what I'd thought, but I will tomorrow. Hard Drive, that's me. I'm still laughing!)

Hi Hard Drive!

I'm okay, yes ma'm. I wish all this work would stop, but after I come back from California only one more gig and then I go on my wonderful vacation. You must start thinking about what I can bring or send you from London or Paris! Or Crete! I still can't believe I'm going.

We must have begun writing at exactly the same moment—I love it. Love you too, Hard Drive!

Got yr pc from SF today—o that city I loved so much way back when— don't remember bad weather ever. Will love hearing about yr stint & if you did manage to see Chan . . . Just to send hello. And love, Hard Drive.

Hi—sorry to use reply but I'm maybe still tired, or maybe tired anew! In any case, two days in a row I have slept for an entire hour with alarm ringing and radio playing 6 inches from my head. How is this possible?

SF so beautiful. The ALA Convention was in one of the buildings of the Moscone Center, only 2 or 3 levels high but the back looks out on a pond that spills over in a waterfall down to some gardens. Wish I could have found postcards of all that instead of the usual old ones. But the light . . . OH! Robert Hass, Chan's former teacher, who snuck her in to the convention, read some of his translations of Czesław Miłosz who has a series of poems called "OH!" All of which, when he finished reciting them, prompted me to respond, "OH!"

Well, your daughter is really something, beautiful and level-headed and smart. I didn't know she'd written poems that won an award at the university, so I tried to encourage her as much as I could.

SOS! I LOST your wonderful long catch-up last night trying to put it in your mailbox . . . finally gave up trying as nothing worked. Would you send it again?

Thanks for description and news of Chan. She never told me about poetry award.

Hi—she said she didn't tell anyone and indeed did not write any more poetry. I can identify, given how long it took me to get my act together.

The Poetry Society of America sent a letter asking me to conduct a 3-hour "seminar" on Beat Poetry in the fall. My heart sank, because I need the money since I lost my Lang class. But oh, now I'll spend the rest of the summer worrying about it. I don't know how to do a seminar, I only teach writing. OH!

Got resend plus!

Too tired to write and need to eat & go to bed. Have spent the day doing picky glass work and again moving stuff around in order to do what I'm doing.

Do not spend the summer worrying about seminar! Every one I've ever been in is just a talk session with someone knowledgeable leading it. Won't be any different than anything else you've done. And by now you sure as shit don't have to prove yourself. You gotta believe that, Hettie Jones.

More tomorrow, Scarlett O'Hara Hard Drive.

Trying to get some light as well as privacy here in "studio" by closing blind low enuff to still let air come in. The summer sounds, by the way, are probably worse for me, being right on street level: screaming kids, car horns, motorcycles, sirens, lawnmowers, neighbors talking, etc.

—of course I forgot to send this. Been working all day & got nothing to show for it. I'd forgotten, in my long hiatus, how exhausting and time consuming working w/the glass is. Doesn't help to have just one small light table & frantically packing stuff in totes. Well never mind. I'm just in one of my very down moods, and shldn't pass it on, but it helps sometimes to wail to a friend. Like Creeley's "you hold it" . . .

At least it's mildly raining now. And I feel better for having you-hold-it-ed.

I didn't mind holding it, certainly she held me. But I also wanted to distract her:

NEW YORK, 6/26

I cut a terrific picture of Louise Bourgeois out of the newspaper today— she's 89 and someone wrote a condescending article about her new piece in Rockefeller Center, which is a giant spider with egg case underneath, under which one walks. Two baby spiders beside her. So what if she's eccentric and focused on her father? She's a fucking genius, and I want to look exactly like her if and when I should make it to 89.

I'm loving that book by Zadie Smith. I cdn't fall asleep last night and read it till 5AM, then got up at 8. I think I better chill. Anyway, I just got a new mail message from Helene Dorn!

• • • • •

GLOUCESTER, 7/3

My kind of weather! Instead of doing errands I walked the boulevard which for once was not overcrowded, everyone at Fiesta. Pleasure boats out in force, but only one schooner way, way out heading into the Atlantic. Got across the bridge as far as the newly erected fisherman's wife's statue. I can hardly wait till they finish whatever they're planning to surround it. Right now it's got a half finished granite wall, lots of gravel, and all kinds of protective fences, but there she is in bronze, standing on a great granite boulder in the wind with her son and daughter, all looking out to sea. I love it.

Hard to resist barbeque smells coming in my windows. Passed, on my way home, lots of yard parties, flags waving in the wind. Now the parade sounds; the seagulls are squawking and having a feast of celebrant droppings. And I've been on the Internet!

Your fault! Library closed, but I found Zadie Smith & have made out online interlib. loan slip to deliver after the 4th. Also found book on Louise B. Then I went to Sherlock which sent me to Britannica & found a bunch of things, tho not the one you wrote abt. Will try again, my eyes gave out.

Hi—You sound wonderful. I'm so glad you're walking, and I love the fisherman's wife even w/o seeing her. Got the usual Megawatt [Fred's band] schedule in the mail this week. I was supposed to do a workshop Aug 24–25 but it's been canceled and I see that they are doing a "Blues Cruise" that weekend. Maybe I'll come if you would like? I don't know how wiped out I'll be after my great excursion but . . . I am now going to TRY to send you my itinerary as an attachment. I've got to keep practicing these skills! Anyway before I leave on 13th I'll be in Great Barrington, Mass. from 10th–afternoon of 12th. I leave here the next morning at 6:30 am. Kellie says she'll help me take suitcase down the stairs and will drive me to airport. I may let her do it!

The attachment has a weird title because I don't yet know how to rename a file, nor do I know how to put files in folders. One day . . .

Love and Independence!

Hi, glad you got it. I find some of the icons ambiguous. But that's just me. Today have been twice to Barnes & Noble because when I went w/o list, I completely spaced and bought books to read on trip. Second time to get French phrase book and a novel by Penelope Fitzgerald, whom I've never read, have you? Probably everyone has but me, as usual. But about ten years ago, I found a poem by Charlotte Mew, English, in *Penguin Book of Women Poets*, now yellowing and dry in my bookshelf, and never found any others, but now it appears that Penelope F. has written biography of her. Maybe I can find in library or somewhere. Her "Rooms" begins:

> I remember rooms that have had their part
> In the steady slowing down of the heart.
> The room in Paris, the room at Geneva,
> The little damp room with the seaweed smell,
> And that ceaseless maddening sound of the tide—

The phrase book was downstairs in the large, unhip, messy basement of the store, so while there I asked guy if memoirs were around, because not considered impt enough or hip enough I guess to warrant better placement. And there was one lone copy of *How I Became*, so I took out my pen and found guy and asked (he'd been pleasant) if he'd like me to sign it. So he forthwith made a big fuss and looked up all my books on the computer and told me I ought to do a reading, etc etc. It was a sweet encounter—he was funny, weird, obviously deaf, kept cupping his ear!—an Englishman—his name Mark "they don't allow me to have a last name yet"—and I came home happy and minus much money.

GLOUCESTER, 7/7/01

Spent many minutes trying to find Heraklion in index of my Readers Digest Atlas of the World (1987) which has never failed me, but it warn't in thar. So I went to Greece, which was, and found it on the northern shore of Crete. Spelled Iraklion. Am I right? Oh that Mediterranean! I only knew it from the coast of northern Spain, but that blue! And soft, cool water.

Plus London, and Paris . . . Paris!

Well! Just with the thought of where you'll be and when, you've sent me on a memory vacation. Thank you, Ma'm. What'll you do in London to celebrate your 67th?

Mas tarde. Love, H

NEW YORK, 7/9

Hi—I'll be in London only a week, and want to just walk around, usual touristy kind of things.

I loved your Paris memories. There I just want to walk too, in fact Joyce gave me a nice book of "Paris Walks"—the f'ing guidebooks weigh 3 lbs.

Yes, Heraklion is indeed Iraklion, on the coast. I'm gonna try to send postcards from wherever I get to. Great excitement! Love & kizzes.

• • • • •

In her last letter before I left—on my very first trip to Europe—Helene said she'd continue to write "so I don't feel so lonely . . . I'll miss you!" And she did, then sent her letters all together via regular mail. There's a drawing on the first page; looking at it once again I miss her hand, her true signature, her "Love, H." But her voice survives, and her eager investigations:

7/24: There you are in gay Paree. A very humid 82 degrees in here despite all fans going full speed. Walked in the heat . . . limped back here, fell into chair, drank 5 glasses of water and spent the rest of the afternoon, my legs up on a stool, reading Fitzgerald's *C. Mew & Her Friends*, drinking beer & smoking cigarettes. Ain't you glad you're where you are??? (Yes, I know, avoid alcohol in hot weather.)

7/25: Finished the book except for Fitzgerald's selection of poems . . . will read them tonight when hopefully it is cooler. It's a fascinating book. I can't bring up how it is that I did know of Mew when you sent me "Rooms" — maybe when I was reading V. Woolf & then her letters & of course Vita . . .

7/27: Here's a quote from *C.M. & Her Friends*: ". . . they appeared in *The English Woman*, a short-lived monthly edited by Elisabeta Allen, the discarded wife of the publisher Grant Allen." Off to fix food. Love, wherever you are . . .

Discarded Wife.

So! There was a name for us—a category! Because I didn't see these letters until several weeks later, I didn't get to respond to such a revelation. That would have to wait.

8/1 already: That delightful Picasso came in mail today. Thinking abt. you as I read MIT's collection of L. Bourgeois' writing & interviews etc. . . . interesting certainly, but the photos of work she's talking abt. are small and not at all clear. Frustrating. Have been doing a lot of work (masks) which is also frustrating because what I see in my mind's eye is usually technically impossible with the tools I have to work with.

8/2: My kitchen space is filled with paint mixtures, sink loaded with tools that have to be kept wet, plaster of paris all over. Chan once said, looking at stuff I'd done, "Oh, I wish you cld go to art school." At the time I felt it was a putdown; after a day like today, I think I agree. At least I wld. have learned how to deal with the technics. I *had* been to a bunch of night classes at Ann Arbor, but that was all about drawing and painting.

Yes, she should have gone to art school, a workshop with space and supplies and ideas. But she did what she could on her own, with what resources she could find. Which of its two words defines the term "outsider artist"?

At first we laughed about "Discarded Wife," but though we shared the definition it held her tighter in many ways. Still, I did think of her as the survivor she was. Her letter of 8/2 continues:

> Wonderful end to a day of frustrating work: the Mustang that has been sitting for at least 3 weeks right outside my kitchen window while upstairs teenagers have been working on it (male & female), is FIXXED! and back on the road . . . and just now I look out after enduring the awful sound of the mower & the doors to the basement clanging open & then closed, and watched the lovely young girl who'd done the mowing swing on the little kids' play set with such joy & abandon, hair flying in the wind . . . it was so beautiful!

• • • • •

NEW YORK 8/11 JUST TURNED ON COMPUTER

HELLO! I've been home since Tues night and today's Saturday but this is truly the first moment I've been able to lift the lip of the laptop.

How are you? I just read all your emails at once.

I had a wonderful time everywhere. In Crete all I did was swim and eat too much and look at the amazing moon and stars of another sky.[1] But Paris—oh, seeing those Impressionist paintings I'd seen repros of all my life . . . Van Gogh's intensity, the light—even Whistler's Mother! And Rodin . . . Well, it's just too much to describe and I've been away from words a while—these the first I've written in what seems like a very long time. I hope you still have all the info on that Charlotte Mew book as I'd like to get it. Oh, I was reading Colette in Paris right across from the Palais Royale, where she was living when she wrote "My Mother's House," and what an experience that was, to come across the reference while lying in bed across the street!

I might add that I was greeted by my precious daughters who had brought along a tall man to hold up the sign that said "Welcome Home

---

1. All courtesy of the painter Jack Whitten and his wife, Mary, longtime friends.

Figlet." Have brought you some presents. Am I still invited to come up for Blues Cruise?

Rita Marley has offered my price! I came home to urgent phone message: call immediately! My agent is in Africa with her boyfriend, meeting the gorillas, but I spoke with her contracts man, and it's true. Actually, I still don't believe it.

OK. I'm trying to remember what I wrote you just before I left, but whatever it was it disappeared from my brain as soon as I got on the plane. But oh, the British Museum!

OK again. Thanks for writing so steadfastly to welcome me home.

Love and kisses!

GLOUCESTER, 8/12/01

What a blessing! to find yr. email just now . . . like the proverbial shot-in-the-arm.

NEW YORK, 8/14/01 QUICK NOTE

Hi—I'm still a bit woozy but from now I'm going to be very respectful of people who say they are jet lagged. A whole week! Many, *many* thanks for all the little notes. Also thank dear Fred for putting us on the Blues Cruise. It sounds as if you've been having a more sociable time than last winter, and that makes me *extremely* happy as I often feel that you isolate yourself and then depression sets in which inspires more isolation, etc. But that you are working is also fabulous. Have to stop writing. I can't wait to see you.

GLOUCESTER, 8/15/01

Bits of my ceiling in studio are falling down and Rachel (upstairs) came last night to look & said the only answer was scrape. Holy Mary, Mother of God (Catholic version of oy vey).

Rachel sd. it would be a terrible mess. I said "Shit!" She agreed. It's not the actual ceiling, just some cheap plasterized paint, so it's not life-threatening, but definitely work threatening, and just when I'm into it. I think the gods are trying to tell me something.

You're right abt. my isolation, but I think my depression comes from living in a house I hate. I shld. not bitch, but sometimes I want to take an axe to the paneled walls, keep the blinds down day & night, tear up the ugly carpet in the kitchen—I would go on but that's not worth your time or mine . . . I'm not happy in this house.

Hopefully the scraping will be done and cleaned up before you get here.

What has happened since Rita and all those $?

8/17/01 BELL JAR

That thought came out of the blue when I was in the kitchen having given up trying to do anything more in studio. Rachel and a bunch of the teens who come & go upstairs were sitting on the steps right outside the windows I need for light, and once again I felt so exposed and cldn't pay attention to what I was doing. You can work on, and indeed write, your poems, no matter how many people are around. But writing is private, always. Who wrote *The Bell Jar*? Sylvia Plath? An image that has obviously stayed with me for a lotta years.

NEW YORK, 8/18/01 RE: BELL JAR

Yeah, it was Sylvia Plath. No, I can't work with people around, either. If I had people in my ears or within sight I'd be freaked, just like you. I can't even listen to the radio when I'm working because it distracts me, even music, forget about words.

GLOUCESTER, 8/19/01

Have fussed all day w/little mask I shld. have made a big one. My little Discarded Wife sits in front of fan going full speed for my comfort and to dry her ears that I had to add on because the fish teeth didn't work.

8/20/01 TIMER ASKEW

Jeese, my dear, I suddenly realized late this afternoon that it is *this* weekend you're coming for the Megawatts cruise. Called Fred: boat leaves at 7:30pm, we need to be there at 7:00.

NEW YORK, 8/23/01 RE: TIMER ASKEW

Hi—I think I should be there about 3pm. Now I have a cell phone that claims to work all the way from western PA to Maine, so all I need do when I get close is pull over and call. We'll see!

Doesn't matter if wharf is not within walking distance as I can drive us there. On the ferry from London to Greenwich we passed many wharves, many disused, and origin of "wharf" was explained as Ware House At River Front!

Looks like rain, but maybe not. Just dull gray, a perfect day for sitting here at desk. I'm gonna eat early and sit tonight as long as my ass holds out.

GLOUCESTER, 8/23/01 WHEE!!

Bring a warm jacket or sweater as Steph tells me they play on the upper deck, which will be more fun but a lot colder than it is on land.

Soon as it gets dark enuff to feel right about putting down the blinds, I'm gonna get in the shower and wash my hair which is a big deal because I gotta be deaf till it dries.

So many things I want to ask you about.

NEW YORK, RE: CLEAN, BUT . . .

I revved up the car this morning. You've inspired me, I'm gonna go wash my hair. See you tomorrow!

This was the last good time I spent with Helene, dancing to Fred Buck's Megawatts Blues Crushers, who in 1996 won the Boston Battle of the Blues Bands, and had gone on to Memphis. Defeated there, yet as he put it, "What a different thing, to be in Memphis, and on stage, no less." And they were champions enough for us, out there on the cold water, lights of Boston bright in the distance.

NEW YORK, 8/27/01

I had a wonderful ride home in the dark, straight down 95, stopping to pee and refill water bottle; at one stop took my wallet thinking to buy coffee, left it in the john! Ran in a tizzy from water fountain, and there it was, ugh . . . But I got here in record time, at 2:04am.

It was so good to see you and to take that lovely walk on that perfect day. Also to see you looking okay and working and reading and in general going forward. Because why not? Look at the Fisherman's Wife! I love the Fisherman's Wife! I agree, she could be corny but she isn't. And look at what she overlooks, shit, nothing corny about that!

Such a treat to have that time with you, but, of course, I realized after you left how many questions didn't get asked or answered. But just quick, you shld. know I don't at all think of myself now as "discarded"; it was an image that really struck me, because it said something I'm sure I felt, but never thought of, even way back then, when I *was* discarded. (Ed: "I guess I want a bright new coin.")

And if I can manage to do it I got 3 masks in mind. And I don't intend any of them to be other than the Fisherman's Wife!

love, H

13

I dreamed a pronouncement
about poetry and peace.

"People are violent,"
I said through the megaphone . . .

"People do violence
unto each other. . . ."

"Poetry," I shouted . . .
"changes none of that . . .

But a poem is a living thing . . .

and as life
it is all that can stand

up to violence."
　　　　　—*Elizabeth Alexander*

Studying now the clear beginning to our ever more complicated twenty-first century, and America's last week of (mis)perceived innocence, I wonder why this correspondence counts. Still, it's as if I'm peering into an archeological dig I can't abandon. Everyone kept talking about the weather.

GLOUCESTER, 9/3/01

Beautiful day! Ditto yesterday . . . made it to Larry's opening & on way home was amazed to see, a few doors down, big STORE CLOSING SALE in window of a shop of very nice things too expensive for me. (Though once I bought 2 champagne glasses.) The owners (man & wife) I used to see all the time when I lived at 90 Middle, and I'd thought of putting my glass there, but didn't because they wanted exclusive rights.

Hi—Your story of the couple saddened me. Closing because real estate too high? When will it all stop going higher? Do we have to have a real depression before the rich stop seizing things?

Forgot to tell you this weird thing. Stuck in traffic yesterday, I was listening to the Columbia Univ. radio station when the very young DJ mentioned the date, Sept 5th, and I suddenly remembered that it was Marion Brown's birthday. And then in the next moment the kid said he was going to do a switch in the kind of music he was playing and announced Marion's first recording, and the best song on it, "Capricorn Moon." Lovely melody, inventive rhythm. And there I was, in the car, with almost a visitation!

I am still in denial about having to start teaching and the homework and the Prison Writing Committee, and the weather is so beautiful, ah.

Turns out my friends are closing that store because they simply want a change. How nice to be able to sell one's house in Rockport and move to the house in Florida!

I think a real depression, by the way, would never stop the rich from seizing things. It's just something they do, no matter.

You'll laugh. This morning while eating breakfast I read another of Louisa May Alcott's early stories . . . book I brought home from lib. yesterday. "Perilous Play," published anonymously. 1869. Young Dr. tosses out hashish to bored young people at a party. One of the "thrillers." I dunno, I've smoked a lot of hash, thanks to Tom Raworth, in England, where it was more available than pot, still have his handwrit recipe for hash fudge & brownies; never had such reactions as she writes about. But it is an engrossing story.

Quick note to tell you I'm wearing my Greek apron, I love it but am worried abt. how to wash it.

And I've just washed the last of the tomatoes you brought. The lovely herbs still sit on table because I can't figure out where to hang them. This is a thank-you I don't think I've said in emails since your visit.

Much love.

I warmed up a bit to the Fitzgerald book about Charlotte, but as usual I'm less interested in whether someone was homo, hetero, bi or whatthefuck, than I am in the work they did. I do love that she was called Lotti, my mother's name, and that she was small. The main thing is that I really like some (not all) of her poems. The librarian here printed "Moorland Night," which knocked me out. Let me know if you'd like me to send a copy; also "She Was a Sinner" (I think I'm going to really like this librarian)! And I found the 2 poems that had attracted me in the first place. Shit, I suppose it's enough to write a few good poems in one's life.

After the championship tennis match between the Williams sisters (which I didn't watch because I was working), my phone rang, and it was Lisa saying "The Big Sister Beat the Little Sister Again, Boo Hoo!"

That's hilarious about the hash and Alcott. Speaking of which, there's to be a musical, of all things, based on that old film *Reefer Madness*. Or at least it'll bear that title. I dunno! I'd better close . . . have to sneak out my garbage, since in all the years we live here, there is no provision for garbage collection for this block. Amazing.

Aprons, tennis, hash, garbage — and then:

It seems ridiculous to think an email will go thru when calling is impossible; Fred tried around noon and got a busy signal. Yr. Gloucester family is anxious to hear that you & K&L are okay. I think abt. the close vicinity of the lethal smoke that may be blowing into your house.

What a shock, that call from Fred telling me to turn on TV "all Hell's broke loose." All these hours later, CNN, etc.

What a mess. And as always, none of the responsible people were touched. Bush looks alive & well & is bravely (?) returning to Washington. Can't help thinking we've had this coming. What a mess, I repeat! Still gorgeous weather here, lovely sunset. The universe cldn't care less. Will try to call later.

Quick reply as it's 3pm; I actually heard the plane and the explosion while doing my exercises this morning. I'm trying to write this but really want to watch TV because it's so terrifying. Wash apron by hand in cold water, or put it in hot water by itself and let it bleed if it's going to. More later.

Got yours just now. Didn't think to check before sending mine figuring if phones didn't work, emails wldn't either. A relief to know you're OK. Me too glued to TV. Called Fred and repeated your message, minus the apron washing. He was relieved & sd. he'd call the kids. Obviously, everyone here was thinking abt. you!

What a beautiful day, said Jerry the newsstand man at Astor Place. He saw the plane, as did the guys who own the pizza place 2 doors up from me. People dazed, walking the streets. A group of women at newsstand wanted to know the best way to walk home to Brooklyn via the Manhattan Bridge, as all subways were closed and they'd obviously been sent off the trains without any clear idea where they were. Then there were some young people arguing about which way to go to the Bronx. Thank god I managed to direct them. Girl said, Are you lost too?

The smoke was hideous, angry, boiling, black and gray and white. Crowds of people in my neighborhood walking uptown and down. On 1st Ave, where Bellevue Hospital is, traffic was being directed to 3rd Ave. by a boy-child in uniform, prob. Natl Guard. None of the drivers wanted to believe him, but 3rd Ave *was* clear, so I told a cabbie, and the other cars started following him, at least for the while I noticed. Some young man walking downtown said, "I'm worried about my sister, she works on the 80th floor." But his lack of panic told me he had just come off the subway and hadn't been told anything.

Now it's totally quiet out there, and cool. The smoke is horizontal against the sky instead of billowing upward. Straight to Brooklyn. I must have talked to my children at least 10 times. Each time I went out they wanted me to take my cell phone and report when I returned. Now the sirens are growing more frequent, after a lull, so I suppose they're finding the bodies. Not real frequent, just enough time to feel normal again and then another one. But all day there was a lot of screeching and the buzz of people on the street.

What's most distressing is nowwhat. More sirens, cop cars. It's 11:45pm.

More sirens, an ambulance. Cop cars. OK, this is probably upsetting you too and I shouldn't go on. Mostly it's the eerie quiet. All traffic prohibited in lower Manhattan. Kellie's friend Lorna Simpson who called earlier told me she'd walked from Cooper Union down to Soho but had to sneak around barriers. A show of her work had been scheduled to open.

Before they built the World Trade Center I used to take my dogs every Sunday on a long walk to that neighborhood. There were empty lots with butterflies and other wildlife, tall weeds. Then they began to build the thing, on landfill, which on my walks I watched them arrange. Along the way I used to climb through fences to get to the water, but the dogs wanted to go in and I eventually discouraged them. I so resented the making of that land, though came to appreciate the park that was created (the one you and Marie and I walked along).

GLOUCESTER, 9/12/01

A nightmare! Thank you for your long midnight letter. I'm still stunned; it's weird depending on the media, watching what they choose to show. I think abt. that young man who was worried abt. his sister. Bless you for yr. letter. The quiet must be unnerving.

Marie called last night, and we talked abt. our walking around that park. She'd lost yr email, so I immediately sent it & you'll probably hear from her.

The sirens must be awful. And the silence worse. I love you, H. Yeah, and now what? It's all scary.

9/13/01

Turned on TV, though I'd vowed not to, and CNN tells me more injured bldgs. are falling & sending out terrible clouds of lethal air and I'm freaked, this far away.

NEW YORK, 9/13/01

Yeah, air is not good. I've been wearing a mask outside and closed all windows and roof door last night after a rather panicky call from Joyce at about 11pm. This is the "frozen zone" so there's still no traffic except for trucks from the site and the cops and fireguys and ambulances, though those are less frequent than yesterday. I keep gravitating to the TV set but can only get one station because the rest had antennas on the Trade Center. The mayor keeps insisting there's no asbestos in the air, but that doesn't reassure me about the other stink. Someone mentioned the furniture—all that furniture—which also burned, so you have to think of plastics, lots of plastics. Today the wind's high at times and blowing every which way. Rain is predicted for tomorrow but I don't know whether that'll help. I didn't realize it had been hard to get through here via phone until this morning I had a call from my sister who said she'd been trying for 2 days. Katy Neighbor is stuck in Pennsylvania because they're still not letting cars in below 14th St. When I rode bike in search of newspaper yesterday I had to present ID in order to get home. It's strange.

GLOUCESTER, 9/13/01

What a weird world you're living in. At least you DID have your ID . . . bet you'll never again leave your house without it. The media hasn't included such details as the TV antennas, and nothing abt. air quality and what's in that smoke; I just instinctively knew it must be lethal, watching it on the screen . . . of course didn't think about plastics. Holy Mary.

NEW YORK, 9/15/01

Hi—a quick note in case I don't get to write later. The kids are picking me up and we're going to an opening and then out to dinner. Rudy Giuliani, whom I've loathed until this event, said that NYers mustn't hide themselves. "Go out to dinner," he said. So we're doing that. But I've just read today's paper and learned that 9 of the firefighters from around the corner, the guys who saved us years ago when this building was set on fire, 9—nine—have died. Tomorrow I'm going to bring them something. Today the air is just fine; maybe the rain helped. But they say the bodies are starting to smell. The stories in the paper just break your heart; I seem to be near tears all the time. A young woman passed me on the street saying to boy she was with—"So I said to him, 'War, war, let's talk about peace!'"

Hi—yesterday in motion all day long. My favorite bike route is gone now, so rode uptown. But I missed the pretty downtown gardens. They're covered with ash. Ah.

The library around the corner is still closed. People beating up Indians mistaken for Afghanis, poor luckless gas station attendant in Arizona. It's too hard to "get back to normal."

GLOUCESTER, 9/20/01

Took Louisa back to library today, and Xeroxed an excerpt from novel she published in 1873 to send you. I can hear you sputtering abt. the writing, but there are some really nice bits. Read it sometime.

I'm still dazed, like everyone else. The necessary trip to library was a lovely respite. I just browsed. Happened on people I haven't seen for years, like Jeanne P. from Senior Home Care, my first supervisor, a dancer who way back then used to dance through the long halls delivering messages. I loved her.

On my way home I met a fat brown dog who looked like he wanted to say hello . . . oh such beautiful brown eyes! His owners were in driveway working on car. I said something silly to them like "You're not feeding him enough." We all laughed. It was so nice to have those few positive hours.

NEW YORK, 9/23/01

Haven't turned on email for a couple of days as I've just been too dispirited by everything and busy besides. In fact I haven't done my homework and it's 2:45 in the afternoon and I'm procrastinating. Rode my bike downtown to see the site but the police barriers keep you on Broadway, 2 long blocks away. It's eerie and smelly, same smell that periodically drifts in through my open windows. When I got home my teeth felt gritty.

Have heard from so many people out of town—everyone concerned, it's comforting. But nothing dispels this feeling of helplessness. Re the firemen: I finally took flowers over there last Sunday—the one I knew who used to live on 5th St. was there and that was some relief, because as I was walking over I kept thinking, suppose he died, I don't even know his name.

I've spent hours reading the capsule stories—a whole life in a paragraph!—of those who died. It's heartbreaking and so frustrating. I've signed petitions. I went to a PEN meeting. At the copy shop I started to cry talking to the woman who runs it, who came here 10 years ago from Bangladesh. I'm getting around to going to the shoe repair, where the guys who own it are Jews from Uzbekistan. There's so much flag-waving but it does nothing except incite revenge.

I could just keep on like this but all I'm doing is depressing myself and you. It's so hard to get over it, and I have the smell to remind me. Anyway let's just hope Bush doesn't act in a way that will burst the whole world's bubble. According to one article I just read, bin Laden has already disappeared from where he was known to be last week. And there are many to take his place. I got an email suggesting "Bomb Them With Bread."

GLOUCESTER, 9/24

I can't imagine what it must be like for you, it's bad enuff here. I woke up this morning thinking abt. the children involved. How many are now orphans . . .

It's like a slow burn, knowing this country has done the same to others. The flags all around me are scary. Steph said it seems the only way people can respond. Why?

Who was it, Kissinger? who said 3rd world war wld start in Mideast . . . I don't think there's much hope for Bush's not bursting the whole world's bubble. I've got myself drunk with the dilemma which ain't gonna help anything. I love and worry about you . . .

NEW YORK, 9/26/01

Hi—this was supposed to be a real letter but it got late before I realized it and now at 11pm I really need to take off the clothes I've been wearing all day and sit in my rocker and drink tea. Last night did begin poem about the dust, which we are breathing, of the dead. Weepy, weepy.

NEW YORK, 9/28

Hi—I guess it's best in face of everything to immerse yourself in something outside yourself—chores or whatever. For the last couple of days I've cut and pasted material for the 3 workshops I have to teach next weekend, upstate, to the ex-offender group. It's kept me from thinking.

Now I'm trying to force myself to respond to the National Book Foundation's request that I submit material for their website called The Book That Changed My Life. Well, I don't know that books changed my life, life itself changed my life!

Yesterday I secured (just that word) a van for us to drive to S. Carolina for Thanksgiving.

I feel like a totally boring person but that's better than feeling frightened and sad. I'm glad I can't get CNN—in fact I haven't turned on the TV at all. The photos in the *Times* are enough; yesterday and today we got views of the wrecked subway stations, as well as one of a group of relatives of the incinerated who were led onto the site "to grieve." Oh, godhelpus. Oops. I didn't mean to descend into the current and inescapable morbidity. One cheerful note: they've reopened one lane on the Brooklyn Bridge and one in the Holland Tunnel. But—estimates of 100,000 jobs lost don't improve anyone's mood. To my mind, the terrorists have accomplished their task, in spades. All the flag waving doesn't make money; neither do the tales of heroism. Lots of dishwashers out of work.

OK, I've been bad, brought you down! But I'm really all right, and my diet has been working; I was finally able to fit into my pants.

GLOUCESTER, 9/29/01

Yeah, you're right. But jeese, unlike homework & obligations which I ain't got, chores don't really work because doing them doesn't stop my head. Still, I'm doing them.

No, m'dear, you didn't bring me down any more than I already was. All that shit is swirling around in my addled head, with or without yr. input. It's a mess, the whole political world and its gods.

You'll laugh, I'm reading the "Iliad." When I get really depressed, I read HD's "Helen in Egypt." Why, I dunno, except the music of her verse is soothing. I pulled it out of the bookcase one of those days last week, and after a couple days of soothing verse, I wanted to know the story. Hadn't read it for years and years.

GLOUCESTER, 9/30/01

Letter Lost!

I spent a lotta time telling you the funny story of my day, this last one of September. But the funniest bit of it all is that I must have hit some key I shldn't have, because it is now all gone. Zap. That hasn't happened to me for a long time. I really can't now start over, mebbe tomorrow. It was all abt. a cat and the crazy Feline Rescue lady I called, and it really was funny.

Meant to send you a cheery note in the midst of this scary time. There is a proverb abt. good intentions.

NEW YORK, 10/1/01

Hi—funny thing—I got a completely blank message titled "October Eve."

Went in haste at 4:30 to a wedding I didn't want to go to; by 8:30 I realized I was exhausted, having been to the greenmarket and then to yoga earlier in the day, so I just slipped out without saying goodbye, something I seldom do. I was so fucking tired after waiting for the train home that it was all I could do to undress and crash. Woke at 3:30am then at 4:30 and that was all—from 2 glasses white wine. I lay there pissed off and still tired, but got up at 6—and it was so cold in here! I had to remove screens from back windows so I could close the windows, wash screens, but before doing so had to move the overgrown plants in front of windows shutting out whatever light comes in at this season. Then I managed to take off my pajamas and shower and find something to wear in this 50-degree weather. By the time I finished I had a little bit of time to eat and then get to Martha King's reading; walked through the rain to 6th Ave. but was glad I did as the story Martha read was way better than anything else she's written!

The stuff I have to do is starting to back up, and I think I'm still nervous about this seminar. But I shouldn't complain because this is the life I have chosen and I am not dead like some others.

I know this is disjointed and self-involved but I don't seem to have peace of mind. The old Jews always said "as long as you have your health" and I've always thought they were right. Hope you have yours and all of yours have theirs. Love and kisses, H

GLOUCESTER, 10/1/01

I'll never learn!

I got a reprieve from "thinking" when I woke this (late) AM to find my whole kitchen sink area soaked with cruddy water . . . figured it was the little kids overrunning the bathtub which has happened 3 times since I've lived here. No one home upstairs, of course. This time it was really drastic, water weighing down the plastic cover of the ceiling light fixture. Looked like it would break. Opened cupboard to get cup to make coffee; water everywhere there too. It's a funny story, really.

Turns out it was TOILET overflow, not bathtub. I can't turn on light till it dries out, but managed to wash all the cupboard dishes while I had daylight. The gods do take care of us somehow. In the midst of my fury and dismay and cleaning (I had to wash every dish & glass, etc.) I could DO something, not "think."

Guess you've had days like mine. And please don't ever again apologize for being "self-involved." You're just freaked like me and everyone else I know.

Here's to the old Jews and health. I'm still pulling an ostrich re news. It's too scary. I've signed some things, via the web, but wonder what good that does. Really.

NEW YORK, 10/3/01

Hi—It's 7:40 in the morning and I've been up since 5—I hate having this happen twice in one week.

I can't believe your story, it's just ghastly and I certainly admire you for saying "it's a funny story, really." When oh when can you get out of there? Maybe if you make a list of all the stupid shit you've had to endure—capping it with TOILET OVERFLOW INTO DISHES—they'll bump you to the top of the list at Central Grammar. Maybe I should light a candle for you. Yesterday I lit 3 for 3 different problems, one of which has to do with This Building, once again. Landlord told Katy that work would be starting next week on the middle (empty) floor. Oy vey.

I've been working on a poem, some meager response to the WTC thing—no one knows what to call it—tragedy? disaster? Poem has to do with the fact that for the 2 weeks prior to the day I started it we had been breathing in the incinerated bodies. (I've written you about the smell.) Anyway after I finished my homework I turned my attention to that, and in the midst of it got up to get water. My study windows were closed so I wasn't aware while working that the smell was back, after having disappeared for as long as, I think, a week. I've a bunch of stuff to send you and was going to include an article that reported people's reaction to this smell. But I lost it in the pile of papers . . . anyway some people insist that the smell is from lost souls, or displaced souls, something like that.

So I walked into the kitchen, and it was just overpowering and I kind of freaked, thinking—because the poem asks us to keep breathing this dust until we have absorbed it into ourselves and thus given life to the dead—I had somehow called them out, attracted them. Of course the phenomenon had probably to do with cloud cover, but you know we always have had what other people call "overactive imaginations."

Re: I'll never learn

Dealing w/the smell of the dead is a lot more ghastly than toilet water. It was a bitch, but could be dealt with.

Yeah. Oh Central Grammar! Can't find out where I am on list till the 11th when all their update info is in. But I figure I probably have another winter to deal with.

NICE thing happened tonight as I was closing my blinds: next door neighbor was cutting a bouquet of the magnificent daises from the bush that comes into this yard as well. I told her thru open window that it was "my garden," asked if she thought they wld. keep, cut. She didn't know, had never done it before. "I'll bring you some, how big a vase do you have?" She didn't wait for my answer. While I was checking my cupboard, she knocked on my door, huge bouquet in hand plus a bunch of fresh-cut catnip. Cats went wild. That sez a lot more than flags. And was like a candle answered. This is no answer to your letter, but I need to eat. Have had ditto interrupted sleep. Weird.

Hi—Funny, the letter you sent today replying to my last tale of woe, was piled right on top of mine—I thought wow, what a gas to have a continuous letter, then of course it'd become too lengthy to send—I guess it was sort of a Kerouac moment, big scroll, yeah. On the outside of the envelope I sent you I wrote today's date and "smell still here" and then after I mailed it the air cleared and I felt stupid and overly dramatic. However the smell came back, letting me off the hook.

Bought a new vacuum cleaner because I'd been using Kellie's. First thing I did with the new vac was plug the hose into the wrong end (fit just fine) and then freak when the vac blew, not sucked. That sounds like a dirty joke. In any case I grew more and more amused as the day went on!

In the line at the P.O. the young woman behind me was telling another about a project she'd thought of—photographing post offices, some
of which, she said with passion, were really beautiful old buildings. Of
course I'm so nosy I turned to her presently and said, forgive me for listening but this P.O. was built by the WPA do you know what that was?

As a reward for this history lesson went to the Salv Arm across the
street and bought a cozy pair of fleece sweatpants—whoa!—to wear in
the mountains where I will be this time tomorrow night. If I can find a
place to buy gas, as the station where I have bought gas these last 15 or so
years has closed, abruptly.

You should look in today's *Times* for Mohammed Atta's will—found
at Logan Airport—in which he describes what he wants for his funeral. It
starts according to Islamic law but then gets a bit more "developed," let's
say. Those who wash his body have to wear rubber gloves around his geni-
tals, as he doesn't want those touched. No women at his funeral—or any
other unclean person. Too bad he turned to ash so all that cdn't happen.

Maybe you should ask your upstairs to check their toilet before leaving
house. That'd be simple, no? Though lightning never strikes twice same
place, a piss poor image for these times!

10/10

Hi—You Okay?

I've been busting ass trying to write this lecture for the seminar. Which
is taking days to do. Pound says in one of the essays that he hates to write
about art, that his first essay was about how he hated, etc.

The leaves in the mountains were beautiful and the air so fresh. Here,
today, it's smelly on and off. I don't think I've written since then, nor
heard from you. So just let me know you're okay.

GLOUCESTER, 10/11/01

I'm OK. Just totally nettled. Am going to copy letter from today's GDT
editorial page.

The letter was all about terrorism, war, the need for diplomacy, etc. The
fact that war would create more terrorism. Everything we knew to be true
and that has come to pass.

Hi—the seminar is done. It was such a lot of work, like designing a whole course to fit in 3 hrs. But the people liked it, I think, esp. when the historical, theoretical stuff was over and they could get to the poetry and could say smart analytical stuff which is really just what one likes and the other doesn't. So much to do with personality. Several said they enjoyed my supplying the context for the poetry, and the antecedents like Pound and Fenollosa and Williams. Anyway how else to explain? Shit. I am so glad it's over!

The piece you sent was wonderful, really well written. Amazing how the papers can print a lot at times and then sometimes it's just all Calvin Klein. But everyone is so fucking . . . well, sad is how so many put it. And the assholes telling us what to do are just that, and so bizarre and contradictory it's hard to take anything they say seriously. They just wanted to hit back and they did and now they don't know who they're fighting, the same *meshugenas* who drove out 19th century Brits, then Russia. Why don't they read their history? Why didn't they fucking know not to say "Crusade" in one speech? Do they only drink beer and play football?

It feels better to start to get angry.

One very good thing has happened. I had a call from the movie people.[1] This is a long story, but anyway we're having this conversation and one of them says, by the way, we have rethought the story and we now don't see it as a love story a la *The Way We Were* but now more as a coming of age story and we want to focus on your journey instead of the relationship between you and Roi. When I heard this it was as though some hideous tension in me relaxed. I had been terrified of these women.

Now if I could just deal with the Taliban.

Woke at 5:45 the other morning the smell so strong, such a reminder. Today gone, okay. Will it keep appearing and reappearing like that, on the wind? You see, even though I try to think about everything else, this is all I come back to.

---

1. Left out of this selection of these letters is the saga of the movie rights to my memoir, because the agony never produced the ecstasy, though the option payments did pay the rent. Then a script was submitted, and I could do nothing but blubber.

Thank you! for liking the letter from *GDTimes* . . . I'd sent off copies to other people but no response and began to feel totally isolated. I don't have that smell coming in my windows, but it's in my head and there are times I just cry.

Went yesterday to shoe store and brought home shoes you told me about. Have evaded the present by reading Dashiell Hammett. Book I pulled from "New Fiction" shelf in lib. I always stop at lib. on my way, to rest. Mebbe these new shoes will let me walk without having to stop to rest! Anyway, his stories are totally absorbing. Like Chekhov. I lack discipline, and can't help starting a new story, no matter I know I'll be glued to the book for a couple of hours when I should be doing other things. I really need to stop and eat. So here you are . . . Kerouac scroll (Fred tells me we could, email will take a lotta text). Love, H

OK, why not? We'll just scroll. Re "sometimes I just cry," well, Marie Ponsot said she doesn't care if she does. And I don't either, though it's weird, I caught myself reading the obits or some editorial about them and realized I was crying again—that moment of self-consciousness when you try to swallow it. But fuck it, cry. It shit sure is worth crying about, no?

I have a funny story to tell about the Pakistani (or Afghani?) cab driver who carried a beautiful old chest into my hallway but I'll have to wait until tomorrow or Tues. It's raining. I'm sleepy. Poetry book by Naomi Shihab Nye, *Words Under the Words*, is dynamite.

Just now realized I hadn't thanked you for sending clips from newspaper. I dunno, Het. We all gotta die at some point, it's the people left behind, really. Mebbe I read those pages wrong, but they bothered me. I distrust the media, and it seemed like they were a call to arms, not sadness. I dunno, I dunno, I dunno. And now we're bombing the shit out of Afg, and leaving a lot of other people empty.

· · · · ·

About the same time as the destruction of the World Trade Center there had been an anthrax scare—letters containing deadly spores were sent to several media offices and a couple of Democratic senators, killing five people and infecting more than a dozen others. It was at this time that I mentioned to Helene a friend of mine's refusal to leave the city unless she had the antibiotic Cipro, which was used to counteract anthrax poisoning. Helene, having had extensive experience with this very strong drug, replied that Cipro wasn't to be entirely trusted, and since she was then reading Hammett, sent me this remarkably prescient quote: "Doctor Semich is a very mild, elderly scholar with no knowledge whatever of worldly affairs . . . easily the greatest of living bacteriologists, but he'll tell you: 'Mankind must learn to live with bacteria as friends . . . our bodies must adapt themselves to diseases so there will be little difference between having tuberculosis, for example, or not having it. That way lies victory. This making war on bacteria is a futile business.'"

NEW YORK, 10/17/01

Hi—Thank you for the quote! Hammett so smart, right? Of course that would be the ultimate "antibiotic"—to be a benign host to hitherto unfriendliness.

Re the obits: I guess they're so human, amid all the clamor of the rest. These past few days the *Times* has been running lots more photos of people over there. Which is to the point, really. Rouse a little sympathy for those who are under attack. Maybe a groundswell of "stop the war I want to get off."

I never wrote you my story about cab driver and chest?

I came out in a hurry, saw lovely old pine chest with fabulous drawer pulls sitting beside our tree. Looked inside and all drawers lined with sweet old wallpaper, yellow daisies on blue ground. I opened and closed, opened and closed, decided to hurry on. Cab driver parked there began honking. I turned back. Do you want me to carry it in for you? For free? Would you, I asked. Sure! And so he did, into the hall. I thanked him profusely, hurried to copy shop. On way, though, should I have been worried that he'd "give me anthrax" because he was Pakistani or Uzbekistani (like my shoemakers). Who can tell? I can't live suspecting people. The chest has corner braces, old, in many places. If it hadn't been for that cab driver I wouldn't have it.

Normal life, normal life. I just want it back, to go about my business as if there were such a thing. Not that I'm happy the way I was before; no one is. And most of us are not in jail, where I was last night with Kathy and Judy and Miriam, but then I came home and they didn't. And it was, really, a beautiful, sunny day even if windy. Now I find myself crying.

GLOUCESTER, 10/18/01

Bless that taxi driver . . . HOW cld. you have even considered anthrax??? Jesus, the world is really crazy. No wonder you're crying! I did too this afternoon when Marie called and we talked for at least an hour. OK, here's the queued letter from last night plus a lot of love.

The letter was a quote from Louise Erdrich's *The Last Report on the Miracles at Little No Horse*, in which Father Damien discusses time with Nanapush, who begins:

> "We see the seasons pass, the moons fatten and go dark, infants grow to old men, but this is not time . . . nor are your whiteman's clocks and bells, nor the sun rising and the sun going down. These things are not time."
>
> "What is it then?" said Father Damien.
>
> "Time is a fish," said Nanapush slowly, "and all of us are living on the rib of its fin."
>
> Damien stared at him . . . and asked what type of fish.
>
> "A moving fish that never stops. Sometimes in swimming through the weeds one or another of us will be shaken off time's fin."
>
> "Into the water?" asked Damien.
>
> "No," said Nanapush, "into something else called not time."
>
> Father Damien waited for Nanapush to explain, but after he'd lighted his pipe and smoked it for a while, he said only, "Let's find something to eat."

After explaining that she'd sent the quote "to take the place of my arms around you," Helene closed her letter with "Amen."

GLOUCESTER, 10/20/01

Sitting just now at table, waiting for food to heat, looking at little mask I'd almost finished before the shit hit the fan. She's actually nice, and I should finish her and let everything else sit. Not sure I can do that. But I thought about the poem you're writing, and realize I'd not asked you if you'd had time to work on it.

Hi—THANK YOU for the "fish and time" section from Louise E, and for taking the time to type all that out. The image of being "shaken off time's fin" is so wonderful.

Have had two glorious days to myself, spent entirely in restoring that old chest—all it took was steel wool to get whatever finish was on it off, and there was the original old pine, which I slathered with lemon oil and presto! It's so beautiful I want to take a picture of it.

Listening to NPR most of the day. Some voices of reason at least. Still, voices don't stop bombs. Jerry, my newsstand guy, is sure we've learned our Vietnam lesson, but I think lessons are soon forgotten. My shoe-makers from Uzbekistan are worried about friends and family. Re my poem, and thank you for asking: it now exists in 3 parts and I need to retype it. I always go through a stage of weird reluctance to retype but finally force myself to do it, because the retyping changes things. Then I'm always glad I've done it!

All this housecleaning has helped me to hide out; next week is "social event" week and I had to prepare for it with a bit of silence. Sometimes you just have to show up as part of the game: people notice you, then they think of you when stuff comes up. It's all work, as I know you know.

Hope you'll get back to that little mask you wrote about.

OK. 9:40 and the nightlife is gonna start under my window so I better get to concentrating before the distractions prove too distracting.

Too zonked to answer your last. Just to say thank you, it was so nice to find it.

Woke up to hear that 2 postal workers have died from anthrax. At first I really did believe it was some loony right-winger, or someone like the unabomber [as it has proved to be]. Amazing, isn't it, how vulnerable we are.

Well, shit, at least my house is in order, though I'm thinking of hiring a cleaning service to wash all the floors. I'll probably think about it until I end up doing it myself. Possibly because the floors are in many places made of duct tape. OK, just wanted to say hello. Hope you're doing ok and have started back on that mask. There's nothing else to do, is there. Just like Beckett's "I can't go on, I'll go on."

Hi—it's Sat. afternoon and I've done nothing but go to yoga and then to the greenmarket.

Tonight a book party and then Dorothy White's salon, so tomorrow I'm not going anywhere and may not even talk to anyone. No one! Though I did promise to wash Katy's hair [she had broken her collarbone]. But that's hardly like having to get dressed up and be all smiley-faced and pleasant in 2 different places, first the white place and then the black place. Of course I know I'm blessed to be able to go to both, but always I'm heartsore thinking that so many of the people at either place would enjoy the company of the others. Which makes me wish I had the energy to give parties. But I don't. And now it's 4pm so I'd better start the search for something to wear. Suitable for both parties. Aaaarrrgghh, like all those comic book people used to say.

Well, hullo! Now it's Saturday, 8:52pm, which will be tomorrow at this time 7:52pm. I'm ready to "fall back" in more ways than readjusting the clocks. Like to when my legs worked properly, I worked on masks, my computer allowed me to get on the Internet, and my head was not quite so boggled as it is right now. I can't even think what I've done since I last wrote. Hope this goes thru—I no longer trust this machine. Plus a lotta other things. Like what more than already has happened is gonna happen, now that the new law has been passed, to a lot of innocent people in the name of "War on Terrorism."

Much more would happen, including the return of the very dailiness we'd felt was gone forever:

Hi—I know I haven't written in a long time but I am in a FUCKING FIT. I had just sat down to work for the first time in days, turned on the surge suppressor to start my computer, and the light bulb blew and all the electricity in the front part of my house went out and the circuit breaker stayed still and it's all just fucking gone. So I spent 2 hours rewiring everything.

Hello. Halloween and the eve of a full moon. I wish life were simple, I wish I could ease you out of the fit . . . Are you fooling around with wiring??? Now I'M IN A FUCKING FIT. And I figure it's too late to call . . .

Have been diagnosed as depressed, reason for my long sleeping, among other things and given samples of pills . . .

Well I'm better and here to reassure you. I "rewired" by gerry-rigging extension cords last night. This morning I bought new ones and did a neat job of it. When landlords bought building they put more electricity into my kitchen than needed while I begged them to put some in front but they wouldn't. Sometime after that I bought wire and plugs and outlets and brought some juice in here from the kitchen. So I just put everything on it hoping it won't blow. Have called landlord, electrician, etc.

Of course you're depressed, I could have told you that, you! Why not? Living somewhere you don't feel "home" and all that leg trouble. But you are a resilient one. Take meds if suggested . . . be careful side effects. And be sure to keep walking.

Landlords!!! And the need for power (just plain old electrical kind). Bummers both. When I was a kid the most magical time in my life was our family's spending each summer in my aunt & uncle's "cabin" on the shore of Lake Pokegama. I loved the soft light of the kerosene lamps, and the ritual of lighting them. And the trip to the ice house with Jack to replenish the ice box. The ice house had a wonderful smell: big chunks buried in sawdust so they would last thru the summer. It was fun to pump water at the sink, wind up the big old victrola so it would play the ancient records. And feel the soft dirt road on my bare feet when I was allowed to go visit my Cherokee friends who lived in an incredible shack down the road (that's another story).

Then power hit the area. All the magic gone. Zap! I cried for days. Of course it made life a LOT easier for my mother.

You ain't the only one w/a big mouth, this was to be a quick response!

Hi—I was just going to read this and not write because it's 11:30pm and I have to be up and at'em by 7:30 . . . I have finally got the recalcitrant poem and the reading together for Sunday, but am just becoming aware that the New York Marathon is to be run that day and some of Bklyn's streets will be closed and I have to get to a place I want to drive to . . . aarrghh. I loved that story of the cabin. Do you remember any particular stories? You should write them down. I thought, by the way, that you were writing something (got this 3rd hand when you sent me a letter you'd sent to Marie). Why don't you put yourself on a schedule to do some of it every day. It'd help the depression, blimey! Oh god, it's 11:45. Good night.

Hi—I know I answered you once but I am pooped and it was just as easy, and anyway weren't we going to make a scroll?

Have you tried pills for your depression? You can always stop them if you hate them. Are they speed or what? Re all that, I neglected to include the main thing you're surely depressed about, which is your hearing. For shit's sake, you're entitled! All the more reason to spend some of Kate's $$ on new machines. Kate would no doubt approve.

Hi—what are you doing? Haven't heard from you in eighteen years and am getting worried, so just let me know you're okay.

I've gotten my turntable fixed, and have been listening to all my old records. Playing "Solo Monk" right now—oh! I now acknowledge what all the knowing people always say, records have better sound than CDs. It's as if Monk were in the next room.

The Marley project may indeed go through. I still don't believe it, and neither does my agent. But she ran into the editor in chief of Hyperion Books, who said they really want me, etc etc and that Hyperion would pay, not Rita. Anyway Agent Barbara says in her Brooklyn accent, "Don't let's count our chickens." Hope you're thinking about getting new ear machines, and if you don't think you can afford them, you can ask me, as I'll be so fucking rich!

Write, please.

11/15/01

Hope you're okay. If I haven't heard from you by weekend, I'll call.

GLOUCESTER, 11/16/01

I'm OK. Nothing's up . . . been all down! Machine not broken, but I was.

Feeling better today. Dunno whether I had a bug or those purples did it, probably a combination. Gave the pills ten days, then quit them: found I was much worse on them, in a strange spaced nightmare of days walked through, I dunno really what I did other than sit & watch TV, piled w/ clothes & still those damn fever chills. I really must have caught a bug, the pills wouldn't have done that, but they did fuck up my head. I'd just as soon forget it, and continue being just normally depressed. Yeah!

NEW YORK, 11/19/01

What were those damn purples? Downers? Seems to me they'd give you uppers, which certainly wouldn't reduce you to sitting in a chair and watching TV. Have you spoken to whoever it was that prescribed them to find out what in the world they were? You should let the MD know your reaction—who knows, you could have been given the wrong pills, it's been known to happen. But I'm glad you're coming out of it, I was beginning to think they'd poisoned you or something. And maybe they did.

Anyway, I'm glad you're back to yourself. Though of course I'd prefer you weren't depressed. Are you getting out enough? Getting enough sunlight on these short days? Oh I'm always full of advice, aren't I?

GLOUCESTER, 10/11/01

Never mind abt. me & depression . . . nothing more than a funny story. See Dr. (Ali—Physician's Assistant) on 26th and am going to say some things abt. how she shouldn't hand out pills with such little info from me. It all started w/my complaint that I was sleeping at least 10 hours per day. I mentioned it because I thought it was due to b.p. pills. "Are you depressed?" "Yes," sez I, honestly. Well, no more questions other than what do you want to do about it to which I replied what do you suggest. Answer, the pills. So really, once again, it's all my fault.

Hi—well, that's a pretty weird way to get diagnosed as "depressed"! (By which I mean clinically.) All these chemicals rolling around in your system can do great harm! As you have seen . . .

Rena Oppenheimer was here last week, took me to lunch and we had a great time. Like all of us, she's mellowed. I hope I've mellowed, but I don't really know!

OK, I'm glad it's just a funny story about those pills, but you've got to watch these health professionals.

I better get busy, though I'd love to get busy to sleep, because I have to get up at 3:45am in order to be awake enough to drive. When I come home from S. Carolina, I going to have a nice, light schedule. Can you believe it?

Love, and Happy Thanksgiving. We should, I suppose, be giving mucho thanks for just being here. So lets.

• • • • •

Hullo,

To cool my mind I turned on machine & played this game called "Shangrila." I love it! If you win, you get a cookie with the usual inane fortune. After abt. an hour I finally won, & have to send on my cookie message:

"Moderation in all things should be practiced sparingly." Hope it brings you the laugh it gave me.

OK, love, seems a long time since I've sat down & writ a real letter. And now it's "the season." Got my legs working enuff to get to the bookstore to pick up the book I'd ordered for Steph's birthday. And there was Gerrit whom I haven't seen for ages and that was nice and we are having lunch next Friday.

Gotta go eat. Love, H

Hi. Looks like Rita Marley is coming through for real; they're working on the contract. Also there's a contract about moving Katy upstairs in this building; it's 31 pages and requires our lawyer. So I'm upset, I think. More later. Love, H

Hi. It never ends, this confusion. Rita Marley, though given a deadline of 12/7, has failed so far to agree to contract terms. Agent's money man called today to say that maybe Rita won't sign and that it's not a sure thing after all. I was up sending business emails last night until 12:40 after having been up since 8 in the morning and teaching 2 classes in 2 places. I am going to smoke a joint and ponder my fate.

Hi—it's again, and as always, 10:25 pm, and I have just enough energy to write that—ta da!!!!!—today at about 6pm I signed the contract with Rita Marley Productions, after an entire day of phone calls, faxes, etc. At 4:50, just as it was nearly full dark, my agent's man called to say it was ready, and that it would be a good idea to sign it right then just in case anyone decided to change anyone's mind. So I jumped on my bike and rode to 27th St. and 6th Ave in the middle of rush hour. Funny thing was that no one recognized me when I got there. I was locking my bike outside the building when my agent herself came rushing out, and when I yelled "Barbara!" she looked at me funny and I had to identify myself! And then when I walked into the office, 3 people stared blankly at me until I said, "I'm Hettie!"

Spoke to Rita herself this morning; around her neck she was wearing, she said, 3 cell phones, and they were all ringing at once. Have you seen those attachments that make it possible to simply talk into the air? Yesterday I walked past a woman who was speaking very loudly and angrily at someone—I thought she was nuts until I realized she was on the phone. Godawmighty. This isn't really a letter, but just to tell you the good news. The completed 300 pages must be turned in by June 2003. She says we'll go to Ghana! Hope you're okay. I'm going to be very rich and wish I could buy you something so start thinking about it.

Well, keed, it's 12:10 am as always, but I've just enuff energy to send a hoooraaayy! Merry Xmas! What a lovely funny story. No, I ain't yet seen those attachments. Three cell phones, all ringing, I can't imagine a worse Hell. Lady, you just enjoy time in Ghana, enjoy being rich, and don't think about buying me anything.

A Lovely Day!—though I stirred into it only to open the roof door and sniff the air for a while.

Friday I went to Macy's. Amazing, so much stuff. Got a couple presents for the kids and then went to the bathroom near the bathrobe section. Well I'd been meaning to get a bathrobe because the only other one I'd ever bought I finally and reluctantly threw out last spring (Kellie 13, Lisa 11, I bought them each one too, theirs long gone).

So I wandered through a few aisles of bathrobes, all of them insipid pink or blue, baby colors, an affront to women! I despaired but forced myself on, and there, hanging all by itself in a sea of pastel was a bright red robe. As I neared I saw it was truly small, and the label, when I got to it, said xs/s. Ecstatic I fling my packages to the floor and dump my jacket on top and throw on this robe—which was on sale! The only one of its kind! (I asked.) Of course it became my robe and once I put it on that night I could not take it off.

Now if you were a writer, what would you do with that? Would you include spotting the red robe right after a pleasant encounter in the narrow bathrobe aisle with two middle-aged or older, maybe as old as I, black women, as we passed each other and laughed and spoke about the tight fit as we pushed ourselves into the hanging bathrobes to make way. As though they were angels, harbingers of good luck. Anyway I have the most beautiful red robe, a fine velour on the outside and terry inside. The sleeves are even the right length!

Must be cold up in Gloucester MA. Let me know how you're doing with heat, etc. Are you walking in the cold? Have you had snow?

Bathrobes! Too wasted to really answer, but oh how lovely to think you are wrapped in red velour with terry inside, yet!

Have got most of the studio stuff stashed and wreaths up & deco-
rated plus little fake tree on light table. Xmas! Paul tells me I'm crazy to
do it, but he's not a great-grandmother. Little kids expect more than just
food. And I'm too egotistic (?) to ignore that. I hate Xmas. But the soft
light from my little tree is nice. Though I'm not sure what it's celebrating.
Love, H

DUST—A SURVIVAL KIT 9/11–10/11 2001

9/25
Two weeks breathing the dead
each breath marking each
stunning absence

ourselves as coffin,
winding sheet, urn
worm
but oh, of what is God made?

10/2
We lived among blossoming words
until some of them exploded, like one
human exploding another

Say *human* again
try to feel the word on your lips

10/11
The dead have dispersed.
It has rained on them twice
they have drifted to sea
ascended in mist

Breathe them once again

and begin

14

Praise grief all you want,
More loss is coming . . .
Can you find a sliver of soap,
Comb what's left of your hair? . . .
Breathe in again.
Again.   Please

Don't tell me you can't
Sing

—*Joan Larkin*

Happy New Year! Figure you're resting up from last night's parties.

Happy New Year to You! Had fun at both. But the people who live in the downtown loft may be evicted, and someone else, a painter, just lost his loft.

People still speak of the moment they first felt the squeeze, understood that we longtime artist-citizens of once-abandoned downtown Manhattan were in the way and would soon be among the displaced. Like the morning I stood on my street with a man whose arms were raised to embrace the space around us. "But Hettie," he said, "this place is *changing*." I wanted to tell him I'd noticed this for forty years. But that's not what he meant.

There's a telephone wire outside my study window, and I can tell just how windy it is because it flips and flops against the air conditioner; just now it was going crazy. Think I'm a bit crazy too, trying to stay ahead of the game. I dunno, H.D., sometimes I'm as flippy and floppy as that wire.

Flippy and floppy, yes indeed, Mama, me too; I think the whole world's that way. Went to *NYT* and browsed the headlines long enuff to learn poor cloned Dolly has developed arthritis. Amen.

Oh you sound so happy and lively and I have such bad news: Fielding Dawson died yesterday.

Well. By now I should be used to being told people in my life are gone. But of course I'm not. Vibrant, fast-talking, sometimes a pain-in-the-neck, Fee. Whew!

Had the meeting this afternoon re PEN Prison Writing Contest that was supposed to have been at Fee's; it seemed strange to be working with mss. he had marked for prizes, though I was pleased that some did win.

Picked up my first Rita Marley check and then, oops, went to accountant, where I learned I owed taxes. High finance. Talking about it this afternoon with one of the women on the PEN judging committee, learned that handling money and being in control of it is "empowering." But oh, I just can't wrap my mind around it. Must I be interested?

I called Rena last night, to let her know about Fee, and she said, "Oh Fee, that boy!"

OK. Sorry for all my complaining—I love the word *kvetching* but I'm not sure it applies here.

Kvetching . . . Had in my hands a Yiddish dictionary once, probably from library, it ain't in my hands right now, but that word sounds so right. Don't fret!

With Bush and his Madmen blundering everywhere, we're rapidly going downhill. Maybe the bottom will appear soon. Inshallah. Yeah, people have been saying that a lot around here these days. Jews say it all the time, though I can only remember the English, "god willing" though there must have been a way to say it in Hebrew or Yiddish. I need that dictionary!

Don't know where the last 3 days have gone. And I seem to have lost this one as well. At least the cat box got changed, garbage dragged out, and work table cleared . . . I wonder if I'll ever get back to work? Yes, Helene, you will. Inshallah. I love that word.

The post-9/11 paranoia had a long reach, though. A few days after these letters I was denied entry into the Bedford Hills prison, where I'd held my workshop since 1989. No room for me, they said. "Where," I wrote Helene, "are we headed???" The answer to that came the following week, when I tried again and was escorted, by the Deputy Superintendent for Security, all the way out to the parking lot.

Some days later Helene reported paranoia up the coast, quoting Gloucester's newspaper: "Yesterday morning a [fire] crew went to the hospital's French Center to examine a suspicious package addressed to an employee. They found it contained two live lobsters."

And flying into the new world of Homeland Security was a little like the prison I'd just left:

NEW YORK, 2/20

. . . bought a bra without an underwire so that I wdn't set off the scanning device at the airport, having read an article about women complaining that guys were feeling them up. The guard I used to flirt with at Bedford would manage to skirt the "danger zone" while looking straight into my eyes!

Finding this letter a decade hence, I suddenly recall agreeing to guest teach at Bedford one night some years after I'd been sent away. Since my official dismissal letter in 2002 had stated, "Your ID will be destroyed and your number given to someone else," arriving that later day I was all new information. Except to the man described above, who embraced me shouting my name, and then said, "I never thought I'd see you again in this life." For a dozen years, waiting for the gates to be opened to us, I'd had weekly, sometimes hour-long encounters—with guards, nuns, teachers, relatives—people with varying roles in and opinions about our penal system. All of us equally aware of, and constrained by, its failures.

· · · · ·

A specialist in Boston had told Helene to move, as in walk. But she was already frail. "Walking is so scary," she wrote. Reading was preferable:

GLOUCESTER, 2/24/02

Hullo. Actually made it to lib. this afternoon to pick up book I'd ordered—*Yiddish, a Nation of Words*. It looks interesting, but sits on my table for later. Before I quit, am going to try another attachment, bits I culled from [Zora Neale] Hurston book I had to return to lib today.

NEW YORK, 2/26/02

Hi—I LOVE that stuff from ZNH! Funny, we were discussing her today in my essay class when issue came up about what to do with dialect. One of my students, who cannot form an English sentence without at least ten "likes" in it, told me that her, like English teacher, was the one who like, discovered, like, Eatontown, and like, started the ZNH festival down there. I can't bear to listen! Okay, it's 9:40 and I'm going to bed early. Plane leaves at 9:30am arrives 12:45, giving me 3 hours when of course I'd like to be, like, sleeping instead of like, homeworking.

· · · · ·

Yet death and destruction had no momentum against money; nothing stopped the squeeze:

NEW YORK, 3/4/02

The real estate guy was here this evening. I told him I was not interested in moving and gave him a copy of my memoir, told him this building was on a literary walking tour, told him the Landmarks Commission had asked to put up a plaque celebrating Roi (though I had refused). He's not a bad guy, real estate, and so was (somewhat) interested. But. Oh.

GLOUCESTER, 3/4/02

Did! think abt. you yesterday, about the time you were telling people to turn to each other and shake hands in Fee's honor. I truly don't know why

I'm still alive while all these others are not. Call from Gerrit this aft. telling me John Wieners[1] died last Thurs. Sweet John, I have such wonderful memories of time w/him.

Oh, dear John Wieners! But the thought of him and Fee sailing up to heaven together is quite pleasant—they can outdrink each other along the way . . .

I think you are alive because it is necessary that you be so.

Death-as-subject led, naturally, to our own. Helene wanted her ashes tossed into the waters of the beach where she had gathered all the glass for her sculpture. "So perfect for you," I wrote. "Today I told K&L I wanted to be put into a little urn with a waistline because in my life I never had one. And a memorial service like Fielding's where everyone told funny stories about pissing in the same bowl."

Three days after that service, after our morning yoga class, I walked Fee's widow Susan Maldovan home. "As we get closer to her house," I wrote Helene later, "she says, 'Uh oh, there's my landlord.' Later when I called she told me that her building (where Fee lived 38 years and she 25) has been sold and she will probably be evicted."

• • • • •

Hullo. I've spent most of the afternoon and evening filling out my rent asst. form which I'm convinced is worse than income tax forms. But I wonder, given all the cutbacks, if it's all for nothing. I'm blathering. Need to talk to someone and can't go out to buy the paper, like you, and see people on the street. Been reading Kundera who I somehow missed when I'm sure everyone else was reading him. *The Book of Laughter and Forgetting*, 1980.

You can blather all you want, you know. Especially at me, and even more especially because I blather at you all the time. But are your legs so bad

---

1. John Wieners (1934–2002), poet, professor, publisher.

that you can't get out at all, even to go for a walk? I thought you were supposed to . . .

I'm still in a funny, withdrawn mood—making small talk and being sociable and interesting seems to take so much effort these days. I don't know why. I know I'm totally fucking worried that the world will burst into flame because of the Jews and the Palestinians.

I am often anti-Semitic but never forget that I'd have to wear a star if anyone decided . . .

GLOUCESTER, 4/10/02

I'm not up to letter, but you keep your star—it's total mess. Hard to concentrate, so much shit coming in . . . I dunno, mebbe it's finally Armageddon?

4/12/02

Got Tom Clark's bio of Ed late this afternoon. Am 46 pages into it and impressed with the care T.C. had in the writing. But also in that pit of remembrances. Life. Wish I had a scanner so I cld send you the Creeley quote on our breakup. Interesting to see how other people saw it, & even more interesting that TC included it.

It's getting late again, I've spent so much time thinking abt. the past, what a stupid occupation.

Yes, stupid to us, maybe, but Boyland had meant much to many, and I felt we owed the future its interviews, biographies, summations, interpretations, and, where possible, resuscitations. Pontiac was promoting a new car called Vibe, and—"God forgive us for cozying up to Mammon," I wrote Helene—paying to associate it with the Beats. Joyce Johnson, Janine Pommy Vega, and I were billed as "Beat chicks Live!" though we got the small print. "When I saw that Baraka and I were on at the same time in 2 different places," I added, "and that his was the hot ticket, I just had to laugh!"

GLOUCESTER, 4/13/02

Took time out to send note to Tom & Angelica Clark . . . In her answer to my last night's email, Angelica sent this: "P.S. The young freelance designer who worked with us on the book was greatly impressed with you as the 'heroine' of the story (she said she thought 'Helene would like it'; I'd hoped she would be proven right)!"

Which I certainly don't see so far, except for Creeley's "Helene was the pioneer." Life is weird.

Hi—I'm delighted that someone has given you credit for being the "pioneer" that you were. Most of these books pay scant attention . . . The only way to counteract that is tell your own story. As soon as I read the "definitive" book on Bob Marley, I knew right away why Rita wanted to write hers.

Lisa came to the reading last night for a brief moment with her new boyfriend, and all I got to do was shake his hand in the semi-darkness before it was time for me to read. He looked cute, but I want a better look! [Reader, she married him!]

What's going on? Haven't heard from you in a while, so as always, I start to worry. Went to see Elizabeth Murray's show of small watercolors and have just left her a message asking if I might use one on the cover of my new poetry book. They are zany and terrific.

We're both in arrears, but I've ceased worrying abt. you, knowing your pace. Still in the back & forths of E. bio. Troubles my sleep.

I understand . . . The only thing that works is to get involved in something else, distracted by a problem that needs to be solved. I worry that you can't work because of legs and wonder what kind of artmaking/problem solving would be attractive that you could do sitting down. Does anything interest you? Once I shook hands with Chuck Close, who is in a wheelchair. Anyway his work is huge and so good—do you know it?

I did vacuum today and feel better. Also stuffed some torn-apart mouse skins w/cheesecloth and sewed them. I discovered these mice (real skin! O dear) which keep Rocky occupied but he tears them apart and has gone thru the supply I had & getting to store to get more is beyond my legs right now. So I retrieved some leftovers. It was nice to work with needle & thread. Such mundane "creativeness" is a start. My problem is not standing, it's getting my head out from under the burden of remembering. I've been zapped w/it for almost 2 years it seems, but it's probably only 1. The book in hand seems only to intensify . . . not relieve. Oh well. At 75 I shld know better, but knowing doesn't stop emoting. Or something.

But sewing is only "mundane" because someone put a value on "art"— sewing is good re "getting my head out from the burden of remembering." The concentration is so relaxing, so calming. Your mind does go into what they call "flow," no? I think of you putting all those tiny beads on those masks.

There was no way, though, to distract her. There she was, in ink, another Discarded Wife. Heroine once, pioneer—what she had asked of herself in her twenties and thirties, and even forties, she couldn't summon at seventy-five. But I couldn't stop asking, suggesting, encouraging, either because I didn't understand, or felt, somehow, that my persistence was of some value. I still don't know.

Central Grammar called today with iffy message. And I sit here wondering what it meant. I should find a home for one of my cats, they only allow one per apartment, do I have enuff $ in bank to pay May–June rent, but I am NOT first on the list, etc. etc.

So here I sit with the iffies. It will hurt to send Rocky away. Keeps looking at me w/his green owl eyes and stays close to me, whatever I'm doing. Heavy. On top of the iffiness.

Took a cab to Central Grammar to get phone call straight. She'd used "May to June" simply as an example, cld be many more months. I left the bldg. still dizzy with iffiness. Walked slowly home, the light was beautiful. Lovely Gloucester. I think this every time I make that trek.

OH! The Indecision Game. Persevere, my dear. You'll get to Central Grammar and then you'll be Grand Central!

I've been in this room trying to clean out some files to make room for Rita, who has been stashed in a not very accessible bottom drawer. Yesterday I cleaned out two old wooden "in/out" boxes; one was labeled PEN and the other Bedford, and I not only triaged their contents but peeled off their labels. It's giving me some kind of perverse pleasure to look at them, empty and unidentified, and I don't have any regrets. I'm sure something new will come along to divert me from "my own work"!

Of course the diversion was Rita herself—a year-plus project that would take "me" away, though for a worthy enough cause. Nevertheless, I depended on writing to Helene to find my "lost" self, and every so often felt compelled to tell her:

It's 11:25pm. I should be out of this room by now. But I remember years ago writing to you would bring me back to my own mind, to the self not embroiled in dailiness of little kids and my job at *Partisan*, and Roi, etc. etc. At least I could think from the center of something I felt was true. Well, 11:40! Love, H

Laughing, and probably a little bit mad, 'nother weird day, 9:27pm and just now at last! saw a star in what I'd thought was a very clear sky. Here's a wonderful story:

Was feeling really all awry, shaky & lightheaded—the bp pills probably. I always blame them—and went out, in desperation, to walk a little & get some sun and fresher air.

Met my 86-year-old neighbor on my way to boulevard. He's a sweet man, we've had chats before. But today he was full of some kind of grace he wanted to share with everyone. Explained to me the doctor had told him to walk every day. "That's what I'm doing," I said, "I feel fine everywhere except my legs. It's my legs." Then he asked me how old I was. I told him to guess. He looked at me for a minute at least and said "82." When I told him I was 75, he wasn't at all daunted, just grasped my hands and said "You're a BABY!" Then, still holding my hands, said "God bless you," and when we parted, he on his way home, me off to the boulevard, I turned & called to him, "God bless us all!" He smiled and nodded yes. And I smiled all the way to the boulevard and back.

NEW YORK, 6/09/02

Subject: More Computer Hell!

I'm just writing to "vent," as they say now. The hardware techie from Dell finally arrived today, after promising yesterday, and it turns out that nothing can be done about the speakers that perform imperfectly. It's just something bad about this particular model, blah blah, he has the same one himself. So I called one computer place that wdn't answer the phone, and then got on my bike and went to the closer one, where I bought speakers that I was assured would plug right in and solve the problem.

OK, I came home with speakers. But it turned out that the techie had closed the program in some way that made reopening it a problem and the computer was telling me my files were incompatible and I thought that by plugging in these speakers I had broken the computer, of course. I called the help line for the speakers, in Washington State, to find the correct way to plug them in. The techie there had to ask questions and said she'd call back. By the time she did I was beside myself because I couldn't get any sound to come out. In the midst of my fear, Lisa called, and began to therapy me by saying maybe none of these new things were worth the trouble and I should go back to old tape recorder, etc. etc. and I almost lost my temper, though I didn't because I knew she was trying to help. But I got off the phone and fooled around some more and then called the guy who had installed all this new shit and told him the audio stream wasn't working and we made a date for tomorrow morning and then I turned off the computer, and then turned it back on, and waited while it detected the system error and fixed itself—something I did not expect, because the fact that I know nothing about what's inside this machine leaves me incredibly vulnerable. And then everything worked fine. So I called back the Washington State techie to say that everything was working, how should I plug them in. I did, but there was radio noise in the background. Oh, she said, that sometimes happens, you should get blah blah and maybe more expensive speakers. And I called the nice young man who had installed the programs and said don't come it's fixed (not "I fixed it"). Tonight I made another demo file, having turned up the teeny digital recorder as loud as it will go. And I can be heard well enough over the radio noise. The techie in Washington said maybe in Jamaica there'd be less interference. That when people in Texas use this model speaker for their DVD's, they sometimes get Spanish language stations.

Tomorrow I must wait for the FedEx containing my ticket that did not come as scheduled this morning because they forgot to send it. After that I may go back to the store and investigate more expensive speakers but then again, I may not. But maybe I should, since Rita can't be asked to shout into the damn recorder. Perhaps sleep will show me the way.

I just thought you'd be amused at this story. I am going to sit in my kitchen soon and drink tea and calm down. I have been working on the proposal material every night this week and I'm kind of pooped, but maybe it's not me, it's just the humidity.

"As long as you have your health."

It was a gorgeously sunny day, t-shirt weather. After all this shit happened I gave up and went for a walk, and told my problems to John, who sells porno videos on the corner of Astor Place and was a writer in some phase of his life, and my neighbor Sam, who was visiting John at his sidewalk enterprise. After having described all this, I felt much better, came home and ate a can of mackerel filets and some asparagus and an apricot and some tofu, and got my clean white clothes off the roof where all day they had been bleaching. And right then, about 5pm, all the birds in the neighborhood were having dinner and making marvelous music over my head. There must be a nest high up on a ledge in one of the buildings across Cooper Square, because a bird came whizzing out of it singing so loud I couldn't believe it—and winging its way to one of the buildings I can see on 6th St. (Which I won't be able to see in a year or so.) Anyway, well, just anyway. Hope you're doing okay. Let me know.

Love, H

Hello. Just quick. Thinking abt. you & how you must be going nuts with packing decisions. Spent long time today cleaning out saving-for's myself & other people that were piled up on my table and desk. Most of which I ended up tossing and it felt good to do so . . . I'm tired of living with my pack-rat clutter. A new phase of being? I did keep this list of masks in my head that I jotted down on a dirty scrap of paper: "A long time ago, Lost earrings, I used to sew." I can still see them, but will I ever get my head & body out of "life" & into that other world? Who knows. But it's a list that shld. bring you a laugh in the midst of packing.

Hi—Ticket finally arrived today; Rita called this morning, excited . . .

Actually I've been having fun structuring this book. Her sentences have some pleasant lilt and unexpected word usage. And she comes, as she says, from one underpants. Belonging to Robbie Marley, which she washed out every night "so he could be fresh for the studio."

And I am determined to get along and work hard, as this moola is a giftoola!

Wow! A little window has just slid up informing me that I have received an email from Helene Dorn!

And having read it—having read those titles—which are terrific, I'd love to see each and every one. You say "if only I cd get to it"—out of life into that life. Maybe the form itself is keeping you from your ideas. Which, from the titles, get right to the heart of the matter. "I Used to Sew" indeed. Maybe, for you, and this is just supposition on my part— it's the same as it was for me, a gradual change from prose to poetry that sort of happened in spite of itself, because I like writing stories but came to understand that I wasn't "writing enough" because the sensibility was for the flash of insight one expects from a poem (or I do anyway). You're always working with wet stuff, not that those masks aren't great, but would it be possible for you to find a form that's less arduous and as satisfying and useful to carry the emotion?

I laughed at her "coming from one underpants." Shld be the title of the book. What wife of famous male hasn't done that? Re the "work": You're probably right, I got to find some better way. More on that when you get back . . .

Well, you've probably guessed. Rita has put off my trip until Monday. After being disgusted in the extreme I got over it and rode my bike down to Orchard St. where I bought a suitcase of reasonable size, not the one big enough to sleep in that I'd borrowed from Lisa. Kellie called from Germany to wish me bon voyage but now I'm picking her up at the airport on Friday and she'll take me to the airport on Monday! Whew. Hope you're thinking about those fabulous titles. I mentioned "I Used to Sew" to my friend Winnie Bendiner and she gave a great whoop of laughter and said, "That's a good one!"

All this delay is making me drift back into myself till it's almost hard to believe I'll ever actually leave. How do you get weather on the internet— do you know?

Try weather.com. Works here but may not in NY. Am going to try to get Jamaica weather before I go offline. (I've been offline since the day I was born).

It did work, but of course is all in Spanish.

Thanks for the weather info. Can't imagine why Jamaica stuff is in Spanish when Jamaicans speak English. But I suppose it's the general Caribbean lingua franca, pardon my French. Offline, indeed!

• • • • •

HEY!

I'm working on an ergonomically correct keyboard, and have to keep looking at it, because one false move and you never know where you'll end up.

Having a fine time in this fabulous house renovated by architecture students from maybe? the local university. We've been laughing a lot! And did a lot of good work today.

Right now it's just about 8pm and the "Helper" who has been living here with me has fed me three times today, and I'm totally stuffed and will be fat as a pig by the time I get home. I've got two choices in front of me: transcribe more of the 21 folders I got today or chill out with some of the "stuff" Rita left for me. She is well loved and I can see why. Lisa calls me "mother to the masses" but Rita truly is. And she has insight into her own behavior.

I'm a happy camper. The water pressure's low and hot water not always hot, but I've not minded filling a bucket to flush the toilet up here or taking a chilly shower this morning. Hey, there are worse things, no?

GLOUCESTER, 6/21/02

Hello. Got yrs of last night but too tired to answer. Have been given a "claudication exercise program" which is walking over and above that I ordinarily do. I started today. As long as it's decent weather that won't be hard. But what's HARD is quitting cigarettes, which I have to do. I will, somehow. So that's my story.

KINGSTON, 6/22/02

Hi—We've been doin a lot of talking. Jeez, that woman's got a lot on her plate, payrolls, children, etc. Lots of money responsibilities the likes of which neither you nor I have ever had to deal with.

Re your walking, I'm curious—faster, uphill, or what? What will you do in bad weather? When you finally move, could you get a little tread-mill thing or an exercise apparatus? I'm sure you'll stop smoking, since you've done it before.

OK—I'm excited to be able to write to you.

6/24/02

Everything is fine, but . . . guess what?

You guessed. Rita has changed her mind and is sending me home end of June. She has to go to LA 3rd of July.

Went to beach with her and boyfriend today and for a long long ride to get there. It was great. But you haven't guessed the second part!

I'm going to Ghana in August. Whoa!

So tired I can't write more, just thought you'd like to hear! Irie!

I'm laughing! Gonna stop marking dates on my calendar.

Lovely surprise call from Paul this a.m. He arrived with Ben 1:30pm, went on my claudication trek on Blvd. and then we had lunch at Portuguese place. Then he bought me a case of beer & picked up the books I'd ordered from library—my current infatuation w/Milan Kundera. They had come up from Danvers to get an amp for Ben's guitar that he can take w/him to Germany. My eldest grandson is so interesting. The trip to Germany for some weeks of living w/family & learning language. While Paul & I were talking, he was going thru bookcase in my bedroom, informed me I was missing 2 vols. of Dante's Divine Comedy! It's strange to think I won't be here to watch his life & what he does w/it. Anyway, he's a pleasure.

I gotta hang up my handwash and go to bed. Stay happy!

Hi—it's truly 8:10 and I've been up since something after 6, with alarm—even in the tropics where everyone else gets up at 5:30am with no trouble at all.

But you have to get up early here to beat the hot sun. I've spent much time this morning talking to Miss Paulette, the lady who lives here with me. Kind and funny and sweet and generous. She of course gets up at 5:30. And has already cleaned house. And is now fixing my breakfast. Although I'm freaked about being served . . .

Re Miss Paulette. Nice you are so fond of her, whew! the stories. I always felt uncomfortable being served at the Bucks. Clara, the cook+, was the same kind of person—I used to spend a lot of time w/her in the kitchen and it was so weird when she came thru the swinging doors, white aproned, and "served" us. So formal. If there was some dish she thought I might not recognize, she'd manage to whisper what I shld. do w/it as she bent down to hold the serving plate for me. [In-laws] Glad & Fred Buck were nice people, but dinners were very formal. I never got used to it.

Good morning—this is going to be short because the mosquitoes are wicked around me at 6:45am and I have to get ready to go up to Rita's house to look at photos and then go to the mountains to have lunch with her and two of her girlfriends whom I met yesterday. One white, one black. Oldest friends with stories about having trashed one of the "girlfriend"'s rooms after Bob died. And would do it again, one of them said!

I finally got enough sleep by closing off the world and sleeping in the a/c so bloodsucking mosquitoes wouldn't get me any more than they have. But it's a losing battle, I'm a mess!

Keep on walking, cookie!

Mosquitoes—hadn't thought abt. that, only that you were in some kind of Shangri-la while earning your living. Why do we ever think there is any such thing as "heaven"?

I have no idea why there isn't a screen to be seen in Jamaica. It's insane, everyone slapping themselves, etc, but no precautions. Well, anyway, that's my only complaint. It's almost 7:30 and I'm full of yesterday . . .

The girlfriend trio took me up to the (rich white) girlfriend's home in the mountains, where we had a fabulous lunch (cooked by servants of course). But I have on my recorder a little story of how each of the girlfriends met Rita, and will get (today I hope) her version of them. Will put in book, as I did with you in mine. Oh we had such fun. When Rita took a nap, the girlfriends and I retreated to a little gazebo overlooking the house and grounds and smoked a joint and just talked shit. They started Jamaica's first feminist organization in the 70s and are still active in such things in many ways. They present themselves (with Rita who is very dark) as the rainbow tribe of Jamaica women.

The best thing about it is the amount of goodwill and cooperation and encouragement.

Re: yr time with girlfriends in gazebo, the front pg. of today's *Glos. Times* ran long article on the Unitarian Church "Statement of Conscience" proposing legalizing marijuana. Just to give you a smile before you head back! I've no idea when you'll be leaving on Monday and am sure you won't have time tomorrow to check mail. Anyway, in case this gets to you before you start packing up, bless you for sharing your journey.

I have been left on my own all day, though this morning Rita said she'd "be here later." But it's the Sabbath for her, that is, she don't like to work weekends!

I'm so glad you're doing this walking. Maybe you should try the nicotine patch and see if that'll start you off. OK kid, maybe I should let Miz Paulette feed me as it's getting on to six oclock. I let her give me a bagel with cheese and some mango juice for lunch, at 1:30, after having cereal with fruit and an orange in the morning.

Bless you for keeping me company on this journey. Wish I could take you to Africa, and maybe, since I'll be staying in a hotel, I will.

Love and kisses, and mucho irie! H

Good Sunday morning!

As to where in Jamaica I am: the city of Kingston, in the "uptown" area, suburban except for the presence of the Queen's House—or Kings, I forget which—across the road. Sort of in the country, but actually around the corner from a busy two-lane suburban highway.

When this building was given to Bob Marley and his band (in lieu of cash) by the man who owned Island Records, there was a scandal.

It's nice to have someone cook for you, yes, but it would be nicer to have exactly the food you want. And no one ever eats enough greens to suit me . . . I am ready to go home, actually—I'm feeling walled-in. This house is kept locked and security guards patrol the grounds night and day. And I mean locked, re the house, which has gates on all the doors, which are kept padlocked at all times.

I'm glad the Fiesta nonsense is over, or maybe that's the wrong word since no one would want to deny people the right to fiest! At least the noise will subside. I imagine you hear the noise worse than people who simply tune out with natural ears . . . ? Every time I see ads for new improved fabulous hearing aids I want to get rich and buy you some.

But first I want to finish this book!

GLOUCESTER, 6/30/02

Good Sunday Evening!

Didn't dream I'd find word from you, what a nice surprise. Fiesta hasn't come to an end yet but this is the last day and the Blessing of the Fleet. Today hit that and on my 3rd stop watched St. Peter statue being carried to a platform in front of the fisherman's statue, some cardinal or other delivering the blessing. Strangely impressive, weird bit, the mixture of carnival & faith, so totally human. This is a WELCOME HOME!

15

From desire to desire . . .
                              it was thus and thus
repeats the head, the fantasist.
                    No matter:
the wind sweeps forward
again—life itself.
                         irregular . . .
           So
one smiled, another turned pages
                         —Denise Levertov

Hi—

A developer has bought the air rights over this building, and is negotiating with the remaining property owners on the block.

Boy, was I happy yesterday.

Het, you're looking at the very worst scenario. A lot of things cld. happen in the meantime. No point in dealing with it before you actually have to. Anyway, I love you. Dinna worry, somehow things always work out.

Hi—this is not really an answer because it's 12:30AM and I've been up longtime. Thanks for your words which I've just read hurriedly. The worry over house has been supplanted by more immediate woe—computer fan isn't working. I had to call the techies and now they'll come and replace the motherboard. Had 3 shots today . . . polio, typhoid, and something else, I forget. Malaria meds cost $125!

Thanks again for your encouragement. I'm wiped. Love, H

Machines! And their terminology—"motherboard"!   Holy Mary!

I have to laugh at the term too. Weird, right? When the guy said replace it I thought oh god, and asked whether I should back up everything. Well no, said he, the hard drive is a separate thing. So the motherboard controls . . . what? Not the contents? Oh blessed mothers!

Why I love you—who else would have such fun with a motherboard?

Fortune—"Things just get curiouser and curiouser" Won! 1st time around—thought of you and your apt. and your motherboard. Anyway just to say hello. Hope yr motherboard ain't so shot that you can't get mail. Much love.

Landlord called to say that info from real estate agent was "premature." That we're to ignore. I refuse to ignore. But since things are supposed to get curiouser: cap on molar came off last month and I put it on until I could see dentist, who said I'd done such a good job I should leave it there and go to Jamaica. The 2nd day I was there it came off and I failed to get it back on. The dentist is away. The gum below is now swollen and here's my curiouser dilemma: Shall I begin the course of penicillin the dentist gave me "just in case" on top of the yellow fever immunization I got today? It's 11:05 and this is hardly a letter but a silly recitation.

OH yes, I'll be up to visit in August. All I want to do that month is clean this house that I'm apparently going to live in until the premature matures. I've had a mouse living with me this week but finally realized what he was eating and removed it so I guess he'll be gone. I know mice are a mess but they're really cute. Why am I writing you this stuff at 11:15pm? I guess I miss wildlife.

Kenneth Koch has died, of leukemia. His last book, *New Addresses*, was really funny. After Allen died Kenneth and I were on a program at the 92nd St. Y together and he was so sweet and friendly. The last poem in my new book, the title poem, "All Told," is "after Kenneth Koch," in form, addressing several subjects unlikely to be linked together. Now it'll have to be "in memoriam," along with a poem for Denise Levertov, also in memoriam, as well as the same for Fee. Wow.

What's going on? Is Mercury in retrograde, or are there other malforma-
tions in the air? They sent me A Bad Motherboard! Meanwhile my mouth
is swollen. The motherfucker (not the motherboard) is throbbing.

Oh I cldn't decide which was worse.

Now I got not only garbage cans on porch by my window, but a bicycle.
And two cars plus mounds of dog shit under my kitchen window. Life cld
be elsewhere but the gods keep me here, and you there.

On my birthday I get to see dentist. I know you think I'm a baby, but 68
seems considerable. Kind of bewildering.

Have you read any of the brouhaha over the estrogen replacement
scandal? If not, and you're interested, I'll send you the *Times* article. It's
all been a boondoggle. All! A horrible scandal! No benefit, it seems, and
actually a detriment to women's health.

I'm reading another wonderful book, this one by Penelope Lively,
Moon Tiger. You'll love it. A woman on her deathbed has decided to write
her memoir, but in the context of the history of the world. Sounds fluky,
and at first I didn't trust it, but then got sucked in. A terrific love story at
the heart of it.

Relax, keed, 68 is no big deal, wait till you hit 70 to get spooked. After
that it's sort of a shrug of the shoulders. It's all nonsense, really. The yester-
days that get lost are still stored somewhere in our overfilled, by this time,
brains. Why else would some happening from 50 or 60 years ago suddenly
pop into my consciousness when I was concentrating on something here
& now? OK. Right now, today, I gotta go hang up my handwash. Goodnight, I love you, H

Going through my head all weekend long: what shall I do, what to do,
what to do about house. They will fight us, I suspect, and I so dread it.

Yes, I've had sudden flashes of the past, for no reason at all. And they might repeat for a day or so, and then vanish. It must be the hard-wiring of the brain. So I'll just let my birthday go past and let the past do as it will.

· · · · ·

Hello Everyone!   [Helene, Kellie, Lisa]

It took two days with only about one hour sleep but we finally arrived last night and were met with much enthusiasm. I'm at the Golden Tulip Hotel in a "junior suite" and am going to Rita's village this afternoon.

The sky's overcast and the wind is blowing and it seems warm/humid but somehow out of this world, though the BBC tells me this morning that stock markets all over are continuing to fall and in LA a teenage girl was beaten up by the cops.

The airport seemed, last night in my exhaustion, like what I imagine one might find in, say, Shreveport, out of date but terribly friendly. NO lights on the road from there to here. But daylight will tell me more, that's for sure.

And okay, Diana Rosses of the large suitcases, mine was the very smallest of those in the group of seven. Rita's a great tour leader, handling tickets and passports, etc. But she rode first and we in tourist. Ah, there went my fancy expectations!

OK, I'm going out to explore. So far I have seen more handsome men than I've seen in a while . . . That'll do for openers.

Love to everyone! Write back!

H Figlet Harv

Hello back! What a pleasure to find word from you! Golden Tulip Hotel! What an image . . .

Hi—

Yesterday went to mountains for a ceremony re some contribution from Rita's foundation to kids immunizations. Dignitaries, drumming, schoolkids, lots of umbrellas, ride back to Accra past many old crumbling colonial buildings, where squatters live, oh Africa.

It's starting to look like it'll be hard to catch Rita. Wish I were just a plain tourist so I could do other things. But then I wouldn't be here!

This is just quick to let you know I'm still here & thinking abt. you there. Big holocaust on street tonight—police cars, Rachel from upstairs going with cops to identify (?) someone in big van . . . I've no idea. Then loud shouts and screaming from house next door . . . and when it all stopped the quiet was unnerving. Also got a call from Marie. She'd gone skinny dipping with friend last night in the aftermath of fierce thunderstorms. My wonderful big sister!

As soon as I stood up to her Rita backed down. And then, since we all know that the gods work in mysterious ways, that very night there was an electrical fire in her house and so she too has moved to the hotel. I think she worries that the accountants get on her ass about money. But she and I have made up very nicely and she's working. In fact she woke me at 6am so we could work before she had to see the insurance people. Her bath-tub melted!

OK, this has to be short. Sorry about all that upstairs drama of yours. Sounds really ominous.

Hi—I'm stunned with nothing to do. This hotel is on the road to the air-port, with widely spaced hotels punctuated by makeshift structures and people living in the most degraded situations. And yet clean. You see lines of wash wherever you go.

This morning Rita disappeared and I went in search of a notebook. Walked for an hour with no luck until I returned to find a small lined pad in the supermarket across the street. Listened to everything I taped of her yesterday, all of which is interesting, but I have no way to transcribe it until I get home and get my computer fixed. I'm bored in a way that I never ever get. A girl at the end of this row of computers is plugging away at her laptop, and I'm totally jealous.

Hi—This morning the driver took me to a stationery store and on the way back found a bookshop for me. I was able to buy *Wuthering Heights*, *Mill on the Floss*, and one African novel from the 70s. So I don't have to watch the Discovery Channel all night.

The driver and I were accompanied by one of Rita's advance men who came along to see that no one cheated me. Weird to be in a country where you have to go miles and miles to find a stationery store. What we take for granted . . .

The African novel, which I started, is so interesting.

Now I'm on my way to Barclay's Bank to get some $$—my remaining dollars have to be saved to pay the cab driver from Kennedy airport, and I have just enough.

· · · · ·

Hello! I'm home!

After I managed to sleep, I called the computer people, and whether it was fate, or the gods, or the cute guy on the phone, I took apart the computer under his direction, and he diagnosed a different problem from the one I was told I had, for which they sent a part I was not able to receive because I was in Africa and they refused to send it to Lisa as I begged. Anyway, as I was talking to this guy, and putting the computer together again, it suddenly started to work. I left it on, he promised to send new parts anyway, and then I put the phone lines in all backwards, because I was so greedy. But lo! when I finally put them in straight—HERE I AM! And aside from the fact that I think I have a tick in my neck, I'm fine.

Can you believe all this? "The Perils of Pauline." But I'm *so* glad to be home. And today is Lisa's 41st birthday.

New York is too hot to bear, and I haven't unpacked, but it feels like heaven to be sitting here writing to you. Hope you're doing okay.

I think I'll go on a cleaning binge. Maybe do yoga on Saturday. Have a regular life! Try to start my car! I wanted so much to come up to visit for the Blues Cruise but I don't think I can go anywhere right now. Write to me! Love, H

Oh I was so HAPPY to check mail just now & find yours! Can't imagine your even contemplating another trip right now. Take a breath, lady. Wish I cld. send you some of our ocean breezes. LOVE, H

Hello, it's Saturday night! The city, besides being hot, is stinky. So odd, to have been away from "myself," unable to determine the next move. Even a regular job was easier than not knowing what would happen from one moment to the next. Ah, this is how servants must feel . . .

Ate my favorite summer dinner of steamed vegetables with fresh corn. Sweet corn. In Ghana, a woman who gave me a lift down from Rita's house one afternoon bought us some corn boiled at the roadside. Hard, thick kernels . . . How spoiled we are . . .

There are new apples in the greenmarket, and I know that means fall, which is always fun and nippy. I have come home to find that the city has finally fixed the depressed manhole cover that I tried from December on to get them to fix — the one that caused the buses to bounce and the house to shake. New York, New York, so nice they named it twice someone said to me at one of the airports. OK, I'm nattering. But what a pleasure. Love, H

My turn — I'm worried abt. you this time. Are you all right??? Send a note. Just "hello, I'm OK." H

Hi — sorry — just too much going on. Rita has called twice to ask when the book will be done (not exactly in those words, but . . .). Yesterday Lisa asked, twice, "Are you going up to see Helene?" I said yes but that I didn't know when. I tell you, babe, I'd like to come right now!

I full-mooned it last night, drank myself stupid and went to bed at 5AM. Dumb! But did manage to make some blueberry/apple muffins tonight for breakfasts — the remaining 6 are in the freezer. Oh I do wish you cld. come right now, and we cld. sit at the table and eat muffins (they're full of fat, but got a lot of wheat germ & wwflour).

If I decided at the spur of the moment to visit you on Labor Day week-end would you freak out? Would it be foolish? Would Gloucester still be too crowded? Should I just keep checking the weather? That's next week-end, mind you.

Friday is OK . . . any time is OK. It will be wonderful to give you a hug and sit at the table gabbing! Just now checked & find I actually have 2 clean sheets. Imagine that!

Yay, I'll come! Don't worry about sheets, food, etc. We will manage as always.

Call from real estate agent—tomorrow he and the developer are coming. It's 10:15. I have been down down down in the dumps but now I'm getting angry angry angry. Unless I get at least a million dollars I'm not moving.

Stay angry. Am sure it accomplishes more than my reticence.

Well, maybe they were startled when I asked for 1.4 million dollars, but they definitely want this building DOWN. No one did any talking but me, but Katy said I was "brilliant." I was prepared with 4 books of lit history, but brilliant or no, when you're dealing with people who only want money . . . Anyway it was all very civilized; I'll tell you about it when I get there. Love, H

I'm laughing, between last nite's letter & meeting today you upped the ante: not 1 but 1.4 million. Well. Guess you might get it if they want that space badly enuff. Wish you cld. have taped the conversation.

Looking at the sequence of events, I could admit that the casual comment made to me about money being "empowering" might be said to apply here. But money can't buy you history any more than it can buy you love, and I would learn soon enough which I preferred.

· · · · ·

. . . 3 hrs. from when I waved you off. Chili is asleep on yr. bed & I'm soon going to be in mine so am writing now to say thank you for your visit, my beautiful Ghana box and the book, & hope you are having a reasonably pleasant drive back. LOVE! H

Murphy's Law, or What I Came Home To:

Hi—I suppose I was totally manic from all the coffee—or maybe just full of energy from having relaxed for two days—but I cleaned up all the huge chunks of plaster (the original, probably pre-1850 ceiling), swept, vacuumed, mopped. It all took 2 hours exactly. I filled a garbage bag, and two large paper shopping bags, with the plaster, but may have some trouble getting them down the stairs, plaster is fucking heavy.

I feel like Calamity Jane, but am trying to be calm, though I keep hearing my voice when I'm talking to other people and it's tense and angry. I wonder if I should start reading more Buddhist theory so I might part with more of my possessions: this morning I caught myself wondering whether I could take the dresser I've had in this closet for 40 years. OH!

I had a lovely time, thank you, and it was really good to see you. Don't know when I've seen two movies in one night. Please keep walking. Love, H

Yeah, I know how heavy plaster is. And the times it happened to me I, too, had to deal w/it at once and get it the fuck out of my house.

Today I rode to Canal St to get some plastic to cover the hole in the ceiling. Had a nice encounter with one of the men who has worked in this plastics store for years — all the years I've had to hang plastic on the roof stairs to keep warm. He rides a bicycle too, and we congratulated each other on looking trim, since he revealed that he was, oh, 66!

Then this evening, after I'd eaten a nice big salad — a feast — I looked at the hole in the ceiling and thought, I can't. But then said, I must. So I did, but it wasn't easy, could only use the staple gun at one side, the other 3 abut the part of the ceiling that's tin, so I had to use nails. One thing I did do, respecting my age, I forced myself to put sneakers on so I'd stand less chance of falling off the ladder. There are now red marks on my shins from leaning against the top step, while nailing over my head. I thought of Rita Marley's Aunty, who raised her, who did stuff like this, and was inspired. But afterwards there was plaster in my ear. And boy, right now I could really use a massage.

We see the lawyer tomorrow at 11 in the morning. Just finished transcribing Rita's admission to having a lover. Good and honest. Fun to hear us both laughing on these tapes. I have another "discarded wife" story but it's too late to tell it. Please remind me where you found that phrase? I think I need to write something about it . . . LOVE! H

9/4/02

Hi — Lawyer beginning what we hope will be a long delaying process . . .

GLOUCESTER, 9/6/02

Won a game of Shangrila and my fortune was: "There ain't no such thing as a free lunch unless you own the restaurant."

NEW YORK, 9/9/02

Hellow! This letter is my reward for having finished transcribing the last session with Rita. You sound good. And are you claud-ing? I must know! OK, I'm kind of stupid, even though I had wanted to reply to yours of loveliness! Love, H

GLOUCESTER, 9/10/02

Totally zapped by UTI. Took me by surprise. Got a dr. on phone & Fred brought the Cipro plus something else turns my urine an elegant red orange.

Well, maybe red orange piss is not so bad, if it works. I kind of remember that one. Hope this finds you better.

SUNY Purchase—where I just last week reluctantly refused a job teaching fiction next semester (afraid it would interfere with the book)—has offered me a month in France on the Riviera, all expenses paid except for food, plus a salary, to teach a poetry class to 10–12 students. I just emailed them that I needed the weekend to think, as I was so anxious about the book, which is due in June. But oh god, that's hard to refuse. What should I do, mama??

Re: offer. Yr "scoreahope" for tomorrow. "Opportunities to do something a little different at work are likely to develop. Jump at the chance to travel . . ."

• • • • •

Whee!

Digital hearing aids in my ears. Can already tell it's a vast improvement! Can listen to the radio, etc. PLUS! call from C.G. Apt. available on Oct. 23. I still don't quite believe it . . . Will see it tomorrow . . . right now I'm dizzy w/ looking around this house seeing all the sorting I'll have to do to fit into a much smaller space. Which is stupid to do before I see the apt., but hard to ignore. It's damp & cold in here . . . Just want to send on my good news.

Yayyyyyy!!!!!! (I suppose this is how everything sounds now.) Congratulations, in fact, congratulations!!!!!! Love, H

You wldn't believe the mess I'm in. Can hardly move in here w/bags of glass to pass on. Hope woman who is going to take them can come soon. I'm crazy.

Bear with it all, cookie; soon everything will be copasetic. You'll be able to do laundry twice a day if you want to, and you can at last have a life minus dog shit out one window and garbage out the other.

I've looked at all the stuff I keep in my "shop," like brackets and hooks and screws and nails. All because they're needed when I need them. It's the kind of living we're used to, don't forget. No one has ever plunked us down and said, here, just get yourself and your clothes and your bed in and we'll do the rest. Ah.

I hope that "glass woman" arrives tomorrow as promised. Maybe she'll take your nails, too? Or else—put them in the metal recycling and think of them coming back to life as a brand new refrigerator for some lucky woman who needs one.

Lady came, 20 some years of my life. All cleaned & sorted. She called later, ecstatic: you've given me $1,000 worth of glass! Unfortunately there's no metal recycle. Still miles to go. O lady, if you too are going to have to move, start clearing. Hilarious bit: Mark [upstairs] came in yesterday to put a new lock on my back door, which they've known for 3 years didn't work. They better not try to do any more fixing till I get out of here, I'll scream & call the cops.

Don't let those people come in on you. Lock the door! That's illegal in New York.

Keep at it, lady, we're rootin for you! You'll be so streamlined you'll be positively modernist!

Totally wasted again, food warming, gonna go eat & fall into bed before I fall like I did last night . . . Managed to extract myself from floor, wedged between bed & make-do nite table, but got on my feet minus injury. Measured yesterday, figure it's abt. ½ space I got here, makes it easier to know what I can bring w/me. There will always be room for you. Moving is a bitch.

NEW YORK, 10/10

No falling allowed. Please make sure that you are eating—even if you have to eat out of cans, or whatever. Order Chinese food. You fell last time because you were starving to death! NO FALLING ALLOWED, THAT'S AN ORDER!

It's 11:10 and I've had too little sleep, so this is just to say, Carry on. You'll do it. But eat eat eat eat eat !

GLOUCESTER, 10/19/02

If you have to move, tell your lawyer 2 mil. Gerrit came yesterday and packed most of the books. Went out for food, bent my ear w/all kinds of literary stuff that I had no head to really listen to, but wow! What a friend.

10 DALE AVENUE, GLOUCESTER, 10/24/02

In!! And computer working. Fred and Steph did it, somehow. Even got TV etc. set up & working. Holy Mary, how can I ever repay them! Gonna love this place once I get it all together. Just to let you know. I'm amazingly reachable.

·····

I keep returning to the word "unsettle," the insecurity it engenders, the red alert of "watch your step":

NEW YORK, 10/25/02

There's a new deal in progress and new person doesn't seem as demanding about this building. But Cooper Union is selling our parking lot, oy vey.

GLOUCESTER, 11/8/02

Haven't heard from you for days, are you alive & well? I feel abandoned . . . handyman I called not answering. I've just spent lotta time untangling wires Fred in his frenzy left in a jumble on floor. You can't imagine the mess.

Hello hello—I've been—where? What have I been doing? Anyway it's 6:15pm and I'm here getting ready to attack this ms. again, which ended up being 72,438 words.

The house situation has heated up quickly: we're to meet the new developer at our lawyer's office on Weds. I'm trying to stay calm.

Have read completely through the first draft as of ½ hr ago. I've got to keep checking to make sure Rita doesn't come off as too "godly" and too naïve. Because she both is, and isn't. It's not an unusual juxtaposition, actually, to be savvy and smart but nonetheless caught up in an aesthetic . . . what do I mean, what do I mean?

Our lawyer is brilliant. Asked what kind of buyout we'd be looking for he very calmly said, "Well, high seven figures." "HOW MUCH?" asked real estate. "You count the zeros," said lawyer.

Had a nice dinner with Marie Ponsot Tues eve—she's so terrific. I also went to hear her read on Weds, after coming home from the lawyer's office, and was so glad I made the effort because I felt much calmer after listening to good poetry. Last night I took Eliz Murray out to dinner, finally, as thank you for book cover. I'm getting so eager/anxious for that book to happen. Also nervous. Write and let me know you're okay and that wires are untangled. Love, H

OK, where are you? Still in moving dilemma but it gets better day by day.

I was sure I'd written but things got crazy, real estate agent, structural engineer, on the phone with Lisa half this night talking over a book, but she got off the phone happy, whew. Shit, if I can't help my own daughter, why teach at the Y?

Found out yesterday that there's to be a HOTEL next door. A fancy hotel. Ah, day by day—

Looks like we might be renovated—lots of disruption. Have one chapter to go before printing out second draft. If there's going to be a ruckus, I'd better finish this book.

Hi—just checking up on you. It's freezing here. Landlord, real estate, and plumber came today to talk about new heating system.

Am ok, just crazy trying to clear people space for Xmas Eve. Trying not to stash heavy stuff where I can't deal w/it, etc. OK. Merry merry, and love!

Hello—Did you have Big Christmas Snow? We were stuck in Jersey overnight. Now I have had lunch out yesterday and brunch today and there'll be dinner New Year's Eve and then dim sum New Year's Day, and by that time I'll want to put my head in the sand and never see another person even if they are nice.

Tomorrow with Katy to the lawyer since all weekend long we have been looking at the plans and working up a list of complaints, amendments, blah blah. This is my new job, I guess, figuring out my living stuff, like you had to do so many times.

Anyway here I am, where are you? Love, H

Fig 15.1 Hettie in front of 27 Cooper Square, 1994. Photo: Chris Felver

16

No matter what the grief, its weight,
we are obliged to carry it. . . .
And then . . . a woman holds the glass door open . . .
All day it continues, each kindness
reaching toward another . . .
Somehow they always find me . . . keep me
from myself, from . . . this temptation to step off the edge
and fall weightless, away from the world.

—*Dorianne Laux*

"Worrisome you!" wrote my student Joy Wosu, mistaking object for subject: "You worry about your father, your mother, your sister, your brother . . ." I worried some about Helene's worrisome health, and she about my worrisome pace: "You really need to take a break somehow . . . cancel some of your appt's, and *rest!*"

But I had always done too much, while she had never done so little.

Thanks for long phone call & making my fingers work . . .

Tired and full of beer, thinking it wld help . . . didn't. Food & bed much better. Which I'm going to do. Again, thank you!

Hope your fingers are better. Try bag balm, or something else with lanolin. It's February and no one has even mentioned Groundhog Day. I guess they're too busy finding pieces of the space shuttle. How dreadful, the death of those young people. And how dreadful will be the deaths of all the young people in Iraq if the fucking bombing is carried out. What hubris. Anyway, and despite all this—one thing: Dan Rice[1] has died. He was sick for a long time, I was told. Did you know him at Black Mountain?

---

1. Dan Rice (1926–2003), painter.

Dan Rice, whew, I certainly did know him! Have a small painting he gave me for my birthday, was on my wall unframed for years, but I got worried that it was getting so dirty, either gave it to Fred to store or have it stashed here. Hope I don't die before I sort all that out. Too many moves.

Too many moves, too many chores. The cat to be walked, the laundry piled up:

Another freaky day. Too late now to attempt washing my hair, just need to eat & get back into bed, but oh! it's going to fall off my head completely from non-care. I need to get it cut short so it's not such a scene to wash & dry (because I have to take out my sound & am deaf until it is dry enuff to put aids back in my ears).

Linos from Lorna [Obermayr] in mail today. She's doing a satirical series on women in the Bible. The 2 she sent are re Mary. The prose that came with them, poems, really, are wonderful. What a wonderfully alive, active mind she has. And puts to use. Makes me feel like a nerd, so much in my mind waiting. I gotta remember that she has someone come clean & do dishes, etc and a studio close by where she can go to work. It makes a difference. But still. I gotta stop and somehow get back to work, no matter aches & pains & fucked up living quarters.

Lorna's poem is, indeed, wonderful, and begins: "God chose Mary / but it was not a bilateral decision." And Helene did add, at the end of that letter, that her living quarters were "a godsend, despite . . ."

Chan once warned me, "You can't fix it." Well, I knew that. But I wanted my friend back. I asked, "Why don't you get someone to cut you a kind of glamorous bob?"

Every time I see Bush's face in the newspaper I shred it. Tho he's just an icon for all the powers that put him where he is — they want their oil. And I'm sure they'll get it. And, you know, war stimulates the economy. God help us and all those innocent people we're on the road to bomb. I'll think abt. my hair tomorrow, like Scarlett. G'nite.

There had been worldwide antiwar protests; in New York our mayor had agreed to a rally only, not a march. Gloucester's marches were beyond Helene. Around the corner to the library was "like a trip to China." "And I'm still just half moved in . . . my books stashed on whatever shelf they fit & I go nuts trying to locate things."

It wasn't her fault, but the veins she'd inherited: "Damn my genes," she wrote.

· · · · ·

My friend Marilyn Colvin once said she'd spent her life transcending her horoscope. To me, blaming one's body on the dead was as useless as depending on the stars. Still, who was I to measure the depth of Helene's heartbreak? And even if I couldn't fix it, why would I ever desert her? So I just kept bringing her along:

NEW YORK, 2/16/03

Hi—This has been exercise day-and-a-half! Had to get on my bike and ride clear across town in the freezing cold to retrieve the roses the kids had FedEx'd to me [for Valentine's Day] because I refused to answer the doorbell last night—thought it was some kook since I didn't expect any flowers! I was the first customer there on Leroy St. in full view of the icy Hudson River.

Rode home with my roses and ate some breakfast and then went up with a small group on the subway to join the Poets for Peace contingent; they let us "march" on the sidewalk 3 blocks to join the group that soon stretched from 51st to 80th St.—but the bummer was not being able to move. I stood for several hours until my feet got so numb I was afraid I wouldn't be able to get home. We were on First Ave., and as I walked west, toward the subway, I saw thousands of people who had not been able to get anywhere near the speeches and thus were pissed and arguing with the police—eventually, and inevitably, there was violence. If they had simply let us march none of that would have happened. And then they closed the fucking subway, so I had to walk from 56th St., where I'd stood, all the way to 42nd St. on my numb feet, and then couldn't get a train that would take me to my stop—so I had to walk from Union Square. My hands were okay but my feet were definitely nokay. None of this activity today was reported in any specific detail by the TV folks—except some of the violence with the police and their horses. I'm sure that by now you've seen some of the marchers all over the world. But I'm worried that nothing will affect these horrible people who have seized control of us so illegally. And they're so stupid! There was a wonderful puppet head of Bush, terrific signs: "empty warhead in the white house" "regime change starts at home." I heard Julian Bond and M. L. King III, and the rally started with the Muslim call to prayer, which affects me so because it uses the same nasal, keening notes as Hebrew, the first music I ever loved. And then a Baptist minister, an American Indian in his fabulous headdress, a rabbi (a woman!). I missed Desmond Tutu, but Kellie said he was great, and Harry Belafonte. Pete Seeger sang, but a poor choice ("Over the Rainbow"). Al Sharpton, and a terrific congressman from Ohio, whose name I didn't get—a white man who could preach as well as a black minister. And the father of a woman killed on 9/11 who had traveled with a group of the bereaved to meet their counterparts in Afghanistan. One of the Israeli soldiers who had refused to occupy the Left Bank (looking so much like my uncle who was killed in WWII). And a reservist from Staten Island who is refusing to go.

You know, my students have for the past few years complained that they had nothing to complain about, that they lived at the wrong time and missed all the excitement of the 60s. Do you think this war will be enough for them?

Susan Maldovan and I are having dinner on Mon eve with Mary Fiore.[2] Do you remember Joe and Mary from Black Mountain? Hope you're not too frozen in up there. Love, H

GLOUCESTER, 2/17/03

Cabin fever! Which I always get in stormy weather . . . But my body ain't up to it. Went to P.O. early this week, had no idea how strong the winds were, and came close to being blown to the ground trying to cross Dale Ave to get home, wld. have but for some passing good Samaritan who took my arm & got me to the sidewalk. I hope I thanked him. I was so freaked all I cld. think of was to get down the walk & inside this blessed building.

---

2. Joseph Fiore (1925–2008), painter. His wife, Mary, had joined the military in World War II, the only woman I've ever met to have done so.

And now we're getting our Feb. storm, I can hear the plows going out-side my window, clearing the sidewalks. Whew! Last such storm I was at 6 Riggs & cldn't get out either door.

You can add my name to the two Maries [Ponsot and Bahlke]. I do so love your "Ode to My Kitchen Sink."[3] I had one like it at 90 Middle, re-member? And one day I walked by and saw it junked in the yard. I just stood there, trying not to cry. It's a good thing the new owner & renovator didn't pass by because for the 1st. time in my life I cld. have murdered . . .

I'm afraid to turn on the news. Hope you're warm. Love, H

NEW YORK, 2/17/03

Hi! Here's a funny story: I was just walking from room to room, think-ing exactly this: "how easily I get cabin fever; if it weren't for the phone I'd probably be outdoors." And then I turned on machine, and there you were with cabin fever!

I'm so pleased you like the kitchen sink poem too. If ever I had to see my sink as you saw yours I think I would have burst into tears immedi-ately and caused a big commotion.

But apart from the sink itself, it just takes all my willpower to write about stuff like that, even though it's such a true experience. No one else is so "ordinary"—except maybe Neruda, from whom I got the idea, of course. But he is special.

Rita says that all the Jamaican versions of "hip chicks" would say, be-hind her back, that she was "so ordinary." The other night I stood in the Strand reading in a book of Jane Bowles's letters, deciding whether to buy it; would I read them? Ah, her self-doubt! And what a writer she was . . . The letters are like yours and mine. Real life. Worried about her spell-ing, of all things. How much of William Trevor have you read? Joyce has always recommended him; I bought a skinny novel the other night as well as that Colette I mentioned and stories by William Maxwell. And, amaz-ingly, a copy of Creeley's *For Love*. They're all on my kitchen table. Now there's another ordinary object—but writing about the table is a bit too ordinary, even for me.

OK. Watch that wind, mama. We don't want you falling. Love, H

---

3. *All Told* (2003).

Just hello—

My windows look like a corny Xmas card, fluffy snow piled on the sill, iced all over, etc. The weather channel is enthralled. I love looking out into all that white knowing I don't have to trudge thru it. Selfish 76!

Haven't read Maxwell, in fact never heard of him . . . ditto William Trevor. Colette I do know, of course. I'm really out of it, literary-wise. I'm out of it period. Whew! Looking for small photo I KNOW I have stashed in some box or other, I ended up reviewing my life, found an envelope marked dreams & notes. I quit at that point. One day I'll open & read.

I dunno what's more important than "ordinary." I've finally got my "kitchen table" cleared of desiderata except for the above envelope. No more new books. I've no place to put them, and don't have that many years left to get them read. Much love, H

That tossed off "years left" stops me now. It didn't then; I simply refused to believe her.

William Maxwell was for 30 years the editor of the *New Yorker*. I read, in a memoir about him, that he had advised writing every word as though it might be read by an intelligent ten year old. Within reason, of course, I thought that a fine idea, because it saved me from worrying about my tendency (drive?) toward simplicity. Which makes me think I'm unsophisticated. Going along with ordinary. But I'd never read anything by Maxwell himself until I found this book. As for Trevor, he's English and writes interconnecting lives.

I'm really enjoying my Parsons students. Usually I have one or two decent poets, but now one girl and four terrific boys (I don't often have boys)—1 white, 1 black, 1 Russian immigrant, and 1 named Cuizon who appears to be either Filipino or Latino—hard to sort out these ethnicities because lots of them are mixtures. But that's one reason for liking to teach there—I love their artiness, too. The girl is Ruggiero, wears her baseball cap sideways.

Quick addendum to such things: I saw, another day, my beloved stove trashed in the 90 Middle courtyard. It had a separate broiler on the side of the oven, no bending to the floor to get to. Geeze, now you pay thousands to put in separate unit . . .

Whoever first invented that broiler near the floor never broiled anything in his life. And I know it was a man, because a woman would have been far more sensitive to the fact that there'd be many a slip between the floor and wherever the (broiling hot) pan was supposed to end up. In NY that stove would have been rescued just like all those claw-footed bathtubs lined up outdoors in a high-end flea market on Houston St. Last developer who came through here I told no way was my tub gonna end up there. Ah, again, back to real estate. Obsession!

Hilarious story: The Great American Lamb Chop Caper. As you know, I haven't been cooking or eating meat for a very long time, though occasionally I'll have fish or chicken in a restaurant. Anyway, after walking 2 miles back from my accountant on Thurs afternoon, I stopped off at one of my favorite discount stores to buy candles, and suddenly found myself so hungry that I couldn't wait to get home; had to have something right then. So I bought a bag of almonds and opened it before I left the store and kept eating. Felt better, but still had some weird kind of craving. Yesterday, though, in the afternoon, after I'd had bike ride to publisher and trip to P.O., I had another hunger attack while in the local supermarket buying toilet paper. As I rounded the aisle on my way to the cash register, I glanced at the meat case and had a sudden, overwhelming desire for MEAT. I bought a lamb chop (not very large, $1.43 doesn't buy you much meat) and took it home, but found that I had no desire for it at all, since there were two beautiful little sweet potatoes all baked and ready, and some greens. So I put chop in fridge. Long about 10:30pm I was about to eat an apple and have a cup of tea when that overwhelming desire returned and even though I thought it would wreak havoc with my digestion I grabbed that lamb chop and put it in a pan and turned the fire up as high as it'd go—eventually setting off my smoke alarm and filling the entire house with lamb chop smell! I was in such a hurry that at first I didn't cook the damn thing enough and tried to eat it half raw—then had sense enough to return it to the pan and cook it some more. Then I ate that sucker—everything I could get my teeth around! When I came to I was sitting at my kitchen table with grease dripping off my fingers, licking my lips and then eventually my fingertips—I wish I had a photo of my glazed eyes! So much for the vegetarian. The last time I had a lamb chop was 1994, in a cowboy-type restaurant in Wyoming, where I'd been taken by Vicki Lindner, the woman who'd hired me, in her great effort to make me eat a steak. I wouldn't though, thus the chop (which was good, I won't deny it).

Today I seem perfectly normal. I guess I can wait a few years before having another lamb chop, but that one last night was fabulous, all $1.43 of it!

I've been so cranky and morose, but haven't spoken to a soul since 1pm, and that helped somewhat, I think. Sat myself down and hemmed 2 pairs of pants, and put new elastic in the waistband of one I made 20, 30 years ago. Took all afternoon but was a pleasant meditative activity—

GLOUCESTER, 2/22/03

What a nice! way to spend this afternoon, at the sewing machine. Funny how our minds somehow connect, thot all day I shld. be sitting in the wicker chair hand sewing similar things. Too sick to face hauling out the little machine, & always have found I enjoy sewing by hand more relaxing. I love the rhythm. I envy you. I'm wailing, sorry.

NEW YORK, 2/23/03

Wail all you want to, and don't be sorry! Last week I overheard my new yoga teacher telling some guy: "Kvetch, kvetch—kvetching is good!"

"Funny how our minds connect"—it is, they always have. Sewing (and hand sewing is wonderful, I agree) is relaxing, it's a meditation. Even machine sewing—which I had to do for hemming jeans, otherwise it's a wasted effort—is a way to get outside yourself and just get lost. I guess that's why I sewed for so many years before I could write.

Great Lamb Chop Caper is the source of much amusement to my chil-

dren. At least something funny has happened to dispel some of the doom/
gloom of the house/world/everything else situation.

I should send you some of my sudden appetite.

A Quick Thank you!

Felt good enuff to get dressed & down to check mail, found yr. pkg. in
box! What a nice surprise. Thank you, my dear friend. I've started w/Max-
well, bigger print & short stories are abt. all I'm up to right now. 2 more
days of Cipro, which is harder on body than the bacteria, I'm convinced.
Tomorrow I'm gonna try to get to store for acidophilus. Jeeze, I really got
zapped this time.

·····

Here I must remind the reader that in 1997 Helene had complained about the
Cipro she had been given, and since then had extensive experience with it. So
I keep rereading the above, sunk in the space between what we know now and
what she was convinced of then—and which predicted what eventually would
do her in. Though Chan had been right—ultimately I couldn't fix it—I sure
wish I could tell Helene she'd had the right diagnosis.

Hi—how are you doing? Tomorrow's a big Moratorium Day—Kellie's
joining a "draw-in" at the Metropolitan Museum, in the Mesopotamian
galleries . . . among all the artifacts from—remember?—the "Cradle of
Civilization." Present day Iraq. An article last week re all the historic sites
that might be damaged . . .

In tonight's *Glos. Times* letters: "We have a weekly Bible class . . . and this
week we decided to participate in a Grass Roots Movement by sending
a ½ cup of rice to the President and a [letter with] a small Bible quote:
'If your enemies are hungry, feed them, Romans, 12:20. Please send this
rice to the people of Iraq. Please do not attack them.' Put the rice in a
baggy, squeeze out air and place in a regular envelope. Postage is only
three stamps." I packed up a ½ cup of rice in a snack bag, perfect size for

envelope. I can't go to marches, am tired of sending emails. Makes me feel better that I bothered. Amen.

Send that rice, babe! What a great idea. I marched for 2 or 3 miles this evening and was going to soak in a hot tub, but my email was broken all day and . . . and . . . now it's midnight and I'm on my way out of town tomorrow and . . . ta dah! it's supposed to snow.

To welcome you home from wherever you've been. Can hear them clearing our sidewalks for the 5th time today. Hope by the time you get home, it will all be melted. The forecast last nite was "few scattered flurries." Hoh!

Hi—thanks for the welcome! I am here relaxing, a bit of a necessity. Where I went: Oneonta, New York, to the State University there, to give a reading, about an hour southwest of Albany. How: On the New York Thruway, crawling. The normally four-hour trip took seven and a half. I left at 11 in the morning, then got delayed by having to get air in my tires. There were several accidents on the Thruway, which had not been plowed by either New York City or Westchester County directly north, so it was rough going, though I discovered that the best way is to drive right behind a big double-tired truck, like walking in someone else's footprints. But then the traffic began stopping, and I noticed that the south road was empty; it took nearly two hours before I arrived at the source of the trouble—several accidents, which meant the highway was closed in both directions so emergency vehicles could get through. I kept having to put on my air conditioning because the heat made the windows steam up; but then the a/c caused ice to form on the outside. Once off the Thruway, having driven 35 miles per hour for about 150 miles, I crept at 30 miles per hour behind a plow on a two-lane highway. All this while my daughters were fuming because I had not canceled this gig—but I'd had to cancel it last year, and refused to cancel it again because I wanted the $ and I was sure it would disappear if I didn't catch it this time. Boy are they getting bossy! When I finally got there (I called them several times on the way, this is why cell phones are useful) they made me promise, "Never again!"

Anyway, once there I was treated to a lovely dinner and even though the audience was small they were appreciative. And then I spent the night in a king sized comfortable bed. This morning I asked at the gas station whether the car wash was open, but the woman said "We usually wait until it hits 20 degrees" and when I asked what the current temp was she said, "Oh, six or seven . . ." So I cleaned what I could reach of the car windows with the mostly frozen window wash I had in the trunk, then ate an enormous breakfast in the diner next door, and drove home. The roads were perfectly clear, as though it hadn't even snowed. But the countryside was gorgeous, under a brilliant sun. Well, to me that was an adventure, even if to my bossy daughters it was too dangerous. And I've got that check ready to go right into the bank.

But there are two "best parts" to this story that I haven't mentioned: first, I had to go to my garage to get air in my tires before leaving since the gas station air was broken. At my garage, people with whom I've been dealing for oh, more than 20 years, the door was shut but one of the guys came out to ask what was wrong, and I kind of begged him . . . Now this guy and I have been flirting for all these 20 years . . . and against his will— "Where are you going? Not the kind of weather to be driving" "Do you have a full tank of gas" . . . etc etc.—he checked and filled all four tires. I know him well enough so that to offer money would have been an insult, so I just said, "Can I give you a kiss?" expecting that he would offer his cheek. But no, he went straight for the lips! A lovely kiss in the midst of the snow, after 20 years of expectation!

Best Part #2: When I got to within 10 miles of my goal yesterday, and knew the whole ordeal would soon be over, the snow stopped and the sun came out, lighting up a few stray clouds, which before my very eyes turned magenta! I'd never seen magenta clouds, they were amazing. And then they were gone, and I was there, at the Super 8 Motel.

It had better not snow next Sunday when I'm on my way up to you! Love, H

• • • • •

Before I got there she had fallen and cracked a rib. In my doggedness—part good deed, part denial—I begged her to go outside soon as the weather improved ("Vitamin D is necessary to mend bone"), promised a leash for the cat so she could walk him, and continued to lay my woes on her because between us there was no power play—we were both Mama—comforter as well as the comforted:

Today I'm the basket case, maybe just tired, but feels more like depressed. The news is all so bad; just now a fierce firefight—a "surprise attack" by Iraqis during the sandstorm they've been reporting all day. But of fucking course, THEY are experienced with sandstorms, not we. Just like the jungles of Vietnam. I can't stand it.

Spent some of today working on the list of scenes in my memoir that will serve as a guide if ever I do get to write a script. So Act II is of course the difficulties the protagonist encounters, which I got into today, and halfway through was plunged into the kind of "I can't deal with this, I just can't" feeling. So I got on my bike and rode over to Elizabeth Murray's current show, way near the river in the new(ish) hot Chelsea art scene, known as the Meat Packing District because until the galleries fled Soho that's what it was. Anyway Elizabeth's wonderful zany paintings cheered me up, some.

Motherless Brooklyn is a good read. Jonathan Lethem. When you get back to the library. It's 10:45 and I think I'll go read it. Though there's a poem I'm working on, might look at that first. Anything to distract me. I'm afraid that somewhere in me is the idea that without this house I'll have no identity, no history. Also my responsibility to be the guardian of a place that's on literary walking tours of NY. How should I act in face of all this, what's the right thing to do. I feel very pressured. Hope you're feeling better. I sent Mary Fiore an invite to my book party and sent your regards along. More tomorrow. I'm wiped out. Love, H

Hettie, please, take a breath & realize no matter what happens, what you may have to give up, you'll NEVER lose your identity! No matter where you live. And you'll always have "a life." It's not the same thing at all, I was only there for some 13 yrs., but 90 Middle was so much a part of me, I took care of that beautiful old house like it was my child, so I do really understand what hell you are in. Oh so much love, & my arms are around you. I'm being my ostrich self again re: war. It's all so awful. Manana.

I wasn't reassured: "I have settled into a kind of frozen dread of what's going to happen." Still, if I had to once again reencounter the past, there were a few bright spots:

Today I came to the place in my book where you and I met, and it was such a delight to read it again and remember. And I do, truly, remember us standing looking into the window of the stocking store—the Bargain Hosiery Center!—and your saying "Bohemia, Momma" when you saw the black stockings.

Half a century past that afternoon, I can still hear her. Bohemia Momma, indeed; she knew what I was into, plus what I was in *for*. The first time I wrote that story, I added: "I loved her at once."

And soon, as I continued to expect, there she was again:

I managed to VACUUM!!!, change the sheet on my bed, store yr. quilt in its right plastic container, & clean the cat hairs off almost everything. My body will probably suffer tomorrow but oh what a boon for my spirits! It's awful to be sick in filthy surroundings.

Anyway, that shld. reassure you that I am okay. But now I do wonder abt. you . . . Tit for tat. Just to send love & share my joy at being able to DO things again . . . I hope things have quieted for you. I hope, I hope! H

In your snail mail letter you said you'd set the clock back—I hope you meant forward, otherwise you'll really be behind! Rereading it now, I realize how much I miss the little, expressive faces you know how to draw. What a gift drawing is. Do you ever want to just draw?

I finally figured out once again how to use the CD on this machine & am listening to Bessie thru my earphones . . . a funny way of making believe I was at yr [book] party [for *All Told*, dedicated to her]. Send pics, when you have to go to P.O. Just for heaven's sake, like my little mama used to say, rest yourself!

I just looked into the mirror and saw an aging witch . . . my dried out, partially gray hairs hanging, the lines on my face . . . it was weird. I've never thought of myself as a witch, but mebbe some part of me is.

No, No! Not a "witch" but a "crone"—much wiser, don't you think? Unless one thinks of oneself as a witch who can alter the course of history. Witches did (do?) indeed have power. (This is called "spin.")

I don't have any pictures but we did have a grand time, with both front and back door open to the lovely weather. Not a morsel of food was left, though plenty of wine was, for the next party. And we sold 58 of the 60 books from publisher. And everyone was gone by 7:15, as they should have been. And today, of course, I have the cold I fought so. But I don't care.

The sequin jacket I bought at Salv Army was a big hit. But I notice it sheds sequins (it's quite old). Yesterday, just before I left, I turned around to flush toilet and saw something black floating . . . panic, then—oh, it's a sequin! I am a tired person right now at 8:45pm. There are 12 emails from Russell Banks in this inbox, all to do with politics, and I'm too wiped to read them.

Have you been having lovely days? It was gorgeous here yesterday and today. Will write tomorrow when I have more of a head, as you always say. The only person really missing from the party was you! Love, H

• • • • •

Can't write. In a bind again. Festering sore on foot, Dr. today. Sent me home w/crutches & meals on wheels, etc. If I don't keep off it & let it heal it'll go into the bone. Mebbe I can figure out how to get semi-prone & use computer, doubt it. Time out. But I'll be thinking abt. you.

What's up? It's all downs here. Seems ages since I've had a word from you, please write to me. I need it. To specialist today, still on crutches & told to keep off my foot. In for many more awful tests. Have some incredible itchy rash all over my face & neck, have to see dermatologist but looks to him to be psoriasis! I feel I've been set upon by devils. Woke this a.m. to eyes almost swollen shut . . . Amen. Am sure you have woes, but mebbe will take a minute to at least send a hello. Steph has been my incredible angel . . . makes up batches of food for freezer, got me to dr. etc., Yma has come to clean, Niva took Chili to animal shelter . . . I miss him, but I can no longer take care of him & god willing she'll find a home for him. oy vey. Ain't life innaresting. H

Oh, I thought you were unable to write, so I didn't want to pile up messages. Sent you a letter via snail, and got yours via snail this afternoon.

Lordy, psoriasis—I know Adele D. says it's from a vitamin deficiency . . . What is causing this sore on your foot—seems like it's been there for weeks, or is it just that I feel as if that's so? I do miss you and your lovely sentences.

This is just a bit of a letter. It's 10:30 on Fri night and I've been sitting here all day with Rita's pages, half the time with Katy on the floor, going over the agreement we're working on re the house. Weds night our hot water heater gave up after 12 years of faithful service, water streaming into the karaoke bar's electric light! So yesterday I spent with plumbers, etc. But at least I only had to boil water one morning . . . We had a new heater by nightfall yesterday, which is kind of amazing.

OK, this goes to you with all my love and hope that all tests come out okay. I'll write more tomorrow. H

Well, here I am again, in the perpetual rain . . .

In my snailmail I mentioned *Angels & Insects* by A. S. Byatt, which I finished last night—what a lovely ride. I'll send you a list of books—let me know which interest you.

Gosh, I wish I could come up there and give you a big hug.

Oh, rereading your letter makes me itch in sympathy. Poor you, damn, wish there were something I could do—magic, that's it! The second part of Byatt's book (the "Angels" section), is about 19th century English seances and has Tennyson as a character, and his sister among others . . . a fun read, with poetry!

We've just had the most torrential rain, howling winds blowing down the roof stairs because I can't stand to have the door closed, the light and air are so wonderful this time of year. Today the longest day but the grayest and rainiest. I have a new poem called "Weather," I'll send it with this.

Are you up to answering? I don't mind if you don't, tho writing would be a distraction for you. But if I don't hear from you I'll just continue to blather. An old boyfriend used to chant, when I'd tell him my chores, complaints, etc: "Gettin thru the day, gettin thru the day" to the tune of "The Farmer in the Dell." Ugh.

OK, it's 11:15 and the rain has stopped. Hope they've at least given you some meds to quell the itchies. Love, H

GLOUCESTER, 6/22/03

Bless you! All them letters. I love "Weather," but just gave it a quick read, took forever to come thru. Tried to print it but printer went awry. Pouring again, and a mere 57 degrees—a truly gloomy Sunday. And I can't sit here any longer—my jerry-rigged foot-up can do only bits at a time, got to figure something better. Meanwhile bless you for writing! And I'll try later today, tho I ain't got much to say.

NEW YORK, 6/23/03

Good evening! Don't worry whether you have much to say, the point is just to get better so you can at least get out into the fresh air before it turns into hot air.

The rest of Rita's pages—minus only the very last 12 or 14—came this morning. I'll get a final version together and email it to her assistant. What a wonderful way to send a ms. When I think of all the times I had to type things over, and then print things out, and schlep paper around . . . Once I was on my bike and a taxi pulling out of a parking space behind me caught part of the bike and knocked me over. I wasn't hurt but the driver was so scared! I'm fading. Surrounded by piles of paper right left and center. Tomorrow! Love, H

6/27/03

Hi—New developer here today. No one wants to see wash on the roof. It's only in a nostalgic scene that a washline is permissible. What will they do with the people in the tenements behind us who are perfectly free to hang their wash between fire escape and roof, or some other arrangement. Hah. I'm just writing to say I will write tomorrow. Hope you are doing much much better, please do! Love and kisses, H

6/28/03

Hi—I've just finished the last Rita pages and my eyes are so blurry I can barely see the screen. But there's such a breeze coming in my window, which has probably a fine layer of silt and lots of those little orange no-see-ums, still it feels sweet and as soon as I've come far enough out of Rita's life I'll go to the corner and get my *NY Times*, in order to get depressed about the world.

Katy has called a meeting at our lawyer's office this Weds but hasn't yet heard from lawyer himself whether he can make it! Someone is supposed to bring a typist who can get our contract into a computer and have us all sign it while we're there. I think this is Mission Impossible but I admire her for trying.

It's 11pm and the breeze has died down but I know it'll be possible to sleep tonight if I don't get too riled up about the quagmire yes quagmire of a desert we're all in.

I hope you're better and that the weather is as lovely for you tomorrow as it has been for us today. How is your foot? Next week I'll send books. I wanted to buy you J. M. Coetzee's *Disgrace* but couldn't remember whether you'd read it. Love and kizzes, H

6/30/03

BOOK DONE!!!

I can't really believe it. It's 1:15pm Monday and I'm going out in a few minutes to get a copy made of the ms—which gained 10 pages with Rita's additions. I told her she should feel very proud of herself. I still can't believe... But we made the June deadline—on June 30th! How are you? I'm writing just to say that now I'll have time to send you those books. All I have to do for the rest of the summer is get together 2 new classes, read lots of kids books,[4] worry about when [and whether] they're going to

---

4. That fall I would begin teaching a workshop in Writing for Children in the Graduate Writing Program at The New School.

start this renovation, and move my car from one side of the street to the other, starting tomorrow.

OK. What are you doing with yourself all day? Just reading? Can you do anything else to entertain yourself? How is your apartment in the heat? Write if you can! Love, H

Re book done: Wonderful!! I'm o.k., just sitting here w/my foot up, telling myself I don't itch, etc. Apt. is awful in the heat but I have the fans going which helps. (70 outside but 80 in here.) No bother really, except when I try to sleep, which I can't because I don't move around all day, etc. Gonna call Dr & scream tomorrow. Mas tarde. My backside hurts, from constant sitting. Otherwise, everything is just hunky dory. I'm still alive and bitchy. Love, H

There's an incredible photo op at the moment: a pink sky with an overlay of blue-gray cloud, like a scrim, and in front of that a water tower . . .

I've just finished a very homemade package of books for you. I've cleared all the Rita stuff off my desk and stuffed it in the Rita drawer— one whole file drawer.

I know I should feel celebratory, but I worked so many hours over the weekend that all I want to do now is—well, the truth is I don't know what I want to do. Of course I'd love to have a new poem to work on, but I think my brain is on hold. Anyway, tomorrow I'm back to things that pertain to me instead of Mrs. Marley. Though I must say she's been terrific this last push—really put her mind to it. And so sweet on the phone . . .

Sky's almost all dark now, though faintly pink where it was so intense. Almost 9pm. Hope this finds you feeling better. Love, H

I owe you lotsa letters, but I'll get back to it one day. Bless you for writing. My life still one of sitting, every time I think of something positive to do, the effort of getting all the implements necessary stops me. But today it seems easier to walk on my sore, mebbe it's curing itself. No word from Dr re tests. Give me a couple more days & mebbe I can get off a decent letter. Lovve! [*sic*]

Hi—Happy 4th to you! A very quick note—I'm worried about your not getting any sunshine, bad for your bones. This is not good! What's wrong with the doctors—if you can't use crutches they should write you a prescription for a wheelchair!

You Angel!!

Knock on my door around 2PM ... my "come in" produced the smiling face of the man who brings P.O. packages ... keep forgetting to ask Fred his name. He's just doing his job, of course, but has that wonderful smile that sez he's happy to bring something I might be waiting for, or mebbe a nice surprise. . . . Surprise today, certainly! He found a place on the table, set it down, smiled, and left. I'd thought it wldn't come till next week.

Your packing job was impressive, must have taken hours! And what a cache inside! Instead of sitting down immediately to thank you, I picked a top one out (Josephine Tey), sat back down w/it and just now came to the last page. It kept me engrossed enuff to ignore my sweating body. Damn near 90 in here still. Bathroom so hot I can't even contemplate cooling myself off with tepid water. And what to eat in this encased heat . . . I keep making sandwiches out of cold stuff. Reminds me of that wonderful alcoholic tramp in Burlington who sd. no thanks to stew I offered, picked out bits of it, asked for bread slices & made a sandwich. Smiling at me, "that's how I gotta eat." And once, he turned very white, his eyes got strange, and he looked at me: "Sorry, DT's coming & I don't want the kids to see," staggered off his chair & was out the door in a flash. I loved that man. Wish I cld. remember his name. He told me wonderful stories of life on the road. All gone now into the nether parts of my brain. Am told it's all still there . . . Poor brain! 76 years of finding a place to stash stuff, can you imagine???

I love you!! I am simply not going to look, but just take one off the top when I need a new one. H

• • • • •

She'd also told this story to Tom Clark, who included it in *Edward Dorn, A World of Difference*, the 2002 biography that had troubled Helene's sleep. Though we'd both gone for that world, I never forget that she'd come to it at an earlier point in time, and had given herself away to it twice as long. When I'd written her that our letters had "validated my existence," I meant the self-direction that despite all hardship I'd never relinquished, which Helene had to wait two decades to reclaim. Thus, as I hope I've made clear, I always thought she had it harder. And if I didn't truly understand, and couldn't fix, at least I could entertain.

This is the only world:
Our opaque lives. Our secrets. And that's all. . . .

Our two eyes see in plurals:
What we understand, and what will fail.
They're both the only world.
        — *Tracy K. Smith*

GLOUCESTER, 7/12/03

Now it's me, wondering where you are & what's happening!

NEW YORK, 7/13/03

Hellooo! There were 68 emails when I turned this on — 67 spam, one you. Thank goodness for you! Where have I been? Trying to figure out my new poetry class, going to the dentist, waiting for the phone company . . .

Today's *Times* has a story about a young (35) Turkish woman who was stoned because she was pregnant and unmarried, and prob raped by a 55 year old known in the village for his "wide eye." While the woman lay dying for 3 months in hosp many women from village came to visit (she couldn't speak, walk, etc but could blink her eyes) and when she eventually died they carried her coffin to the grave, then put the first dirt on it, both no-nos. Oh women! Turkey passed a law against this stoning but "remote villages" still practice old ways. Oh women. I wanted to write a poem, but then on the roof my local robin kept singing and singing . . . what does one celebrate?[1]

Write me about the books you're reading. Love, H

GLOUCESTER, 7/20/03

Am rereading A. S. Byatt. Looking at copyright page, was amazed to discover that "she" had full credits. It had just seemed to be the work of a "he" first time around. Why, I've no idea. I wish she didn't use words like

---

1. "7/13/03 Gifts," *Doing 70* (Hanging Loose Press, 2007).

stoan (two dots above the a) which are not in my dictionary. It's a delight, nonetheless. I'm still a prisoner despite my vow to ignore drs because I was going nuts, but walking got too painful and I'm back on my chair.

I'm fed up with doctors. "If I had no sense of humor, I would long ago have committed suicide." Mahatma Ghandi

Hi! For my birthday Kellie gave me Joe LeSoeur's *Digressions on Some Poems by Frank O'Hara* which I can't wait to read. Joe died this past year and this was published posthumously—I heard parts of it a couple of months ago, and thought it was wonderful. Maybe your library will order it? Right now I'm not allowing myself to read anything but the pile of young adult books on my floor—I've got to start thinking about that new class—though I just heard this afternoon that the copyedited ms. of Rita's book will arrive this Friday and I have 2 weeks to get it looked at and TYPOS ONLY (said editor in caps) can be fixed on first printed proof . . . oy vey. Love, H

Just to let you know 2 days ago Dr. pronounced my foot sore healed and I'm learning to walk again.

Nuts! Using my newly usable legs, had planned a day of starting to clean up 2 + month's accumulation, but instead have spent hours trying to unplug my kitchen sink. Hauling bucketfuls of water to dump in toilet, etc.

Actually, I think the gods or planets are having fun with me, so I might just as well laugh along with them. Love, H

I don't know where the planets are, but they're where they ought not to be. Just when I had my schedule for moving the car down, the TV show "NYPD Blue" has commandeered the fucking street. Anyway, I'm gonna put some clothes on and go out to get the paper. All the bad news of the world will take this focus away. Take care of yourself and take it easy at first. Love, H

Hi. They've gutted the apt below me and my entire apt is full of dust which keeps rising. There's nothing between my floorboards and downstairs except empty space. They'd better put soundproofing in because all the old plaster and lath is now gone and we will hear every fart between here and there. Everything is filthy.

This may be my last letter for a minute or so, though it sure does help to tell you my troubles!

Rita has cooperated by being late! I am cleaning out stuff! There is a dumpster and the construction guys will take out my dumpings!

The tossing is something one shld. do periodically, but never does. I've been thru a lot of that, every move. I don't want to think abt. it, so much here still to be tossed. Stay happy! love, H

Hi—how are you? I guess you figured right, that you'd stop hearing from me at some point. I can't remember when that was. Everything's happening so fast. I've been getting up at 6:30 every day and bathing in the tub on the floor below and using the toilet there.

What's been interesting is seeing how much work I put into gerry-rigging the things I couldn't fix—hiding broken ceilings and walls with plastic sheeting and grass mats. Things I'd almost forgotten I'd done, with a ladder balanced in the bathtub . . . oh! So this is my whole story for the moment. Please write and bring me news of the real world out there. Love, H

Sorry to fail you, but I got no more idea of what's going on "out there" than you do. My hair is fast diminishing, walking remains hard, etc. I'm in a terrible mood. But I'll come out of it and write when I can sluff it. It's called depression, I'm told. In the meantime, know I'm thinking abt. you. Love! H

Re your hair—there was a story in the *Times* this week about pellagra, a deficiency disease no one gets anymore in our over-proteined lives, but I wondered anyway whether anyone thought of that, re your age and thinness, since one of its symptoms is a scaly rash.

OK, this is just to wonder how you are. Love, H

Hi—it'll be 2 weeks Tues that I haven't had a bathroom. Had words with the contractor because he claims he never promised me a toilet even though I cracked the one I have years ago either removing old seat or installing new one. I am tired and dirty and mad at everyone and nervous about the teaching starting in two weeks and the captions for Rita book photos not yet written. And I'm here pissing in a bucket while nothing gets done. How are you? Love, H

Back from Boston. Left here at 2:30, Fred drove. Got to my appt. at 3:30. 5 or 10 minutes w/Dr. after 2 hr. wait! Everything "stable," no "aggressive action" necessary. Start walking but make it gradual, check foot sore every night, etc., & let him know if it starts erupting again. Firm handshake and smile. End of session. It WAS good news, but we were so tired & hot & pissed off at the wait. Friday I'll see the dermatologist and then NoMoreDoctors. My hair is falling out, my scalp full of scales etc. It's too crazy to try to put into words. Just like your house bit. I finally put in the mail some cartoons. It's Orwellian, this world. Mas Tarde, and my love, H

Hope you survived the weather yesterday . . . I sat all day unable to move. Read a mystery set in Manhattan & there was this wonderful quote abt. the weather: "You don't know whether to breathe it or eat it with a spoon."

Saw dermatologist on Friday. Gave me some 100$ worth of scripts, didn't name what I had . . . a ten or fifteen min. exam. Left w/a shot of cortisone in my rear ("to calm it down"). Tonight I must wet my scalp, apply a thin film of oil, put on the cap provided, sleep, and manana wash my hair with shampoo which blurb tells me may very well take a lot of my hair with it, but not to worry, once scalp is thoroughly moisturized, hair

will grow back. I wonder if my new crop of hair will come back grey??
Innaresting. Love, H

Here's where I'd like to remind her she'd predicted this, just as she'd known
what was killing her. Just as she'd remind me that even if I sympathized with
addiction I didn't understand alcoholism. And I was always up for drinking
beer with her, to relax and party. I suppose that's "enabling." But what she did
on her own, for her own reasons, I had no right to question. Nor could I cure
the depression she'd mentioned. So, as always, I just blundered on:

NEW YORK, 8/25/03

The last wash I did yesterday contained dirty rugs. That wash backed
up into my bathtub. It drained slowly, leaving debris, which I cleaned.
At night I took a bath and the water refused to drain. This morning I
used Liquid Plumber and went out for more and came back to find the
plumbers here to collect their tools to go to another job because we have
been abandoned until after Labor Day. Please help I begged. Call the boss
they said. Called the boss, who said that the pipes just needed snaking,
not replacing as the plumber said. Please snake said I. We don't snake,
said the boss. You have to get other plumbers who snake. SPECIALTY
PLUMBERS! I freaked out, called the real estate agent, long story, and new
plumbers, snakers, arrived shortly. Thank god.

But I should be grateful that I have a bathtub (though not yet a shower
because the plumbers "forgot" the shower curtain rod). Other than that, I
am not happy. I don't feel that I can be my real self anywhere. I am terrified that I won't be good in my new class because I'm so distracted. And
which begins one week from tomorrow! Meanwhile, at least I can cook
my own food, though I have been eating out of a stainless steel mixing
bowl. And Ken, Lisa's darling betrothed, has been keeping my car which
is such a great help. But I'm so very very anxious about everything.

OK, now I have complained about it all.

About your head, poor babe: I know how you love your beautiful hair,
but maybe, because it's such a trial to wash, you might think about cutting
it now that it's going to come out. Oh! Have you looked up Adele Davis to
see what causes cradle cap in babies? I'm so certain that all this is fixable
nutritionally, but of course I could be dead wrong. Soon the weather will
be better and all these problems will be bad memories. Lisa keeps telling

me that. OK. I think I'll take a bath and worry about the reading I have to give on Sept 7, which is some distraction from the class I don't know how to teach which starts on 9/2.

Sorry I'm so full of self-regard. That's what I mean, I just am not myself, or maybe that's my true selfish self? Please let me know what happens with your hair. I need to hear from you because else I really do worry. Love, H

I'm in a vile mood. My hair. I'm amused you think I thought it beautiful. I've only thought of it as warmth. I've lived in so many cold places. Ed cut it for me once. As short as yours. I'm sure there are photos to prove it. Now I have bald spot on top. Very little below that. Fuck Adele, I tried all that. I'm cortizoned & steroided, 2003.

Hello Vile Mood, it's still Weds. but at the other end, 9:15pm.

I always thought your hair was beautiful! But anyway, just pull what's left over the bald spot, into a topknot. It will grow back, surely. Love, H

Still in a vile mood. But that steroid shit does seem to be helping. I've spent so much money on scripts; I just take a breath, hand them my credit card. Oh to live in a country that does something abt. medical ripoff.

Last night I started a poem about Vinnie and Michael of All County Sewer, the snakers. That made me feel terrific but I haven't looked at it again to see whether it's real or just something in the heat of the moment. I remember May Sarton writing in her journal about the relief of just being home alone with her poem.

I'm so glad the stuff is working on your hair. I have this present I bought for you a thousand years ago when it was cold. It'll keep you warm even if you don't have any hair. I even know where it is at this moment — a miracle. God willing, I'll get to the post office, inshallah. Feel better! Love, H

Hi—Went out of town with my friend Eric Richards on Friday. We were headed toward the NY-Penna border, at the narrow part of the Delaware River, when we saw a sign "turn left here for the Zane Grey museum"—so we did. And there, presided over by 2 young women from the National Park Service, was the sweetest house, Zane's house, with a long porch overlooking the river. Inside were various exhibits—his corny western novels plus some interesting nonfiction. And the short bridge we crossed from NY was by Roebling, who built the Bklyn Bridge! I'm sending you a postcard.

I came home to the news that the next day workmen were coming to repoint the shaky brick wall in Katy's to-be apt. Promptly at 9:30am a machine started. We'd been warned about dust but this dust filled the entire building and boiled out the windows. A neighbor called the fire dept. Firemen broke the front door lock and dashed up the stairs. Etc. I don't know who got what summons, but the people who left us for 10 days with canisters of flammable gas in the hall and mountains of debris in the back of the building are in for it.

Just wanted to let you know reason for my silence. Tomorrow's my first day of school. Whew. Hope you're doing okay. Love, H

GLOUCESTER, 9/2/03

It's late, and I gotta put something in my stomach. My computer went berserk, like me. Fred came today and somehow fixed it w/this disc he has. Whole bit as weird as my scalp & hair. I'm still losing the latter & the former is improving but not all that much. When it gets really bad, I'll ask you to check the Salvation Army for head scarves. Be interesting to see my hairless head in the mirror, but I think I might be too vain to let anyone other than friends & relations view it. Someone, Yul Brynner? made a fortune w/ his bald head. But a man can do that, a woman can't. That is, if she's 76 & doesn't give a shit abt. a fortune. For all I know it's the rage now, shaving your head.

NEW YORK, 9/2/03

I have a ton of scarves and the Salv Army always has more. Hats are good too. But I understand your vanity, as I'd no doubt have the same reaction.

I just wish doctors could figure out what's causing all this, but they specialize in treating symptoms, as though symptoms were causes.

Yes, it was Yul Brynner, and a few years ago it was Sinead O'Connor, a singer, who made the shaved head popular for women. Lots of girls copied her. Last I saw a photo she'd finished her statement and had let her hair grow. But all the bald guys shave their heads now; it's considered cool.

Take heart. The weather will be cooperating, as it'll soon be too cold to go out without a hat anyway. I wanted one already this morning. Love, H

And a little more than a week later, she had "sluffed it." Hair loss and all, she was back on her feet:

I've had what might be called a purposeful day. Started back w/clauds, took a cab & got my glasses fixed, got Lorna's woodcuts & Chan's self-portrait from 1974 off the wall & stored with care, and now I gotta eat something. My legs & my head are healing, day by day. Love always, take time to breathe, lady. H

Hi—I've had the nicest few hours since this whole thing started—completely alone.

I've also been happy thinking about you doing your clauds and going hither and yon and your head healing.

Ok, momma. It's 11:05 and I'm going out to find out how many people were killed and maimed today in this needless war. No one seems to have a clue as to how to stop the madness. Love, H

Power outage here, due to something on tel. lines—a crow no doubt. Didn't last more than a few hours, but fucked up all my electronic devices. Oh well. In between changing time settings on vcr, microwave, phone, I've read bits of this Slav poet's novel I pulled off the new books shelf. Milorad Pavic. It's intrigueing sp! Also intrigueing (I'll look it up after I send this), is the fact that there were about 5 Slavic titles on the shelf. I wonder why. Anyway here's a wonderful quote I think you shld. use next time somebody tries to get you to do something not on yr. agenda. Change the third person to first, or something:

"... Never was he able to mix the crumbs from lunch with the crumbs from dinner. He was constantly on the move."

And if they question you, tell them you're Constantine of Thessalonica, St. Cyril. Hair thing is getting better, seem to be losing less. We'll see. I don't even anymore worry abt. walking around bald. Save yr. scarves. Love, H

You sound like yourself! I loved that Slavic stuff, thank you, I'm gonna read it again right now . . . Love! H

• • • • •

What's up? Seems long time no hear, but I'm in a netherworld & quickly lose dates & time, etc.

It was an even longer time before I answered:

Hi—It's Sat night and I'm remembering with much nostalgia the pleasant Sat nights I wrote to you from my comfortable desk.

I dunno, Helene. I'm all tuckered out. Hope you're better and doing your clauds and all. Write me some encouragement! Love, H

I've been trying to find words of encouragement, but all I've come up with is that at least it is YOUR apt., it WILL all finally get fixed.

And NOW, all this time later, given I've been sick but! I want to start again, and I can't locate the sketchbook that contains all the color mixing info I need. In the process of hunting thru boxes, I discovered the scale I've been missing but remembered I'd carefully packed. So that adage Ed had at Santa Fe "don't look, it will turn up" seems right, but I wonder how much time I've got.

Mebbe this is some sort of encouragement. I hope you're keeping yrself together no matter the mess. Wish I cld. wave a magic wand & make it all go away. I love you. H

How much time she had. Was this "Why bother to live if you're going to die," or an attempt to get past Ed's instructions? Here, as the past kept resurfacing in the dusty ancient innards of this house, some days I believed the exposure would free me; others I thought it kept me safe. I couldn't decide. If you know, let me know.

Whew! It's taken me until the following Sat. to even reread your letter—that's how it's been around here. But as of this moment everything is, at last, peaceful. And will be for one day, perhaps—

OK, no more about that, though something interesting: This past Monday was the 45th anniversary of my former marriage, which I got through without thinking much about it, though (unavoidably) marking it because it fell on Columbus Day, just as the wedding had that year (1958). Anyway, thinking about Roi a bit this week, not without sympathy.[2] Then this morning, at the greenmarket I ran into Milford Graves, a drummer who was on the scene then. He asked if I still lived here, and I told him about the renovation . . . and he said he was pleased we'd managed to save the place because it was "an historic building" and he'd been thinking about those times as he drove past.

I came home, and looking in on the floor of what will be my study, noted that the sanding had not completely obliterated the burn mark made by a cigarette fallen from Roi's ashtray when he (as often) fell asleep while smoking. . . . I wish I could make a poem about it, but giving that much emotional energy to Roi at this point is not what I want to do.

What am I trying to say here? I think I've already said it enough times, but there will always (I imagine) be reminders that there was another, now distant life here.

Hope you've found that sketchbook by now.

What else to tell you? The weather's been beautiful, and I do get to see some of the turning leaves when I drive up to Purchase. Last week I

---

2. Amiri and Amina Baraka's daughter had been murdered.

left there just at dusk, and the crickets (cicadas, maybe) were loud, and the smell of the earth and trees was, well, divine. I pass an old grave-yard on the way to my car, and the lovely dark stones in that light . . . So there's always something to remark, though I don't have a new poem. I need something like your color mixing notebook. Meanwhile, it's become nearly 9pm. Thanks for your offer to wave a magic wand. Your letter was one. Love, H

10/19/03

Hi—Went to the bookshop for the first time since all this chaos, bought a new *Selected Poems* by Denise Levertov, read three or four poems and was immediately inspired—that word I love because it just means breath—it's literal—

So I was finally able to write something. It's only a first draft really, but herewith. Love and thank you for your continued love as I don't know what I'd do if I couldn't write to you. H

The poem, I'm pleased to note now, is not about that long-ago life, but a later time when all the rooms were mine.

. . . . .

GLOUCESTER, 10/23/03

Forgive me, am too tired and out of it to write. Legs & head hurting. Try-ing to work out how to get Compaq close to printer which will take both. Looked up all my measurements & on same sheet was writ a fortune I'd got when playing Shangrila game on my then new little Apple. "Prayers are always answered. The answer is usually no."

Not exactly encouragement, but I hope will bring you a laugh. And I love the poem, 1st. draft or not, it said a lot to me. So there! Denise, whew! That takes me back years.

10/31/03

You ok?

It's been a hollow Halloween except Ket brought her three, so proud of their costumes. So here I sit with all those left-over chocolates, Ket re-fused to take them with her, grinning at me, "Have fun."

Have played Rapuntzel-with-no-hair for 4 days, elevator out of order due to part needing replacement. Sat here for that time reading mysteries, doing me clauds in the hall, and trying to start organizing all the piles of what-to-do-withs. The laundry has piled up, but instead of doing that when notice came that elevator was back in service, I called a cab & went to the store and walked around just breathing fresh air! My legs are getting better, but to make it both down & up 3 flights I don't think they are ready for and I didn't attempt it. This morning on my way out to P.O. passed by the man in wheelchair I often open the outside door for, wears a baseball cap & has a nice smile, and asked how he'd fared w/no elevator. "Went nuts. 4 days inside!" Me too, sez I. Cabin fever, sez he & then the elevator he was waiting for opened and we parted. And I felt stupid for bemoaning my own state. I cld have made it down the steps, sat for a long time in the lobby and then slowly made it back up again. Felt a total wimp. So are you OK? Long time no email . . . and of course I wonder & worry. Love, H

NEW YORK, 11/1/03

I'm glad you have all those chocolates—better than I who ate the leavings of not one but three bags of candy corn, bought for my classes.

I owe you a letter. There sits the one you sent end of last week, and I kept looking at it and saying, okay, when things calm down . . .

Had what I thought was a true nervous breakdown this week when my car had a leaky fuel line and was uptown and Kellie and Lisa were feuding about who'd bring it down, and AAA wouldn't tow it unless I was standing right there and I had to be in a rental car on my way to Purchase (in the pouring, pouring rain). I boo-hood all over Lisa, then boo-hood all over Kellie . . . Endless story.

Sometime in and around all this drama the contractor arrived one morning and told me he was going to cover up the skylight in my hallway because the plans said it was blocked. This was the architect's mistake who couldn't see with his own eyes that the skylight was not blocked, had never been. He said "only temporarily" but I freaked out, called landlord, realtor, lawyer, everyone, screaming, hanging up the phone. Called Katy, demanding why she didn't give me the fucking plans she'd held on to ever since May . . . which showed NO SKYLIGHT WHATSOEVER!!!!!!!!!!! Although we had gone over and over and over the plans in lawyer's office to everyone's satisfaction and the skylights had been carefully, legally protected.

Then I lost it, really lost it and ended up sobbing and screaming in front of the workmen, all of whom like me and were trying to comfort me. And all day long I just kept crying and crying, it was weird. Then, at the end of the day, the contractor, who had started all this with his obtuseness, came breezing in and said, "Oh, I talked to my brother (who is the new architect on the project) and he said it was okay." By then I was so drained, and so humiliated. The way these people talk to women is more than I could ever stand on a regular basis.

They have put up a fence on the roof that looks like a corral, made of metal pipe that looks suspiciously like plumbing pipe. Anyway it's the perfect height for me to sit on, at a corner, and contemplate the skyline that will soon disappear from my view. It's also totally ridiculous, I don't think that's what our fancy developer had in mind!

My life is still packed, after 3 months. This week I have to teach my 3 classes, have one student conference (last week I had five hour-long conferences). But this week I have to do a reading. I haven't even looked at my poems for days and days. So this is what I'm doing, and trying not to lose it again. And why I haven't written. In between I just sit here and do homework.

Last night after everything got reasonably quiet and I had done 4 hrs of homework, I smoked a joint and tried to come to terms with all this shit. I was looking at the switch in this room, a square gray metal box on a pipe strapped to the wall. Beside it is a nail holding what used to live on my wooden apartment door, a brass knocker with some bells tied to it, one of which is a cowbell Allen Ginsberg brought me from India. I had hung it there temporarily after the guy who took off the door this week handed it to me. The electric box has four markings, which easily become, when one is stoned, the two eyes, the forehead third eye, and mouth of Electric Man; the switch itself is his nose. Beside him is Ms. Door Knocker, who looks for all the world like a Victorian caricature: small head, wide curved bust, narrow waist. So what if her feet are a cowbell from India? I hope the two of them stay together a long time.

I suppose this nonsense is good for me.

Thanks for writing even though I owed you one. You ought to look up that nice man in the wheelchair and offer to meet him in the lobby and open the door for him one day. I love to invent romances for other people. OK, my friend. Much love, H

· · · · ·

But reality trumped romance, and then everything began to go really fast:

I have to be mobile before noon tomorrow to attend brunch for grandson David's 12th and Fred's 55th, so this is short. As of 4:30 p.m. yesterday, Fred has RETIRED from the P.O.!! A lot to tell you but it's gotta wait. Love, H

Re Fred: I was struck again today, I haven't seen him for over a month at least, how very handsome he is, & keeps getting more so. The relief of being shed of the P.O. shows in his whole demeanor. Despite waiting on the returns of biopsy done last week on lump in his throat. I haven't told you because I knew he wouldn't want me to . . . In fact, I'm not even sure he knows I know.

It was a really successful party. I'm always not able to decipher what everyone is saying, but that didn't matter today. I've never seen David so happy.

Wish you cld. have been there to share my grands & great-grands . . . they are all incredible! Ket is unbelievably beautiful, I cldn't take my eyes off her. She always had that wonderful shine in her eyes, but now I was fascinated watching her dealing w/all the kids. I've got to quit . . . Love, H

Hi—I've been flashing on Fred and thinking and worrying. Nothing new here; I just carried 13 boxes from one room to another. OK, on to read a student rewrite. Sure hope it's better than the write. Love! H

What's up? Nothing but bad news here. You got any good to send? Long time no hear.

What is it—Fred? Everything's okay here except for my continuous gnashing of teeth.

Left you a phone message a couple of hours ago.

Got all your messages, including phone. Just cldn't deal with talking abt. it. Fred is due for surgery on 12/10. That fucking cancer shld have latched on to me, not him. It's so fucking unfair! See? I shldn't write. That's why I haven't.

I don't blame you for not feeling up to writing. But Fred is so gutsy . . .

My father had his larynx removed before they'd developed the machine that's in use now. He was 65 and lived to be 85, and for 20 years spoke (clearly enough to be understood, even over the phone) by swallowing air, a technique that didn't seem to take him long to learn. (I saw him, after his operation, in the hospital, and he was able to speak to me— it was the occasion of our first meeting in 10 years.)

I'm telling you this just to encourage you. Please keep me posted. Much Love, H

Thanks, that was a lovely letter and I needed one.

It's a bitch to lose any sense. My sister once told me, in commiseration of my deafness, she'd rather lose her sight than her hearing, because it had to do with communication . . . she's the only one I've ever known to really understand. But at some point in her life she'd worked w/deaf kids, and knew. And speech is similar in that respect. But at least they got machines to help communication, so I figure if you gotta lose something, keep your sight. No news except it's bitchy weather here too, 16 and fierce winds that come thru my windows no matter I've closed them.

Have to quit because I gotta eat and put gook on my hair. Got that shit on my scalp again. My fault, Dr. told me I shld continue to use it once a week to keep it from coming back, but I didn't, afraid it wld make me lose more hair. Now I'm convinced it would be better to be bald. Hope you're snug in your box-filled home & out of the winds that are raising hell outside and managing to come thru my closed windows enough to make my nose cold. The gods are having fun. Love! H

Well, yours was a lovely letter too and I needed one. Oh, I think it has to be hard to lose your ears, your voice, any of it—and I keep trying to remind myself of what *is* instead of what *isn't*. Here I've been whining and all I am is discombobulated and overworked . . . which is probably standard for most people these days.

I wanted this to be a long letter, but now it's 10:30 and I have to go to sleep early because tomorrow I am reading poetry at the library on 53rd St. for all the NY Public Library's nice librarians "to inspire them" in this time of budget cuts (so says the lady from Poets House, who hired me). I didn't want to do it but I hate to disappoint Poets House (they're good people) and it's important to pay attention to our long-suffering librarians, and so I must leave here at 9:45am dressed and breakfasted.

My teaching will be done by 12/17. That doesn't leave too much room for Christmas stuff.

I wish your head weren't itchy, itchy is maddening. Today I discovered an itchy patch on my shoulder, prob reaction to wool or something, bad enough, but your head, oh. Much love, H

Just quick. Freaking out abt. Fred & then suddenly hit me Xmas I gotta deal with too.

Just found out I have shingles, which doesn't surprise me. Yes, Xmas— I feel like playing hooky from it. I lit a Big Red Candle for Fred last night, which still burns. Somewhere I learned that red candles are for strength.

Xmas is something I'd like to just step over. This year especially.

Hi—yes, that's exactly the right way to say it! Stepping over Xmas—Be of good cheer, my dear. Christmas will be over before we know it. But send my love to your wonderful family and take a big chunk of it for yourself!

So—what's up? Haven't heard from you in ages. Happy New Year and let's hope it's all good, or at least some good. Love and kizzes to all, H

Happy New Year to you too, but somehow I stepped over it. Am not sure when the wedding is, but please give Lisa & Ken my love & best wishes. The ups are, re Fred, the surgeon still iffy, but hopeful. I'm living thru a nightmare, so please understand when you don't hear from me.

Hello—Of course I understand. Wedding is 6pm Saturday, and the weather predicted for that day is extreme, so I'm worried about what I'm wearing since I'm always so cold. Courage, babe. Keep yourself well so you won't worry Fred while he's worried about himself. Love, H

Well, it's Friday night & cold!! Suggest you wear a skisuit to the wedding! I was freezing till I went down to get my mail & found the 1st floor toasty warm. Met Joe on my way back to elevator & he explained that I was freezing because the boiler, going full blast, cldn't handle the upper floors & especially those like mine getting the full blast of the wind. 45 min. later he arrived at my door with a miraculous little heater! That's all for now. Love, H

· · · · ·

And that was all. For now and forever. Helene stopped writing and answering the phone. Even her son Paul couldn't reach her. Eventually she was hospitalized, sent to a nursing home, and then back to the hospital where she died, at the end of May, of the incurable bacterial infection we've since come to know is epidemic, familiarly known as *C. dif.*

I couldn't believe her death. For years I was sure she'd willed it. I tried writing to her as though she were alive (useless), I missed her humor and her help, I will always miss Helene. Like her I couldn't keep a diary, nor could any Dear Diary teach me to make garbage soup or nine raisins soaked in gin, or send me quotes from Virginia Woolf to calm me when I was fighting all my battles—literary and otherwise—without precedent and terribly alone.

This book is for the person who saved my life, who sat on her floor surrounded by paper and then wrote, "Such a story, our letters." Which story remains what I'd asked: a conversation with a plainspoken woman, about what we were thinking and doing. The journey that itself was home.

These days, as she'd wished, Helene Dorn drifts in Gloucester Harbor. Her little "Discarded Wife" hangs in my hall, in line with this desk. She's finely textured plaster of paris, a green so dark I sometimes catch her midnight blue. After she lost one shell earring, I gave her a set of silver stars, then added a pair of Helene's that Fred sent—multihued wooden discs like color wheels. Discarded Wife is jazzed, her stubborn mouth almost smiles, everything has come to pass. As has her promise, "to know you're not alone":

"Goodnight, my equally dear dear friend. If I shortly pass out of this world, I'll send you poems from the next one. Yeah. Love, H"

DOING 70

A Passion Play

In memoriam Helene Dorn 1927–2004

ACT I

On the Mass Pike, at the first rest stop past
Boston, the starter breaks. The lights and radio
go on, but there's no click click. It's six
on a hot, humid, summer Saturday.
I'm headed to New York
with a file box of letters in the trunk.

What could have caused this?
Overheating? I'd only been doing 70.

The cashier calls three times for a guy
who appears at last with doped-up eyes
and writes down a number.
The man on the phone says
Look for a truck, but it might take
twenty to thirty and if he doesn't come
call me back.

A pattern? A portent? Well,
a second chance.

I start right away for the car.
The box of letters is heavy every
way. Thirty pounds, four decades,
two women. One dead, the other
stuck. Fuck.

But even as the door of the store closes behind me
a flatbed roars into the sunburnt parking lot.
Waving and pointing, I run the rest of the way,
and soon an audience has gathered, a three-generation family
with two awed children. Everyone likes a driver,

and here's a young, good-looking, acrobatic one.
who parks precisely, load-ready, then
in one quick movement swings out,
takes my keys, turns on the lights and radio, and says
it's probably the starter.

Well I *know* that.
But Ryan, as I'd come to know *him*, notes
at once that I've gone past cause to effect.
He tells me the terms, admits he's been
to New York twice, and not in many years.
(How many years are in him, maybe
twenty-three?) But his self-possession rivals
his grace. I assure him I know the roads.
When we agree, his excitement
parallels my relief. He loads the car
on the bed and me in the cab.
The family watching waves
as we drive away.

This is when I discover that the truck has no a/c
and not too many shocks.

ACT 2

Back on the highway,
the shouting wind is a third rider.
Ryan stays on his phone, all about
getting lucky and going to New York City.

On my mind and in the side mirror
the car on the flatbed, all those old words
stirring. It's the night of a huge blue moon

as July becomes August, and I've been doing seventy
for sixteen days and I'm still new to it.
A broken starter isn't auspicious.
And you, Helene, are not even here
for the humor. Shit.

But so far, nothing has changed about
being here now to get there then. It got us
on this truck. What I have of you is safe
in the trunk. And I'm in the cab
with Ryan. When I ask if he minds
if I take off my shoes, he says
do what you like
we've got a long way to go.

Though of course we haven't gone far
before I'm in love. Every time
we hit rough road the glove compartment
falls open into my lap, and my bare foot
closing it seems
provocative

though I know doing seventy means
giving up the pretty boys

you lust you lose, you hear
the cry of the crows

ACT 3

It's hard to talk over the wind.
Sometimes we travel miles between sentences.
Ryan goes to college on and off for law
enforcement. He's two months into
driving this truck. At the midway stop,
he asks me where we are on the map.
Then he helps me get a drink.
We are to each other a profile only,
yet there's easy body language

between us, some physical trust. I'm sweaty
and dirty and beginning to feel as if
I'm the one who really got lucky.

After the Pike we take 84 to 91 to 95,
Ryan reporting to his dispatcher,
whose staticky voice seems tense,
as if her tracking might not prevent
his transfiguring. But despite a side trip
over the Triboro to Queens (my fault),
he gets us into Manhattan and onto
Second Avenue, where the real fun begins:

It's Saturday night, New York!
The neighbors are out! There are buses, taxis,
bikers, bad drivers, jay walkers,
cell phone talkers, a jabber and clank
of outdoor eaters—

Ryan drives among them all, Second Avenue
end to end.

ACT 4

At the parking lot he once again
commands an audience. After driving
one hundred ninety miles at night on
four unfamiliar major highways,
he backs his load through tight,
curving, graveled spaces, then
slides it gently into place,

and then, ready to turn back,
guns the truck across a double
yellow, yelling "What the hell,
I'm from Worcester, and I'll
just make a u-ie here!"

REPRISE

The box is waiting in my hall
the route I've written out reviewed
and Ryan reminded that he said
he'd take a nap. By now it's eleven,
he won't get back till four. But no,
he'll blast the radio, work
the overnight, why not. He knows
what holds him, lucky Ryan,

and lucky us, my dear Helene,
the dead and living
safely home.

ACKNOWLEDGMENTS

Grateful acknowledgment is made to the following: the New York Foundation for the Arts for the 2009 Nonfiction Literature Fellowship, and AE Ventures for their grant to work on this book. To Kathryn Holmes for her research and computer skills. To Kenneth Wissoker of Duke University Press for his interest and appreciation, and to his assistant Jade Brooks for her attention to detail. To Helene Dorn's family: Marie Bahlke, Paul and Chan Buck, and above all tireless Fred Buck, for his generosity and time and effort supplying names, dates, photos, emails, and all the original letters I drove home from Gloucester that night of the huge blue moon when I had just turned seventy, a sight and situation Helene would have loved. And, as always, to my daughters, Kellie Jones and Lisa Jones Brown, for their forbearance in allowing me the stories I have forever told about them; my sons-in-law Guthrie Ramsey and Ken Brown, for their kindness and support; and lastly to Zoe Margaret Hettie Chapman Brown, who will see her name in this book and have a record of my life after I'm gone.

INDEX

Page numbers in italics refer to illustrations and captions; *pl.* to color plates.

Baraka, Amina, 53, 342n2
Baraka, Amiri (LeRoi Jones), 7, 38, 53, 74n11, 284, 342n2; autobiography of, 51, 54, 130
Barnard College, 17
Barnes, Djuna, 63, 75
Basho, 33
Baxter, Charles, 192
Beat, Beats: books on, 175–76; exhibits on, 160n5; in NYC, 1; poets of, 243; supporters of, 154n3
Beat women, 144, 151, 156, 175, 177, 284; as heroes, 3; literature of, 49, 173
Beckett, Samuel, 271
Bedford Hills Correctional Facility, 101, 101n2, 212, 215; Hettie teaches at, 107, 107n4, 110, 114, 125, 151, 153, 176, 177, 181, 187, 194, 232, 235, 236, 281–82; reading at, 207–8
Belafonte, Harry, 316
Bell Jar, The (Plath), 250
Belushi, John, 111
Belushi, Judy, 111, 117
Bendiner, Winnie, 291
Berkeley Poets Conference, *13*
Berlin, Lucia, 97, 97n10, 222, 223, 239
Berrigan, Ted, 17
besmirching, literary, 51–52
Bible, 230, 314
birth control, 17–18, 59
birthdays: Helene's, 52, 112, 131, 142, 150, 151; Hettie's, 23–24, 106, 127, 134, 146, 198, 246, 299, 334
Black Arts Movement, 7
Black Mountain College, 1, 12, 313, 316
Black Power, 28, 29
blacks, 31, 62; as artists, 111; color of, 134; cuisine of, 103; literature, 86; in white America, 167
Blake, William, 105
Blues Cruise (Boston), 245, 249, 250, 302
bohemia, 119, 325; conformity in, 2; memoirs of, 3; of NYC, 2

Bond, Julian, 316
books, 27, 30, 144, 213, 221, 261, 309
bookstores, 20n9, 36, 137, 155, 178, 182, 245, 275, 343; in Accra, 302; feminist, 130; in Gloucester, 54, 70, 82, 84–85. *See also under names of bookstores*
Boston, 54, 62, 72; art in, 138, 182; Blues Cruise, 245, 249, 250, 251, 302; Helene in, 39, 336; Hettie's reading in, 218; newspapers in, 54, 127, 129
Boston Women's Caucus for Art, 82
Boston Visual Artists Union, 40–41, 54
Bourgeois, Louise, 244, 245, 247
Bowles, Jane, 36, 64, 126, 317
Boyland, 1, 6–7, 202, 284
Boyle, Kay, 3, 64, 167; *Collected Poems* of, 166–67
Brakhage, Jane Wodening. *See* Wodening, Jane
Brakhage, Stan, 97n9
Brando, Marlon, 116
Breath, Eyes, Memory (Danticat), 150
Brecht, Bertolt, *Poems, 1913–1956*, 56
Breger, Brian, 45, 45n6
Brent, George, 127
Breytenbach, Breyten, 167
British Museum, 249
Brontës, 21, 223
Brooklyn College, 58
Brooklyn Museum, 211, 213
Brown, Ken (Hettie's son-in-law), 285, 337, 349
Brown, Lisa Jones (Hettie's daughter). *See* Jones, Lisa
Brown, Marion, 15, 15n1, 19, 24, 26; "Capricorn Moon," 254
Brynner, Yul, 339, 340
Buck, Chansonette (Chan) (Helene's daughter), 11–12, 26, 30, 32, 36n3, 41, 111, 130, 197, 207, 232, 247, 314, 321, 340; as doctoral candidate, 149, 218; Hettie on, 242; poetry award of, 242, 243; removal of dedication to, 51–52;

Close, Glenn, 211, 212

Coetzee, J. M., *Disgrace*, 329

Cohen, Hettie (Hettie Cohen Jones). *See* Hettie

Colchester, Helene in, 15–16, 19, 21, 22, 23, 25, 26, 30

Coles, Jane, *Women of Crisis*, 180

Coles, Robert, *Women of Crisis*, 180

Colette, 248, 317, 318; "My Mother's House," 248

Coltrane, John, 16, 24, 26, 112, 165

Columbia University, 17, 130, 254

Colvin, Marilyn, 173, 176, 315

computers, 102, 118, 141, 142, 155, 219, 271–72, 297–98, 301, 309, 339, 343; games on, 275, 306, 343; Helene on, 90, 126, 148, 149, 184, 186, 188, 189, 191, 231; Hettie on, 86, 151, 157, 288–89, 299, 302; Macs, 241, 242; writing industry on, 86. *See also* Internet

Cook, Sam, 136

correspondence, 253; as harmonization, 3; publication of women's, 2, 92. *See also* letters

Corso, Gregory, 190

Council on Interracial Books for Children, 43

Coyolxauhqui (warrior moon goddess), 227

Creeley, Robert, 3, 5, *13*, 124, 190, 244, 284, 285; *For Love*, 317

Crews, Harry, *A Childhood*, 93

Crouch, Stanley, 59, 106

Cuba, 175

Dante, *Divine Comedy*, 293

Danticat, Edwidge, *Krik Krak*, 163, 166

Dasimayya, Devara, 148

Davie, Donald, 29

Davis, Adele, 327, 337

Davis, Bette, 127

Davis, Miles, 57, 222

Davis, Ossie, 91

Davis, Stuart, 32

Dawson, Fielding (Fee), 187, 280, 282, 283, 298

Death in Venice (Mann), 207

de Beauvoir, Simone, 103

deKooning, Willem, 1

Delillo, Don, 208

Department of Homeland Security, 281

déraciné, 51

Diallo, Amadou, 238

Dickinson, Emily, *Complete Poems*, 217

di Prima, Diane, 172, 173

Dirty Crazy Mean Mike, 81

disappeared, 51–52, 53

discarded wives and women, 4, 32, 33, 45, 234, 247, 248, 252, 286, 306, 350

divorce, 12, 22, 97, 99, 134, 160

Doerr, Harriet, *Tiger in the Grass*, 181

Dole, Bob, 177

Dolly the Sheep, 280

Dorn, Edward (Helene's second husband), 2, *11*, *13*, 26, 27, 29, 31, 67, 91, 96n8, 105, 179, 203, 338, 341; affair of, 30; as author, 22; biography of, 284, 285, 331; cancer of, 192, 193, 200; child support and, 37; as Fulbright Scholar, 13; Helene on, 6, 252; Helene assists, 16, 22, 206; marriage of, 4, 36, 45; papers of, 189, 235; publications of, 19, 23, 34, 51–52

Doyle, Arthur Conan, 19

drug use: cocaine, 65; Helene's, 25, 27, 182, 254; hashish, 254, 255; heroin, 194; Hettie's, 26, 65, 71, 154. *See also* marijuana

Duberman, Martin, 84

Dukakis, Michael, 118

Dunbar, Jennifer (Jenny), 30, 30n16

Duncan, Isadora, 67

Dunlap, Sarah, *Fitz Henry Lane, Family and Friends*, 79n1

Dunn, Adam, 182, 209
Duras, Marguerite, 36, 158; *The Lover*, 82; *The War*, 82

Eady, Cornelius, 153
Eisenstein, Sergei, 169
email, 4, 196, 197, 231, 232, 235, 236, 290, 326; attachments to, 245, 282; Helene on, 239; Hettie on, 240; 9/11 and, 256, 260; problems with, 261–62; spam and, 333
England, 16, 18, 196; class in, 27; Helene in, 13, 15–16, 17–18, 19, 20–21, 23, 25, 26–27, 27–28, 30, 85; hospitals in, 28; London, 27, 57n4; weather in, 15, 17, 21, 27, 29
English Woman, The (monthly), 247
Ensler, Eve, 236
environmentalism, 95
Erdrich, Louise, *The Last Report on the Miracles at Little No Horse*, 269, 270
Exportfinans, 40–41, 43

Faison, George, 241
Fanon, Frantz, 158
faxes, fax machines, 6, 148, 154–55, 159, 180, 181, 193, 199–200, 208, 217, 227; from Hettie, 149, 150, 196
feminism, feminists, 53, 93, 130, 164
Fenellosa, Ernest, 221, 266
Ferlinghetti, Lawrence, 155
finances: poor people and, 66; Helene's, 37, 55, 56, 62, 63, 103, 106, 118, 134, 182, 209, 221, 286; Hettie's, 15, 17, 18, 20, 22, 30, 37, 40, 56, 58, 59, 74, 111, 125, 223, 280
Fiore, Joseph, 316n2
Fiore, Mary, 316, 316n2, 324
Fire Island, 26
Fitzgerald, Penelope, 245; *Charlotte Mew and Her Friends*, 247, 248
Florida, 55, 56, 57

Flowers, Margaret, 70, 75, 76
Fonda, Henry, 127
Ford, Gerald, 130
found objects, 54, 121; discards and, 33, 45; letters and, 191
Franco, Francisco, 31
Franconia, N.H., 120
freelance editing and proofreading: by Helene, 134, 137, 139, 141, 144–45, 159–60, 168, 182, 188, 198, 205, 209; by Hettie, 18, 19, 21, 22, 23, 36, 46, 87, 88, 89, 111, 120, 125
Frontiers (magazine), 131, 131n4
Frost Place, The (Franconia, N.H.), 221

Gandhi, Mahatma, 334
Garland, William "Red," 16, 52
Gates, Henry Louis, Jr. (Skip), 114, 218; *Thirteen Ways of Looking at a Black Man*, 195, 199
Gates, Sharon Lynn Adams, 114
Gaye, Marvin, 136
gays, 53, 130, 255; Gay and Lesbian Coalition, 104; Jews as, 55. *See also* lesbians
Generation X, 216
Genet, Jean, 167
Genêt (pseud. of Janet Flanner), 158
gentrification, 65; in Gloucester, , 62–63; in NYC, 62–63, 64, 75, 109, 279
Ghana, Hettie in, 276, 277, 293, 300–301, 303, 305
ghosts, 19, 21, 25, 26, 220, 222
gifts: from Helene, 55, 108, 142, 147, 350; from Hettie, 60, 64, 76, 138, 139, 161, 249, 305, 321, 331, 338
Gilb, Dagoberto, 157, 158
Ginsberg, Allen, 1, 5, 13, 27, 28, 29, 51, 160,172, 206, 345; death of, 190–92, 298; "Howl," 231
Ginsberg, Eugene, 190
Giotto, 105

Giuliani, Rudy, 258

global warming, 92

Gloucester, Mass., 32, 37, 52, 52n2, 60; art
and artists in, 32, 39, 54, 116, 223, 236,
244, 251, 253; festivals in, 70, 214, 244,
296; fire in, 225; fishing industry and,
66, 231, 302; *Fisherman's Wife* (statue),
250, 251, 252, 257, 258; gentrification of,
62–63; harbor of, 283, 350; Helene on,
60, 116, 287; sea serpent of, 214; Stage
Fort Park in, 35, 116; Ten Pound Island
Bookstore in, 54, 70, 84–85

Gloucester Daily Times (*GDT*), 78, 84, 87,
142, 215, 265, 267, 281, 295, 321

God, 20, 278, 314

Gordimer, Nadine, 101–2, 207

Gordon, Ruth, 116

Grady, Panna, 154, 154n3

Graves, Milford, 342

Greece, 246

Grimm, Jacob, 56

Grove Press, 158, 198, 209; Hettie works
for, 22, 23, 36, 88; *How I Became Hettie
Jones* and, 157–58, 159, 165, 165n2, 172,
182, 209

Guest, Barbara, 147

Guevera, Ernesto (Che), 31

Gulf War, 123, 123n1, 124, 225

Gurdjieff, George Ivanovich, 18

Hagedorn, Jessica, 145; *The Gangster of
Love*, 168

Hale, Nathan, 223

Hammett, Dashiell, 267, 268

Hansberry, Lorraine, 128

Harlem Renaissance, 83

Harlem School of the Arts, 101

Hartley, Marsden, 32

Harvard University, 218

Hass, Robert, 242

Hatch-Billops Collection, 119n11

H.D. (Hilda Doolittle), 261

Healey, Shevy, 146

Hebard, Grace Raymond, 143

Helene (Helene Helmers Buck Dorn), 9,
11, *12*, *13*, *64*, *78*, *pl. 9*, *pl. 10*; as artist,
4, 13, 22, 39, 47, 52, 54, 56, 63, 90, 116,
120–21, 158, 184, 198, 200, 207, 243,
247, 249, 250, 283, 308, *pl. 4*; aunt of,
58, 103, 132; as autodidact, 31; birth of,
2, 11; brother of, 35, 83, 95, 165; childhood of, 272; child support for, 37;
conformity of, 2; deafness of, 48, 54,
67, 114, 195–96, 219, 273–74, 307, 314,
347, 349; death and cremation of,
283, 349, 350; depression and, 203,
236, 249, 272, 273, 274–75, 335, 336;
diary of, 191; divorce of, 12, 128, 128n2;
dreams of, 60; in England, 13, 17–23,
25, 26–30; father of, 40; first meets
Hettie, 1–2, 325; friends of, 67, 67n8,
239; garden of, 91; gets stoned, 25, 27,
148; at Gloucester Manor Nursing
Manor, 37; governmental assistance
for, 97; grandchildren and great-
grandchildren of, 52n2, 187, 197, 212,
278, 346; health medical problems of,
28, 32, 42–43, 48, 75, 90, 91, 103, 150,
193, 197, 198, 199–200, 203, 206, 210,
228, 230, 234, 274, 306, 308, 320, 321,
323, 326–27, 334, 336, 338, 340, 343;
Hettie on, 80, 218, 223, 350; jobs of, 37,
45, 65, 134, 203–4; living situation of,
63, 65, 67, 73, 74, 75, 76, 77–80, 100,
225–27, 230, 232–33, 234–35, 236, 286,
307, 308–9, 314, 335; makes dresses, 6;
marriages of, 2, 12, 36, 45; papers of,
189, 235, 318; in Paris, 22; poems by,
151; removal of dedication to, 51–52;
self-integrity of, 4; sexuality of, 139,
175; smokes, 194, 203, 205, 217, 292;
in Spain, 30, 80; suicidal, 203, 204; as
typist, 45, 48; workspace of, 35; youth
of, 36

Helene's artworks, 4, 13, 22, 32–33, 39, 52;
Baseball/Love Circle, 54, 56; Big Joke

Leach, Henry, 126
Leary, Timothy, 18, 27, 28, 29
Lee, Spike, 91, 106
LeGuin, Ursula, 134; *Fisherwoman's Daughter*, 142; "The Reciprocity of Poetry and Prose," 222
Lemon, Ralph, 85n3
lesbians, 53, 255; Gay and Lesbian Coalition, 104; Jews as, 55. *See also* gays
LeSoeur, Joe, *Digressions on Some Poems by Frank O'Hara*, 334
LeSueur, Meridel, 103, 110
Lethem, Jonathan, *Motherless Brooklyn*, 324
letters, 54, 191, 202, 235, 351; compared to poems, 4; Helene's, *14*, 189, 191–92; Hettie's, 73, 75; of Jane Bowles, 317; as lifesavers, 3; memory and, 71; publication of, 2; stationery and, 25, 151; as story, 350; women's friendships in, 1. *See also* correspondence; email; faxes, fax machines; postcards
Levertov, Denise, 298, 343
Lewinsky, Monica, 228
Lewis, Harry, 45, 45n6
libraries, 43, 48, 51, 63, 94, 112, 148, 195, 214, 259, 293, 334; events and exhibits in, 82, 119, 134, 235, 237, 348; on 42nd Street, 58; Helene on, 105; interlibrary loan and, 75, 86, 245; librarians and, 255, 348
Lindner, Vicki, 320
Listen to Their Voices (Pearlman), 157
literature, 5; African American, 86; feminist, 36, 93
Lively, Penelope, *Moon Tiger*, 299
Lodge, David, *The Art of Fiction*, 175
Lorca, Federico García, *Collected Poems*, 217
Loewinsohn, Ron, 114
London, Hettie in, 249, 250
Lovell, Whitfield, 130, 130n3
Lovisco Gallery, 85

Lowell, Robert, 95
Lumumba, Patrice, 94, 94n6

magazines, 27
Malanga, Gerard, 17, 108, 108n5
Malcolm X, 91, 125
Maldovan, Susan, 283, 316
Manhattan, 2, 62, 354; gentrification in, 279; Lower, 257; Upper, 30. *See also* 9/11
Mansfield, Katherine, 100
marijuana, 71, 254; Helene and, 254; Hettie and, 150, 174, 276, 294, 345; legalization of, 28, 295; social use of, 15, 55
Marley, Alpharita Constantia Anderson (Rita)(Mrs. Bob Marley), 249, 273, 276, 285, 287, 289, 290, 294, 300, 301, 303, 306, 317, 335; Hettie on, 292, 310, 330
Marley, Bob, 240, 285, 290, 294, 295
marriage: risks in, 12; traditional, 2
Marsalis, Wynton, 226
Martin, Andre, 105
Martin, Harry, 67n8, 70, 75, 76
Marxists, 53
Massachusetts, 220
Massachusetts Turnpike, 72, 351
matrix, 191
Maud, Ralph, 154, 154n3
Maxwell, William, 317, 318, 321
McCarthy, Mary, 36
McClure, Joanna, 178, 179, 180
McDarrah, Fred, 65, 175
McLucas, Leroy, 23, 23n13
McNamara, Michael, 77
Megawatts (Fred Buck's band), 214, 245, 250, 251
Melanga, Gerard, 108, 108n5
memory, 299–300
Metropolitan Museum of Art, 101, 321
Mew, Charlotte, 45, 245, 247, 248
Michigan, joint vacation in, 105